D1338027

A GRAMMAR OF SPOKEN ENGLISH

A GRAMMAR OF
SPOKEN ENGLISH

BY

HAROLD E. PALMER

AND

F. G. BLANDFORD

THIRD EDITION

REVISED AND REWRITTEN

BY

ROGER KINGDON

W. HEFFER & SONS LTD
CAMBRIDGE

© R. Kingdon, Mrs. D. Anderson and the Executors
of F. G. Blandford, 1969

First edition, 1924
Reprinted six times
Second edition, revised, 1939
Reprinted three times
Third edition, completely revised, 1969

SBN 85270 016 4

ST. JOSEPH'S COLLEGE OF EDUCATION
TRENCH HOUSE
BELFAST 11

Printed in Great Britain
by W. Heffer & Sons Ltd, Cambridge

Preface to Third Edition

PALMER'S *Grammar of Spoken English* was first published in 1924, and was dedicated to the author's friend, Thomas Beach, with acknowledgement of the advice and encouragement he had given. After several reprints had appeared the author, with the help of F. G. Blandford, who had already collaborated with Palmer in other works intended to facilitate the study of English as a second language, produced a slightly revised edition, which appeared in 1939. In the preface to this second edition the revisers thanked those who had sent comments on the book, mentioning in particular Lilias Armstrong, G. Noël-Armfield, Dr. Sanki Ichikawa and Dr. James Welton. Special mention was made of the sympathy and stimulus derived from "D. J.", and the revisers, declaring that the book owed its inception to Professor Daniel Jones, recorded their gratitude for his inspiration and encouragement.

It is generally acknowledged that Palmer's *Grammar of Spoken English* is a very important pioneer work which has had a decisive influence not only on the presentation of English grammar to foreign students but also on the course of further research work in this field. Many of the ideas put forward by Palmer have met with widespread acceptance and at the same time further advances have been made. This has had the inevitable effect of making Palmer's grammar begin to "date," and I felt, therefore, that a fairly full revision of the work would be justified—firstly in order to carry the author's ideas to their logical conclusion and secondly, by incorporating some of the latest advances and adding a few ideas of my own, to preserve the pioneer spirit of the original work. In consequence, most of the book has been rewritten on the lines described below.

The detailed Table of Contents has been replaced by a skeleton table supplemented by an alphabetical index at the end of the book. The system of numbered paragraphs has been retained, but the paragraphs have been increased in length and the number of examples given has in many cases been increased. All examples are now transcribed in bold type, which avoids the need for frequent use of square brackets.

The phonetic transcription used in previous editions (often known as the E.P.D. system) has been replaced by the Simplified System used by an increasing number of phoneticians in books intended for the teaching of English to foreign students. This system, which was recommended to me personally by the late Professor Daniel Jones, uses fewer unfamiliar symbols and thus makes it easier for the uninitiated to read the examples. Alternative pronunciations have not been given; where these exist the one shown is that which I consider most likely to be used by educated people in fluent speech.

Intonation is shown by means of a system which was favourably commented upon by Harold Palmer, though he did not live long enough to experiment with it. This is the Tonetic Stress-mark System which I developed for use in my own works on English stress and intonation. This system, which requires a minimum expenditure of time and space, makes it possible to give an easily readable outline of recommended intonations for all the examples throughout the book. It must, of course, be understood that in many cases alternative treatments are possible, but in every case the intonation shown is one that might well be used by most native English speakers.

The general arrangement of the book has been adhered to, except that *Part IV, Logical Categories*, has been eliminated, as it was felt that it might be better to use the space for a more detailed analysis of verbal structures.

Part I. This has been renamed *Pronunciation* in order to place Tonetics on an equal footing with Phonetics. While the original arrangement has been preserved the whole section has been re-written and the treatment of intonation has been based on my own analysis of the English tunes.

Part II. Palmer's classification of the Parts of Speech has been followed and treated as definitive, though the now widely used term Determiners has been substituted for his Determinatives. Most of the chapters dealing with the parts of speech have been rewritten, particularly the chapter on the Verb, and in this a number of new ideas of my own have been introduced. These entail a radical change in the presentation of verb structure, which may be regarded as too revolutionary, but experience has convinced me that this presentation enables foreign students to understand the English verb system much more easily than has been possible hitherto. The innovations for which I must take full responsibility are: the placing

Preface

of the negative finites on a par with the affirmative ones; the rejection of Palmer's concept of "compound finites" in favour of a three-tier division into conjugating finites, conjugating verbals and specific verbals; the amalgamation of future and conditional tenses into modal tenses, and a new system of tense nomenclature.

Part III. The original title *Parts of the Sentence* has been changed to *Sentence Structure* since increased space has been given to an analysis of the various structures used in the four forms of the sentence. Using a new set of symbols to identify the various elements that can enter into the formation of a simple sentence, the analysis gives in tabular form examples of practically every possible structure for all the tenses of the verb. The fact that English is able to express unusually fine shades of temporal and modal meaning has led to a belief in some quarters that the tense system is complicated and unsystematic. It is hoped that this new presentation of the verb will help students to understand the system and will convince them that its reputation is undeserved.

I desire to thank Harold Palmer's daughter, Mrs. Dorothée Anderson, for giving me a free hand in revising her father's work, and the publishers for making this revision possible. My best thanks are also due to Professor Frank Palmer and Professor Randolph Quirk for valuable suggestions, and to my wife, Martha Velarde de Kingdon, for the idea developed in §§373–377 and for help in compiling the index.

R. K.

London, October 1968

PUBLISHERS' NOTE

Mr. Roger Kingdon was an assistant in the Department of Phonetics in University College, London, under Professor Daniel Jones. Later he was Director of Studies in the British Institutes in Cairo, Mexico City and Bogotá. He has lectured on English Intonation in the University of Groningen and in various Latin American universities. He is the author of three works on English Stress and Intonation, and has published a number of articles on various aspects of English grammar.

Table of Contents

viii

Table of Contents

Introduction

THE GRAMMAR AND THE DICTIONARY

LANGUAGES are made up of an enormous number of units loosely designated as *words*, each of which has one or more *meanings*. In order to find these we consult a *dictionary*. Thus the dictionary tells us that the word *horse* is associated with a certain animal, or that the word *take* corresponds to certain activities (such as *seizing, conveying, conducting,* etc.), either by describing them or by giving the equivalents of the word in some other language. In similar ways it gives us the meanings of such words as *good, five, quickly,* or *yesterday*. All words having a character comparable to those quoted above are considered by Sweet[1] as being *independent sense-units*, and he terms them Full Words (now generally known as Content Words). But in addition to such full words we find words which have little or no independent meaning, but merely express relations between the different parts of a sentence; instead of having distinct *semantic* functions they have *syntactic* or *grammatical* functions. Such words (e.g. *of, to, the, is*) are termed by Sweet Form-words (now generally known as Structural Words). This distinction is in many ways a convenient one, but it is not always easy to draw a line between the two classes.

The inexperienced student might imagine that it is possible to learn a foreign language on a lexical basis alone, and the authors of some artificial languages seem to have had in view a system for which the dictionary would afford a complete key. But in natural languages we find that certain conceptions of number, time, relation, etc., are not represented by specific *words*, but by devices such as word-order, inflexion, intonation, or the use of affixes; such devices I have termed *alogisms*.[2]

What may be expressed in one language by means of a structural word may be expressed alogistically in another, thus the French *boîte à allumettes* is equivalent to the English *matchbox*, the relational

[1] *New English Grammar*, §§52, 58.
[2] *The Scientific Study and Teaching of Languages*, pp. 12, 39, 41, 45, and Appendix II.

idea represented by the structural word *à* being expressed by the English word-order. Conversely, the English *he will come* is equivalent to the French *il viendra*, the English structural word *will* being expressed by the inflected form of the French verb *venir*. The tendency of English during the whole of its history is to substitute structural words for inflexions.

It would almost seem that the scope of the dictionary should be confined to content words, and that structural words and their alogistic equivalents should be relegated to the grammar-book. This, however, is neither possible nor even desirable, for, apart from the difficulty of drawing a line between the two, a given word may sometimes be one and at other times be the other. Moreover, in many cases a word expresses both a semantic conception and one or more grammatical conceptions. The word *horses* not only evokes in our minds the idea of a certain animal, but it also evokes the conception of plurality. Even the word *horse* conveys, in addition to its primary meaning, the idea of "singularity." The word *took* corresponds to the ideas of seizing, conveying or conducting, etc., but also evokes the idea of "pastness." The word *better* suggests not only goodness, but also *relative* goodness. The word *me* suggests the *ego* and also the objective relation. The word *my* evokes the *ego* and possession.

The dictionary therefore explains content words and structural words alike, while the grammar-book describes and explains all phenomena which can be brought under general rules.[1] It classifies words and states the peculiarities of each category. To do this effectively and economically, it creates as many categories as are deemed necessary or expedient, and designates each by a term which will enable us to recognize it.

---

[1] We have seen that the phenomena of language are of two kinds: those which can be brought under general rules and those which cannot. The only phenomena that can be brought under general rules are those that have something in common, by which they are associated together in the mind by the psychological process of *group-association* by which *association-groups* are formed. There are in every language an endless number of these groups, and one and the same word may belong to several such groups at once. Thus the words *trees, towns, boys,* form an association-group through having the same "inflection" *-s,* and having the meanings "more-than-oneness" in common. Sweet, *New English Grammar,* §20.

Introduction

We do not say *this books*, in educated English speech we do not say *I are*, and no Frenchman ever says *le table*. But in quite another order of incompatibility we do not speak of *warm ice*, for, as far as we know, such a substance does not exist; we do not speak of a *triangle with four corners*, for such a figure is inconceivable; these would be nonsense expressions. But *this books are all mine, I are busy*, or *voici le table* are not nonsense expressions; they make sense but they offend against *grammatical* usage.

The dictionary only gives us such information as will enable us to avoid nonsense expressions, it is silent concerning the grammatical incompatibilities; for information and guidance concerning these, we must have recourse to *grammar*.

THE UTILITY OF A GRAMMAR

Most educationists probably agree that the sort of English grammar which is intended to serve as a series of "directions for use" for the benefit of the foreign adult student of English must differ very widely (if not fundamentally) from the sort of English grammar taught in English schools to English school children.

This *Grammar of Spoken English* is intended to be used chiefly (but not exclusively) by foreign adult students of English, and by all teachers of spoken English. The fact that it is written *in English* shows that it is not intended to be put into the hands of beginners; it is designed to help (*a*) those who are already able to understand written English, and (*b*) the English teachers who teach living English speech.

Such a grammar helps foreign students by economizing time. It is impossible to learn a language by memorizing it word by word and sentence by sentence, for the number of possible sentences in a language is practically limitless. If, when we form original sentences of our own, we build them up synthetically by piecing together the units of which they are composed, what usually results is a foreign caricature of some sentence of our own language. It is clear to-day that we must form original sentences *from analogous sentences which have been* (consciously or unconsciously) *memorized at some previous time*.

The process is that now known as *substitution*; the following example shows how it works: Consciously or unconsciously a foreign student has memorized the sentence *If I'd seen him yesterday I should have spoken to him.* He has also memorized such isolated words or word-groups as *written, met, her, last week,* and has become aware that English grammatical usage allows him to replace *I'd* by *he'd, she'd* or *they'd, seen* by *met, him* by *her* or *them, yesterday* by *last week* or *a few days ago, I should* by *he would, they could* or *we might, spoken* by *written, to him* by *to her* or *to them.* In consequence therefore of having memorized the sentence and the isolated words and word-groups, *and having become aware of certain grammatical categories,* he is able to recognize at first hearing and to produce instantaneously and automatically any of the following 1,728 sentences, all of which (with one exception) are original or non-memorized.[1]

If I'd	seen	him	yesterday,	I should	have	spoken	to him.
If he'd	met	her	last week,	he would		written	to her.
If she'd		them	a few days ago,	they could			to them.
If they'd				we might			

By applying this process of substitution we can form an unlimited number of correct sentences. But to do this the student must know the various grammatical categories, otherwise he may proceed according to false analogies. Having memorized *ought you to go?* he may form by false analogy: *want you to go?* Having memorized *I hope to go,* he may derive from this: *I think to go.* If he is not aware of the limited extent of the category *written, driven, ridden,* etc., he may introduce into it such an invented form as *arriven.*

The chief function of a grammar-book is to furnish the student with categories which will enable him to perform the greatest number of useful substitutions. In many cases the grammar merely sets forth either the whole or the most frequently-used members of each category. In other cases it is possible to frame a "grammatical rule," by which the student can draw up his own category. It is, however, safer to furnish the student with the actual members of the category, for he may feel that it is enough for him to have to learn the contents of a given category without having, in addition, to work it out for himself from abstract rules and formulae.

[1] See my *100 Substitution Tables* (Heffer), *Principles of Language Study,* pp. 175–177 (Harrap), *Systematic Exercises in Sentence-Building, Classroom Procedures and Devices, Mechanism Grammar, Automatic Sentence-Builder* (the last four published by the Institute for Research in English Teaching, Tokyo).

Introduction

In this book the foreign student will find a selection of what the author considers to be the most useful grammatical categories of spoken English. In many cases the actual word-lists are provided, those being drawn in most cases from lists of the 2,000 most useful words. In other cases, the word-lists themselves are replaced by grammatical rules and explanations. The copious examples given to illustrate every rule afford full opportunities for the process of substitution. A serious endeavour has been made to treat each subject according to its importance. The aim throughout has been to show students how to form original sentences rather than to give detailed instructions concerning word-building. Information which can be found in a good dictionary has been omitted, except in a few instances in which the author has judged it expedient to encroach on the scope of the dictionary.

"SPOKEN" AND "WRITTEN" ENGLISH

The terms "spoken" and "written" are open to more than one interpretation. In the present case, the term *Spoken English* should be taken to mean "that variety of English which is generally used by educated people (more especially in the South of England) in the course of ordinary conversation or when writing letters to intimate friends." The term *Written English* may be taken to cover those varieties of English that we generally find in printed books, reviews, newspapers, formal correspondence, and that we sometimes hear in the language of public speakers and orators, or possibly in formal conversation (more especially between strangers).

The terms "spoken" and "colloquial" are frequently used synonymously; when this is the case, the term "colloquial" is assumed to have the connotation used above, and not that connotation which would make it synonymous with "vulgar" or "slangy." Similarly, the term "written" is frequently used as a synonym of "classical" or "literary."

All words and examples are given in phonetic transcription, the only possible procedure to follow when dealing with the spoken form of a living language whose orthographic and phonetic systems are mutually are variance.[1] Moreover, throughout the book the

---

[1] Not only do the aims of grammar teaching need restating, but its methods need radical reform. Nearly all text-books on grammar are written as if English were a dead language. Their rules, examples and exceptions are

examples have been shown with recommended stressing and intonation, since these form an integral part of the grammar of Spoken English.

THE GRAMMAR OF USAGE

One of the most widely diffused of the many linguistic illusions current in the world is the belief that each language possesses a "pure" or "grammatical" form, a form which is intrinsically "correct," which is independent of usage, which exists, which has always existed, but which is now in danger of losing its existence. For, according to this theory, there exist in all lands enemies of the language; those who, from perversity or from neglect, are attempting to defile the well of pure language. Among those enemies are assumed to be the careless slipshod writers who do not trouble to study their grammars, the uneducated who are too lazy to learn their own language, and the slovenly speakers who mumble their syllables instead of articulating them. According to this theory, there also exist Defenders of the Faith (generally assumed to be the "best" authors and the "best" speakers), and there is waged a long and bitter struggle between the followers of Ormuzd and Ahriman. Those who declare themselves as being "on the side of the angels" may indeed confess to certain shortcomings in respect to the "purity" or "correctness" of their personal speech, but endeavour to make up for those regrettable lapses by the zeal with which they pillory the lapses of their fellow-sinners.

"It has now become practically impossible for any writer so to express himself that he shall not run foul of the convictions of some person who has fixed the employment of a particular word or construction as his test of correctness of usage. Should any person

---

expressed in the form of our conventional spellings rather than of the spoken words or syllables which those spellings represent, often very inadequately. Few school grammarians appear to realize that a living language is composed of sounds, not of letters; for example, to state the rule for the plural inflexion of English nouns in terms of spelling without the use of phonetic symbols is quite misleading. \ . . . The teaching must be closely allied with phonetics, since the first fact to be learnt about language is that it is composed of sounds, and since there are some grammatical notions which it is impossible to convey without the use of phonetic symbols.—*Report of the Government Committee on the Teaching of English in England*, §§258, 264.

Introduction

seriously set out to observe every one of the various and varying
utterances put forth for his guidance by all the members of this
volunteer army of guardians of the Speech, he would in process of
time find himself without any language to use whatever."[1]

One of the best proofs of the prevalence of this theory is the
persistence of that age-long series of enquiries "Where is English
best spoken?" "In what part of France do they speak the most
correct French?" "Where is purest German to be found?" etc. etc.
The mere use in this connection of such terms as "best" or "correct"
implies that there is in the mind of the enquirer an implicit belief
in the existence of some standard or super-dialect the superiority
or intrinsic "correctness" of which cannot be questioned. The only
possible answers to such questions are: "The best Scottish-English
is spoken in Scotland"; "The best American-English is spoken in
the United States"; "The purest London-English is to be found
in London"; "The most correct Parisian-French is used in Paris";
"The ideal Viennese-German is spoken in Vienna"; "The only pure
form of Slocum-in-the-Hole-English is used at the village of
Slocum-in-the-Hole."

With this our questioners are not satisfied; they say, "Oh, but
I am not speaking of local dialects and suchlike debased forms of
language; Where is the standard language spoken? Where do they
speak Real English?—Genuine French?—Pure German?" etc. The
answer is: "There is no Real, Genuine or Pure English, French,
etc., and there never has been." But the chimerical idea of a
standard dialect still persists. In vain do the most eminent and
most respected linguistic authorities deny its existence; in vain do
the most erudite grammarians and etymologists assure us that the
sole standard is and always has been that of correct usage. From
the time of Horace[2] down to the time of Hales,[3] Sweet,[4] Lounsbury,[5]

---

[1] Professor Thomas R. Lounsbury in an article entitled *The Standard of
Usage.*

[2] ". . . si volet usus,
Quem penes arbitrium est et jus et norma loquendi."
—*Horace in his treatise on the Poetic Art.*

[. . . if it shall be the will of usage, in whose power is the decision and authority
and the standard of speaking.]

[3] "The vulgar grammar-maker, dazzled by the glory of the ruling language,

Wyld,[1] Jespersen and Bloomfield, the standard of usage has remained supreme and unquestioned by those who have come to understand something of the nature of language. That usage is ruled by grammar is a thesis only defended to-day by the uninformed.[2]

The amateur grammarian or the "member of the volunteer army of guardians of the Speech," while pointing out in the abstract the proprieties or improprieties of speech, is generally perfectly unconscious of the forms of speech which he uses himself. He warns the unsuspecting foreigners against what he calls "vulgarisms," and says to him, "Don't ever use such vulgar forms as *don't* or *won't*; you won't hear educated people using them!" or "Never use a preposition to finish a sentence with!" or he may say, "I don't know who you learn English from, but you are always using the word *who* instead of *whom*."[3] Or we may hear him say, "Oh, I've got something else to tell you: don't say *I've got* instead of *I have*."

---

knew no better than to transfer to English the schemes which belonged to Latin."—J. W. Hales.

[4] "The first object in studying grammar is to learn to observe linguistic facts as they *are*, not as they *ought* to be, or as they were in an earlier stage of the language."—Sweet.

[5] ". . . were grammars and manuals of usage absolutely trustworthy. But no such statement can be made of most of them, if, indeed, of any. It is an unfortunate fact that since the middle of the eighteenth century, when works of this nature first began to be much in evidence and to exert distinct influence, far the larger proportion of them have been produced by men who had little acquaintance with the practice of the best writers and even less with the history and development of grammatical forms and constructions. Their lack of this knowledge led them frequently to put in its place assertions based not upon what usage really is, but upon what in their opinion it ought to be. They evolved or adopted artificial rules for the government of expression. . . . As these rules were copied and repeated by others a fictitious standard of propriety was set up in numerous instances, and is largely responsible for many of the current misconceptions which now prevail as to what is grammatical."—Professor Lounsbury.

[1] "A grammar book does *not* attempt to teach people how they *ought* to speak, but, on the contrary, unless it is very bad or an old work, it merely states how, as a matter of fact, certain people *do* speak at the time at which it is written."—Professor Wyld.

[2] "There is no such thing as English Grammar in the sense that used to be attributed to the term."—The Board of Education's Circular on *The Teaching of English in Secondary Schools* (1910).

[3] See Coleman's *The Kind of English I use in Ordinary Conversation*, as quoted in my *English Intonation*, pp. 99–105.

Introduction

Now in the everyday speech of educated people those (and many other) so-called "vulgarisms" are constantly heard. Sweet calls them "theoretical vulgarisms," and observed their extreme frequency in the speech of those who so hotly denounce them. If such expressions are "ungrammatical" we must conclude that the vast majority of educated persons (not to mention the uneducated) have established *the usage of ungrammatical forms.* In which case the forms cease *ipso facto* to be ungrammatical.[1] The sort of English described and taught in the following pages is that used in everyday conversation by the vast majority of educated speakers of English. In pronunciation, in choice of words and expressions, and in grammatical usage, it represents faithfully the type of dialect which the author has carefully and conscientiously observed in the speech of the majority of those with whom he has generally come into contact. It is, moreover, the only spoken dialect which he feels competent to teach.

There are, of course, many different styles of pronunciation in English, but for the purpose of teaching the language to foreign students it is advisable to choose one that is most widely useful to them. The best dialect for this purpose is probably the one that has been called Received Pronunciation, and it is this that will be represented in this book. It is that given in Professor Daniel Jones's *English Pronouncing Dictionary,* viz. "that most usually heard in everyday speech in the families of Southern English persons whose men-folk have been educated at the great public boarding schools. . . . It is probably accurate to say that a majority of those members of London society who have had a university education, use either this pronunciation or a pronunciation not differing very greatly from it."

SCHEME OF CLASSIFICATION

In books devoted to teaching grammar of the conventional type it is usual to establish two main divisions, these being variously termed:

1. *Accidence, Etymology, Parsing, the Grammar of Words.*

2. *Syntax, Analysis, the Grammar of Sentences.*

---

[1] "Whatever is in general use in a language is for that reason grammatically correct."—Sweet's *New English Grammar,* §12.

Without necessarily objecting to this twofold division, I find it more convenient and more in accordance with the nature of modern spoken English to adopt a different order of classification and to treat the various classes of grammatical phenomena under the following headings:

1. *Pronunciation,* including the study of sounds, stress and intonation.

2. *Parts of Speech,* their forms and functions.

3. *Parts of the Sentence,* or the syntax of the sentence.

For ease of reference, the whole of the material has been divided into paragraphs.

Pronunciation

A. Phonetics

ELEMENTS OF PRONUNCIATION

1 The English phonemes. In the same way that written language is made up of letters, spoken language consists of speech-sounds. Such sounds vary according to context and from one speaker to another, even in the same dialect, but such variations are held within limits that prevent their being confused with any other speech sound used by the same speaker. The sounds used in speaking a language are therefore divided into a number of families, known as phonemes, each of which has a definite significance. If the substitution of one sound for another can change the meaning of any word in the language, those two sounds belong to different phonemes of the language. Thus the existence of the words rʌm, rʌn, rʌŋ in English proves that m, n and ŋ belong to three different phonemes in that language, whereas the clear l and dark l (see §7) belong to the same phoneme, since the substitution of one for the other cannot change the meaning of any word.

2 Phonetic transcription. Again, for the purpose of teaching English to foreign students, its sounds must be represented by a system of phonetic transcription in which each phoneme is shown consistently by an appropriate symbol. The system used in this book is that of the International Phonetic Association in its most simplified or "broadest" form; it is the form that uses the smallest possible number of "strange" symbols consistent with representing all the phonemes. In some works on the phonetics of English "narrower" systems are used; these employ a greater number of symbols and less familiar ones, and are more adapted to works concentrating on dialectal and individual differences in pronunciation and less suitable for a work like the present one.

3 English consonant sounds.

Symbol	Example		Short Description
			Plosives
p	piː	pea	Bilabial, voiceless
b	biː	bee	Bilabial, voiced
t	tuː	too	Alveolar, voiceless
d	duː	do	Alveolar, voiced
k	kiː	key	Velar, voiceless
g	gou	go	Velar, voiced
			Nasals
m	mai	my	Bilabial, voiced
n	nau	now	Alveolar, voiced
ŋ	siŋ	sing	Velar, voiced[1]
			Lateral
l	lou	low	Alveolar, voiced
			Fricatives
f	feə*	fair	Labio-dental, voiceless
v	vau	vow	Labio-dental, voiced
θ	θin	thin	Linguo-dental, voiceless
ð	ðen	then	Linguo-dental, voiced
s	soun	sown	Alveolar, voiceless
z	zoun	zone	Alveolar, voiced
ʃ	ʃou	show	Palato-alveolar, voiceless
ʒ	ˈpleʒə*	pleasure	Palato-alveolar, voiced[1]
h	hai	high	Laryngal, voiceless[2]
			Semi-vowels
w	wei	way	Bilabial and velar, voiced[3]
r	roː	raw	Post-alveolar, voiced[3]
j	juː	you	Palatal, voiced[3]
			Affricates
tʃ	tʃəːtʃ	church	Post-alveolar, voiceless
dʒ	dʒʌdʒ	judge	Post-alveolar, voiced

4 English vowel sounds.

No.	Symbol	Example		Short Description
				Pure Vowels
1	iː	siː	see	Front, close
2	i	sit	sit	Front, close to half close[4]
3	e	set	set	Front, half close to half open[3]
4	a	sat	sat	Front, half open to open[3]
5	aː	faː*	far	Back, open
6	o	got	got	Back, open, rounded[3]
7	oː	soː	saw	Back, half open, rounded
8	u	fut	foot	Back, half close to close, rounded[4]
9	uː	tuː	too	Back, close, rounded
10	ʌ	ʌp	up	Central, half open, unrounded[3]
11	əː	fəː*	fur	Central, half open to half close
12	ə	ə'gou	ago	Central, half open to half close[5]
				Falling Diphthongs
13	ei	mei	may	Narrow, front
14	ou	nou	no	Narrow, central to back
15	ai	mai	my	Wide, front
16	au	nau	now	Wide, back
17	oi	boi	boy	Wide, back to front
				Centring Diphthongs
18	iə	diə*	dear	Front, half close
19	eə	peə*	pair	Front, half open
20	oə	koə*	core	Back, half open
21	uə	tuə*	tour	Back, half close[1]

* Indicates that r is added when the word is followed immediately by one beginning with a vowel or diphthong.

[1] Never occurs in initial position in native English words.

[2] Never occurs in final position and is weakened or completely elided when it occurs at the beginning of an unstressed syllable.

[3] Never occurs in final position in native English words.

[4] Never occurs in stressed final position in native English words.

[5] Never occurs stressed in native English words.

The foregoing tables of English consonant and vowel sounds contain all the English phonemes and provide a reference enabling the reader to interpret the symbols which will be used consistently in all the examples given in this book.

The modifiers used with these symbols are described in the next two paragraphs, while the significance of the tonetic stress marks is given in §31.

5 Vowel length. The sign (ː) is used as a mark of vowel length. The vowels iː, aː, oː, uː and əː are intrinsically long, that is to say, they are longer than the other vowels when they occur in a similar phonetic context and are pronounced with the same degree of stress and the same intonation. The diphthongs have about the same length as the long vowels.

Shortening. Vowels are shortened when they are followed by voiceless consonants. Thus the vowel iː is shorter in the word biːt (=beat) than in the word biːd (=bead).

Lengthening. Vowels are lengthened when they occur at the end of a sentence, more particularly in open syllables. Thus the vowel uː is longer in ˋðei ˌduː than in ˋðei ˌduː it. They are still further lengthened if a kinetic tone falls on them, more especially if this happens to be a Tone III (see §31, 37). Thus duː in the group ai ˅duː is a great deal longer than in the group ai ˈduː ˅laik it.

6 Miscellaneous signs. In addition to the 45 symbols (simple and compound) figuring in the above lists, the reader should note the following special signs:

(ˌ) placed under a consonant (generally m, n or l) indicates that the consonant has a syllabic value. Such words as prizm̩, bʌtn̩ or piːpl̩ contain two syllables. In the present work *all* syllabic consonants will be marked in this way.

(*) indicates that r is to be added when the sound immediately following is a vowel (or diphthong). Thus the word spelt *near* is transcribed and pronounced as niə*, but *as near as* would be transcribed and pronounced əz niər əz, and the comparative and superlative forms *nearer, nearest* are niərə*, niərist.

One or more words which may be omitted are enclosed within parentheses ( ), while a phonetic symbol printed in parentheses means that the sound for which it stands is often omitted or is inaudible in rapid speech.

SPECIAL POINTS IN PRONUNCIATION

7 The l phoneme. The English l phoneme has two principal members, and the choice between them depends on their phonetic context. Both are articulated by placing the tip of the tongue against the teeth-ridge and lowering one or both sides of the tongue to allow the breath stream to escape between the tongue and the back teeth, but they are distinguished by a secondary articulation.

One member, known as the "clear l," is made by raising the front of the tongue to the neighbourhood of the hard palate, which produces a resonance similar to that of the vowel i. This variety is used whenever a vowel or j follows the l.

The other member, known as the "dark l" is made by raising the back of the tongue to the neighbourhood of the soft palate, which produces a resonance similar to that of the vowel u. This variety is used whenever a vowel or j does not follow the l. Examples:

Clear l: lein, glʌv, fiːliŋ, koːl aut, wil ju.
Dark l: bul, waild, fiːl, koːld aut, ai tould ju.

Since the choice of variety of l follows the rule given above, it is unnecessary to distinguish the two kinds in a phonetic transcription.

Some English-speakers (chiefly in Ireland and Wales) use clear l in all positions, while others (chiefly in the United States) use dark l in all positions.

8 The r phoneme. There are several varieties of r used in English, but undoubtedly the commonest, and therefore the most acceptable for teaching to foreign students, is the *semi-vocalic* r. This sound, like w and j, occurs only before vowels or syllabic consonants and is made by moving the vocal organs from a close to a more open position—in this case the tongue tip, slightly retroflexed, from a position near, and slightly behind, the teeth-ridge to the more open position of the succeeding vowel. It is the variety used by the great majority of speakers of Received Pronunciation when the r sound occurs in a stressed syllable, and sometimes in other positions, particularly before syllabic consonants.

There are two other varieties of r which many of these speakers use in special phonetic contexts. They are:

The *tapped* r, made by tapping the tip of the tongue lightly against the teeth-ridge. This is used after the consonants θ and ð, as well as intervocalically when the r begins an unstressed syllable. The *fricative* r, made with audible friction between the tip of the tongue and the teeth-ridge. This is used after the consonants t and d. A few speakers still use a slightly fricative r in all positions instead of the semi-vocalic one.

Other varieties of r occur as dialectal or individual peculiarities; these need not be dealt with here, and students should confine themselves to the three varieties described above, giving preference to the semi-vocalic r.

Examples:

> *Semi-vocalic:* əˈraund, ˈriːzn̩, greit, spred, ðə ˈrest.
>
> *Semi-vocalic or Tapped:* ˈveri, ˈhʌri, ˈfjuəri, ˈiriˌteit.
>
> *Tapped:* θril, θrout, ˈsʌðrən (southron).
>
> *Fricative:* truː, inˈtriːt, ˈentri, drai, əˈdres, ˈloːndri.

9 Nasal plosion. When one of the six plosive consonants is followed by a nasal consonant the air is expelled through the nose instead of the mouth, thus producing nasal plosion. In many such cases the nasal consonant is syllabic, especially in a final position. Examples:

Non-syllabic Nasal		*Syllabic Nasal*	
−pm−	ˈʃopmən	−pm̩	ˈoupm̩[1]
−bm−	ˈkabmən	−bm̩	ˈribm̩[1]
−tn−	ˈlaitniŋ	−tn̩	ˈritn̩
−dn−	ˈgudnis	−dn̩	ˈwudn̩
−kn−	ˈrekniŋ	−kŋ̩	ˈrekŋ̩[1]
−gn−	ˈsmʌgnis	−gŋ̩	ˈoːgŋ̩[1]

10 Lateral plosion. When one of the plosive consonants t,d is followed by the lateral consonant the air is expelled through an opening between the sides of the tongue and the back teeth instead of at some point on the centre line of the mouth. This type of articulation is known as lateral plosion, and the l is often syllabic, especially in a final position.

---

[1] Many speakers avoid nasal plosions in these cases.

Examples:

Non-syllabic Lateral		*Syllabic Lateral*	
–tl–	ˋbʌtlə*	–tl	ˋbot‖
–dl–	ˋmidliŋ	–dl	ˋmid‖
–tl–	ətˋlantik	–tl–	ˋset‖mənt
–dl·–	ˋendlis	–dl–	ˋaid‖nis

11 Incomplete plosion. When a plosive is followed by another plosive, the two are so merged together that the explosion of the second serves for the two. When two identical plosives come together they are pronounced as one plosive, with a closure of double length. If the plosives are not identical the mere closure of the first is enough to indicate its difference from the second.

–p p–	'raip ˋpeə*		–b p–	'rob ˋpiːtə*	
–p b–	ˋsoup ˌbʌb‖		–b b–	'rʌb ˋbriskli	
–p t–	ˋkʌp ˌtai		–b t–	'skrʌb ˋtwais	
–p d–	'diːp ˋdaun		–b d–	ˋkab ˌdraivə*	
–p k–	ˋpaip ˌkliːnə*		–b k–	ˋbob ˌkeim	
–p g–	'diːp ˋgoːdʒ		–b g–	'grab ˋgould	
–t p–	'wet ˋpeint		–d p–	'ruːd ˋpiːp‖	
–t b–	ˋpokit ˌbuk		–d b–	ˋkaːdboːd	
–t t–	'ðat ˋtrein		–d t–	'gud ˋtaim	
–t d–	'greit ˋdiːl		–d d–	'bad ˋdei	
–t k–	'not ˋkiːn		–d k–	'red ˋkʌvə*	
–t g–	'wait ˋguːs		–d g–	'bad ˋges	
–k p–	'silk ˋpəːs		–g p–	ˋflagpoul	
–k b–	ˋiŋk bot‖		–g b–	ˋdogˌbiskit	
–k t–	'blak ˋtai		–g t–	ˋragtaim	
–k d–	'pʌblik ˋdjuːti		–g d–	'dig ˋdaun	
–k k–	'blak ˋkat		–g k–	ˋegkʌp	
–k g–	'paːk ˋgeit		–g g–	'big ˋgəːl	

When a plosive is followed by a fricative or a semi-vowel various sorts of glides occur, the nature of which hardly comes within the scope of this grammar.

12 Elision. The delivery of speech is often speeded up by the omission of various sounds which would otherwise interrupt easy and familiar sound-junctions. This tendency is known as elision, and the following are characteristic examples:

Elision of Vowels

ə'laud tends to become |'aud in *we're not allowed to.*
eni   „ „ „   ɳi   „ *I haven't got any more.*
ən'til   „ „ „   ɳ'til „ *wait until I'm ready.*
'raːðər „ „ „   'raːðr „ *rather a good thing.*

Elision of Consonants

məst   tends to become məs   in *I must go.*
dʒʌst „ „ „   dʒʌs „ *just come here.*
laːst „ „ „   laːs „ *last month.*
ənd   „ „ „   ən   „ *here and there.*
səm   „ „ „   sə   „ *some more.*
frentʃ „ „ „   frenʃ.
saundz „ „ „   saunz.

13 Assimilation. Another device used in order to make speech easier and more rapid is that of avoiding awkward and difficult sound-junctions by modifying one of two adjacent sounds. This process is called assimilation. It will be noticed that in some of the following examples elision occurs as well as assimilation:

Devoicing of Voiced Consonants

widθ   tends to become witθ.
ʃəd əv „ „ „   ʃt f in *I should have thought so.*
kəd   „ „ „   kt   „ *I could take it.*
faiv   „ „ „   faif „ *fivepence.*
əv   „ „ „   əf   „ *of course.*
z   „ „ „   s   „ *as far.*

Various Consonant Modifications

tj tends to become tʃ in *last year, question, natural, etc.*
dj „ „ „   dʒ „ *would you, soldier, during, etc.*
sʃ „ „ „   ʃʃ „ *horseshoe, of course she does, etc.*
zʃ „ „ „   ʒʃ „ *has she, does she, etc.*
nk „ „ „   ŋk „ *enquire, in company, etc.*
ng „ „ „   ŋg „ *engage, in good condition, etc.*
pɳ „ „ „   pm̩ „ *open, soap and water, etc.*

Note.—When assimilation takes place in the body of a single word, the actual pronunciation is transcribed, thus *question* is shown as kwestʃn and not as kwestjn. But when the final sound of a word is assimilable to the initial sound of a following word, it would be a cumbrous proceeding to include the possible variants in the word-lists and explanatory matter of a grammar-book, and indeed it is often considered inexpedient to give the modified form even in connected texts.

In such cases it must be left to the student to deduce the exact pronunciation by means of the rules and conventions furnished in text-books of English phonetics.

WEAKENING

14 Weak forms. Certain frequently-used words are given a weakened pronunciation when they are unstressed. In a few cases the use of weak forms is optional, but about fifty words have what may be called essential weak forms, which are used automatically when the words are unstressed. In such cases the use of strong forms gives an artificial and foreign flavour to the speech and destroys the natural rhythm of the language; it is therefore important for foreign students of English to pay special attention to this point in their pronunciation.

Grammatically, the words having essential and optional weak forms belong to the following parts of speech. (An explanation of the terms used will be found in §47.)

	Essential	*Optional*
Determiners	16	2
Conjugating verbs ..	18	2
Prepositions	6	1
Connectives	7	2
Miscellaneous	4	1

While the great majority of these words have only one strong form (which must be used on the comparatively rare occasions when the word is stressed), most of them have several weak forms, the choice between these depending on the phonetic context in

which the word occurs, and the speed of delivery. In the following
tables the weak forms are classified under these headings:

> *Normal:* used when none of the other circumstances obtain;
> *Initial:* used when the word begins a sentence or sense-group;
> *Pre-vocalic:* used when the word is followed by another beginning
> with a vowel;
> *Post-vocalic:* used when the word is preceded by another ending
> in a vowel;
> *Final:* used when the word ends a sentence or sense-group;
> *Rapid:* used in rapid speech when extra weakening is needed.

In a few cases there are variant forms used (*a*) as a result of
assimilation, (*b*) in the neighbourhood of sibilant consonants
(s, z, ʃ, ʒ, tʃ, dʒ) or (*c*) in special contexts. These are indicated
in notes at the foot of each table.

This classification is given, not as a hard and fast rule, but as
a guide to the circumstances in which each form is most likely to
be used. Numerous examples of the use of the different weak forms
will be found in the specimen sentences given in the chapters
describing the respective parts of speech.

A more generalized manifestation of weakening consists of the
use in unstressed syllables of a shorter and more centralized (and
therefore more obscure) vowel where a longer and more distinctive
vowel or diphthong would be used if the syllable were a stressed
one. In English there are three weak vowels that occur in such
positions:

> i, which may replace iː, ei *or* ai
> u, which may replace uː or ou
> ə which may replace almost any other vowel.

It should be noted that unstressed i and u are rather more
centralized in quality than the stressed i and u, while if they are
representing the diphthongs ei and ou respectively many speakers,
particularly in the English countryside and in the United States,
use an abbreviated diphthong; others prefer a centralized pure
vowel, so that one may hear pronunciations varying from sʌndei to
sʌndi and from windou to windu. Since foreign students of English
tend to use vowels that are too strong for unstressed syllables, the
latter transcriptions will be preferred in the present work.

15 Determiners.

The determiners having weak forms are of several kinds.

Strong Forms		Ortho-graphic Form	Weak Forms			
Normal	Pre-vocalic		Normal	Initial	Pre-vocalic	Rapid
Personal Pronouns						
ˈhiː		he	i	hi		
ˈʃiː		she	ʃi			
ˈwiː		we	wi			
ˈjuː		you	ju			
ˈmiː		me	mi			
ˈhim		him[1]	im	—		
ˈhəː	ˈhəːr	her[1]	ə	—	ər	
ˈʌs		us	əs[2]			
ˈðem		them[1]	ðəm[3]			ðm̩
Possessives						
ˈmai		my[1]	mi			
ˈhiz		his	iz	hiz		
ˈhəː	ˈhəːr	her	əː	hə[4]	ər[4]	
ˈjoə	ˈjoər	your[1]	jə		jər	
Articles						
ˈei	ˈan	a, an	ə		ən	
ˈðiː		the	ðə		ði	
Partitive						
ˈsʌm		some	səm			sm̩

Optional weak forms:

any, strong form ˈeni, has the weak forms n̩i and ni.

such, strong form ˈsʌtʃ, has the weak form sətʃ.

The word body, strong form ˈbodi, is often weakened to bədi in the semi-pronouns ˈsʌmbədi, ˈenibədi, ˈnoubədi.

[1] The weak forms are used in forming the expanded pronouns.
[2] A special weak form s is used in the collocation let s.
[3] A weak form əm, from the O.E. pronoun hem, is widely used.
[4] A weak form hər is used in initial pre-vocalic position.

16 Conjugators. When they are used unstressed in conjunction with a specific verbal (§124–5) the affirmative forms of most conjugating finites (§146) have a weakened pronunciation. In other cases a strong form is used, even in unstressed positions.

| Strong Forms | | Ortho- | Weak Forms | | | | |
Normal	Pre-vocalic	graphic Form	Normal	Initial	Pre-vocalic	Post-vocalic	Final
Temporals							
ˈam		am	m	əm			am
ˈiz		is	z¹	iz			iz
ˈaː	ˈaːr	are	ə		ər		aː
ˈwoz		was	wəz				woz
ˈwəː	ˈwəːr	were	wə		wər		wəː
ˈhav		have	əv	həv		v	hav
ˈhaz		has	z²	həz			haz
ˈhad		had	əd	həd		d	had
ˈduː		do	də³		du		du(ː)
ˈdʌz		does	dəz				dʌz
Modals							
ˈwil		will	l̩	wil			wil
ˈʃal		shall	ʃəl		ʃl	ʃl	ʃal
ˈkan		can	kən				kan
ˈmʌs	ˈmʌst	must	məs		məst		mʌst
ˈwud		would	ud, əd	wəd		d	wud
ˈʃud		should	ʃəd				ʃud
ˈkud		could	kəd				kud
Verbal							
ˈhav		have	əv				əv

Optional weak forms occur in the case of two verbals:
be, strong form ˈbiː, weak form bi.
been, strong form ˈbiːn, weak form bin.

¹ The sibilants s, z, ʃ, ʒ, take the form iz after them, and the voiceless consonants p, t, k, f, θ are followed by the assimilated form s.
² The sibilants s, z, ʃ, ʒ take the form əz after them, and the voiceless consonants p, t, k, f, θ are followed by the assimilated form s.
³ A special weak form, d, is used before unstressed juː.

17 **Prepositions.** The weak forms of these are not used when they occur finally in their clause in the circumstances described in §294.

Strong Forms		Ortho-graphic Form	Weak Forms			
Normal	Pre-vocalic		Normal	Pre-vocalic	Final	Rapid
ˋat		at	ət		at	
ˋbʌt		but	bət		ˋbʌt[1]	
ˋfoː	ˋfoːr	for	fə	fər	foː	fr
ˋfrom		from	frəm		from	frm̩
ˋov		of	əv		ov	v, ə
ˋtuː		to	tə	tu	tu	

Optional weak forms:

by, strong form ˋbai, weak form bi (in certain contexts only).

[1] In the expressions 'oːl ˋbʌt and 'eniθiŋ ˋbʌt.

18   Connectives.

Strong Forms		Ortho-graphic Form	Weak Forms			
Normal	Pre-vocalic		Normal	Pre-vocalic	Post-vocalic	Rapid
Conjunctions						
ˈan	ˈand	and	ən	ənd		n̩, n̩d
ˈbʌt		but	bət			
ˈaz		as	əz			
—		than[1]	ðən			ðn̩
—		that[1]	ðət			
Relatives						
ˈhuː		who	u		hu	
—		that[1]	ðət			

Optional weak forms:

   or, strong forms oː, oːr, weak forms ə, ər.
   nor, strong forms noː, noːr, weak forms nə, nər.

---

[1] The strong forms of these words are normally used only in naming them; the demonstrative "that" has no weak form.

19 Miscellaneous.

Strong Forms		Ortho-graphic Form	Weak Forms			
Normal	Pre-vocalic		Normal	Pre-vocalic	Post-vocalic	Rapid
ˈðeə	ˈðeər	there[1]	ðə	ðər		
ˈnot		not[2]	n̩	n̩t	n, nt	
ˈseint		saint[3]	sn̩	sn̩t		sm̩, sŋ̩
ˈsəː	ˈsəːr	sir	sə	sər		

Optional weak forms:

so, strong form ˈsou, weak forms su, sə.

---

[1] This word is not the adverb of place, but the precursory "there" used with the verb "to be."

[2] The weakened form of "not" occurs only as an element in the formation of the negative conjugating finites (§146).

[3] The assimilated form sm̩ is used before names beginning with p, b or m, and sŋ̩ occurs before names beginning with k or g.

B. Tonetics

FACTORS IN INTONATION

20 Scope. The term tonetics may be said to cover all those elements of speech (sometimes referred to as supra-segmental features) that help to express a speaker's meaning or feeling, or his attitude towards what he is talking about. It covers such factors as stress, loudness, rhythm, pitch, intonation, speed of delivery and voice quality, all of which affect the relative prominence of words and syllables. The factors that most concern us here are stress, pitch and intonation.

21 Stress. Stress is the force used in speaking. It is rare for stress to remain constant over successive syllables. Strong stress usually gives the impression of greater loudness, though in dramatic passages it is sometimes used without increasing the loudness of delivery. There are infinite gradations of stress, but for practical purposes it is sufficient to distinguish three degrees, and syllables may be classified as fully stressed, partially stressed and unstressed. The object of stressing certain syllables in speaking is to make them stand out from the others, thus giving greater prominence to the words of which they form part.

22 Pitch. The relative height or depth of the voice is referred to as pitch. Some stressed syllables are pronounced on a level pitch and may be said to have Level or *Static Stress*. Others are associated with a more or less marked glide upwards or downwards—or both —and this glide may be complete on the stressed syllable itself or may be spread over a following series of unstressed syllables. Since the precise incidence of the glide is not significant and is determined by the distribution of stressed and unstressed syllables it is convenient to regard the syllable in either case as having Moving or *Kinetic Stress*.

23 Prominence. Pitch and pitch change have considerable effect on the prominence of a syllable. Given equal degrees of stress, syllables pronounced on a high pitch give a hearer the impression of greater prominence than do those pronounced on low pitches, and those bearing a kinetic stress have greater prominence than those bearing a static stress. Further, among the kinetic stresses the downward glide gives more prominence than the upward glide.

24 Word stress. This is a convenient term for designating the stressing of the various syllables of a word when it is pronounced in isolation. Word stress is the foundation on which sentence stress and intonation are laid. The final full stress in any complete utterance is always a kinetic one; if, therefore, a word is pronounced in isolation it is automatically given a kinetic stress on one of its syllables. Thus when words such as ˋiːzi, ˋkʌvəriŋ or ˋevidəntli are pronounced in isolation (or as the last stressed word in a group) the first syllable will in each case take a kinetic stress, but when words such as məˋʃiːn, diˋtəːmind or disˋkʌvəri are used in similar circumstances it is the second syllable that takes the kinetic stress.

25 Multiple word stress. Many English words take two stresses, and a few very long ones take three or more. In these cases the last stress is the kinetic one and those that precede it are static ones. There are two main causes of multiple stressing:

1. In many polysyllabic words the kinetic stress falls on a syllable later than the second; in such cases a static stress is used on one of the first two syllables:

ˈʌndiˋtəːd, ˈkɒnvəˋseiʃn̩, igˈzamiˋneiʃn̩.

2. In many words composed of two elements each element retains a stress:

ˈɑːftəˋnuːn, ˈgudˋwil, ˈʌndəˋgradjuit, ˈilˋtriːt,
ˈsʌbˋkɒntinənt, ˈouvəˋdʌn.

Examples of words having three or more stresses:

ˈsjuːpəˈfiʃiˋaliti, ˈinəkˈsesiˋbiliti, ˈmisprəˈnʌnsiˋeiʃn̩,
ˈekstrəˈteriˈtɔːriˋaliti.

26 Rhythm. English speakers show a preference for separating stressed syllables by one or more unstressed ones, and for placing stresses at more or less equal time intervals. Words that have multiple stress in isolation are particularly influenced by this habit, and many of them may lose one or other of their stresses in connected speech, the rule being that if they are closely linked in meaning

17

with a neighbouring stressed word, the stress falling nearest to that word will be very much weakened or will disappear altogether. Taking the double-stressed word ˈaːftəˈnuːn, we find:

ˈaːftənuːn ˈtiː *but* ə ˈfain aːftəˈnuːn.

27 Sentence stress. The stress modifications noted in the previous section are one aspect of what is known as sentence stress, i.e., the stressing of words in the sentence. In connected speech even single-stressed words may lose their stress if their function in the sentence is an unimportant one, or if they are being repeated, having just been used by the same or another speaker in a conversation, or if they are being modified in some important respect by the addition of another word.

28 Intonation. The term intonation refers specifically to those pitch changes that are significant. In "expressionless" speech the voice does not continue on a dead level, but follows a very slowly descending scale. Since this gradual descent is consistent its presence can be assumed, and in marking intonation only the significant rises and falls need be indicated. In a complete utterance these may be quite complicated, but they can be reduced to a manageable number if those pitch changes that can occur on a single syllable are regarded as the basic tones. When looked at from the point of view of intonation, the static and kinetic stresses will be called static and kinetic *tones*.

29 Static tones. These add prominence or emphasis to the word on which they are used, but do not normally add meaning or feeling. They may occupy any pitch within a speaker's voice range, but for practical purposes it is sufficient to distinguish two levels, high and low. Emphasis tends to raise high tones and to lower low tones.

30 Kinetic tones. These add meaning or feeling to the word on which they are used, and this meaning or feeling extends in suitable cases to the whole sense-group in which they occur. As there are five different kinds of pitch change that may be concentrated on a single syllable, five kinetic tones must be distinguished, but it must be remembered that in many cases the tone is extended over a series of unstressed syllables following the stressed one.

31 Tonetic stress marks. Thanks to the connection between pitch variation and stress it is possible to indicate both phenomena by a single set of symbols, known as tonetic stress marks. With the exception of the high pitch mark, all the marks are placed before a stressed syllable, and the five kinetic tone marks—those preceded by roman numerals in the following list—indicate the stressed syllable on which a significant pitch change occurs or is initiated.

	High (')	or Low (ˌ)	Level or Static Tone.
I	High (´)	or Low (ˏ)	Rising Tone.
II	High (ˋ)	or Low (ˎ)	Falling Tone.
III	High (ˇ)	or Low (ᵥ)	Falling-Rising Tone.
IV	High (ˆ)	or Low (ʌ)	Rising-Falling Tone.
V	High (˜)	or Low (ᵳ)	Rising-Falling-Rising Tone.

(˙) A weak stress of any pitch (except the lowest) which does not interfere with the flow of the intonation.

(⁻) An unstressed syllable of high pitch.

Specially emphatic tones are shown by doubling the first stroke of the tonetic stress mark, e.g., (ˮ, ˶, ˇ).

ANALYSIS OF A TUNE

32 Nature of tunes. A sense-group containing a nuclear tone is called a tone-group, or more conveniently a *tune*. It may or may not be grammatically linked with other sense-groups having their own tunes, but with few exceptions any tune must contain a kinetic tone to form its nucleus, thereby acquiring its special character. In most tunes there will be other words besides the nuclear one that require stresses, and these other stresses may have either static or kinetic tones associated with them.

33 Simple tunes. Tunes in which all tones except the nuclear one are static may be referred to as *simple tunes*. The following example shows the parts into which a simple tune may be divided.

Prehead	*Head*	*Body*	*Nucleus*	*Tail*
ju ʃəd əv	'tould	joː 'brʌðə tə 'giv wʌn tu	ˌiːtʃ	əv ðəm

34 Prehead. This consists of any unstressed syllables at the beginning of a group. Normal preheads are pronounced on a rather low pitch, but there are two contexts in which high preheads are used, and these must then be marked with the high pitch mark:

1. As a normal element in the intonation of certain words and short phrases conveying salutations, warnings, apologies or encouragement. The nuclear tone is a low rise:

‾gud͵bai. ‾bi ͵keəf|. ‾ai m ͵sori. ‾oːl ͵rait.

2. As a device for increasing the prominence of an immediately following low tone by introducing a strong pitch contrast:

‾hi ͵oːt tə bi. ‾wot ə ʃeim. ‾ai ͵nou ͵ðat.

35 Head. This is the first fully stressed syllable of a group containing more than one stressed word. A normal head has a High Level tone, except before a Low Rising nucleus, when a Low Level tone is normal.

'mei ai 'teik wʌn?   'dʒon fə'got it.   wi 'aːnt ͵leit.
ai 'didn̩t 'nou ͵ðat.   it ͵izn̩t im͵poːtn̩t.

36 Body. This consists of any syllables, whether stressed or unstressed, lying between the Head and the Nucleus. In a normal body containing level stresses each of these is pitched slightly lower than the preceding one, and any unstressed syllables occupy the same pitch as the stressed syllable with which they are most intimately linked. Thus, in the following example, each of the internal groups is slightly lower than the one that precedes it:

ju ʃəd əv | 'tould | joː 'brʌðə | tə 'giv wʌn | tu ͵iːtʃ | əv ðəm

37 Nucleus. Since this is the most important intonational element in a group it falls on the word to which the speaker wishes to give the greatest prominence. Any of the other elements in a tune may be absent, but, except in a few special cases, a kinetic tone must always be present to form a nucleus. In some cases the form taken by a nuclear tone varies according to whether or not it falls on the final syllable of its group. The following diagrams show the form taken by each of the five nuclei when they are final.

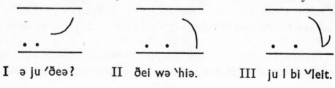

I   ə ju 'ðeə?   II   ðei wə 'hiə.   III   ju l bi 'leit.

20

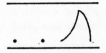

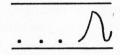

IV   ai m sə^praizd.   V   wi wər in ⌄taim.

38 Divided nuclei. The final rise which is characteristic of
Tones III and V may occur on a later syllable than that which
bears the fall (of Tone III) or rise-fall (of Tone V). This delayed
rise may occur on the syllable immediately following the fall (or
rise-fall), or it may be separated from it by a series of unstressed
or weakly stressed syllables. As it may be placed on a different
word from that bearing the initial element, these tones may even
embrace the whole sense-group. This transfer of the rising element
of the nucleus has the effect of increasing the prominence of the
word on which it is placed.   It is important to note that all inter-
vening syllables between the two parts of the nucleus must be
pronounced on a low tone, even when they are stressed, and that
the nucleus does not lose its tonetic unity in spite of being divided.

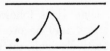

IIID ⌐ðat ˌizŋt ˌrait.   VD ðə ^plei z ˌgud.

39 Tail. This consists of any unstressed or weakly stressed
syllables that follow the nucleus. The examples given in §37 showed
how the five nuclear tones can each be completed on a single (final)
syllable; those given below show the form taken by the same nuclei
when a tail is present. The unstressed syllables in the tail afford
a means of completing the various pitch changes in a more leisurely
fashion, and advantage is always taken of this in the case of the
tunes that end in a rise; in the case of those that end in a fall
the pitch change may or may not be completed on the stressed
syllable.   Tails therefore fall into two classes, the rising tail and
the low level tail, of which the tails of Tones I and II may be
regarded as typical respectively.

When Tone I is followed by a tail the syllable bearing the nuclear
stress is pronounced on a low, or comparatively low, pitch, and the
rise is expressed on a series of unstressed or weakly stressed syllables
rising regularly to a higher point.   While this series may occupy

any range of pitches, the range used for questions is generally mid-pitch to high, and that for statements low-pitch to mid.

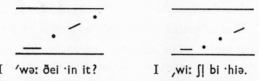

I 'wəː ðei ·in it?   I ‚wiː ʃ| bi ·hiə.

When Tone III is followed by a tail the syllable bearing the nuclear stress falls to a low, or comparatively low, pitch, and the rise is expressed on the tail, as in the case of Tone I. The range used for the rise is generally the bottom half of the voice range. Tone V has a similar tail, with the stressed syllable taking the initial rise and fall.

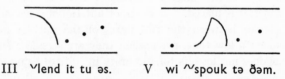

III ᵛlend it tu əs.   V wi ᴬspouk tə ðəm.

When Tone II is followed by a tail the syllable bearing the nuclear stress may be pronounced with a rapid fall from a high, or comparatively high, pitch, to a low one, or it may remain level on the high pitch, with a slight suggestion of a fall at the end. In either case the tail consists of a series of unstressed or weakly stressed syllables on a low pitch. If there is no fall on the nuclear syllable the impression of a fall is conveyed by the sudden drop from the high pitch of the nucleus to the low pitch of the tail.

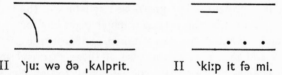

II ˋjuː wə ðə ‚kʌlprit.   II ˋkiːp it fə mi.

The tail of Tone IV has the same form, but the nucleus may be spread over either two or three syllables instead of one.

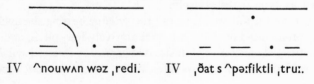

IV ᴬnouwʌn wəz ‚redi.   IV ‚ðat s ᴬpəːfiktli ‚truː.

40 Nuclear incidence. It has been stated that the nuclear tone is placed on the word to which the speaker wishes to give the greatest prominence. Since a speaker's feeling as to which idea is most important in a sentence will vary with the conversational context, it follows that almost any stressable word in a sense-group may bear the nuclear tone. The following are examples of nuclear tone shift, with suggestions as to the context in which each might be used. Two incidental points should be noticed: the adjustments made in the static and partial stresses to adjust the rhythm of the utterance, and the tendency of Tone III to divide when the fall comes early in the sentence.

Tune I. Rise.

həz 'dʒon ˙red ˙ðis ′buk?	(Simple question)
həz 'dʒon ˙red ′ðis buk?	(and not the other one) .
həz 'dʒon ′red ðis ˙buk?	(not just glanced at it)
həz ′dʒon ˙red ðis ˙buk?	(and not someone else)
′haz dʒon ˙red ðis ˙buk?	(I doubt it)

Tune II. Fall.

ai 'soː ˙dʒon hiə ˏjestədi.	(Emphasis on time)
ai 'soː ˙dʒon ˎhiə ˌjestədi.	(Emphasis on place)
ai 'soː ˎdʒon hiə ˌjestədi.	(Emphasis on person seen)
ai ˎsoː dʒon ˌhiə ˌjestədi.	(Emphasis on fact)
ˎai soː ˌdʒon hiə ˌjestədi.	(Emphasis on person seeing)

Tune III. Fall-Rise.

'ðat iznt ˙oːl ai ˯wont.	(but it may be all I shall get)
'ðat iznt oːl ˯ai ˙wont.	(Contrast with someone else)
'ðat iznt ˯oːl ai ˙wont.	(only some of it)
ˌðat ˯iznt ˌoːl ai ˌwont.	(contradiction of affirmative)
˯ðat iznt ˌoːl ai ˌwont.	(Simple protest)

USE OF THE TUNES

41 Functions and meanings. In the following sections the most important functions and meanings of Tunes I, II and III are explained. Tunes IV and V, being more complicated in form and feeling and only occasionally essential, will be used as little as possible in the present work. For ordinary purposes a mastery of Tunes I, II and III will equip a speaker with an adequate English

intonation, it being nearly always possible to use Tone II instead
of Tone IV and Tone III instead of Tone V, though there will,
of course, be a certain loss of expressiveness. For detailed descriptions of the more complicated tones the reader is referred to specialist
works on intonation.

Below are tabulated the principal types of utterance on which
Tunes I, II and III are used.

	I. Rise	*II. Fall*	*III. Fall-Rise*
Questions	General	Special	—
Statements	—	Simple	Implicatory
		Straightforward	Doubtful
		Definite	Hesitant
Imperatives	—	Familiar	Polite
		Commands	Entreaties
Exclamations	Interrogative	Normal	—
Salutations	—	Greetings	(Farewells)
Apologies	—	—	Normal
Warnings	—	Urgent	Normal

Notes. The rise referred to in the table is a high one. *All* the
types of utterance shown can be given a perfunctory flavour if they
are given a low rising nucleus with a low head or prehead.

General questions are those, beginning essentially with an anomalous finite, which can be answered by "Yes" or "No."

Special questions are those, beginning essentially with an interrogative word, which cannot be answered by "Yes" or "No," but
require a specific, detailed answer.

The fall-rise on *farewells* is typical of American intonation; in
Britain they are given a high prehead followed by a low rise.

42   Tune I, Rise. When used interrogatively the nucleus tends
to start on a medium pitch and rise to a high one; in statements
it generally starts from a low pitch and rises to a medium one.
Tune I is used in:

General questions.

With a low prehead these have a casual sound.

kən ju ˈtʃeindʒ it?   məst ai ˈrait tu im?

A high level head on the conjugating finite suggests that the question is being asked with interest.

'kan ju 'tʃeindʒ it? 'mʌst ai 'rait tu im?

A high prehead with an emphatic nucleus gives an exclamatory effect.

‾kən ju ″tʃeindʒ it? ‾məst ai ″rait tu im?

Special questions.

When, in order to temporize, a speaker repeats a special question asked by another, he changes the intonation from the normal fall to a rise, thus suggesting the introduction: Did I understand you to ask ...?

wot 'iz it? ˌwen did ai ə'raiv?

If the interrogative word is given a high head the repetition becomes rhetorical.

'wot 'iz it? 'wen did ai ə'raiv?

The rhetorical effect is increased if a high prehead is used, especially with an emphatic nucleus.

‾wot ″iz it? ‾wen did ai ə″raiv?

When a special question is used in order to ask for a repetition of information that has already been given (having been either not heard, not understood or forgotten) a rising nucleus is placed on the interrogative word.

'wot did ju ˙sei? 'weə did ʃi ˙bai it?

An emphatic nucleus makes such questions rhetorical or exclamatory.

″wot did ju ˙sei? ″weə did ʃi ˙bai it?

Imperatives.

A low rising nucleus makes these sound laconic and often suggests that the hearer ought not to have needed prompting. The head must be low.

ˌput it ˌdaun. ˌɑːsk im fər əˌnʌðə.

Exclamations.

Interrogative force is given to these by a high rising nucleus,

25

while a low rise makes them sound laconic. If the nucleus is not
on the first syllable a high prehead is used.

ˈou.   ˌou.   ¯hʌˈlou.   ¯hʌˌlou.

43 Tune II, Fall. This nucleus starts on a high or medium pitch
and falls to a low one. It is the decided tone, but the decisiveness
is sometimes reduced by stopping the fall short of the bottom of
the speaker's voice range. It is used in:

General questions.

These are given a falling nucleus in two cases:

1. When a speaker repeats a question which has already been
asked, but which has not been answered. This indicates that the
speaker is insisting on an answer.

ˈaː ðei ˋkʌmiŋ?   ˈhav ju ˈleid ðə ˋteib| jet?

2. When a speaker uses a question as an exclamation and expects
the hearer to agree with him. In British English the negative form
of the conjugating finite is always used in these questions.

ˈizn̩t it ˎwʌndəf|?!   ▪wount ðei bi ˎpliːzd!

A high prehead before a low emphatic fall is very much used.

¯izn̩t it ˎwʌndəf|!   ¯wount ðei bi ˎpliːzd!

The nuclear tone may fall on the conjugating finite (§146).

ˋizn̩t it ˌwʌndəf|!   ˋwount ðei bi ˌpliːzd!

Special questions.

This is the normal intonation for this type of question. The
interrogative word usually takes a high level head.

ˈweə dəz i ˌliv?   ˈhau mʌtʃ | it ˌkost?

If special emphasis is needed on the nuclear word, this must fall
from a higher pitch than that occupied by the head.

ˌweə dəz i ˋliv?   ˌhau mʌtʃ | it ˋkost?

Statements.

This is the normal intonation for simple, straightforward, definite
statements. Usually both head and nucleus are of the high variety.

ʃi z ˈgetiŋ ˋtiː ˌredi.   ai ˈdount θiŋk it s ˋtruː.

26

Without changing the tonal arrangement changes can be made in the respective pitches to give greater prominence to either the head or the nucleus.

ʃi z 'getiŋ ˌtiː ˌredi.   ai 'dount θiŋk it s ˌtruː.

ʃi z ˌgetiŋ ˋtiː ˌredi.   ai ˌdount θiŋk it s ˋtruː.

The whole tune can be lowered to give a somewhat perfunctory flavour.

ʃi z ˌgetiŋ ˌtiː ˌredi.   ai ˌdount θiŋk it s ˌtruː.

Imperatives.

A falling nucleus on these gives them the nature of commands, though in familiar speech this tune is often used without a suggestion of impoliteness.

'kʌm ən sit ˌdaun.   'dount ˌwʌri mi.

Exclamations.

This is the normal intonation for most exclamations. There is often a suggestion that the surprise is mixed with satisfaction if the nucleus is high, and with dismay if it is low. The fall is often emphatic.

ˋou! ˇou! ˋaː! ˇaː!   ˌou! ˌou! ˌaː! ˌaː!

Salutations.

This is the formal intonation for greetings. The word **gud** is very seldom stressed.

gud ˋmoːniŋ.   gud 'aːftəˌnuːn.   'hau d ju ˌduː.

Warnings.

An urgent warning may take a falling nucleus.

ⁿluk ˌaut!   bi ˋkeəfl̩!   ⁿmaind wot ju ə ˌduːiŋ!

44 Tune III, Fall-rise. This nucleus combines the high or low fall of Tune II with the low rise of Tune I to convey an implication, apology or warning, or to soften utterances that might sound too harsh if said with a blunt Tune II. Whether the nucleus is concentrated on one word or divided between two has no effect on the underlying feeling of the tune; the difference is in the relative prominence given to the words involved. This tune is used almost

exclusively for statements (including apologies) and imperatives
(including warnings); it is hardly ever heard on questions or
exclamations.

Statements.

These always have an implication, that is to say, something
unexpressed which the hearer is intended to understand. Various
feelings or attitudes are thus conveyed.

1. Doubt.

    hi ˇmei bi ˌðeə.   (but I ˎdoubt it.)
    wi I 'kʌm if wi ˇkan.   (but we 'can t ˎpromise.)

2. Reservation (low nucleus.)

    it 'izn̩t ˎbad.   ('nor is it very ˇgood.)
    hi z 'veri ˎklevə.   (but 'not very ˇnice.)

3. Concession (high nucleus.)

    ðei ə 'raːðər əˇtraktiv.   (one must adˇmit.)
    ai 'laik ðə ˇfəːst ˙paːt.   (I conˇcede ˌthat.)

4. Protest.

    ju ˇnevər iŋˌkʌridʒ mi.
    ai m ˇtaiəd əv ˌkworǀiŋ.

5. Excuse.

    ðei 'weitid ˙ten ˎminits.   (ˌsurely ˌthat was eˌnough.)
    wi ˇaːskt ju if ju ˌwontid wʌn.   (so 'why ˙blame ˇus?)

6. Warning.

    it s 'gouiŋ tə ˎrein.   (so 'take your ˇraincoat.)
    ðei 'wount ˎlaik it.   (so 'don't ˇdo it.)

7. Unwelcome news.

    ai 'kaːnt ˙weit eni ˎloŋgə.   (I'm aˈfraid.)
    hi 'wount bi 'hiə təˎdei.   (I'm, ˌsorry to ˌsay.)

8. Apologies.

    ai m ˇsori.
    ai ˇbeg joː ˌpaːdn̩.

Imperatives.

This is the tune for polite imperatives or requests. If the whole nuclear tone falls on the complement or object it gives it a certain prominence, but various other arrangements are possible. A fall on the verb, or in the negative on "don't," gives the feeling of an entreaty.

ˈweit fər ˬʌs.	ˈdount ˙ʃʌt ðə ˇwind(o)u.
ˋweit fər ˏʌs.	ˈdount ˋʃʌt ðə ˏwind(o)u.
ˇweit fər əs.	ˋdount ˌʃʌt ðə ˏwind(o)u.
ˇweit ˙foːr əs.	ˋdount ˏʃʌt ðə ˙wind(o)u.

This is also the normal tune for warnings.

ˋluk ˏaut.	ˋmaind wot ju ə ˏduːiŋ.

45 Special tune for farewells. A tune that is probably a weakened form of Tune III is used for farewells. It consists of a high prehead followed by a low rise.

ˉgud ˏiːvniŋ.	ˉgud ˏnait.	ˉgudˏbai.

This same tune is also used on a number of short phrases of a miscellaneous nature. (See also §34.)

ˉoːlˏrait.	ˉnot ˏbad.	ˉkʌm ˏin.	ˉou ˏjes.
ˉai m ˏsori.	ˉit | ˏduː.	ˉveri ˏwel.	ˉbi ˏgud.

46 Compound tunes. When a sense-group is pronounced with more than one kinetic tone it may be said to have a compound tune. In such cases the last of the kinetic tones is the nuclear tone, while the first performs the function of a head to the tune—unless it happens to be preceded by a level head. Any kinetic tones occupying an intermediate position may be regarded as forming part of the body of the tune. Almost any combination of the five tones is possible, but some combinations are much more used than others. Examples are given below of the most frequently occurring combinations of the first three tunes.

I + I, Rising head, rising nucleus.

This compound uses high elements in general questions to give them animation, and low elements in statements and imperatives to give them reassurance or friendliness.

ˈiz it ˈðeə?   ˈkɑːnt ju ˈhiə mi?
ˌðat ǀ ˌduː.   ðə z ˌplenti əv ˌtaim.
ˌkʌm ən sit ˌdaun.   ˌgiv im əˌnʌðə wʌn.

I + II, Rising head, falling nucleus.

The head of this compound is usually a low rise, which gives
the tune more animation than that possessed by the simple Tune II.
It may suggest mystification or impatience, according to the context
in which it is used. It can be used in both types of question as well
as in statements, imperatives and exclamations.

ˌhav ju ˈleid ðə ˋteibl̩?   ˌweə dəz i ˋliv?
ʃi z ˌgetiŋ ˋtiː ˌredi.   ˌai dount ˋlaik ˌðat soːt əv θiŋ.
ˌkʌm ən sit ˋdaun.   ˌwot ə ˌpriti lit̩l ˌhaus!

II + II, Falling head, falling nucleus.

The usual form of this compound is a high fall on the head and
a low fall on the nucleus, though other combinations may occur.
It is very energetic, and tends to sound dogmatic. It can be used
on both types of question as well as on statements, imperatives
and exclamations.

ˋaː ju ˌredi?   ˋweə wə ði ˋʌðəz?
it ˋiznt ˌfeə.   ðat s ðə ˋlaːst ˌstroː.
ˋduː sit ˌdaun.   ˋwot ə ˌnjuːsn̩s!

III + II, Falling-rising head, falling nucleus.

The fall on the head of this compound emphasizes the word on
which it is placed, while the rise gives a softer effect than do the
two blunt falls of the previous compound. On account of the
presence of a Tone III this compound is not much used on questions.
The Tone III may be divided, and either high or low, while the
nuclear tone is usually high.

ˇweə dəz i ˋliv?   ˌðat ˌiznt ˋrait.
ðei ˇmaitn̩t bi ˋredi.   ˌwiː ʃl̩ biː in ˋlʌndən.
ˇgiv im əˋnʌðə wʌn.   hau ˇnais əv ju tə ˌsei sou.

II + III, Falling head, falling-rising nucleus.

In this compound the fall on the head usually stops before
reaching the bottom of the voice range, and the nucleus is a lowered

Tonetics

one. The tune is implicatory, with a strong stress on the head word. It is used on statements, imperatives, apologies and warnings, and most frequently conveys a feeling either of apology or of warning, according to the context in which it is used.

wi ˈdid ˬwoːn ju.

ˈteik ˬsʌm əv ðəm.

ai ˈbeg joː ˬpaːdn̩.

it ˈwoznt ˬdifik|t.

ˈdount ˬwoːk tə ði ˌofis.

ˈduː bi ˬkeəf|.

PART II

Parts of Speech

47 A functional classification. In conventional grammars it is usual to recognize the following eight parts of speech: *Noun, Pronoun, Adjective, Verb, Adverb, Preposition, Conjunction* and *Interjection.*

This classification has been adhered to as closely as is consistent with the objects of this book, but experience shows that the following modifications are justified on grounds of both logic and expediency. They are based partly on recommendations in the Report of the Joint Committee on Grammatical Terminology (1915).

1. All pronouns, demonstratives, articles, numerals, etc., are grouped together under the general heading of *Determiners*, because most of the members of this category may be used indifferently as pronouns or as qualifiers of nouns.

2. Participials functioning as qualifiers are grouped with adjectives.

3. Relatives and interrogatives are grouped with conjunctions under the general term *Connectives.*

In this book, therefore, the eight parts of speech will be:

A. Nouns.
B. Determiners (with Semi-Pronouns and Pronouns).
C. Adjectives (including Participials).
D. Verbs (Finites and Verbals).
E. Adverbs (and Adverbials).
F. Prepositions (and Phrases).
G. Connectives (with Relatives and Interrogatives).
H. Interjections (and Exclamations).

A. Nouns

FORMAL CLASSIFICATION

48 Varieties of nouns. A noun is defined as a word used to name a person or thing. Nouns vary greatly in form and degree of complexity, from words such as ˈkat, ˈbuk, ˈman, which are simple roots, through forms like ˈprezn̩s, ˈmesidʒ, əˈriθmətik, which are for all practical purposes indecomposable, and others such as ˈhait, ˈfren(d)ʃip, riˈsiːt, formed by adding more or less obsolete affixes to recognizable roots (many of which are modified in form or meaning) to words like ˈdrainis, ˈtiːtʃə, ˈoupniŋ, imˈpruːvmənt, which are clearly derivatives, being formed from existing words by adding living affixes.

All the foregoing examples consist of simple roots or roots to which affixes have been added and which may therefore be called derivatives, but a further stage is reached when two or more roots are joined to form what is known as a compound word. These also show variations in form, ranging from intimate combinations such as ˈgran(d)faːðə, ˈpainap|, ˈwaitwoʃ through more obvious combinations like ˈteib|ˌkloθ, ˈriːdiŋˌlamp, ˈʌndəˌklou(ð)z to words in which the independent meaning of each component remains undimmed, as in ˈgudˈwil, ˈwiːkˈend, ˈθaŋksˈgiviŋ.

49 Simple and derivative nouns. The following categories, ranging almost imperceptibly from one extreme to the other, will give some idea of the various formal characteristics of these nouns.

a. ˈkat, ˈbuk, ˈman, ˈteib|, ˈfraːns, ˈwind(o)u.

b. ˈreiliŋ, ˈsiːliŋ, ˈstokiŋ,

c. ˈlektʃə*, ˈpiktʃə*, ˈmikstʃə*,
ˈmeʒə*, ˈpleʒə*, ˈpreʃə*,
dʒiˈolədʒi, əˈstronəmi,

əˈriθmətik, fəˈnetiks, ˈmaθ(ə)ˈmatiks,
ədˈvaːntidʒ, ˈkʌridʒ, ˈmesidʒ,
ˈprezn̩s, ˈabsn̩s, ˈdistəns, ˈkonʃn̩s,
ˈleŋθ, ˈbretθ, ˈdepθ, ˈtruːθ,
ˈhait, ˈθeft,

33

d. ˈkiŋdəm, ˈfriːdəm, ˈwizdəm,
ˈtʃaildhud, ˈneibəhud, ˈpriːsthud,
ˈfrendʃip, ˈtʃeəmənʃip,
ˈdrainis, ˈilnis, ˈgudnis.

e. əˈtendənt, ˈsəːvənt, ˈstjuːdn̩t, lefˈtenənt, iˈkwivələnt,
ˈaːtist, ˈkemist, ˈsouʃlist,
ˈprinˈses,
ˈkauntis, ˈhoustis,
ˈdʒapəˈniːz, ˈpoːtjuˈgiːz,
ˈrʌʃn̩, əˈmerikən, iˈtaljən, noːˈwiːdʒən,
ˈdifik|ti, ˈdʒenəˈrositi, ˈopəˈtjuːniti,
ˈkonvəˈseiʃn̩, kəˈlekʃn̩, ˈinstiˈtjuːʃn̩, əˈsousiˈeiʃn̩,
diˈviʒn̩, diˈsiʒn̩, əˈkeiʒn̩, əˈpinjən.

f. əˈreindʒmənt, imˈpruːvmənt, iŋˈgeidʒmənt, ədˈvəːtizmənt,
ˈtiːtʃə*, ˈraitə*, fəˈtogrəfə*, biˈginə*, ˈforinə*, ˈdoktə*,
ˈeditə*, ˈoːθə*,
ˈfiːliŋ, biˈginiŋ, ˈoupniŋ, ˈmiːniŋ, etc. etc.

50 Compound nouns. There are many classes and varieties
of compound nouns. Examples:

a. ˈblakbəːd, ˈblakboːd, ˈgranfaːðə*, ˈiŋgliʃmən.
b. ˈskuːlrum, ˈiŋkstand, ˈteib|kloθ, ˈlanloːd, ˈsʌnʃeid.
c. ˈbukˌbaindiŋ, ˈhandˌraitiŋ, ˈwudˌkaːviŋ, ˈblʌdˌpoizn̩iŋ.
d. ˈpaundzwəθ, ˈʃiliŋzwəθ, ˈpeniwəθ *or* ˈpenəθ.
e. ˈkaːviŋˌnaif, ˈswimiŋˌmatʃ, ˈwoːkiŋˌstik, ˈsitiŋrum.
f. ˈbrʌðərinˌloː, ˈfaːðərinˌloː, ˈdoːtərinˌloː.
g. ˈskuːlˌtiːtʃə*, ˈboksˌmeikə*, ˈkloθˌmanjuˌfaktʃərə*.

There are also many established collocations that may be regarded
as compound nouns. Notice the differences in stress in the following
examples. Words taking the stress-pattern (ˈ ˌ) are said to be
single-stressed, while those taking the pattern (ˈ ˈ) are said to be
double-stressed.

Noun + noun

ˈbei ˈwindu   ˈgaːdn̩ ˈsiti
ˈkamp ˈtʃeə*   ˈmeidn̩ ˈneim
ˈfaːm ˈhaus   ˈseilə ˈhat

Possessive noun + noun

ˈbə:dz ˌnest ˈfraiəz ˋbo:lsm̩

ˋdeθs ˌhed ˈkwi:nz ˋkaunsļ

ˋleidiz ˌmeid ˈseiləz ˋnot

Present participle + noun

ˋbo:diŋ ˌhaus ˈka:stiŋ ˋvout

ˋlendiŋ ˌlaibrəri ˈli:diŋ ˋa:tikļ

ˋraitiŋ ˌdesk ˈwə:kiŋ ˋkla:s

Past participle + noun

ˈka:st ˋaiən ˈoild ˋsilk

ˈkʌt ˋgla:s ˈspotid ˋfi:və*

51 Dual function words. Some words function as either nouns or verbs without undergoing any change of form:

ˋhelp, ˋtʃeindʒ, ˋpuʃ, ˋdʒʌmp, ˋa:nsə*, ˋla:f, ˋwo:k, ˋwə:k, etc.

Some of these combine with adverbial particles to form compound or group-words:

ˈtʃeindʒ ˋouvə*   it s ˈtaim fər ə ˈtʃeindʒ ˏouvə.

ˈlai ˋdaun   ai m ˈgouiŋ tə ˋhav ə ˈlai ˏdaun.

ˈluk ˋraund   ˈlet s ˋhav ə ˈluk ˏraund.

Certain nouns differ slightly from verbs with which they are related. The examples on the left are different in spelling as well as pronunciation, while those on the right differ only in pronunciation and therefore require special care.

Noun.	*Verb.*	*Noun.*	*Verb.*
ˋlaif	ˋliv	ˋju:s	ˋju:z
riˋsi:t	riˋsi:v	ˋreko:d	riˋko:d
ˋfu:d	ˋfi:d	ˋekstrakt	ikˋstrakt
ədˋvais	ədˋvaiz	ˋinsʌlt	inˋsʌlt.

A certain number of words that usually function as adjectives (including past participles) are used also as plural nouns.

ðə ˏritʃ   = ˈritʃ ˏpi:pļ

ðə ˏfrentʃ   = ðə ˈfrentʃ ˏpi:pļ .

ðə ˈkild ən ˏwu:ndid   = ðə ˈkild ən ˈwu:ndid ˏpi:pļ .

ði ˏindʒəd   = ði ˈindʒəd ˏpi:pļ .

INFLEXIONS OF THE NOUN

52 The two inflexions. The noun is subject to only two inflexions: 1. Plural. 2. Genitive.

The noun is not inflected for gender or for any other case than the genitive. The limitations in the use of the genitive are set forth in §56.

53 The plural inflexion. The regular plural of nouns is formed by adding to the singular:

- *a.* iz after the sibilant consonants s, z, ʃ, ʒ;
- *b.* s after the voiceless consonants p, t, k, f, θ;
- *c.* z in all other cases.

a. *Plural in* iz:

hoːs	ˈhoːsiz	saiz	ˈsaiziz
pleis	ˈpleisiz	praiz	ˈpraiziz
ˈpromis	ˈpromisiz	disˈgaiz	disˈgaiziz
boks	ˈboksiz	feiz	ˈfeiziz
fiʃ	ˈfiʃiz	eidʒ	ˈeidʒiz
diʃ	ˈdiʃiz	dʒʌdʒ	ˈdʒʌdʒiz
intʃ	ˈintʃiz	ˈkaridʒ	ˈkaridʒiz
tʃəːtʃ	ˈtʃəːtʃiz	ˈlaŋgwidʒ	ˈlaŋgwidʒiz

b. *Plural in* s:

kʌp	kʌps	paːt	paːts	seif	seifs
stamp	stamps	striːt	striːts	ruːf	ruːfs
strap	straps	buk	buks	klif	klifs
ʃop	ʃops	klok	kloks	mʌnθ	mʌnθs
hat	hats	foːk	foːks	deθ	deθs
nait	naits	woːk	woːks	tenθ	tenθs

c. *Plural in* z:

kab	kabz	ˈpensl	ˈpenslz	flai	flaiz
koːd	koːdz	kiː	kiːz	kau	kauz
leg	legz	staː*	staːz	boi	boiz
neim	neimz	loː	loːz	aiˈdiə	aiˈdiəz
pen	penz	ʃuː	ʃuːz	peə*	peəz
θiŋ	θiŋz	fəː*	fəːz	ʃoə*	ʃoəz
lʌv	lʌvz	dei	deiz	kjuə*	kjuəz
leið	leiðz	tou	touz		

54 Irregular plurals. A certain number of nouns in f, θ and one in s replace these voiceless consonants by the corresponding voiced one in the plural.

The following replace f by vz:

liːf	liːvz	louf	louvz	-self	-selvz
θiːf	θiːvz	naif	naivz	ʃelf	ʃelvz
haːf	haːvz	laif	laivz	wulf	wulvz
kaːf	kaːvz	waif	waivz		

The following replace θ by ðz:

paːθ	paːðz	juːθ	juːðz	ouθ	ouðz
baːθ	baːðz	truːθ	truːðz	mauθ	mauðz

The following replaces s by ziz:

haus   ˈhauziz

A certain number of nouns form the plural quite irregularly· The chief of these are:

man	men	tuːθ	tiːθ	maus	mais
ˈwumən	ˈwimin	guːs	giːs	oks	ˈoksn̩
tʃaild	ˈtʃildrn̩	fut	fiːt	ˈpeni	ˈpens[1]

A few foreign words have special plural forms. The chief of these are:

'meməˈrandəm	'meməˈrandə	ˈsiəriz	ˈsiəriːz
pəˈrenθisis	pəˈrenθisiːz	ˈdʒiːnəs	ˈdʒenərə
fiˈnominən	fiˈnominə	ˈfoːmjulə	ˈfoːmjuliː[2]

The prefix-title ˈmistə forms its plural in ˈmesəz, but this is generally avoided by saying mistə ˌsmiθ ənd mistə ˈbraun or ðə 'tuː mistə ˈbraunz.

---

[1] Weakened in compounds to pəns or pn̩s. Example ˈsikspəns. ˈpeni forms a regular plural in ˈpeniz when meaning *coins* and not the value of the coins. The word ˈsikspəns (meaning the coin) forms a regular plural ˈsikspənsiz.

[2] Or ˈfoːmjuləz.

The following nouns are invariable:

diə*	diə*	fiʃ	fiʃ[1]
ʃiːp	ʃiːp	traut	traut
ˈdʒent|mən	ˈdʒent|mən	kod	kod
ˈwəːkmən	ˈwəːkmən	ˈsamən	ˈsamən[2]
ˈiŋgliʃmən	ˈiŋgliʃmən	pleis	pleis[2]
and other compounds of -mən.		and a few other names of fishes.	

A few nouns exist only in the plural. The chief of these are:
ˈpiːp\|,[3] ˈdeitə,[4] klouðz, ˈkat\|, ˈvəːmin, ˈwiskəz, ˈweidʒiz.[4]

Adjectives and participles used as nouns are plural in meaning, but are not marked by any plural inflexion:

ðə ˌritʃ, ðə ˌpuə, ðə ˌfrentʃ, ðə ˌwuːndid, ðə ˌdaiiŋ.

55 The genitive inflexion. The genitive is marked by adding to the preceding noun (or, in some cases, to the last member of the noun group):

- *a.* iz after the sibilant consonants s, z, ʃ, ʒ;
- *b.* s after the voiceless consonants p, t, k, f, θ;
- *c.* z in all other cases.

a. Genitive in -iz:

	hoːs	ˈhoːsiz	(mistə) welz	ˈwelziz
	niːs	ˈniːsiz	(mistə) ˈstiːvn̦z	ˈstiːvn̦ziz
	nəːs	ˈnəːsiz	(mistə) maːʃ	ˈmaːʃiz
(mistə)	koks	ˈkoksiz	(mistə) buʃ	ˈbuʃiz
	dʒeimz	ˈdʒeimziz	dʒʌdʒ	ˈdʒʌdʒiz
(mistə)	dʒounz	ˈdʒounziz	dʒoːdʒ	ˈdʒoːdʒiz

b. Genitive in -s:

ˈbiʃəp	ˈbiʃəps	djuːk	djuːks	ˈdʒouzif	ˈdʒouzifs
wosp	wosps	ˈkritik	ˈkritiks	smiθ	smiθs
kat	kats	θiːf	θiːfs	iˈlizəbəθ	iˈlizəbəθs
ˈinfənt	ˈinfənts	waif	waifs	ruːθ	ruːθs

---

[1] Also ˈfiʃiz.
[2] Traditional spellings *salmon* and *plaice*.
[3] In the sense of "persons," not of "race."
'Except in the phrases ðə ˌdeitəm ˌlain and ə ˈlivin ˌweidʒ.

Nouns 56

c. Genitive in -z:

rob	robz	dʌv	dʌvz	dei	deiz
frend	frendz	fuːl	fuːlz	krou	krouz
dog	dogz	'leˋsiː	'leˋsiːz	kau	kauz
lam	lamz	ʃaː	ʃaːz	boi	boiz
man	manz	ʃoː*	ʃoːz	meə*	meəz
kiŋ	kiŋz	kruː	kruːz	ˋdoktə*	ˋdoktəz

Irregular plural nouns formed without adding iz, s or z (§54) form
their genitive according to the rule:

men	menz	ˋwəːkmən	ˋwəːkmənz	giːs	ˋgiːsiz
ˋwimin	ˋwiminz	ˋpiːp|	ˋpiːp|z	diə	diəz
ˋtʃildrn̩	ˋtʃildrn̩z	mais	ˋmaisiz	ʃiːp	ʃiːps

Plural nouns formed by adding iz, s or z (§53) are used as genitives
without any modification:

ˋdʒʌdʒiz	ˋdʒʌdʒiz	ˋbiʃəps	ˋbiʃəps	frendz	frendz
ˋhoːsiz	ˋhoːsiz	aːnts	aːnts	ˋdoktəz	ˋdoktəz
		klaːks	klaːks		

56 Uses of the genitive. In Spoken English the genitive inflexion is almost exclusively used in connection with:

a. Names of Persons:

'dʒonz ˏbuk = ðə 'buk biˈloŋiŋ tə ˏdʒon.
mistə 'harisiz ˏhat = ðə 'hat biˈloŋiŋ tə mistə ˏharis.

b. Names designating Persons:

mai 'brʌðəz ˏhaus = ðə 'haus biˈloŋiŋ tə mai ˏbrʌðə.
ðə 'beikəz ʃop = ðə 'ʃop biˈloŋiŋ tə ðə ˏbeikə.
ðə 'menz ˏkleimz = ðə 'kleimz ˈmeid bai ðə ˏmen.

c. Names of Pet Animals:

'tabiz ˏbaːskit = ðə 'baːskit weə ˏtabi (ðə ˏkat) ˌsliːps.
'faidouz ˏken\| = ðə 'ken\| weə ˏfaidou (ðə ˏdog) ˌsliːps.

d. Names designating Animals:

ə 'kats ˏwiskəz = ðə 'wiskəz on ə ˈkats ˏfeis.
ðə 'dogz ˏkolə = ðə 'kolə ðət ə ˏdog ˌweəz.
ðə 'hoːsiz ˏteil = 'ðat 'paːt əv ə ˈhoːs koːld ðə ˏteil.
ə ˋlaiənz den = ə 'den ˈokjupaid bai ə ˏlaiən (*or* ˏlaiənz).
ə ˋwosps nest = ə 'nest ˈbilt ənd ˈokjupaid bai ˏwosps.

39 C

e. Certain words logically intermediate between nouns and adverbs of time and duration:

təˈdeiz ˌpeipə	=	ðə ˈpeipə ˈpʌbliʃt təˌdei.
ˈjestədiz ˌmeil	=	ðə ˈmeil ˈritn̩ oː riˈsiːvd ˌjestədi.
ˈlaːst wiːks ˌnjuːz	=	ðə ˈnjuːz riˈsiːvd ˈlaːst ˌwiːk.
ə ˈθriː ˈjiəz ˌstei	=	ə ˈstei əv ðə djuˈreiʃn̩ əv ˈθriː ˌjiəz.

It will be noticed that the examples of the genitive given in §55 all come under one of the above categories.

57 Theory of the genitive. On logical grounds the genitive may be considered as an independent word coming under the heading of *syntax*, for it may be separated from the noun and attached to the last member of the noun-group:

> ðə ˈman aiˈsoː ˈjestədiz ˌfaːðə = ðə ˈfaːðər əv ðə ˈman ai ˈsoː ˌjestədi.

> ðə ˈkiŋ əv ˈiŋləndz ˌkraun = ðə ˈkraun əv ðə ˈkiŋ əv ˌiŋglənd.

Traditionally, however, it is an inflected form of the noun to which it is nominally attached. In justification of this view it is urged that with plural nouns in **z**, **s** or **iz**, the plural inflexion and genitive modification are merged together:

> ðə ˈpjuːplz ˌeksəsaiziz may mean ði ˈeksəsaiziz əv ðə ˌpjuːpl or ði ˈeksəsaiziz əv ðə ˌpjuːplz.[1]

It would seem to be more convenient to regard such a collocation as ðə kiŋ əv iŋgland as a grammatical unit. If we then, following Sweet and others, treat the genitive as an inflexion, it will naturally (since it is a suffix) be added to the end of the unit.

QUALIFICATION OF NOUNS

58 Position of qualifier. Nouns may be qualified by various parts of speech, some of which precede the noun, while others follow it, as shown in the following list:

---

[1] These two meanings are differentiated in traditional spelling by the two forms: *The pupil's exercises* and *The pupils' exercises*.

Preceding the Noun	*Following the Noun*
Nouns	Nouns in Apposition
Possessive Nouns	A few Adjectives
Determiners	Relative Clauses
Adjectives	Prepositional Phrases
Verbals (Participles)	Verbals (Infinitives)
Adverbs	

The stressing of the collocations that consist of a noun and its qualifier is variable, and will be explained in the next two sections.

59 Qualifiers preceding the noun. The normal stressing of this arrangement is a static stress on the qualifier (except for the articles) and a kinetic stress on the noun.

a. Nouns qualifying nouns.

'poːk ˏpai	'oksfəd ˏroud	'loːd ˏmeə*
'fiʃ ˏsoːs	'oksfəd ˏavinju	'foːpni ˏstamp
'oliv ˏoil	'tʃaːnsəri ˏlein	'ʃiliŋ ˏfeə*
'stiːl ˏpen	'lestə ˏskweə*	'tenʃiliŋ ˏnout
'leðə ˏbag	'tʃeəriŋ ˏkros	'kʌntri ˏwoːk
'kamp ˏtʃeə*	'lʌndən ˏbridʒ	'gaːdn̩ ˏwoːl
'ʃop ˏwindu	'douvə ˏhaːbə*	'famili ˏsəːkl̩

However, the kinetic stress is transferred to the qualifier when it is desired to give it a sense of contrast or contradiction:

ə ˋpoːk ˌpai z ˌnaisə ðn̩ ə ˏviːl ən ˌham ˈpai.

ˋlʌndən bridʒ iz ˌniərə ðn̩ ˏwesminstə ˈbridʒ.

ə ˋʃiliŋ ˌfeə, 'not ə ˋtuː ˌʃiliŋ ˌfeə.

Names of thoroughfares containing the word striːt as their second component take the stress on their first component. In this they differ from other names of thoroughfares such as roud, lein, kros, etc.

ˋhai ˌstriːt   ˋkwiːn ˌstriːt   ˋoksfəd ˌstriːt

As shown in §50, there are collocations of noun + noun which may be regarded as compound nouns. This is particularly the case when such collocations are normally single-stressed, with the kinetic stress falling on the first element, or qualifier, as it does in the following cases:

41

ˈiŋkpot	ˈletəˌboks	ˈgeitwei
ˈaiˌglaːsiz	ˈnjuːsˌpeipə*	ˈkoulˌselə*
ˈtiːpot	ˈhausˌkiːpə*	ˈkoulˌmain
ˈbiskit ˌtin	ˈmilkmən	ˈeəpoːt
ˈteiblˌkloθ	ˈwulˌməːtʃn̩t	ˈlan(d)maːk

b. *Possessive nouns qualifying nouns.*

Both single and double stress are used in these collocations:

Single-stressed	*Double-stressed*
ˈbəːdzˌnest	ˈkam|z ˌheə*
ˈkatsˌmiːt	ˈprintəz ˌink
ˈleidizˌmeid	ˈtravləz ˌtʃek
ˈbiːzˌwaks	ə ˈwiːks ˌholidi

c. *Determiners qualifying nouns.*

All the determiners except the pronouns and semi-pronouns can be used to qualify nouns. Copious examples supplementing the following will be found in §§71–94.

mai ˈpen	sm̩ ˈtikits	ˈsiksti ˌmen
ˈðiːz ˈbuks	ˈveəriəs ˌʃops	ðə ˈθəːd ˌtaim
ə ˈhaus	iˈnʌf ˌtrʌb|	

d. *Adjectives qualifying nouns.*

When this type of collocation becomes established it acquires the status of a compound noun and frequently takes single stress, but the great majority of cases where an independent adjective qualifies a noun have double stress:

ˈgud ˌbuk	ˈould ˌeidʒ	ˈbritiʃ ˌkomənˌwelθ
ˈbig ˌruːm	ˈhapi ˌbəːθdei	ˈpraim ˌministə*
ˈmein ˌdek	ˈpʌblik ˌskuːl	ˈwait ˌelifn̩t

As in the case of nouns qualifying nouns, the kinetic stress may be transferred to the qualifier to give it a sense of contrast or contradiction:

ˈðis iz ðə ˈmein ˌdek, ˈnot ðə ˌbout ˈdek.

A considerable number of stress doublets occur, in which double stress gives a general meaning and single stress a specialized meaning to these collocations, especially if the adjective denotes a colour. In the following examples the double-stressed collocation is to be

42

taken literally; the specialized meaning of the single-stressed compound is given:

'bro:d ˌʃi:t	ˋbro:dʃi:t	(leaflet)
'da:k ˌru:m	ˋda:k‚ru:m	(photographic laboratory)
'hot ˌpleit	ˋhot‚pleit	(part of a stove)
'grei ˌbiəd	ˋgreibiəd	(old man)
'gri:n ˌhaus	ˋgri:nhaus	(glass building for plants)

e. Participles qualifying nouns.

Nouns may be qualified by either the present (active) participle or the past (passive) participle.

The single-stressed examples of this combination may be said to be established compound words, usually written with a hyphen; the collocations are all double-stressed in normal contexts.

Active Participles	*Passive Participles*
ən 'intristiŋ ˌbuk	ə 'spoilt ˌtʃaild
ə 'taiəriŋ ˌdei	'broukən ˌgla:s
'rʌniŋ ˌwo:tə*	ə 'kʌt ˌfiŋgə*
ðə 'raiziŋ ˌtaid	ði ju'naitid ˌsteits
'mu:viŋ ˌpiktʃəz	ə 'komplikeitid məˌʃi:n

f. Adverbs qualifying nouns.

From the logical point of view a certain number of adverbs are used to qualify nouns.[1]

hi z 'kwait ə ˌman!	ʃi z 'riəli ən ˋonlukə.
it s ˋmiəli ən əˌpinjən.	ði ə'bʌv igˌza:mpǀz.
hi z ˋounli ə ˌtʃaild.	auə 'neks·do: ˌneibəz.
ðat s 'skeəsli (*or* 'ha:dli) ə 'feər ˌa:gjumənt.	
ju 'ko:l ▪ðat ə ⸗hil! it s ˌo:lmoust ə ˋmauntin.	
'niəli ə ˋjiə ‚pa:st bi‚fo:r ai ˌhə:d frəm im əˌgein.	

60 Qualifiers following the noun. These cases have more the nature of a sentence structure, and the kinetic tone will normally fall on the qualifier as the last important element in the sense-group. The noun takes a static stress.

[1] "A noun-modifying adverb evidently approaches very near in function to an adjective. In such a construction as *he is quite a gentleman* we feel that *quite* is not an adjective, because if it were, it would come after instead of before, the article *a*."—Sweet's *New English Grammar*, §312.

a. *Nouns qualified by nouns in apposition.*

Each of the two parts of the apposition takes the same kinetic tone:

did ju 'siː 'braun ðə 'loːjə?   ai ˌsoː ˏbraun ðə ˏloːjə.

ˏlʌndən, ðə 'kapitəl əv ˏiŋglənd.

ˏbraun, ðə 'man ai wəz 'toːkiŋ əbaut dʒʌst ˏnau.

b. *Nouns qualified by post-positional adjectives.*

In a limited number of cases the adjective is placed after the noun it qualifies. These cases are mostly of an historical, religious or official character and may nearly all be considered as established compounds. The following are among those usually written as separate words:

'batǀ ˏroiəl   'kʌzn̩ ˏdʒəːmən   'eər əˏparn̩t
'biʃəp ˏsʌfrəgən   'envoi iksˏtroːdn̩ri   'pouit ˏloːriit
'kəːnǀ 'komənˏdant 'gʌm ˏarəbik   'treʒə ˏtrouv

c. *Nouns qualified by relative clauses.*

ðə 'man u 'keim ˏhiə.   ðə 'man ai wəz ˏspiːkiŋ tu.
ðə 'man ai 'soː ˏjestədi.   ðə 'letər ai ri'siːvd laːst ˏnait.
ðə 'wʌn ðət wəz in ði 'ʌðə ˏruːm.
ðə 'man uːz ˏhaus wi wə ˏlukiŋ at ˏlaːst ˏwiːk.

d. *Nouns qualified by prepositional phrases.*[1]

ðə 'striːts əv ˏlʌndən   ðə 'bei əv ˏneipǀz
ðə 'top əv ðə ˏhil   ði 'end əv ðə ˏdei
ðə 'buk on ðə ˏteibǀ   ðə 'man in ðə 'nekst ˏhaus
ðə 'wʌn in ˏkwestʃn̩   ðə 'man frəm ˏkuks
ðə 'haus ˙ouvə ðə ˏwei   ðə 'man wið ə ˏbiəd

e. *Nouns qualified by infinitives.*

'wot s ðə 'best θiŋ tə ˏduː?
'hiə z ə ˏbuk fə ju tə ˏriːd.
ˏðis iz ðə ˏtriː tə bi ˏkʌt ˏdaun.

[1] Logically, however, the prepositional phrase sometimes contains the more important noun. "The nucleus of the group *a piece of bread* is *bread*, for *piece*, although grammatically the head word of the group, is really little more than a form-word."—Sweet's *New English Grammar*, §120. See also *Ibid.*, §61.

LOGICAL CLASSIFICATION

61 Logical categories of nouns. The following is a useful scheme of classification of nouns according to their logical categories.

$$\text{Nouns} \begin{cases} \textit{Abstract (dei)} \\ \textit{Concrete} \begin{cases} \textit{Proper (dʒon)} \\ \textit{Common} \begin{cases} \textit{Material (wɔːtə)} \\ \textit{Class} \begin{cases} \textit{Collective (kraud)} \\ \textit{Individual (buk)} \end{cases} \end{cases} \end{cases} \end{cases}$$

Abstract nouns.

These name non-material objects, ideas, qualities, states or actions:

ˈdei, ˈnait, ˈweðə, ˈʃad(o)u, ˈnoːθ, ˈbjuːti, ˈdaːknis, ˈleŋθ, ˈsaiz, ˈkonvəˈseiʃn̩, ˈpruːf, ˈtʃois;

and are opposed to *Concrete nouns*, such as:

ˈdʒon, ˈiŋglənd, ˈlʌndən, ˈwɔːtə, ˈfəːnitʃə, ˈkraud, ˈskai, ˈtʃoːk, ˈbuk, ˈman,

which are subdivided into *Proper nouns* and *Common nouns*.

Proper nouns.

These name a single person, animal or place:

ˈdʒon, ˈflʌʃ (dog's name), ˈiŋglənd, ˈlʌndən,

and are opposed to *Common nouns*, such as:

ˈwɔːtə, ˈfəːnitʃə, ˈkraud, ˈskai, ˈtʃoːk, ˈbuk, ˈman,

which are subdivided into *Material nouns* and *Class nouns*.

Material nouns.

These name substances:

ˈwɔːtə, ˈsand, ˈkloθ, ˈwul, ˈtʃoːk, ˈwud, ˈaiən,

and are opposed to *Class nouns*, such as:

ˈkraud, ˈkʌmpəni, kəˈlekʃn̩, ˈbuk, ˈhaus, ˈman,

which are subdivided into *Collective nouns* and *Individual nouns*.

Collective nouns.

These, though they have a singular form, name a number of individuals:

ˈkraud, ˈkʌmpəni, kəˈlekʃn̩, ˈaːmi, ˈklaːs.

Individual nouns.

These name individuals that belong to a class:

ˈbuk, ˈtʃeə, ˈhaus, ˈtriː, ˈman, ˈhoːs.

The body referred to by a collective noun may be regarded either as an entity or as a collection of individuals. In the former case the noun should be treated as singular and in the latter case as plural. The elements affected are pronouns, possessives and finites, which must agree in number with the collective noun, and care must be taken not to mix singulars and plurals in the same sentence.

Singular: ðə ˈkaunsl̩ əz ˈdeligeitid its ˈpauəz tu ə kəˈmiti.

Plural: ðə kəˈmiti ə kənˈsidəriŋ ˈweðə ðeə ˈpauəz ə səˈfiʃn̩t.

62 Countables and uncountables. Nouns which stand for things which can be *counted* are called Nouns of Discontinuous Quantity,[1] or more succinctly, *Countables.* They may be singular or plural: ˈwʌn ˈbuk. ˈtuː ˈbuks.

Nouns which stand for things which cannot be counted (but which may sometimes be *measured*) are called Nouns of Continuous Quantity, or more succinctly, *Uncountables.* These are always singular, but cannot be qualified by the indefinite article or the numeral wʌn.

Uncountables may be concrete or abstract:

a. Concrete.

ˈwud, ˈwul, ˈaiən, ˈkloθ, ˈpeipə*, ˈgraːs, ˈglaːs, ˈtʃoːk, ˈstoun, ˈsand, ˈmiːt, ˈbred, ˈwoːtə*, ˈfəːnitʃə*, ˈklouðiŋ, məˈʃiːnəri.

b. Abstract.

ˈhapinis, ˈbjuːti, ˈdaːknis, ˈlait, ˈhelθ, ˈkwiknis, ˈsʌnʃain, ˈloː, ˈmjuːzik, ˈweðə*, ˈrein, ˈwind.

---

[1] *Cf.* Sweet's *New English Grammar*, §232.

Many uncountables, however, may become countables when used in the sense of "a kind of":

'tuː 'difrənt ˋbredz	= two different kinds of bread.
ˋgraːsiz	= different kinds of grass.
'ðiːz ˋwulz	= these qualities of wool.

Certain nouns may be uncountables or countables according to the meaning in which they are used:

Uncountables	*Countables*
ˋaiən (the metal)	ən ˋaiən (used for making linen smooth).
ˋloː (jurisprudence)	ə ˋloː (a statute, etc.).
ˋglaːs (the substance)	ə ˋglaːs (for drinking, telescope or mirror).
ˋwud (the substance)	ə ˋwud (a collection of trees).

63 Grammatical functions of nouns. From the grammatical point of view nouns may function in any of the following capacities:

a. As subject of a sentence:

ðə 'man keim ˌhiə.

b. As subject-predicate:

'ðat s ə ˋman.

c. As direct object:

ai 'met ə ˋman.

d. As indirect object:

ai 'geiv ðə ˙man ðə ˌbuk.
ai 'got ðə ˙man ə ˌdʒob.

e. As prepositional object:

ai 'geiv it tə ðə ˌman.
ai wəz 'weitiŋ fə mai ˌfrend.

f. As object-complement:

ðei i'lektid im ˋprezidənt.

g. As qualifiers of other nouns:

ðə 'gaːdn ˌwoːl.   'lʌndən ˌbridʒ.

B. Determiners

THE TEN CLASSES

64 Definition. There exists a class of words which may be
used, like adjectives, to qualify nouns, or, like pronouns, to stand
instead of them. In other words, they may be used either adjectivally or pronominally, though in a few cases they differ in form
according to which of these two capacities they are used in. Some
grammarians consider these words to be pronouns that can be used
adjectivally, while others consider them as adjectives that can be
used pronominally.

In view of this difficulty in drawing any clear line of demarcation
between their grammatical functions, and since they all serve, like
the pronouns proper, to indicate or determine what person or thing
is being referred to, the simplest and most rational plan would
seem to be to add the pronouns proper to these words in order to
form a general category of *determiners*, and to specify in the case
of each word whether it may be used as an adjective, as a pronoun
or as either.

65 Classification. A convenient classification of words coming
under the heading of determiners is the following:

1. Semi-Pronouns: wʌn, sʌmbodi, nʌθiŋ, etc.

2. Pronouns: ai, him, juː, ðəm'selvz, etc.

3. Possessives: mai, jɔə, həːz, auər 'oun, etc.

4. Demonstratives: ðis, ðat, ðiːz, ðouz.

5. Articles: ei, an, ðiː.

6. Partitives: sʌm, eni, nou, nʌn.

7. Article-Analogues: bouθ, iːtʃ, seim, etc.

8. Quantitatives: mʌtʃ, les, lots (əv), etc.

9. Numericals: tuː, θəːti, meni, fjuə*, etc.

10. Ordinals: fəːst, fɔːtiiθ, nekst, laːst, etc.

Each of these classes will now be described in detail, and examples
will be given of their use.

THE SEMI-PRONOUNS

66 The semi-pronoun wʌn. In addition to its functions as an indefinite pronoun (§§68–70) and as a numerical determiner (§88) the word wʌn has a special role in combination with adjectives, certain determiners, and the conjunctive and interrogative witʃ. It is then comparable in meaning to *individual, variety* or *species*, and since it has a plural form wʌnz it can indicate whether the word with which it is associated refers to one, or more than one, person or thing. The collocation into which it enters has the status of a noun. Sweet calls it an unmeaning noun-pronoun, or a prop-word. The following are examples of its use.

With Demonstratives (usually confined to the singular).

ai ˌwont ˋðat wʌn, ˈnot ˏðis wʌn.

With Articles.

ˈjuː ˏaːr ə ˌwʌn.   ˋðis iz ðə ˏwʌn.
ˈðat s ðə ˙wʌn ai ˈsoː ˋjestədi.

With Article-Analogues.

ˋaiðə ˌwʌn | ˏduː.   ai ˈwont ə ˋhoul wʌn.
wi ˈspouk tu ˈiːtʃ ˏwʌn.   ˈðat s ðə ˋseim wʌn.
ˈmaːk ˋevri ˌwʌn, ˈnot ˏevri ˋʌðə ˏwʌn.

With Ordinals.

ðə ˋfəːst wʌnz wə ðə ˏbest. ˈgiv mi ðə ˋsekənd wʌn.
ˋai ˏlaik ðə ˈfoːθ n̩ ˋfifθ wʌnz.

With Adjectives.

ˋðis iz ə ˏgud wʌn.   wi ˈwont sm̩ ˋbetə wʌnz.
ðə ˈbig wʌn z ˙on ðə ˋteibl̩. ju v ˈbroːt ðə ˋroŋ wʌnz.
ˈteik ə ˋlaːdʒ wʌn; ˋdount ˌteik ə ˏsmoːl wʌn.

With the Conjunctive and Interrogative witʃ.

ai fəˋget ˌwitʃ wʌn ju ˏtʃouz. ˈaːsk im ˈwitʃ wʌnz i ˏwonts.
ˈwitʃ wʌn d ju ˙laik ˏbest?   ˈwitʃ wʌnz əv ðei ˏteikən?

67 The compound semi-pronouns. The partitives sʌm, eni and nou are compounded with bodi, wʌn and θiŋ to form words which, being both noun-like and pronoun-like in function, are best placed in the semi-pronoun class of determiners. They cannot be qualified by the qualifiers that precede the noun, but may be qualified by relative clauses, prepositional phrases and infinitives (§60) and by a few adverbs, notably els. The complete list of these semi-pronouns is:

Affirmative	˅sʌmbodi	˅sʌmwʌn	˅sʌmθiŋ
Indefinite	˅enibodi	˅eniwʌn	˅eniθiŋ
Negative	˄noubodi	˄nouwʌn	˄nʌθiŋ
Plenary	˅evribodi	˅evriwʌn	˅evriθiŋ

The element **bodi** has an optional weak form **bədi** when used in these compounds.

Like the partitives (§§75–77) which enter into their construction, these semi-pronouns are subject to certain limitations in their use. Their effect on the structure of the sentence is dealt with in §§365–6.

All these semi-pronouns may form collocations with the adverb els to give the meaning "——other person or thing," thus:

did ju 'miːt ˙eniwʌn ʹels ?   'sʌmbodi ˅els ˌtould mi ˌðat.

'nʌθiŋ ˅els wəz ˌmisiŋ.   'woznt ˙evribodi ˙els ʹʃokt ?

When these collocations are used in a possessive capacity they are generally treated as a unit, the possessive termination being added to els, thus:

'ðis iz ˙sʌmbodi ˅elsiz ˌhat.   'noubodi ˅elsiz ˌtiː wəz ˌspilt.

˅eniwʌn ˌelsiz ˌpen | ˌduː.   ai v ˅siːn ˌevriwʌn ˌelsiz ˌwəːk.

THE PRONOUNS

68 Definition. These are words that are used instead of the noun that names a person or thing already identified. Traditional grammar usually recognizes Personal, Reflexive, Reciprocal, Possessive, Demonstrative, Relative and Interrogative Pronouns, but in a functional analysis the last two are regarded as Connectives, and are therefore described under that heading, while the Possessives and Demonstratives, being both adjectival and pronominal, have their own headings as determiners. Only the first two classes are dealt with under the present heading of Pronouns. For Reciprocal Pronouns see §95.

Most of the pronouns have weak forms, which are used when the

word is unstressed. In the following table the weak forms are
shown in brackets.

Singular	Nominative	Oblique	Emphatic	Reflexive
1st pers.	ai	miː (mi)	maiˋself	miself
2nd pers.	juː (ju)[1]	juː (ju)	joːˋself	jəself
3rd pers.				
masculine	hiː (hi, i)	him (him, im)	himˋself	imself
feminine	ʃiː (ʃi)	həː* (hə*, əː*, ə*)	həˋself	əself
neuter	it[2]	it[2]	itˋself	itself
indefinite	wʌn[2]	wʌn[2]	wʌnˋself	wʌnself
Plural				
1st pers.	wiː (wi)	ʌs (əs)[3]	auəˋselvz	auəselvz
2nd pers.	juː (ju)	juː (ju)	joːˋselvz	jəselvz
3rd pers.	ðei[4]	ðem (ðəm, ðm̩)[5]	ðəmˋselvz	ðm̩selvz

In an older stage of the language there were pronouns in general
use for the second person singular (ðau, ðiː) corresponding to the
"familiar" pronouns of many other languages. Except in one or
two very conservative dialects these words have now fallen completely out of use, and the second person plural pronoun (juː) is
used in addressing one person as well as more than one. Apart
from the essential distinction made between singular and plural in
the expanded pronouns (joːself—joːselvz), the pronoun juː is now
the only one used to refer to the person or persons addressed, and
students should note that as the pronoun is really a plural it is
always so treated grammatically. When, therefore, it is the subject
of a tense that has different finite forms for singular and plural
(§§130, 154) the plural form of the finite must always be used.

[1] The sequence juː aː is generally weakened to ju ə or joː ə, which latter
is homophonous with the possessive determiner joə (spelt "your"). To avoid
confusion this combination will be shown as ju ə.

[2] it rarely takes a kinetic tone; wʌn never does.

[3] Becomes s in the expression let s.

[4] The sequence ðei aː is generally weakened to ðe ə which is homophonous
with the possessive determiner ðeə (spelt "their") and the adverb ðeə (spelt
"there"). To avoid confusion this combination will be shown as ðei ə.

[5] In rapid and familiar speech əm.

69 Personal pronouns. Five of the personal pronouns and the interrogative and relative huː are the only words retaining different forms for the nominative and oblique cases ; juː, it and wʌn do not vary for case.

Nominative pronouns as subjects:

ˋai ˌsoː it.   ai ˋsoː it.   ai m ˇredi.   ʃl ˊai ˙teik it?   ʃl ai ˊteik it?
ˋjuː ˌwent ðeə.   ju ˋwent ðeə.   ju ˌsiː ... ju ə ˋbizi.   did ju ˊgou?
ˋhiː wəz ˌðeə.   hi ˋwoz ðeə.   if ˋhiː ˌkeim.   if i ˇkeim.   did i ˊkʌm?
ˋʃiː ˌsed sou.   ʃi ˋsed sou.   wil ʃi ˊkʌm?   iz ʃi ˊredi?
it s ˋhiə.   it ˈluks laik ˋrein.
wʌn ˋofn̩ ˌdʌz ˌθiŋz laik ˌðat.
ˋwiː did it.   wi ˇdid it.   wi ə ˇredi.   ʃl ˊwiː gou?   ʃl wi ˊgou?
ˋðei ˌsoː it.   ðei ˇsoː it.   did ˊðei siː it?   did ðei ˊsiː it?

Oblique pronouns as direct objects:

hi ˈsoː ˋmiː.   hi ˋsoː mi.   dəz i ˊwont mi?   dəz i ˈwont ˊmiː?
ai ˈtould ˌjuː.   ˈðat s wot ai ˋtould ju.   ai ˋtould ju ˌsou.
ai ˈwont ˋhim.   ai ˋwont im.   did ju ˊsiː im?
ai ˈsoː ˇhəː.   ai ˋsoː əː.   ai ˈsoː ər in ðə ˌstriːt.   ˈtel ər ai ˌwont əː.
ðei ˇdid it.   ai l ˈduː it tə ˋmoru.
ˋðat soːt əv ˌθiŋ sə ˋpraiziz wʌn.   it ˈmeiks wʌn ˋwʌndə.
hi ˈtould ˇʌs.   hi ˋtould əs.   ˈlet s ˋgou.
ai ˈwontid ˋðem.   ai ˋwontid ðəm.   ai ˋwontid əm.

Oblique pronouns as indirect objects:

ˈgiv ˌmiː wʌn.   ˈgiv mi ˌðat wʌn.
ai sent ˋjuː ˌðat wʌn.   ai ˈsent ju ˋðat wʌn.
ai ˈʃoud ˋhim ðə ˌletə.   ai ˋʃoud im ðə ˌletə.
ai ˈofəd ˋhəː ðə ˌmʌni.   ai ˋofəd ə ðə ˌmʌni.
ai ˈθoːt ðə ˙dog wəz ˌhʌŋgri sou ai ˈgeiv it ˙sʌmθiŋ tu ˋiːt.
ðei ˌgiv wʌn ðə ˈbest əv ˋevriθiŋ.
hi ˈgeiv ˋʌs wʌn.   hi ˋgeiv əs ˌwʌn.
wi ˈʃoud ˋðem ðə ˌpeipəz.   wi ˋʃoud (ð)əm ðə ˌpeipəz.

Oblique pronouns as prepositional objects:

ˈgiv it tə ˌmiː.   ˋgiv it ˌtu mi.
ai ˈboːt ˈðat fə ˋjuː.   ai ˋboːt it ˌfoː ju.
ˈai lukt ət ˋhəː.   ai ˋlukt at əː.
ai ˈgot ðə ˙letə frəm ˋhim.   ai ˈgot ðə ˇletə ˙from im.

ai 'geiv 'ten ˎʃiliŋz foːr it.

ˋðat s ðə ˌsoːt əv ˌθiŋ ðət 'nevər əˋkəːz tə wʌn.

hi wəz 'weitiŋ fər ˋʌs.   hi wəz ˋweitiŋ ˌfoːr əs.

it wəz 'veri ˙kaind əv ˋðem.   it wəz 'veri ˋkaind ˌov (ð)əm.

Pronouns as subject-complements.

In the case of the five pronouns still possessing different nominative and oblique forms much divergency of opinion exists among grammarians and others concerning which form should be used as subject complement, and the unfortunate student, whichever form he uses, will be corrected and warned against that particular "fault." This difference of opinion frequently leads to angry disputation, but the facts seem to be as follows:

In careful and deliberate speech, especially between strangers and among women-folk, when one is on one's guard against possible criticism from purists, the forms ai, hiː, ʃiː, wiː and ðei are generally heard. Those who have cultivated a bookish or formal style of speaking almost invariably use these forms.

On the other hand, in the normal and spontaneous speech of everyday life, especially between friends and in the conversation of men-folk, the forms miː, him, həː, ʌs and ðem are usually heard, as shown in the following examples:

it s ˋmiː.   ðei 'θoːt it wəz ˋmiː.

it s ˋhim.   it 'mait əv bin ˋhim.

it s ˋhəː.   ai ˋtould ju it wəz ˌhəː.

it s ˋʌs.   wi ˋnjuː it əd bi ˌʌs.

it s ˋðem.   ðei ə ˋʃoər it | bi ˌðem.

When pronouns occur in isolation the oblique forms are similarly used:

'huː z ˋðeə? — ˋmiː.   'huː ˋwoz it? — ˋðem.

It may therefore be stated as a general rule that in natural speech the nominative form is used only when the pronoun is the subject of a verb, and that the oblique form is used in all other cases.

70 Expanded pronouns. These are made by adding -self in the singular and -selvz in the plural to the adjectival possessives of the 1st and 2nd persons (see §71) and to the oblique pronouns of the 3rd person. They are stressed when emphatic and unstressed when reflexive.

Examples:

Emphatic pronouns:

   ai 'soː it maiˋself.
   'juː joːˋself ˌtould mi sou.
   hi 'didṇt ˙kʌm himˇself.
   'wai ˙dʌzṇt ʃi 'duː it həˋself?
   ðə 'buk itˋself ˌgivz ðə ˌfigəz.
   wʌn ʃəd bi 'eibḷ tə ˙duː ðis wʌnˋself.
   wi 'beik auə ˙bred auəˋselvz.
   ju məs 'gou joːˋselvz.
   'ðei ðəmˋselvz diˌsaidid tə ˌliːv.

Reflexive pronouns:

   ai v 'dʒʌs ˋkʌt miself.
   'hav ju ˊhəːt jəself?
   hi z ˋweiiŋ imself.
   ʃi 'dʌzṇ ˙giv əself ə ˋtʃaːns.
   ðə 'faiə z ˙bəːnt itself ˋaut.
   wʌn məs biˋheiv wʌnself ˌhiə.
   wi inˋdʒoid auəselvz ət ðə ˌpaːti.
   ˋpliːz ˌmeik jəselvz ət ˌhoum.
   ðei 'praid ðṃselvz on ðeə 'nolidʒ əv ˋkukiŋ.

These expanded forms may be reflexive and emphatic at the same time. In such cases they are stressed:

   ai ˋnevə ˌʃeiv maiˏself.
   did ˊjuː ˙kʌt əː, oː did ʃi 'kʌt həˋself?
   wʌn 'mʌsṇ ˙preiz wʌnˏself.
   'didṇt ðə ˙tʃildrən 'woʃ ðəmˊselvz?
   (*Compare:* 'didṇt ðə ˙tʃildrən ˊwoʃ ðṃselvz?)

When they follow bai or oːl bai these words may be said to have an isolating function:

   hi 'did it bai imˋself.   ə ju 'oːl bai jəˊself?

THE POSSESSIVES

71 Description. These are words that may serve as answers to the question huːz? They have different forms according to the number (and in the 3rd person singular the gender) of the possessor, not of the person or object possessed.

Except in the 3rd person singular masculine they have different forms for adjectival and pronominal use; these are generally referred to as "possessive adjectives" and "possessive pronouns" respectively.

There are also emphatic possessives, which are made by adding **oun** to the adjectival forms. These may be used either adjectivally or pronominally.

Some of the adjectival possessives have weak forms, and these may be used in the emphatic compounds. In the following table the weak forms are shown in brackets.

	Adjectival	*Pronominal*	*Emphatic*
Singular			
1st *pers.*	mai (mi)	main	mai ˋoun
2nd *pers.*	joə* (jə*)	joəz	joər ˋoun
3rd *pers.*			
masculine	hiz (iz)	hiz	hiz ˋoun
feminine	həː* (hə*, əː*)	həːz	hər ˋoun
neuter	its	—	its ˋoun
indefinite	wʌnz	—	wʌnz ˋoun
Plural			
1st *pers.*	auə*	auəz	auər ˋoun
2nd *pers.*	joə* (jə*)	joəz	joər ˋoun
3rd *pers.*	ðeə*	ðeəz	ðeər ˋoun

Examples:

ðis iz ˋmai buk; it s mai ˋoun buk. ˌðat s ˋmain; it s mai ˋoun.

'weə z joə ˋpen? 'iz it joər ˋoun pen? iz 'ðat ˈjoəz? 'iz it jər ˋoun?

iz iz ˈneim ðeə? iz 'ðat iz ˈoun ai ˙diə? 'weə z ˋhiz? 'wai didn̩t i ˙teik iz ˋoun?

'hiə z əː ˌhat; ai ˋθink it s ˌhəːz. it 'mʌs bi hər ˋoun.

it s əˈnoiiŋ tə ˌluːz wʌnz ˌglaːsiz. wʌnz 'oun wei z ˅best.

ˋðiːz ər auə ˌnouts; wi 'meid auər ˋoun; ðei ər ˋauəz.

ˋðeər ə ˌðeə buks. ðei 'briŋ ðeər ˌoun. ˋðiːz ə ˌðeəz.

THE DEMONSTRATIVES

72 Forms and functions. Demonstratives are used to indicate persons or things by suggesting their proximity to or remoteness from the speaker. They may be used either adjectivally or pronominally. They are invariable for gender but have different forms for singular and plural. They are nearly always stressed and have no weak forms.

Singular	Plural	
ðis	ðiːz	specifying the less remote.
ðat	ðouz	specifying the more remote.

The following examples show the differences in reference:

ˋðis aiˌdiə z ˌgud   (the one I'm speaking about now).
ˋðat aiˌdiə z ˌgud   (a previous one, or somebody else's).
'ðiːz ˙buks ə ˋmain   (the ones near me).
'ðouz ˙buks ə ˋjoəz   (the ones not so near me).

Examples of adjectival use:

'trai 'ðis ˙bred ən 'ðat ˌdʒam.
'ðiːz ˙teiblz ə 'laːdʒə ðən 'ðouz ˌdesks.

Examples of pronominal use:

'wot s ˌðis?   'ðis iz ə ˌbuk.   ai I 'teik ˋðis.
'wot s ˌðat?   'ðat s ə ˌpen.   ai I 'teik ˋðat.
'wot ə ˌðiːz?   'ðiːz ə ˌbuks.   ai I 'teik ˋðiːz.
'wot ə ˌðouz?   'ðouz ə ˌpenz.   ai I 'teik ˋðouz.

The singular forms are used in combination with the semi-pronoun wʌn. (See §66.)

'ðis wʌn z ˋjoəz; ai I 'teik ˋðat wʌn.
'ðat wʌn z ˋmain: 'teik ˋðis wʌn.

The plural forms do not usually enter into this combination.

THE ARTICLES

73 Forms of the articles. There are two articles, the definite and the indefinite, which are invariable for number and gender and which are never used pronominally. Both articles have strong and

weak forms, the latter being used almost exclusively, as the articles
are nearly always unstressed. The various forms are:

	Normal Form		Pre-Vocalic Form	
	Weak	Strong	Weak	Strong
Definite Article	ðə	ðiː	ði	ðiː
Indefinite Article	ə	ei	ən	an

The strong forms are used only when the articles are isolated (*a*)
or stressed (*b*); in all other cases the weak forms are used (*c*).

The definite article:

a. wi ə 'gouiŋ tə ˙toːk əbaut ðə 'definit ˙aːtik| "ˏðiː."
b. ai 'didn̩t sei "ˏmai" buk; ai sed "ˋðiː" buk.
c. ðə ˋman, ðə ˋgəːl, ðə ˋbuk, ðə ˋmen, ðə ˋgəːlz, ðə ˋbuks.
   ði ˋaːnt, ði ˋʌŋk|, ði aiˋdiə, ði ˋaːnts, ði ˋʌŋk|z, ði aiˋdiəz.

The indefinite article:

a. ði in'definit ˙aːtik| iz "ˏei" oːr "ˋan."
b. ai 'wozn̩t ˙spiːkiŋ əv ˋmai ˏtʃeə, ənd əv ˋmai ˌaːmˌtʃeə; ai wəz
   spiːkiŋ əv ˋei ˏtʃeə, ənd əv ˋan ˌaːmˌtʃeə.
c. ə ˋman, ə ˋgəːl, ə ˋbuk, ən ˋaːnt, ən ˋʌŋk|, ən aiˋdiə.

When used with plural nouns and uncountables the indefinite
article is alogistic, i.e. is not represented by any word.

   ˋmen, ˋgəːlz, ˋbuks; ˋwoːtə, ˋsand, ˋhapinis.

The indefinite article is not used pronominally, but is replaced by
wʌn, sʌm or eni.

   'did ju ˙siː ə 'buk? ˋjes, ai ˋdid ˌsiː wʌn.
   iz 'ðat ˋwoːtə? if ˏsou, ai ˋwont sʌm, ai 'dount ˋwont eni.
   ə 'ðouz ˏmatʃiz? if ˏsou, ai ˋwont sʌm, ai 'dount ˋwont eni.

74 Use of the articles. To many foreign students the distinctions made between the definite and indefinite articles are exceed-
ingly difficult to grasp. Indeed, in many cases such distinctions
can hardly be formulated at all, and the English usage can be
acquired only by dint of continual observation and imitation. The
following rule is given in Sweet's *New English Grammar*.

"The Definite Article is put before a noun to show that the idea
expressed by the noun has already been stated, and to refer back

to that statement. If, on the other hand, the idea is new, the noun expressing it is accompanied by the indefinite article."

The following examples may help to make this clear:

'niə mai ˌhaus ju I siː ə ˌtʃəːtʃ ənd ə ˅faktəri. ðə ˅tʃəːtʃ iz 'veri ˌould ənd 'veri piktʃəˌresk, weəraz ðə ˅faktəri iz 'veri ˌnjuː ənd 'veri ˌʌgli.

The use of the definite article in the second of these sentences shows that we are referring to a particular house and to a particular factory, which were identified in the first sentence. If the indefinite article were used in the second sentence it would imply that churches in general are old and picturesque, and that factories in general are new and ugly.

Another frequent use of the definite article is the following:

˅ðis iz ˌmai rum; 'not ə veri ˅kʌmfətəbl ˌrum; ðə 'siːliŋ z ˌlou, ðə 'windou z tuː ˌsmoːl, ən ðə 'doə dʌznt ˅ʃʌt ˌpropəli.

Here the definite article shows that we are referring to the ceiling, the window and the door *belonging to the room in question*.

When we say ðə ˅faiəz ˌaut we mean "the fire belonging to this room" or "the only fire in the house."

When we say 'let s ˙gou əz 'faːr əz ðə ˌbridʒ we mean "the bridge which is near here," or "the only bridge in this particular neighbourhood," or "the bridge that we both know of."

Sometimes the definite article "makes the noun into what is practically a proper name" (Sweet):

ðə juː'naitid ˌsteits, ðə 'hauziz əv ˌpaːləmənt.

Again according to Sweet, "the indefinite article has two distinct functions: the introductory article singles out the idea expressed by the noun, and makes us expect further information about it."

wi 'went ˙on til wi 'keim tu ə ˌbridʒ.

"The absolute article does not single out, and has the purely indefinite sense of eni . . . it simply picks out an individual at random to serve as the representative of a class":

ə 'hoːs iz ən ˌaniml.

THE PARTITIVES

75 The affirmative partitive. This has three forms, sʌm, səm, sm̩.

The *weak* form səm or sm̩, when used with uncountables and plural nouns, is intermediate between the article-like determiners and the quantitatives or numericals. It is *article-like* in that it closely corresponds in function to the indefinite article, but *quantitative* in that it is almost synonymous with ə ˈlitl̩, and *numerical* in that it is almost synonymous with ə ˈfjuː.

  ai ˌtuk ə ˌbuk, ə ˌpen, səm (= ə ˈlitl̩) ˌiŋk ən səm (= ə ˌfjuː) ˈʃiːts əv ˌpeipə.

Before plural countables the weak form serves as a plural of the indefinite article:

ðəz ə ˈrok ˌhiə.	ðər ə sm̩ ˈroks ˌhiə.
ə ˈsoŋ wəz ˌsʌŋ.	sm̩ ˈsoŋz wə ˌsʌŋ.
ai ʃl̩ ˈniːd ə ˌpin.	ai ʃl̩ ˈniːd sm̩ ˌpinz.

The indefinite article cannot, of course, be dispensed with in such cases, but sm̩ may be omitted to give the plural sentences a more formal, impersonal, objective or detached feeling.

  ðər ə ˈroks hiə.   ˈsoŋz wə ˌsʌŋ.   ai ʃl̩ ˈniːd ˌpinz.

Before uncountables the weak form is a true partitive:

  ðei ˈwont sm̩ ˌpeipə.   wi ˌtuk sm̩ ˈtiː ən sm̩ ˌkofi.

When this partitive is pronominal the strong form is used, even in unstressed positions:

  ai ˈwont səm ˌpeipə; ai səpouz ˈjuː ˌwont sʌm ˈtuː

  ai ˈtuk səm ˌbuks; ai θɔːt ˈjuː ˌtuk sʌm ˈtuː.

The *strong* form sʌm when used with or standing for uncountables and plural nouns means ˈnot ˈɔːl, ə ˈpaːt. It may be used either adjectivally or pronominally:

  ˈnot ˈɔːl ˌglaːs iz transˌpeərənt; ˈsʌm ˌiz ən ˈsʌm ˈizn̩t.

  ˌsʌm piːpl̩ ˈlaik ˌðat sɔːt əv θiŋ; ˌsʌm ˈdount.

When a stressed sʌm is used with singular countables, it may be considered as an emphasized variety of the indefinite article, often having a more or less disparaging sense.

ʃi woz 'tɔːkiŋ tə 'sʌm ˌman (ai 'dount ˙nou wot ᵛsɔːt əv ˙man, 'probəbli 'noubədi ˙veri imᵛpɔːtn̩t).

hi z 'raitiŋ 'sʌm ˌbuk (='sʌm ˋbuk ər ʌðə, ai 'dount ˙nou wot it s əˌbaut, ɔː 'weðər it s eni ˌgud).

This variety of sʌm has no weak form and is never used pronominally.

76 The indefinite partitive. In interrogative, negative, conditional, hypothetical, and dubitative sentences, sʌm, səm is generally replaced by unemphatic eni occasionally weakened to n̩i, especially after t or d.

	With Uncountables	*With Plural Nouns*
Interrogative	did ju 'siː eni ˊiŋk ðeə?	did ju 'siː eni ˋbuks ðeə?
Negative	ai didn̩t ˙siː eni ˌiŋk ðeə.	ai 'didn̩t ˙siː eniˌbuks ðeə.
Conditional	if ju 'siː eni ᵛiŋk ðeə …	if ju 'siː eni ᵛbuks ðeə …
Hypothetical	if ju 'soː eni ᵛiŋk ðeə …	if ju 'soː eni ᵛbuks ðeə …
Dubitative	ai 'wʌndə weðə ðə z eni ˋiŋk ðeə.	ai 'wʌndə weðə ðər ər eni ˋbuks ðeə.

Pronominal use:

ˋgiv mi ˌwʌn! bət ai ˌhavn̩t ˙got eni tə ˋgiv ju.

həv juː ˊgot eni? ˋnou, ai 'havn̩t ˌgot eni.

When eni is used in affirmative constructions it is stressed, and is then equivalent to 'nou matə ˌwot kaind əv.

" 'θiŋk əv ə ˌwəːd!" — "'wot ˌkaind əv ˌwəːd?" — "it 'dʌzn̩t ˙matə wot ˌkaind əv ˌwəːd; ˋeni ˌwəːd."

ˋeni bed z ˌbetə ðən ˌnou bed.

ˋeni fuːl kən duː ˌðat!

it ˋdʌzn̩t ˌmatə wot ˌsɔːt əv ˙iŋk ju ˙du it wið; ˋeni ˌiŋk | ˌduː (= ˋeni ˌkaind əv ˌiŋk).

ai 'wont səm ˌtʃeəz." — "'wot ˌsɔːt əv ˌtʃeəz?" — "it ˌdʌzn̩t ˋmatə; ˋeni ˌtʃeəz | ˌduː əz ˌloŋ əz ðei ə ˌstroŋ."

Pronominal use:

ᵛðis wʌn z 'betə ðən 'eni ai v ˙evə ˌsiːn.

"d ju ˌwont ˊlaːdʒ wʌnz ɔː ˌsmoːl wʌnz?" — "ðə 'saiz ˙dʌzn̩t ˌmatə, ˋeni | ˌduː."

77 The negative partitive. In this the adjectival form is nou,
and the pronominal form nʌn. It is partly *article-like* and partly
quantitative-numerical, in that it constitutes the negative of the
indefinite article and partitive as well as of quantitatives and
numericals. For the reason given in §366, it probably occurs most
frequently after precursory ðeə* (§231):

ðər 'izn̩t eni ˋtaim.	ðə z 'nou ˋtaim.
ðər 'aːnt eni ˋbuks.	ðər ə 'nou ˋbuks.
ðə 'wozn̩t eni ˋðeə.	ðə wəz 'nʌn ˋðeə.

It is also widely used in the subject position:

'nou ˙njuːz iz ˋgud ˏnjuːz.	ˋnʌn əv ju məst ˏliːv ˏjet.
'nou 'taim məs bi ˏlost.	'nʌn wə tə bi ˏfaund.

Some speakers favour its use in the present and past tenses of
the verb tə hav, in order to avoid the anomalous negative structure
referred to in §156C:

ðei ˏhad 'nʌn ˏleft.	wi ˏhav 'nou ˋmʌni wið əs.

In other cases nou and nʌn are replaced by ə or eni in conjunction
with a negative finite:

ai 'ʃaːnt ˙hav ə ˋtikit.	ju 'didn̩t ˙send mi ən ˋaːnsə.
it 'wudn̩t ˙meik eni ᵛdifrn̩s.	wi 'havn̩t ˋteikən eni ˏjet.

In referring to singular countables, pronominal nʌn may be
replaced by wʌn in conjunction with a negative finite:

'iz ðər ə ˊkiː?	ˋnou, ðər ˋizn̩t wʌn.

With uncountables and plural countables eni replaces wʌn.

'iz ðər eni ˊwoːtə?	{ ˋnou, ðə z 'nʌn ᵛhiə. { ˋnou, ðər 'izn̩t eni ᵛhiə.
'aː ðər eni ˊbuks?	{ ˋnou, ðər ə ˋnʌn ˏhiə. { ˋnou, ðər 'aːnt eni ˏhiə.

In classical English the word nʌn (= *none*) is considered to be
the equivalent of not wʌn (= *not one*), and is therefore held to
be singular even when it refers to plural countables. In spoken
English it is more often used as a plural in such cases.

Sing. 'nʌn wəz ˏðeə.   *Plur.* 'nʌn wə ˏðeə.

78 Table of demonstratives, articles and partitives. The following table gives an analysis of the ways in which these three types of determiner are used, with particular reference to the type of noun they precede when used adjectivally. The demonstratives and partitives are also used pronominally with similar references.

	Used with Singular *Countables*	Used with Singular *Uncountables*	Used with Plural nouns
Demonstratives	ðis ðat	ðis ðat	ðiːz ðouz
Definite Article	ðə, ði	ðə, ði	ðə, ði
Indefinite Article	ə, ən	(*alogistic*)[1]	(*alogistic*)[1]
Emphatic Article	sʌm (§75)	(*not used*)	(*not used*)
Affirmative Partitive	(*not used*)	səm, sʌm	səm, sʌm
Indefinite Partitive	(*not used*)	eni	eni
Negative Partitives	nou not ə, not ən	nou not eni	nou not eni

[1] *Note.*—Foreign students, especially those to whom the study of the article is difficult, should distinguish between those cases in which the alogistic indefinite article is used, and those cases in which no article (alogistic, or other) is used at all.

In the sentence **ai ˈlaik ˌtʃiːz** the word **tʃiːz** is modified by the alogistic article, and means "cheese, in general."

In the sentence **ai ˈlaik ˌlʌndən** the word **lʌndən** is not modified (nor is it modifiable) by any article whatever.

THE ARTICLE-ANALOGUES

79 Definition. This class, which comprises a group of words similar in function to the demonstratives, articles and partitives, comprises the following determiners:

bouθ, aiðə*, naiðə* (denoting duality);
houl, oːl, iːtʃ, evri (denoting totality);
veəriəs, veri, səːtn̩, sʌtʃ, seim, ʌðə* (denoting selection).

Some of them are modified or modifiable by the articles.

80 Determiners denoting duality.

bouθ is used only before plural nouns and precedes any other determiners. It has nearly the same meaning as ðə tuː.

Adjectival:

ˈbouθ buks ə ˌhiə.   ˈbouθ mai ˌbuks ə ˌhiə.
ˈbouθ ðə buks ə ˌhiə.   ˈbouθ ðouz ˌbuks ə ˌhiə.
ðei ə ˈnot ˌbouθ ˌded (= ˈwʌn əv ðəm z ˌded; ði ˈʌðər ˈizn̩t).

Pronominal:

ðər ə ˈtuː ˌbuks, ənd ˈbouθ ə ˌhiə.
ðə wə ˈtuː ˌbuks, ənd ai ˈtuk ˌbouθ.

aiðə* is used only before singular countables and has the same meaning as ˈwʌn oː ði ˌʌðə*.

Adjectival:

ˈaiðə ˌmeθəd z ˌgud.   ai ˈdount laik ˈaiðə ˌmeθəd.
ju kən teik ˈaiðə ˌbuk; ai ˈdount ˈmaind ˌwitʃ.

Pronominal:

ˈhiər ə ˈtuː ˌbuks; ju kən ˈteik ˈaiðə.
ˈhiər ə ˈtuː ˌfoːmz; ˈaiðər | ˌduː.   ai ˈdount laik ˈaiðə.

naiðə* is used only before singular countables, and is not used with any other determiner. It has nearly the same meaning as ˈnot ˌðis ənd ˈnot ði ˌʌðə.

Adjectival:

ˈnaiðə ˌmeθəd z ˌgud.

When used as an object (direct or indirect) naiðə* is generally replaced by a negative finite and aiðə.

ai soː ˈnaiðə buk = ai ˈdidṇt siː ˈaiðə buk.

Pronominal:

ˈwitʃ əv ðə ˈtuː d ju ˌlaik? ai laik ˈnaiðə (*or* ai ˈdcount laik ˈaiðə). ai ˈtraid ˈbouθ ˌmeθədz, bət ˈnaiðə wəz[1] satisˌfaktəri.

In the dialect with which this book deals, the semi-pronoun wʌn is never used after the three determiners denoting duality.

81 Determiners denoting totality.

houl is always used with singular countables and must be preceded by a possessive, a demonstrative or an article. It is synonymous with inˈtaiə*.

Adjectival:

mai ˈhoul ˌlaif wəz ˌspoilt. ðis ˈhoul ˈpeidz iz ˌroŋ. ðə ˈhoul ˌprougram ʃəd bi ˌtʃeindʒd. ə ˈhoul ˈdei wəz ˌweistid.

Pronominal:

This use is formal and comparatively rare.

ə ˌhoul z ˈoːlwiz ˈlaːdʒə ðən ˈwʌn əv its ˌpaːts.

houl used as subject-complement has a different meaning and is then an adjective synonymous with kəmˈpliːt.

it wəz ˈhoul wen wi ˌboːt it (it ˈmust have been ˈbroken ˈsince).

oːl is rarely or never used before a countable, but is replaced by ðə houl.

Adjectival:

oːl θiŋz and oːl ðə θiŋz are generally replaced by the semi-pronoun ˈevriθiŋ.

oːl pipḷ and oːl ðə piːpḷ are generally replaced by the semi-pronouns ˈevribodi or ˈevriwʌn.

oːl pleisiz and oːl ðə pleisiz are generally replaced by the adverb evriweə*.

---

[1] wəz is sometimes replaced by wə*, though not by careful speakers.

Pronominal:

This use is rare, except as an antecedent to relative clauses introduced by ðət or hu.

'ɔːl hu ˙keim wə 'griːtid iˈfjuːsivli.
wi ˌhav 'ɔːl (ðət) wi ˌwont.

A common mistake made by foreign students is to say ɔːl wot instead of simply ɔːl or ɔːl ðət.
This word has many grammatical functions. Sometimes it has the nature of an adverb rather than a determiner.

iːtʃ is similar in meaning to ˋevri. ai ˌtould 'evri ˙membə tə ˌkʌm, however, may imply that the members were told in a body, whereas ai ˌtould 'iːtʃ ˙membə tə ˌkʌm implies that a separate communication was made to the members individually.

Adjectival:

iːtʃ is never used with the articles. When unaccompanied by cardinal numbers it is used only with singular countables.

'iːtʃ 'membə 'brɔːt iz ˙kontriˌbjuːʃn̩.
ai ˌspouk tu 'iːtʃ ˙pəːsn̩ ˌsepəritli.

Pronominal:

iːtʃ is used as a pronoun either alone or in the collocation 'iːtʃ ˋwʌn.

ai ˌgeiv 'tuː tu ˌiːtʃ (*or* tu 'iːtʃ ˌwʌn).
'iːtʃ (wʌn) ˙keim ət ə 'difrənt ˌtaim.

evri is never used with the articles. When unaccompanied by cardinal numbers it is used only with singular countables.

Adjectival:

'evri ˙membə wəz ˌpreznt̩ = 'ɔːl ðə ˙membəz wə ˌpreznt̩.
ai ˌlukt ət 'evri ˙rum in ðə ˌhaus = 'ɔːl ðə ˙rumz in ðə ˌhaus.

Pronominal:

evri itself is not used as a pronoun, but may be followed by the semi-pronoun wʌn, the two words constituting a compound (or group-) pronoun.

ˌevri ˌwʌn wəz ˌðeə (= ˌevri ˌpəːsn̩ *or* ˈevri ˌobdʒikt wəz ˌðeə).

ai ˌlukt ət ˈevri ˌwʌn (= ai ˌlukt ət ˈevri ˌpəːsn̩ *or* ˈevri ˌobdʒikt).

The collocation ˈevri ˈwʌn is distinct from the semi-pronoun ˈevriwʌn (meaning ˈevribodi *or* ˈevri pəːsn̩).

For collocations of evri *see* §97.

82 Determiners denoting selection.

veəriəs is always used with plural nouns, generally in the indefinite sense, but occasionally with the definite article.

Adjectival:

ai soː im on ˈveəriəs əˌkeiʒn̩z.   ˈveəriəs ˌkaindz əˌkəː.

Preceded by the definite article:

ðə ˈveəriəs əˈkeiʒn̩z on witʃ ai v ˌsiːn im.

Pronominal:

veəriəs is occasionally used pronominally.

it s ˈsʌmtaimz kənˈviːnjənt tə diˈvaid ˈwəːdz intə ˈfoː ˌklaːsiz: ˌnaunz, ˌvəːbz, ˌadʒiktivz, ənd ˈveəriəs.

It may also be used with wʌnz.

wi ˈtraid ˈveəriəs wʌnz bət ˈnʌn əv ðəm wə ˌsjuːtəb|.

The determiner ˌmisəˈleiniəs is a frequently-used synonym of ˈveəriəs.

veri as a determiner is preceded by the definite article and has the sense of igˈzakt. It is not used predicatively.

Adjectival:

ju ə ðə ˈveri ˈman ai ˈwontid tə ˌsiː.   in ðə ˈveri ˌmid|.

Pronominal:

veri may be compounded with wʌn, and so form a pronoun: ðis iz ðə ˈveri ˌwʌn.

səːtn̩ is preceded by the indefinite article (expressed or alogistic), of which it is generally an intensified equivalent; it is used only with singular countables and plural nouns.

Adjectival:

ai 'koːld iz ə'tenʃn̩ tu ə 'səːtn̩ ˌpasidʒ (= tə 'wʌn pə'tikjulə ˌpasidʒ).

'səːtn̩ (= 'sʌm, ə 'fjuː) ˙θiŋz 'strʌk mi əz ˌkjuəriəs.

ðər ə 'səːtn̩ (= 'sʌm, ə 'fjuː) ikˌsepʃn̩z tə ˌðis ˌruːl.

The determiner səːtn̩ is indistinguishable from the adjective səːtn̩ except by context or by stress. Thus:

ə 'səːtn̩ ˌman = a man, one man.
ə ˋsəːtn̩ ˌman = a man who is certain.
ə 'səːtn̩ ˌθiŋ = a thing, one thing.
ə ˋsəːtn̩ ˌθiŋ = a certainty.

Pronominal:

səːtn̩ is used pronominally only when combined with the semi-pronoun wʌn, wʌnz, but this is rare.

ə 'səːtn̩ ˙wʌn ə'traktid mai əˌtenʃn̩.
'səːtn̩ ˙wʌnz 'strʌk mi əz ˌkjuəriəs.

sʌtʃ implies a comparison between two things, the second of which may be left unexpressed or else introduced by the particle əz. See also §326.

Adjectival:

sʌtʃ is always followed by the indefinite article when used with a countable in the singular.

ai v ˈnevə ˌhəːd əv sʌtʃ ə ˌkeis (əz ˌðis).
it ud əv bin ə ˋpiti tə ˌmis sətʃ ən ˌopəˌtjuːniti (əz ˌðis).
ai ˈnevə ˌhəːd sʌtʃ ˌnonsəns (əz ˌðis).
ˌai dount ˙θiŋk sətʃ ˙θiŋz (əz ˙ðis) igˌzist.
in 'sʌtʃ 'laŋgwidʒiz əz ⱽiŋgliʃ. . . .

Pronominal:

sʌtʃ is occasionally used as a pronoun, either alone or compounded with the semi-pronoun wʌn.

ai v ˈnevə ˋhəːd əv sətʃ ə ˌwʌn (əz ju ˌmenʃn̩).
ai 'kaːnt əkˈsept sətʃ ˙wʌnz əz ˌ√ðiːz.
in ˋsʌm ˌlaŋgwidʒiz, sʌtʃ əz ˌiŋgliʃ. . . .
ðei ə sʌtʃ ˌdifik|t wʌnz.   it s sʌtʃ ə ˌgud wʌn.

In the last two examples sʌtʃ is practically indistinguishable from an adverb of degree (i.e. the modifier of an adjective).

ðə seim implies "not different from the one we have in mind." It is invariably associated with the definite article.

Adjectival:

it s ðə 'seim ˎbuk. it 'izn̩t ðə ˙seim ˎθiŋ.
it s ðə 'seim ˎsand. it 'izn̩t ðə ˙seim ˎstʌf.
ðei ə ðə 'seim ˎbuks. ðei ə 'not ðə ˙seim ˎneimz.

Pronominal:

'ðis iz ðə ˋseim, *or* 'ðis iz ðə 'seim ˎwʌn.
'ðiːz ə ðə ˋseim, *or* 'ðiːz ə ðə 'seim ˎwʌnz.

ʌðə* means "not the one we have in mind." It may be preceded by either article, as shown in the following table. The singular indefinite article combines with it. When used pronominally, ʌðə has a plural form:

		Indefinite	*Definite*
Singular		əˋnʌðə	ði ˊʌðə
Plural	Adjectival	ˊʌðə	ði ˊʌðə
	Pronominal	(sm̩) ˊʌðəz	ði ˊʌðəz

All the singular forms may be combined with the semi-pronoun wʌn or with the numericals.

'hiər ə ˙tuː ˎbuks; 'ðis wʌn z ˎmain, ði 'ʌðə z ˎjoəz.
'hiə z əˋnʌðə (buk). ai 'dount nou ˋhuːz it ˎiz.
if ju ˎdount laik ˎðis wʌn, teik əˋnʌðə (wʌn) (= ə ˋdifrn̩t wʌn).
if 'wʌn izn̩t ˎinʌf, teik əˋnʌðə (wʌn) (= ən ˋekstrə wʌn).
'hiər ə 'siks ˎbuks; 'ðiːz tuː ə ˎmain; ði ˎˊʌðəz (*or* ði ˎˊʌðə wʌnz) (*or* ði ˎˊʌðə foər) ə ˋjoəz.
'sʌm əv ðiːz ˙piːpl̩ ˙kʌm frəm ˎfraːns; 'ʌðəz frəm ˎitəli, 'ʌðəz frəm ˋspein.

The expression ʌðə wʌnz is rarely used.
When ʌðə* is used with uncountables it implies "kind of."

'wud ju priˈfəː ði ˊʌðə (˙kaind əv) ˙dʒam?
'eni ˎʌðə (ˎkaind əv) ˎbʌtə wəd ˎduː.

For the collocations of ʌðə* see §§95, 97 and 98.

THE QUANTITATIVES

83 Function of the quantitatives. These are words or group-words that may serve as an answer to the question 'hau ˋmʌtʃ? They can refer only to uncountables, and may be used either adjectivally or pronominally.

ai 'wont ə lit| ˏmʌni. ai ˋhav ə ˏlit|.

They form two groups:

(*a*) Those that do not add ov when used adjectivally:

'moə ˋmʌni. ðə 'slaitist ˋtʃaːns.

(*b*) Those that add ov[1] when used adjectivally:

'plenti əv ˋmʌni. ə 'glaːs əv ˋwoːtə.

84 Quantitatives not adding ov. In the following general list nou is adjectival and nʌn pronominal; all the other quantitatives may be used in either capacity.

oːl	'mʌtʃ ˋmoə*	ðə ˋmoust
'not ˋoːl	moə*	'tuː ˋmʌtʃ
mʌtʃ	sm̩ (eni) ˋmoə*	iˋnʌf
sʌm, sm̩	ə 'lit| ˋmoə*	'tuː ˋlit|
eni	ə 'lit| ˋles	ə ˋlit|
nou	les	ðə ˋliːst
nʌn	'mʌtʃ ˋles	ðə ˋslaitist

Examples:

Adjectival	*Pronominal*
'not ˋoːl ˏglaːs iz ˏtransˏpeərənt.	wi ˋoːl ˏwont tə ˏgou.
ai 'wont səm ˏmʌni	ai ˋwont ˏsʌm.
həv ju 'got eni ˊiŋk?	həv juː ˊgot eni?
ðə z 'nou ˏbʌtə ˏleft.	ðəz 'nʌn ˏleft.
'ad ə lit| ˏwoːtə tu it.	ˋad ə ˏlit|.
'ðat ǀ ˙meik ˋles ˏtrʌb|.	'ðat ǀ ˙meik ˋles.
wiðˏaut ðə ˋliːst ˏdifik|ti.	ˋjuː v got ðə ˏmoust.
wiðˏaut ðə 'slaitist ˏdifik|ti.	'ai v got ðə ˋliːst.
'dount ˙put in 'tuː mʌtʃ ˯woːtə.	'dount ˙put in 'tuː ᵛmʌtʃ.
'wai dount ju ˙ad moə ˏwoːtə?	'wai dount ju ˙ad ˏmoə.
'huː z ˙got ðə 'moust ˏmʌni?	'huː z ˙got ðə ˏmoust?

[1] Always in its weak form əv.

69

ai 'wont səm ˙moə ʃugə.   ai 'wont səm ˌmoə.
həv ju 'got i˙nʌf ˊmilk?   həv ju 'got iˊnʌf?
ðə z 'nou moə ˙tiː ˌleft.   ðə z 'nou moə ˌleft.
'put ə ˙lit| moə ˌsoːlt in it.   'put ə lit| ˌmoər in it.
ðə z 'mʌtʃ moə ˙wəːk ðən ju ˌθiŋk.   ðə z 'mʌtʃ 'moə ðən ju ˌθiŋk.

85 **Quantitatives adding ov.** These are generally used adjectivally, but may be used pronominally by omitting the **ov,** or by
adding **it** after the **ov.**

Indicating degree of quantity

Adjectival	Pronominal
ə ˋlot əv, ˋlots əv,	ə ˋlot.
ə ˋkwontiti əv, ˋkwontitiz əv,	ə ˋkwontiti, ˋkwontitiz.
ə 'smoːl ˋkwontiti əv,	ə 'smoːl ˋkwontiti.
ə 'gud ˋdiːl əv,	ə 'gud ˋdiːl.
ə 'greit ˋdiːl əv,	ə 'greit ˋdiːl.
ə 'laːdʒ əˋmaunt əv,	ə 'laːdʒ əˋmaunt.
ə 'smoːl əˋmaunt əv,	ə 'smoːl əˋmaunt.
ˋplenti əv.	ˋplenti.

Examples:

hi 'mʌst hav ə ˙lot əv ᵛmʌni.	hi 'mʌst hav ə ᵛlot.
ðə wə 'greit ˙kwontitiz əv ˌsand.	ðə wə 'greit ˌkwontitiz.
it teiks ə 'greit diːl əv ˌᵥtaim.	it teiks ə 'greit ᵥdiːl.
ðə z ˌplenti əv ˌwoːtə.	ðə z ˌplenti.

Weights and Measures

Adjectival	Pronominal
ən ˋauns əv, 'tuː ˋaunsiz əv.	ən ˋauns, 'tuː ˋaunsiz.
ə ˋpaund əv, 'θriː ˋpaundz əv,	ə ˋpaund, 'tuː ˋpaundz.
ə ˋpaint əv, 'θriː ˋpaints əv,	ə ˋpaint, 'θriː ˋpaints.
ə ˋkwoːt əv, 'θriː ˋkwoːts əv,	ə ˋkwoːt, 'θriː ˋkwoːts.
ə ˋgalən əv, 'tuː ˋgalənz əv,	ə ˋgalən, 'tuː ˋgalənz.
ə ˋspuːnful əv, 'tuː ˋspuːnfulz əv,	ə ˋspuːnful, 'tuː ˋspuːnfulz.
ə ˋkʌpful əv, 'θriː ˋkʌpfulz əv,	ə ˋkʌpful, 'θriː ˋkʌpfulz.
ə ˋglaːsful əv, 'foə ˋglaːsfulz əv,	ə ˋglaːsful, 'foə ˋglaːsfulz.

ən ˈɪntʃ əv, ˈsiks ˈɪntʃiz əv, | ən ˈɪntʃ, ˈsiks ˈɪntʃiz.
ə ˈfut əv, ˈfaiv ˈfiːt əv, | ə ˈfut, ˈfaiv ˈfiːt.
ə ˈjaːd əv, ˈtuː ˈjaːdz əv, | ə ˈjaːd, ˈtuː ˈjaːdz.
ˈhaːf ə ˈjaːd əv. | ˈhaːf ə ˈjaːd.

Examples:

ai wont ə ˈpaund əv ˌbʌtə. | ai I ˌteik ə ˌpaund.
ˈad ˈθriː ˈspuːnfulz əv ˌwoːtə. | ˈad ˈθriː ˌspuːnfulz.
ai tuk ˈtuː ˈjaːdz əv ˈblak ˌribən. | ai tuk ˈtuː ˌjaːdz.

Containers

Adjectival

ə ˈglaːs əv, ˈtuː ˈglaːsiz əv, | ə ˈdʒʌg əv, ˈθriː ˈdʒʌgz əv.
ə ˈkʌp əv, ˈθriː ˈkʌps əv, | ə ˈtjuːb əv, ˈfoə ˈtjuːbz əv.
ə ˈbotl̩ əv, səm ˈbotl̩z əv, | ə ˈpleit əv, ˈtuː ˈpleits əv.
ə ˈpot əv, ə ˈfjuː ˈpots əv, | ə ˈbag əv, ˈθriː ˈbagz əv.
ə ˈboul əv, ˈtuː ˈboulz əv, | ə ˈsak əv, səm ˈsaks əv.

Examples of pronominal use:

ˈmei ai ˈofə ju ə ˈglaːs əv ˈwain?—if ˈðat s ˇwain, ai I ˈhav ə ˌglaːs.
ˈθriː ˈbotl̩z əv ˌbrandi.—ai ʃəd ˈlaik ə ˌglaːs ov it.

86 Partitive units. These correspond to the "auxiliary numerals" of certain oriental languages.

Adjectival

ə ˈpiːs əv, ˈtuː ˈpiːsiz əv, | ə ˈgrein əv, səm ˈgreinz əv.
ə ˈlʌmp əv, səm ˈlʌmps əv, | ə ˈkeik əv, ˈtuː ˈkeiks əv.
ə ˈbit əv, ˈbits əv, | ə ˈboːl əv, ə ˈfjuː ˈboːlz əv.
ə ˈblok əv, ˈθriː ˈbloks əv, | ə ˈstik əv, ˈsiks ˈstiks əv.
ə ˈʃiːt əv, ə ˈfjuː ˈʃiːts əv, | ən ˈiər əv, səm ˈiəz əv.
ə ˈdrop əv, ˈθriː ˈdrops əv, | ə ˈbleid əv, ˈsevrəl ˈbleidz əv.

Examples of the application of the partitive units:

ə ˈpiːs əv ˌtʃoːk (ˌwud, ˌleðə, ˌkloθ, ˌpeipə, ˌstoun, etc.).
ə ˈlʌmp əv ˌkoul (ˌəːθ, ˌklei, ˌʃugə*, etc.).
ə ˈbit əv ˌglaːs (ˌwud, ˌtʃoːk, ˌpeipə, ˌstoun, etc.).
ə ˈblok əv ˌwud (ˌstoun, ˌaiən, etc.).
ə ˈʃiːt əv ˌpeipə (ˌkaːdboːd, ˌaiən, etc.).
ə ˈdrop əv ˌwoːtə (ˌwiski, ˌblʌd, etc.).

ə 'grein əv ˌsand (ˌsoːlt, ʃugə*, etc.).
ə 'keik əv ˌsoup, etc.
ə 'boːl əv ˌstriŋ, etc.
ə 'stik əv ˌlikəris, etc.
ən 'iər əv ˌkoːn (ˌwiːt, ˌbaːli, etc.).
ə 'bleid əv ˌgraːs.

THE NUMERICALS

87 Function. The numericals are words or group-words that may serve as an answer to the question 'hau ˌmeni? With the exception of the numeral wʌn they refer only to plural nouns, and may be used either adjectivally or pronominally. They form two general groups:

(a) Those that do not add **ov** when used adjectivally:

'sevr| ˌpiːp|.   ə 'fjuː moə ˌbuks.

(b) Those that add **ov** when used adjectivally:

ə 'nʌmbər əv ˌpiːp|.   ə 'kʌp| əv ˌbuks.

88 The cardinal numbers. In most contexts these belong to class (a). Their pronunciation and stressing are shown in the following table.

1 wʌn	11 iˈlevn̩	21 'twenti ˈwʌn
2 tuː	12 twelv	22 'twenti ˈtuː
3 θriː	13 'θəːˈtiːn	30 ˈθəːti
4 foə*	14 'foːˈtiːn	40 ˈfoːti
5 faiv	15 'fifˈtiːn	50 ˈfifti
6 siks	16 'siksˈtiːn	60 ˈsiksti
7 sevn̩	17 'sevn̩ˈtiːn	70 ˈsevn̩ti
8 eit	18 'eiˈtiːn	80 ˈeiti
9 nain	19 'nainˈtiːn	90 ˈnainti
10 ten	20 ˈtwenti	100 ə ˈhʌndrid

101 ə 'hʌndrid n̩ ˈwʌn	500 'faiv ˈhʌndrid
102 ə 'hʌndrid n̩ ˈtuː	1,000 ə ˈθauzn̩d
200 'tuː ˈhʌndrid	2,000 'tuː ˈθauzn̩d
201 'tuː 'hʌndrid n̩ ˈwʌn	100,000 ə 'hʌndrid ˈθauzn̩d
202 'tuː 'hʌndrid n̩ ˈtuː	1,000,000 ə ˈmiljən

Stress is an important element in helping to distinguish between the double-stressed "teens" and the single-stressed "tens," as is shown in the following examples:

'fif'tiːn ˌmen.   ʃi z 'dʒʌst fifˌtiːn.
'fifti ˌmen.   ʃi z 'dʒʌst ˌfifti.

In counting, however, the sense of contrast causes the "teens" to become single-stressed:

ˌθəːtiːn, ˌfoːtiːn, ˌfiftiːn, ˌsikstiːn, ˌsevn̩tiːn, ˌeitiːn, ˌnaintiːn.

The indefinite article that normally precedes certain cardinal numbers (ə ˋhʌndrid, ə ˋθauzn̩d, ə 'hʌndrid ˌθauzn̩d, ə ˌmiljən and the compounds ə 'hʌndrid n̩ ˌwʌn, etc.) is omitted when another determiner is used with the numeral, thus:

ðə 'hʌndrid ˌdeiz.   'ðis 'fəːst ˙hʌndrid ˌθauzn̩d.
'evri 'hʌndrid ˌmailz.   hiz 'miljən ˌriːzn̩z.
'sevr̩| 'θauzn̩d ˌpaundz.   ə 'fjuː ˙miljən ˌpiːp|.

After sʌm and meni (and sometimes after sevr̩|) the numerical is pluralized and is followed by ov.

'sʌm 'hʌndridz əv ˌpeidʒiz.   'sʌm 'hʌndridz əv ˋθauzn̩dz ov ðm̩.
'sevr̩| ˋθauzn̩dz əv ðm̩.   'meni ˋmiljənz əv ˌpiːp|.

But if sʌm is used with a singular numerical in the sense of əˋproksimitli it is not followed by ov.

ju | 'faind it 'sʌm (= əbaut ə) 'hʌndrid ˙peidʒiz 'fəːðər ˌon.

The cardinal numbers may themselves be modified by various words such as articles, əˋbaut, igˋzaktli, 'ounli (which precede), and moə* (which follows), but ounli may follow a cardinal number used pronominally.

Adjectival	*Pronominal*
'ounli ˋθriː moə ˌstamps.	ai 'ounli ˋsoː əbaut ˌsiks.[1]
'θriː moə ˌdeiz.	ðər ər 'ounli ˋθriː ˌmoə.
'ounli ˋθriː ˌwiːks.	ai ˌsoː 'θriː ˋounli.
əbaut 'foːti ˌpiːp|.	igˋzaktli ˌθəːti
ˋwʌn buk, ˋtuː buks,	ai v 'ounli got ˌwʌn
ˋθriː buks, etc.	(ˌtuː, ˌθriː, etc.).[1]

When a cardinal number (other than wʌn) is followed by a noun indicating a weight or measure the latter is in the plural if it is

[1] Note that in spoken English ounli generally has the same position as oːlwiz.

acting in a substantive capacity; if, however, it is followed by another noun it is then acting adjectivally, and remains in the singular. Examples:

it 'weiz ˙ten ˌpaundz.   but it s ə 'ten ˙paund ˌtəːki.

hi z 'siks ˙fiːt ˌtuː.   ,,   hi z ə 'siks ˙fut ˌman.

it s 'θriː ˌmailz.   ,,   it s ə 'θriː ˙mail ˌwoːk.

The cardinal numbers are followed by ov when they are used to indicate a certain number of persons or things extracted from a larger collection. In this case the noun is preceded by another determiner.

ai ˌwont 'foər əv ˙ðouz ˌbuks.

hi 'geiv mi 'ten əv iz ˌtʃeriz.

When the cardinal numbers are preceded by words such as nʌmbə*, peidʒ, buk, tʃaptə*, paːt, to form ordinal equivalents, the article is not used.

'weə z nʌmbə ˌwʌn?   ju l 'faind ˙ðat on 'peidʒ ˌwʌn.

wi 'got əz ˙faːr əz 'tʃaptə ˌθriː ˌlaːst ˌtaim.

89 Numericals not adding ov. In the following general list nou is adjectival and nʌn pronominal; all the other numericals may be used in either capacity.

oːl	'meni ˋmoə*	(ðə) ˋmoust
'not ˋoːl	'sevrḷ ˋmoə*	'tuː ˋmeni
ˋmeni	moə*	iˋnʌf
sʌm, sm̩	sm̩ ˋmoə*	'tuː ˋfjuː
ˋeni	'eni ˋmoə*	ə ˋfjuː
nou	ˋfjuə*	fjuː
nʌn	'meni ˋfjuə*	(ðə) ˋfjuist

Examples:

Adjectival	*Pronominal*
'oːl 'plaːnts hav ˌruːts.	'ðiːz ər 'oːl ˌmain.
wil ju 'get mi səm ˊstamps?	wil ju ˊget mi sʌm?
həv ju 'got eni ˊstamps?	həv ju ˊgot eni?
ðər ə 'nou ˌmatʃiz.	ðər ˋaː nʌn (*or* ðər ˋaːnt eni).
ai v got 'sevrḷ ˙θiŋz tə ˌtel ju.	ðər ə ˋsevrḷ.
kən ju 'speə mi ə ˙fjuː ˊmatʃiz?	kən ju ˊspeə mi ə ˙fjuː?

ðər ə 'fjuə 'piːpl ðən ai ˏθoːt.
'huː z ˈmeid ðə 'fjuːist misˏteiks?
ˋmeni ˏpiːpl̩ ˏθiŋk sou.
ju 'oːt tə ˈləːn 'moə ˋwəːdz.
ˋjuː v ˏmeid ðə ˋmoust misˏteiks.
ai 'wont səm ˈmoə ˏstamps.
həv ju 'got i ˈnʌf ˊmatʃiz?
ðər ə 'nou moːr ˏenviloups.

ˋnot ˌmoə; ˊfjuə.
ˋjuː v ˏmeid ðə ˏfjuːist.
ai ˋhavn̩t ˏmeni.
ðər ə 'moə ðən ai ˋθoːt.
'huː z ˈgot ðə ˏmoust?
ai 'wont səm ˌmoə.
həv ju 'got iˈnʌf?
ðər ə 'nou moə ˏleft.

90 Numericals adding ov.

Indicating degree of quantity

Adjectival	*Pronominal*
ə ˋlot əv, ˋlots əv,	ə ˋlot, ˋlots.
ə ˋnʌmbər əv, ˋnʌmbəz əv,	ə ˋnʌmbə*, ˋnʌmbəz.
ə 'gud ˋnʌmbər əv,	ə 'gud ˋnʌmbə*.
ə 'greit ˋnʌmbər əv,	ə 'greit ˋnʌmbə*,
'greit ˋnʌmbəz əv.	'greit ˋnʌmbəz.
ə 'smoːl ˋnʌmbər əv,	ə 'smoːl ˋnʌmbə*.
ə ˋkʌpl̩ əv,	ə ˋkʌpl̩.
ə ˋhiːp əv, ˋhiːps əv,	ə ˋhiːp (ov ðəm).
ə ˋmas əv,	ə ˋmas (ov ðəm),
ˋmasiz əv,	ˋmasiz (ov ðəm).
ˋplenti əv,	ˋplenti.
ˋbouθ əv,	ˋbouθ.

Mixed examples:

> ju I faind ˋlots əv igˏzaːmpl̩z laik ˏðat.
> ju ˏsiːm tə hav ə ˏgud ˏnʌmbər əv ˏbuks hiə.
> 'hau ˈmeni d ju ˏwont? —ou, əbaut ə ˏkʌpl̩.
> 'teik əz ˈmeni əz ju ˏlaik, ai v got ˋhiːps (ov ðəm) ət ˏhoum.
> hi ˏsiːmz tə hav ˏplenti əv ˏfrendz.

Weights and measures

These are identical with the weights and measures shown as quantitatives in §85.

Containers

These are identical with the containers shown as quantitatives in §85.

Collectives

These are generally used adjectivally.

ə ˈpeər əv, ˈpeəz əv,   ə ˈgruːp əv, ˈgruːps əv,
ə ˈset əv, ˈsets əv,   ə ˈkʌmpəni əv, ˈkʌmpəniz əv.
ə kəˈlekʃn̩ əv, kəˈlekʃn̩z əv,   ə bəˈtaljən əv, bəˈtaljənz əv.
ə ˈsiəriz əv, ˈsiəriːz əv.   ə ˈredʒmənt əv, ˈredʒmənts əv.
ə ˈbʌntʃ əv, ˈbʌntʃiz əv.   ən ˈaːmi əv, ˈaːmiz əv.

   ə ˈpeər əv ʃuːz (ˌbuːts, ˌsoks, etc.).
   ə ˈgruːp əv igˌzaːmp|z, etc.
   ə ˈset əv ˌtiːθ (ˌdroəz, etc.).
   ə kəˈlekʃn̩ əv ˌstamps (ˌspesimənz, etc.).
   ə ˈsiəriz əv igˌzaːmp|z, etc.
   ə ˈbʌntʃ əv ˌgreips, etc.
   ə ˈkʌmpəni əv ˌsouldʒəz, etc.

By omitting the word **ov**, such group-words may occasionally be used pronominally, but it is more usual to replace **ov** by **ov ðəm**, thus making compound pronoun-equivalents.

91   Equivalents of quantitatives and numericals.   In addition to the foregoing lists of quantitative and numerical determiners, there exists another (and almost unlimited) series of collocations used to express quantity, number and fractional parts.   The distinguishing difference appears to be this:

The quantitatives and numericals proper may qualify *nouns which are unaccompanied by an article or a similar determiner*; in such cases they *replace* the article, etc.

   ə ˈlit| ˌmʌni, ə ˈlot əv ˌmʌni;
   ˈtuː ˌbuks, ə ˈfjuː ˌbuks, ə ˈkʌp| əv ˌbuks, etc.

The quantitative and numerical equivalents, on the other hand, qualify nouns which are already qualified by an article or a similar determiner; in such cases they *do not* replace the article, etc.

   ðə ˈhoul əv ðə ˌmʌni, ə ˈkwoːtər əv ən ˌauə,
   ə ˈpaːt əv mai ˌmʌni, ˈnʌn əv ˑðiːz ˌpiːp|, etc.

In such cases it is difficult to say which is head-word and which is qualifier.   In ə ˈpaːt əv mai ˌmʌni it may be considered that the noun ˌpaːt is qualified by the phrase əv mai ˈmʌni; or it may be

held that ˋmʌni is the chief noun, and that this is qualified by
ə ˌpaːt əv and by ˋmai.

The following is a list of the more important determiner equivalents that serve as quantitatives:

ˋmʌtʃ əv	ə ˈgud diːl ˋmoər əv
ə ˋlitl əv	ə ˈgreit diːl ˋmoər əv

The following serve as numericals:

ˋmeni əv	ə ˈgud meni ˋmoər əv
ˋsevrl̩ əv	ə ˈgreit meni ˋmoər əv
ə ˋdʌzn̩ əv	ˋwʌn əv
ə ˋfjuː əv	ˋtuː əv, etc.

The following serve as either quantitatives or numericals:

ˋmoust əv	ˋmoər əv
ˋsʌm əv	sm̩ ˋmoər əv
ˋeni əv	eni ˋmoər əv
ˋnʌn əv	ˈnou ˋmoər əv
ə ˋpaːt əv	ˋhaːf əv
ˋoːl əv	ə ˋθəːd əv
ðə ˋhoul əv	ə ˋkwoːtər əv

The corresponding pronominals to the above are formed

(*a*) By simply suppressing the ov.

ˈjuː v ˈgot ə gud ˋmeni ˌbuks, bət ˈai v got ə ˈgud meni ˋmoə.

(*b*) By replacing the ov by ov it for the quantitatives and
by ov ðəm for the numericals.

if ju ˋlaik ðat ˌpeipə, ju d ˈbetə ˈbai səm ˋmoər ov it.
if ju ˋlaik ðouz ˌbuks, ju d ˈbetə ˈbai səm ˋmoər ov ðəm.

92 Restricted use of mʌtʃ and meni. The words mʌtʃ (used
with uncountables) and meni (used with countables) are almost
invariably replaced by ə lot, ə laːdʒ nʌmbə*, ə laːdʒ kwontiti,
plenti, ə gud diːl, etc., except in the following cases:

1. When used in negative sentences:

ðər ˋiznt̩ ˌmʌtʃ. ðər ˋaːnt ˌmeni.

2. When used in general questions:

   'iz ðə 'mʌtʃ? 'aː ðə 'meni?

3. In clauses introduced by weðə* or if:

   ai 'dount nou ˙weðə ju I ˎsiː ˌmʌtʃ (*or* ˌmeni).

4. When preceded by az, sou, tuː and hau:

   ai v ˌgot əz 'mʌtʃ (*or* 'meni) əz ai ˎwont.
   ai 'ʃudn̩t 'teik sou ˎmʌtʃ (*or* ˎmeni) if ˌai wə juː.
   ju v 'givn̩ mi 'tuː ˎmʌtʃ (*or* ˎmeni).
   'hau mʌtʃ (*or* meni) d ju ˎwont?

5. When modifying or standing for the subject of the sentence:

   'mʌtʃ əv ˙ðis | 'hav tə bi ˌtʃeindʒd.
   'meni piːp| ˙θiŋk it 'oːt tə bi ˌtʃeindʒd.

Similar rules of usage are found in connection with the adverbs
faː* (distance) and loŋ (time), which are replaced by ə loŋ wei
and ə loŋ taim, respectively.

THE ORDINALS

93 General list. This class of determiners includes the ordinal
numbers and the two words nekst and laːst. Of all the determiners,
they approach nearest grammatically and semantically to adjectives.

1st fəːst	11th iˎlevn̩θ	21st 'twenti ˎfəːst
2nd ˎsekənd	12th twelfθ	22nd 'twenti ˎseknd̩
3rd θəːd	13th 'θəːˎtiːnθ	30th ˎθəːtiiθ
4th foːθ	14th 'foːˎtiːnθ	40th ˎfoːtiiθ
5th fifθ	15th 'fifˎtiːnθ	50th ˎfiftiiθ
6th siksθ	16th 'siksˎtiːnθ	60th ˎsikstiiθ
7th ˎsevn̩θ	17th 'sevn̩ˎtiːnθ	70th ˎsevn̩tiiθ
8th eitθ	18th 'eiˎtiːnθ	80th ˎeitiiθ
9th nainθ	19th 'nainˎtiːnθ	90th ˎnaintiiθ
10th tenθ	20th ˎtwentiiθ	100th ˎhʌndridθ

101st 'hʌndrid n̩ ˎfəːst	500th 'faiv ˎhʌndridθ
102nd 'hʌndrid n̩ ˎsekənd	1000th ˎθauznd̩θ
200th 'tuː ˎhʌndridθ	2000th 'tuː θauznd̩θ
201st 'tuː 'hʌndrid n̩ ˎfəːst	100,000th 'hʌndrid ˎθauznd̩θ
202nd 'tuː 'hʌndrid n̩ ˎseknd̩	1,000,000th ˎmiljənθ

94 Uses of the ordinals. The ordinal numbers are generally preceded by other determiners:

ðə 'fəːst ˌtaim.   mai 'sekn̩d ˎjiə.

They serve as qualifiers or as pronouns:

ai 'tuk ðə 'fəːst ˌbuk.   ai 'tuk ðə ˌfəːst.

They may occasionally be used predicatively:

ai wəz ˎfəːst.

They may be used with or without the semi-pronoun wʌn:

'did ju ˙teik ðə ˎfəːst (wʌn) oː ðə ˌsekənd (wʌn)?

laːst is used without the definite or other articles when compounded with nait, wiːk, mʌnθ, jiə*, taim, and the names of the seasons to form adverbials of past time in the sense of "immediately before this."

nekst is used without the definite article when compounded with wiːk, mʌnθ, jiə*, taim and the names of the seasons to form adverbials of future time in the sense of "immediately after this."

ai 'soː im ˙laːst ˌnait.   hi z 'kʌmiŋ hiə 'nekst ˌmʌnθ.
it 'reind ˙evri ˌdei ˌlaːst ˌwiːk   'betə 'lʌk 'nekst ˌtaim.
wi 'went tə ˎskotlənd ˌlaːst ˌsʌmə.   ʃi z 'gouiŋ əˎbroːd ˌnekst ˌwintə.

To give the sense of "concluding" or "following" the definite article is used.

ai 'went ðeə ðə 'laːst ˌwiːk (= ðə kənˎkluːdiŋ ˌwiːk).
ai 'went ðeə ðə 'nekst ˌwiːk (= ðə ˎfoluiŋ ˌwiːk).

Note the use of the ordinals in royal titles:

(kiŋ) 'dʒɔːdʒ ðə ˌsiksθ. (kwiːn) iˈlizəbəθ ðə ˌsekənd.

The ordinals fəːst, nekst and laːst may be modified by **veri**, which serves to intensify the meaning of each:

ðə 'veri 'fəːst ˌtaim.   ðə 'veri 'nekst ˌdei.

COLLOCATIONS OF DETERMINERS

95 Collocations of ʌðə*. This determiner enters into two collocations to form what are sometimes called reciprocal pronouns, since they can act as pronouns with verbs to express a mutual activity.

iːtʃ ʌðə* generally implies two persons:
wi 'dount ˅spiːk tu iːtʃ ʌðə ˌnau.
'tuː əv ðə ˙stjuːdn̩ts ə ˅helpiŋ iːtʃ ʌðə.

wʌn ənʌðə* generally implies more than two persons:
'juː ˙piːp| ʃəd ˅help wʌn ənʌðə ˌmoə.

The reciprocal pronouns may be used as possessives:
'ðouz piːp| 'siːm tə bi in˙dʒoiiŋ iːtʃ ʌðəz ˅kʌmpəni.
wi 'dount veri ˙ofn̩ dis'kʌs auə ˌplanz tə‚geðə, bikoz wi ə 'not
veri ˙intristid in wʌn ənʌðəz ˅wəːk.

96 Collocations of bouθ and oːl. The determiners bouθ and
oːl form collocations with the plural personal pronouns as shown
in the following table:

Subject:	*Subject or Object:*	*Object:*
wi ˅bouθ	˅bouθ əv əs	əs ˅bouθ
ju ˅bouθ	˅bouθ əv ju	ju ˅bouθ
ðei ˅bouθ	˅bouθ əv ðəm	ðəm ˅bouθ
wi ˅oːl	˅oːl əv əs	əs ˅oːl
ju ˅oːl	˅oːl əv ju	ju ˅oːl
ðei ˅oːl	˅oːl əv ðəm	ðəm ˅oːl

Those shown in the first column are used only in the subject
position and those in the third column only in the object position.
Those in the middle column may be used in either position.

wi ˅oːl ˌspouk tə him.   hi 'spouk tu əs ˌoːl.
˅oːl əv əs ˌspouk tə him.   hi 'spouk tu ˌoːl əv əs.

97 Collocations of evri. The determiner evri forms collocations
with the cardinal and ordinal numbers. These collocations may be
either adjectival or pronominal.

Adjectival:

ai 'gou ðeər əbaut 'evri ˙θriː ˌdeiz əz ə ˌruːl.
ə 'repri˙zentətiv z i˙lektid fər 'evri ˙hʌndrid ˌmembəz.
ðə z ə 'lamppoust in ˙frʌnt əv 'evri ˙fiftiːnθ ˌhaus.
wi 'gou ðeər 'evri 'θəːd ˙wiːk in ðə ˌmʌnθ.

Pronominal:

ai 'niːd sm̩ ˅briks ; ai I 'giv ju ə ˙peni fər 'evri ˙faiv ju ˌbriŋ mi.
in'sted əv ˙teikiŋ wʌn evri ˅θəːd dei, 'trai ˙teikiŋ wʌn
evri ˅foːθ.

evri forms with ʌðə* a collocation which has two different
meanings, and context alone determines which meaning is intended.

Adjectival:

(a) ˅ai sed ˅jes", bət 'evri ˅ʌðə ˌpəːsn̩ sed ˅nou".
   ('evri ˙ʌðə ˙pəːsn̩ = 'evribodi ˅els, *or* 'oːl ði ˅ʌðə ˌpiːpl.)

(b) hi 'didn̩t ˙koːl ət ˅evri ˌhaus, bət ət ˙evri ˅ʌðə ˌhaus.
   ('evri ˙ʌðə ˙haus = 'evri oːl˅təːnit ˌhaus.)

Pronominal:

(a) 'ðis iz ði 'ounli ˙peidʒ ˅left ; ai v dis˅troid evri ˌʌðə.
   ('evri ˙ʌðər = ˅oːl ði ˌʌðəz.)

Sometimes not even the context will show which meaning is
intended: 'evri ˙ʌðə ˙boi in ðə ˙klaːs wəz ˅roŋ may mean that all
the other boys were wrong or that every alternate boy was wrong.

98 Collocations of sʌtʃ. The determiner sʌtʃ forms collocations
with oːl, evri, meni, sʌm, eni, nou and ənʌðə* which express a
similarity to something already in mind. Though they are usually
adjectival, some of them may be used pronominally.

Adjectival:

'oːl sʌtʃ ˙θiŋz ə bi'jond mai ˅miːnz.
'evri sʌtʃ ˙pəːsn̩ əz bin i˅limi ˌneitid.
˅meni sʌtʃ mis ˌteiks əv bin ˌmeid.
˅sʌm sʌtʃ ˌtrʌbl̩ wəz ˅baund tu ə ˌkəː.
ai 'wount ək˙sept 'eni sʌtʃ ˌfoːlti wʌnz.
ai ˌment 'nou sʌtʃ ˌθiŋ !
ə˅nʌðə sʌtʃ iks ˌpiəriəns wəd bi ði ˅end əv mi !

Pronominal:

wiː I ˌhelp 'oːl ˙sʌtʃ əz ə˅griː wið əs.
˅meni ˌsʌtʃ əv ˅feild in ˌlaif.
həv ju 'evə ˙met ə˅nʌðə ˙sʌtʃ ?

C. Adjectives

TYPES OF ADJECTIVES

99 Definition.   Adjectives may be defined as qualifiers of nouns; that is to say, they describe or indicate the person or thing denoted by the noun.   They are marked in general by the following characteristics:

(*a*) They serve to answer the questions *what kind of . . . ?* and *what . . . like?*

(*b*) They may serve to answer the question *which . . . ?*

(*c*) They may be used to qualify nouns attributively or predicatively (i.e., as subject-complement).

(*d*) They may usually be modified by adverbs of degree.

(*e*) They can usually form adverb-derivatives by adding li (-*ly*) and noun-derivatives by adding nis (-*ness*).

The following classes of words are therefore excluded from this category:

(*a*) Possessive nouns.

(*b*) Nouns qualifying other nouns.

(*c*) Participles proper.

(*d*) Determiners.

Adjectives may be grouped into the two following classes:

(*a*) *Adjectives Proper*; simple, derivative and compound.

(*b*) *Participials*, which may be either *Active* or *Passive*.

100 Adjectives proper.   It is difficult, if not impossible, to draw a rigid line of demarcation between simple and derivative adjectives. Words such as **gud, wait, fri:** are obviously simple and indecomposable; words such as ˋreini, ˋmʌnθli, ˋwaitiʃ, ˈʌnˋseif, formed from existing words by means of living affixes, are clearly derivatives.   But between these two extremes we find adjectives such as ˋobviəs, ˋevidənt, ˋbriljənt, which are for all practical purposes indecomposable, and others, such as ˋnoːðən, ikˋspensiv, riˋmaːkəbl, ˋhoulsəm, formed from recognizable roots (many of which are altered in form or meaning) and more or less obsolete affixes;

these cannot be considered as simple words, and yet they do not belong to the class of derivatives that may be built up synthetically.

The following categories, ranging almost imperceptibly from one extreme to the other, will give some idea of the various formal characteristics of adjectives.

(a) gud, bad, wait, laːdʒ, smoːl, friː, etc. (For fuller list see §114.)

(b) ˈjelou, ˈklevə*, ˈsimpl̩, ˈkomən, pəˈlait, siˈviə*, ˈbizi, ˈpriti, etc. (For fuller list see §115.)

(c) ˈneitiv, ˈbriljənt, ˈhansəm, ˈoːkwəd, ˈliːgl̩, iˈmens, kənˈviːnjənt, ˈevidənt, ˈsailənt, ˈkjuəriəs, ˈobviəs, ˈlaikli, ˈhandi, frentʃ, ˈiŋgliʃ, ˈhoulsəm, ˈlounli, ˈnoːðən, ˈsʌðən, ˈiːstən, ˈwestən, ˈspaniʃ, ˈswiːdiʃ, ˈdʒapəˈniːz, ˈtʃaiˈniːz, ˈkworəlsəm, ˈsensibl̩, fəˈnetik, ˈenəˈdʒetik, ˈdefinit, ˈaktiv, ˈrelətiv, ikˈspresiv.

(d) ˈwudn̩, ˈwulən, ˈmanli, ˈaŋgri, ˈhʌŋgri, ˈnoːθwəd, ˈwestwəd, ˈhoumwəd, ˈposibl̩, ˈprobəbl̩, riˈmaːkəbl̩, kənˈsidərəbl̩.

(e) ˈdeili, ˈdəːti, ˈfʌni, ˈiːzi, ˈreini, ˈwindi, ˈstoːmi, ˈsʌni, ˈfogi, ˈfrosti, ˈklaudi, ˈhoupfl̩, ˈkeəfl̩, ˈhelpfl̩, ˈjuːsfl̩, ˈpeinfl̩, ˈtʃiəfl̩, ˈhouplis, ˈkeəlis, ˈhelplis, ˈniːdlis, ˈjuːslis, ˈpeinlis, ˈriːdəbl̩, riˈlaiəbl̩, ˈtʃeindʒəbl̩, ˈgloːriəs, ˈfeiməs, ˈnəːvəs, diˈpendənt, ˌaːˈtistik, miˈtalik.

(f) ˈrediʃ, ˈwaitiʃ, ˈkouldiʃ, ˈswiːtiʃ, ˈʌnˈtaidi, ˈʌnˈseif, ˈʌnˈtruː, ˈʌnˈwaiz, ˈʌnˈkaind, ˈinəˈfensiv, ˈinsinˈsiə*, ˈiŋkəmˈpliːt, ˈindiˈpendənt, imˈposibl̩, imˈpəːfikt, ˈimpəˈlait, imˈprobəbl̩.

Examples of Compound Adjectives:

ˈpitʃ ˈdaːk, ˈskai ˈbluː, ˈdaːk ˈred, ˈlait ˈgriːn, ˈtʃaildˌlaik, ˈspriŋˌlaik, ˈnon-igˈzistənt, ˈgudˈlukiŋ, ˈouvə-pəˈlait, ˈsemiˈadʒikˈtaivl̩.

101 Participials. A certain number of participles (both present and past) are used with the functions of adjectives, and differ very little from adjectives proper. They may be termed *Participial Adjectives*, or simply *Participials*. It is not always easy to distinguish participles proper from participial adjectives. One test is to ascertain by ear whether they may be modified by adverbs such as veri, tuː, inʌf, hau, etc. If they are so modifiable, they may be considered as participial adjectives; if not, they must be considered simply as participles, in which case they are modifiable by such words and word-groups as mʌtʃ, veri mʌtʃ, tuː mʌtʃ, etc.

102 Active participials. Certain words which are sometimes purely adjectival in function are derived from the *ing*-form of verbs, from which these are therefore indistinguishable in form. The following are selected from those most commonly used:

ə'mjuːziŋ	dis'kʌridʒiŋ	'laːstiŋ	'pʌzliŋ
'tʃaːmiŋ	iŋ'kʌridʒiŋ	'lʌviŋ	ri'freʃiŋ
'tʃiəriŋ	ik'saitiŋ	'misiŋ	'ʃokiŋ
'kʌmfətiŋ	ig'zoːstiŋ	'mis'liːdiŋ	'straikiŋ
kən'fjuːziŋ	'graːspiŋ	ə'blaidʒiŋ	sə'praiziŋ
kən'vinsiŋ	'intristiŋ	'pliːziŋ	'temptiŋ
'defniŋ	in'vaitiŋ	'presiŋ	'teri,faiiŋ
'disə'pointiŋ	'nouiŋ	'promisiŋ	

103 Negative active participials. Their adjectival character is particularly brought out by the fact that many of them have negative forms in ʌn-, though the corresponding verbs cannot be so modified, e.g., 'pliːziŋ—'ʌn'pliːziŋ, correspond exactly to 'pleznt and 'ʌn'pleznt, though the corresponding negative modification of the verb is dis-.

'ʌn'tʃeindʒiŋ	'ʌnfə'giviŋ	'ʌnəb'zəːviŋ	'ʌn'satis,faiiŋ
'ʌnkəm'pleiniŋ	'ʌn'heziteitiŋ	'ʌnə'fendiŋ	'ʌnsəs'teiniŋ
'ʌndi'zəːviŋ	'ʌn'intristiŋ	'ʌn'pliːziŋ	'ʌn'temptiŋ
'ʌniŋ'kʌridʒiŋ	'ʌnin'vaitiŋ	'ʌn'promisiŋ	
'ʌn'flatəriŋ	'ʌnə'blaidʒiŋ	'ʌnri'freʃiŋ	

ai v ˌhəːd 'veri ʌn'flatəriŋ ə'kaunts ov im.

ði ə'kaunts ai v 'həːd ov im ə 'veri ʌnˌflatəriŋ.

ə ˌmoust ʌnˌintristiŋ ˌbuk.   ˌðis 'buk s 'moust ʌnˌintristiŋ.

The participials in this section can hardly be considered as present participles proper, for no such verbs exist as tu 'ʌn'tʃeindʒ, tu 'ʌnkəm'plein, etc.

104 Compound active participials. A certain number of these adjectives may be used in composition with an adverbial or other prefix, though such adverbs or other prefixes would not be so compounded with the corresponding verbs. Examples:

'friːkwntli-ə'kəːriŋ	'nevə'feiliŋ	'wel'miːniŋ
'self-di'dʒestiŋ	'haːd'wəːkiŋ	'wel'fitiŋ
'self-sə'poːtiŋ	'faː'siːiŋ	'gud 'lukiŋ

The stress falls on the first element when these words are used as qualifiers, while the kinetic stress falls on the second element when they are used predicatively:

ə 'wel-fitiŋ ˋkout.　　　　'ðis ˙kout s 'welˋfitiŋ.

Many adjectives of this type may be used as qualifiers, but when used as subject-complement the present participle together with biː may constitute simply the progressive form of the verb. Thus in hi z əˋmjuːziŋ the word əˋmjuːziŋ is a true adjective, equal to such adjectives as ˋkomikļ or ˋfʌni. But in hi z ə'mjuːziŋ ðə ˌtʃildrən the word əˋmjuːziŋ is the present participle of the verb əˋmjuːz forming the present tense of the verb in the aspect of activity. In hi z ˋkʌmiŋ, ˙hi z ˋliːdiŋ, etc., however, the words ˋkʌmiŋ, ˋliːdiŋ, etc., are simply present participles, not participial adjectives.

Note also that a present participle, as such, is not modifiable by such adverbs as veri, tuː, etc. Thus we say hi z 'veri əˋmjuːziŋ, but not hi z 'veri ə˙mjuːziŋ ðə ˋtʃildrən, and we never say hi z 'veri ˋkʌmiŋ.

The following are typical cases of present participles that are seldom used as subject-complements.

ˋkʌmiŋ, igˋzistiŋ, ˋfoluiŋ, iŋˋkriːsiŋ, ˋliːdiŋ, ˋliviŋ, priˋsiːdiŋ, riˋmeiniŋ, səˋraundiŋ.

105 Passive participials. These consist generally of the past participle form of certain verbs. The following are selected from those most commonly used:

ˌʌpˋset[1]	əˋstoniʃt	ˋkompliˌkeitid	səˋpraizd
diˋsaidid	əˋfendid	kənˋfjuːzd	ˋseliˌbreitid
diˋlaitid	ˋfeidid	kənˋtentid	ˋsivilaizd
diˋvoutid	ˋfraitņd	ˋkraudid	ˋspoukən
'disəˋpointid	ˋhʌrid	ˋkwolifaid	ˋʃeltəd
'diskənˋtentid	ikˋsaitid	ˋnoutid	ˋteriˌfaid
disˋkʌridʒd	igˋzoːstid	ˋpliːzd	ˋtaiəd
disˋtiŋgwiʃt	iksˋpiəriənst	ˋpʌzļd	ˋwʌrid
ˋdrʌŋk[2]	'iniksˋpiəriənst	riˋzəːvd	
əˋmjuːzd	ˋintristid	ˋsatisˌfaid	

it s ə ˋsivilaizd ˌkʌntri. ðə 'kʌntri z ˌsivilaizd.

hi z ə 'veri iks'piəriənst ˌtiːtʃə. hi z 'veri iksˌpiəriənst

[1] Only used as subject-complement.

[2] ˋdrʌŋkən when used as qualifier.

106 **Negative passive participials.** In addition to the past participles of a few verbs in ʌn- (e.g. ˈʌnˈduː, ˈʌnˈtai), there are a considerable number of passive participials in ʌn- to which there are no corresponding verbs, for the ʌn- is a purely negative prefix and might be replaced by not or non-. The following list includes the commonest negative passive participials:

ˈʌnˈbʌtn̩d	ˈʌndisˈtəːbd	ˈʌnˈhəːt	ˈʌnˈpoliʃt
ˈʌnˈkoːld foː*	ˈʌnˈdremt ov	ˈʌnintəˈrʌptid	ˈʌnpriˈpeəd
ˈʌnˈklasifaid	ˈʌnˈdrest	ˈʌninˈvaitid	ˈʌnˈpruːvd
ˈʌnˈkukt	ˈʌnˈiːtn̩	ˈʌnˈnoun	ˈʌnˈkwolifaid
ˈʌnˈkoːkt	ˈʌnˈedjukeitid	ˈʌnˈmarid	ˈʌnˈsiːn
ˈʌnˈkʌvəd	ˈʌnikˈspektid	ˈʌnˈmauntid	ˈʌnˈset|d
ˈʌnˈkʌt	ˈʌnfoːˈsiːn	ˈʌnˈnoutist	ˈʌnsəˈpoːtid
ˈʌnˈdamidʒd	ˈʌnˈfiniʃt	ˈʌnˈokjupaid	ˈʌnsəsˈpektid
ˈʌndiˈsaidid	ˈʌnˈhəːd ov	ˈʌnˈoupənd	ˈʌnˈtʌtʃt

107 **Compound passive participials.** A certain number of these may be formed, on the model of: ·

ˈwel-biˈheivd	ˈbadliˈdʌn	ˈwelˈlaitid
ˈbadli-biˈheivd	ˈhaːfˈdʌn	ˈbadliˈlaitid
ˈwelˈbilt	ˈʌndəˈdʌn	ˈwelˈmeid
ˈbadliˈbilt	ˈhaːfˈdraund	ˈbadliˈmeid
ˈhaːfˈbilt	ˈhaːfˈiːtn̩	ˈrediˈmeid
ˈwelˈkliːnd	ˈwelˈdrest	ˈwelˈmanidʒd
ˈhailiˈkʌləd	ˈbadliˈdrest	ˈbadliˈmanidʒd
ˈselfˈkonstitjuːtid	ˈhaːfˈdrest	ˈwelˈpeid
ˈwelˈkukt	ˈwelˈedjukeitid	ˈbadliˈpeid
ˈbadliˈkukt	ˈhaːfˈedjukeitid	ˈouvə-səbˈskraibd
ˈhaːfˈkukt	ˈgudˈhjuːməd	ˈwel-θoːtˈaut
ˈwel-diˈfaind	ˈwel-inˈfoːmd	ˈgudˈtound
ˈwel-diˈdʒestid	ˈwelˈkept	ˈhaːfˈwoːmd
ˈwel-disˈpouzd	ˈbadliˈkept	ˈkliːnˈʃeivn̩
ˈwelˈdʌn	ˈhoumˈkild	

When such compounds are used as qualifiers, the stress falls on the first element; when they are used predicatively, the kinetic tone (if any) falls on the second:

ðəi ə ˈwel-biheivd ˌtʃildrən.   ðəi ə ˈwel-biˌheivd.

COMPARISON OF ADJECTIVES

108 Comparative of superiority. This is formed in two manners:

a. By placing the adverb **moə*** before, and the conjunction **ðən**[1] after the adjective. This is the non-inflexional mode of comparison:

    'ðis buk s ˈmoər ˎintristiŋ (ðən ˏðat wʌn).

b. By using the comparative inflexion of the adjective, followed by the conjunction **ðən**[1]. This is the inflexional mode of comparison:

    'ðis buk s ˎlaːdʒə (ðən ˏðat wʌn).

109 Comparative of equality. This is expressed by placing the adverb **əz** before, and the conjunction **əz** after, the adjective.

    'ðis wʌn z əz ˈgud əz ˏðat wʌn.
    ðis iz ˎdʒʌst əz ˌgud ən ˌig¡zaːmpḷ əz ði ˏʌðə.
    ˌmain z ˎdʒʌst əz ˌlaːdʒ əz ˏjoəz.

When the sentence is negative, the adverb **əz** is often replaced by **sou**:

    ˌðis wʌn 'izṇt əz (*or* sou) ˈgud əz ⱽðat wʌn.
    ˌðis wʌn 'izṇt əz (*or* sou) ˈgud ən igˈzaːmpḷ əz ði ⱽʌðə.

110 Comparative of inferiority. This is expressed by adding the adverb **les** before, and the conjunction **ðən**[1] after, the adjective:

    it s 'les ˈkould ðən it ˈwoz ⱽjestədi.
    ⱽðis wʌn z 'iːvṇ 'les ˈintristiŋ ðən ði ˎʌðə.

But this mode of expression is generally felt to be rather formal and bookish, and it is generally replaced by the negative form of the comparative of equality:

    it 'izṇt əz ˈkould əz it ˈwoz ⱽjestədi.
    ⱽðis wʌn 'izṇt ˈiːvṇ əz 'intristiŋ əz ði ˎʌðə.

---

[1] The latter part of the comparison (beginning with the conjunction **ðən**) may be omitted.

III **Superlative of superiority.** This is formed in two manners:

a. By placing the adverb **moust** before the adjective. This is the non-inflexional mode of comparison:

> it s ðə ˌmoust 'intristiŋ ˙buk ai v 'evə ˌred.

b. By using the superlative inflexion of the adjective:

> ˌðis iz ði 'iːziist ˙buk ai v 'evə ˌred.

A superlative expression is often completed

a. By a clause beginning with **ðət** (expressed or understood):

> ði 'iːziist ˙buk (ðət) ai v 'evə ˌred.

b. By a phrase introduced by the preposition **in**:

> ðə 'laːdʒist ˙kʌntri in ˌjuərəp.
> ðə 'fainist ˙θiŋ in ðə ˌwəːld.

Other prepositions are also used according to the meaning to be conveyed:

> ðə 'fainist ˙θiŋ on ðə ˌmaːkit.
> ðə 'fainist ˙θiŋ ʌndə ðə ˌsʌn.

II2 **Superlative of inferiority.** This is formed by placing the adverb **liːst** before the adjective:

> ˌðis iz ðə 'liːst ˙intristiŋ ˙buk ai v 'evə ˌred.
> ˌðis iz ðə 'liːst ʌndə˙standəbl̩ ˙buk ai v 'evə ˌred.

But the superlative of inferiority is almost invariably replaced by the superlative of superiority of an adjective expressing the contrary meaning:

> ˌðis iz ðə ˌmoust ʌn'intristiŋ ˙buk ai v 'evə ˌred.
> ˌðis iz ðə ˌmoust əbs'kjuə ˙buk ai v 'evə ˌred.

INFLEXIONAL COMPARISON

II3 **General rule.** The general rule for forming the inflexional comparison of adjectives is to add **-ə*** for the comparative and **-ist** for the superlative. Example:

Positive degree: ðə 'weil z ə ˙laːdʒ ˌaniml̩.

Comparative degree: it s 'laːdʒə ðən ən ˌelifn̩t.

Superlative degree: it s ðə 'laːdʒist ˙animl̩ in ðə ˌwəːld.

The inflexional method of comparison is not used for participals. It is used for practically all monosyllabic adjectives and for dissyllabic adjectives having certain final sounds.

The non-inflexional method of comparison is used for other dissyllabic adjectives, for adjectives of more than two syallables and for participials.

114 Monosyllabic adjectives. These are divided into four classes.

a. Certain adjectives that form their comparison irregularly.

Positive	Comparative	Superlative
ˋbad	ˋwəːs	ˋwəːst
ˋfaː*[1]	{ ˋfəːðə* / ˋfaːðə*	ˋfəːðist / ˋfaːðist
ˋgud	ˋbetə*	ˋbest
ˋil	ˋwəːs[2]	ˋwəːst[3]
ˋrait	ˋbetə*	ˋbest
ˋroŋ	ˋwəːs	ˋwəːst
ˋwel[1]	ˋbetə*	ˋbest

b. In the following three cases the comparative and superlative are formed by adding respectively -gə* and -gist.

ˋloŋ	ˋloŋgə*	ˋloŋgist
ˋstroŋ	ˋstroŋgə*	ˋstroŋgist
ˋjʌŋ	ˋjʌŋgə*	ˋjʌŋgist

c. Monosyllabic adjectives ending in a vowel susceptible of adding "linking-r" (marked by the sign *) form their comparative and superlative respectively by adding -rə* and -rist.

ˋbeə*	ˋbeərə*	ˋbeərist
ˋdaiə*	ˋdaiərə*	ˋdaiərist
ˋfeə*	ˋfeərə*	ˋfeərist
ˋkliə*	ˋkliərə*	ˋkliərist
ˋkwiə*	ˋkwiərə*	ˋkwiərist
ˋmiə*	ˋmiərə*	ˋmiərist

[1] faː* and wel form their degrees of comparison in the same way when used as adverbs.
[2] Occasionally moər il.
[3] Occasionally moust il.

89

‵niə*	‵niərə*	‵niərist
‵pjuə*	‵pjuərə*	‵pjuərist
‵puə*	‵puərə*	‵puərist
‵reə*†	‵reərə*	‵reərist
‵skweə*	‵skweərə*	‵skweərist
‵soə*†	‵soərə*	‵soərist
‵ʃuə*	‵ʃuərə*	‵ʃuərist

d. The majority of monosyllabic adjectives follow the general rule for inflexional comparison. Examples:

Positive	*Comparative*	*Superlative*
‵big	‵bigə*	‵bigist
‵blak	‵blakə*	‵blakist
‵bluː	‵bluːə*	‵bluːist

Other adjectives that follow this rule are given below. Some of these (marked with the sign †) may also be compared non-inflexionally.

‵bould	‵friː	‵lou	‵smoːl
‵brait	‵ful	‵mad	‵soft
‵braun	‵gei	‵maild†	‵stiːp
‵breiv	‵glad†	‵miːn	‵stif
‵broːd	‵grei	‵nais	‵stil
‵daːk	‵greit	‵ould†	‵streindʒ
‵damp	‵greiv†	‵peil†	‵streit
‵diːp	‵griːn	‵plein†	‵swiːt
‵drai	‵haːd	‵prompt†	‵ʃaːp
‵dʌl	‵hai	‵raip	‵tait
‵fat	‵hot	‵raund	‵teim
‵faːst	‵kaːm†	‵red	‵truː†
‵fain	‵kaind	‵ritʃ	‵θik
‵feint	‵kliːn	‵ruːd	‵θin
‵fəːm	‵kould	‵saund†	‵waid
‵fit†	‵kuːl	‵sad	‵waild
‵fond†	‵kros†	‵seif	‵wait
‵foːls	‵kwik	‵sik	‵waiz
‵flat	‵laːdʒ	‵skeəs†	‵wet
‵fraŋk†	‵lait	‵slait	‵wiːk
‵freʃ	‵leit	‵slou	‵woːm

115 **Dissyllabic adjectives.** Many of these form their comparison by the non-inflexional method only, but those having certain terminations are usually inflected. Even here, however, some speakers may use the non-inflexional method in a few contexts. The inflected dissyllabic adjectives in most frequent use are shown below in their various groups.

a. Adjectives ending in -ə* or in one of the diphthongs having -ə* as their second element form their comparative and superlative by adding -rə* and -rist respectively. Example:

Positive	*Comparative*	*Superlative*
ˋbitə*	ˋbitərə*	ˋbitərist

Other adjectives following this pattern are:

osˋtiə*	diˋmjuə*	ˋklevə*	ˋtendə*
siˋviə*	məˋtjuə*	ˋslendə*	
sinˋsiə*	əbsˋkjuə*	ˋsoubə*	

b. Adjectives ending in unstressed -ou (which is often weakened to -u) form their comparative and superlative respectively by substituting -uə* and -uist for the final vowel. Example:

Positive	*Comparative*	*Superlative*
ˋhol(o)u	ˋholuə*	ˋholuist

Other adjectives following this pattern are:

ˋkal(o)u	ˋnar(o)u	ˋʃal(o)u
ˋmel(o)u	ˋsal(o)u	ˋjel(o)u

c. Adjectives ending in -| form their comparative and superlative respectively by substituting -lə* and -list for the |. Example:

Positive	*Comparative*	*Superlative*
ˋaid|	ˋaidlə*	ˋaidlist

Exceptions which retain the |:

ˋbrit|	ˋbrit|ə*	ˋbrit|ist
ˋkru:|	ˋkru:|ə*	ˋkru:|ist

Other adjectives following the pattern of ˋaid| are:

ˋeib|	ˋnimb|	ˋamp|	ˋdʒent|
ˋfi:b|	ˋnoub|	ˋsimp|	
ˋhʌmb|	ˋsteib|	ˋsʌt|	

d. Adjectives ending in -i form their comparative and superlative by adding -ə* and -ist respectively. Example:

Positive	Comparative	Superlative
`ˈaŋgri`	`ˈaŋgriə*`	`ˈaŋgriist`

Other adjectives following this pattern are:

ˈaisi	ˈhapi	ˈmeri	ˈspiːdi
ˈbizi	ˈhaːti	ˈmilki	ˈstedi
ˈblʌdi	ˈheəri	ˈmisti	ˈstiki
ˈbuʃi	ˈheisti	ˈmʌdi	ˈstoːmi
ˈdəːti	ˈhelθi	ˈnaːsti	ˈstouni
ˈdindʒi	ˈhevi	ˈniːdi	ˈsʌni
ˈdriːmi	ˈhili	ˈnoːti	ˈʃeidi
ˈdʌsti	ˈhouli	ˈnoizi	ˈʃoui
ˈdʒoli	ˈiŋki	ˈpriti	ˈtaidi
ˈdʒuːsi	ˈiːzi	ˈredi	ˈtaini
ˈempti	ˈkəːli	ˈreini	ˈtriki
ˈəːli	ˈklaudi	ˈriski	ˈtʃili
ˈfilθi	ˈklʌmzi	ˈroki	ˈθəːsti
ˈfiʃi	ˈkouzi	ˈsandi	ˈθoːni
ˈfogi	ˈlaikli	ˈsili	ˈʌgli
ˈfoːlti	ˈleizi	ˈsilki	ˈwelθi
ˈfrosti	ˈleŋθi	ˈsliːpi	ˈwəːði
ˈfʌni	ˈlounli	ˈsmouki	ˈwindi
ˈgriːdi	ˈlʌki	ˈsnoui	ˈwintri
ˈgriːsi	ˈlʌvli	ˈsori	ˈwudi
ˈhandi	ˈmanli	ˈsoupi	ˈwuli

e. A few adjectives ending in miscellaneous sounds form their comparative and superlative inflexionally:

ˈkwaiət	ˈpleznt	kənˈsais	ˈkomən
pəˈlait	ˈwikid	priˈsais	

MODIFICATION OF ADJECTIVES

116 Adverb position. Adjectives may be modified by the adverbs marked with the figure B2 in the catalogue of adverbs (§262). In this collocation the adverb is usually placed immediately before the adjective. Some of the adverbs frequently used as adjective modifiers are: veri, tuː, sou, əz, kwait, raːðə*, feəli, priti, ikstriːmli, moə*, moust, hau. Examples:

it s 'tuː ˌould.   it s 'sou ˌiːzi
it s 'haːdli ˌnesisri.   ai m 'kwait ˌwoːm.
dei ə 'feəli ˌsimpļ.   ˌðat s 'moust ˌintristiŋ.

The adverb iˋnʌf follows the adjective:

'iz it ˊlaːdʒ inʌf?   ðei 'aːnt ˌgud inʌf.

When the adverb-adjective collocation is associated with a noun taking an article there are four possible orders in which these four words can be placed.

a. With the adverb inʌf the order is: determiner, adjective, adverb, noun.

'iz it ə ˊlaːdʒ inʌf ˙haus?   it 'izņt a ˌgud inʌf igˌzaːmpļ.

b. With the adverbs tuː, sou, əz and hau the order is: adverb, adjective, determiner, noun.

it s 'tuː ˌsmoːl ə ˌhaus fə ˌmiː.   'dount ˙teik sou ˌbig ə ˌlʌmp.
'iz it əz 'gud ə ˙pen əz ˊjoəz?   'hau ˌould ə ˌman ˌiz i?

c. When the adverb modifies the verb rather than the adjective the order is: adverb, determiner, adjective, noun. Among adverbs with which this pattern is used are haːdli, skeəsli, kwait, raːðə, not ət oːl, səːtņli.

it s 'raːðər ə ˋnais ˌvjuː.   it s ˋhaːdli ə ˌdiːsņt ˌwei tə biˌheiv.
it s 'kwait ə 'loŋ ˌwei.   it s ˋskeəsli ðə ˌrait θiŋ tə ˌduː
it s 'səːtņli ə ˋgud ˌbuk.   it 'izņt ət ˙oːl ə ˌbad aiˌdiə.

d. When the adverb modifies the adjective the order is: determiner, adverb, adjective, noun, which may be regarded as the normal pattern. It is used with such adverbs as priti, feəli, veri, ikstriːmli, moust, θʌrəli.

hi z ə 'feəli ˙wel red ˌman.   it s ə 'priti ˙difikļt ˌsʌbdʒikt.
ðat s ə 'veri ˙gud aiˌdiə.   ʃi z ən iks'triːmli ˙klevə ˌgəːl.
ðei ər ə moust 'komik ˌpeə.   ðə z sm̩ 'θʌrəli diˈpresiŋ ˌnjuːz.

93

POSITION OF ADJECTIVES

117 Front position. Adjectives generally precede the word they qualify:

sm̩ 'laːdʒ ˌhauziz.	ən 'intristiŋ ˌbuk.
sm̩ 'broukən ˌbot|z.	ə 'gud˙lukiŋ ˌman.
ðə 'deili ˌpeipəz.	ən 'ʌndə˙dʌn ˌdʒoint.

Two or more adjectives may precede the noun. In this case the one that particularizes most is placed first, and the second, which often suggests a category, is usually unstressed.

ə 'tʃaːmiŋ lit| ˌhaus.	ə 'nais big ˌpiːs.
ə 'diər ould ˌleidi.	ə 'tʃiːki jʌŋ ˌboi.
ə 'greit big ˙hʌlkiŋ ˌfelu.	

118 Rear position—attributive. The adjective always follows the semi-pronouns of the sʌm-, eni-, nou-, evri- group.

'ðis iz ˙sʌmθiŋ ˌnjuː.	it s 'sʌmbodi imˈpoːtn̩t.
iz ðər 'eniθiŋ ʹroŋ?	ðə z 'evriθiŋ ˌnesisri.
ðə z 'nʌθiŋ ᵛdifrn̩t.	ðə z 'noubədi ᵛfeiməs.

In a certain number of collocations, mostly of an historcail, religious or official character, the adjective follows the noun that it qualifies:

'bodi ʹpolitik	'eidʒn̩t ʹdʒenr|.
'gʌm ʹarəbik	'kons| ʹdʒenr|.
'prins ʹriːdʒn̩t.	'envoi ikʹstroːdn̩ri.
'treʒə ʹtrouv	'ministə 'plenipuʹtenʃəri.
'biʃəp ʹdezignit.	'noutəri ʹpʌblik.

In a few special cases the adjective may follow the word qualified, but the style is rather literary:

'adʒiktivz ˌpropə.	'θiŋz dʒapəˌniːz.
'litritʃə ˙pjuər ən ˌsimpl.[1]	

In some cases the adjective (generally a pair of adjectives) is used semi-parenthetically, suggesting book-titles or items in a catalogue:

'edjuˌkeiʃn̩, intiˌlektʃuəl, ˌmorəl ən ˌfizik\|.
ˌmeθədz, 'einʃn̩t ən ˌmodən.

---

[1] "*Pure and simple*" usually follows its noun, but its antithesis, "*common or garden*," being essentially colloquial, always precedes its noun.

119 Rear position—predicative. Adjectives used as subject-complements follow the verb of incomplete predication:

it s ˈred.   hi z ˈoːlwiz getiŋ ˌaŋgri.

Adjectives used as object-complements follow the direct object:

it ˈmeiks mi ˌtaiəd.   ai ˈpeintid ðə ˈdoə ˌgriːn.
ˈget ði ˌʌðəz redi.

When accompanied by prepositional and certain other adjuncts, the adjective usually follows the word qualified:

ə ˈbuk ˈdifik|t tə ˌriːd.   ə ˈhaus ˈθriː ˈstoːriz ˌhai.
ə ˈpeidʒ ˈtoːn in ˈtuː ˌpleisiz. ə ˈrivə ˈwʌn ˈmail ˌwaid.
ə ˈbuk ˈjuːsf| fə ˌsəːtn̩ ˈpəːpəsiz.
ə ˈmeθəd əv ˌwəːkiŋ ˈhaili rekəˌmendid bai ˌsʌm piːp|.
ə ˌsiːn ˈtuː ˈwʌndəf| tə disˌkraib.
ˈoːl ˈsʌbdʒikts ˈwəːði əv əˌtenʃn̩.

FUNCTIONS OF ADJECTIVES

120 Noun qualifiers. Adjectives are used as noun-qualifiers:

ðə ˈlaːdʒ ˌboks.   ði ˈiŋgliʃ ˌlaŋgwidʒ.
ə ˈwait ˌhoːs.   ˈintristiŋ igˌzaːmp|z.
ˈgud igˌzaːmp|z.   ˈspoukn̩ ˌiŋgliʃ.
mai ˈnjuː ˌhat.   ə ˈwel-bilt ˌhaus.
ˈðouz ˈould ˈʃuːz.

Two or more adjectives may be used together:

ə ˈgreit ˈwait ˌboks.   ˈmodən ˈspoukn̩ ˌiŋgliʃ.
ən ˈould ˈwait ˌhaus.

121 Pronominals. The adjective is not used pronominally, but pronominal equivalents may be formed by adding the semi-pronoun wʌn:

did ju ˌsei ðə ˈred wʌn oː ðə ˌbluː wʌn?
ˇðat s ə ˈbroukn̩ wʌn.   ˈðat ˌould wʌn.
ə ˌmoust ˈintristiŋ wʌn.   ju v ˈbroːt ðə ˈroŋ ˈwʌn!

122 Complements. When used as subject-complements, adjectives are preceded by a verb of incomplete predication:

it s ˈred.	ðə ˈweðə z ˌkiːpiŋ ˌfain.
it s 'getiŋ ˌdaːk.	it ˌluks ˈintristiŋ.
ai m 'getiŋ ˌbetə.	it wəz 'moust ʌnˌdʒʌst.

When used as object-complements, they are preceded by the direct object of causative verbs:

ai l 'get it ˌredi.	ðei 'rould ðə ˈgraːs ˌsmuːð.
ai 'peintid ðə ˈdoə ˌgriːn.	'kaːnt ju ˈmeik it ˈlaːdʒə?
hi ˈkʌt mai ˈheə tuː ˌʃoːt.	'ðat s wot ˈmeiks it sou ˈintristiŋ.

123 Nouns. Adjectives are occasionally used as Plural Nouns, in which case they are generally preceded by the definite article:

ðə 'ritʃ ən ðə ˌpuə.	ðə 'liviŋ ən ðə ˌded.
ðə 'kild ən ˌwuːndid.	

D. Verbs

FORMAL CLASSIFICATION

124 The two kinds of verb. Briefly defined, a verb is a word that asserts something about a person, animal or thing. It refers to an action or state of its subject, and through its tenses, moods and voices indicates the time, manner and incidence of its occurrence or non-occurrence.

In many languages the tenses are distinguished by a system of inflexions known as the "conjugation" of the verb, but in English they are almost always formed by placing one, two or three auxiliary verbs before the principal verb. Since it is usual to apply the same term "conjugation" to the various arrangements of auxiliaries that form the English tenses, it may be permissible and helpful to refer to these auxiliaries as *conjugators*. Further, since the function of the verb that is being conjugated is to specify the action or state of the subject of the sentence, it can be suitably referred to as the *specific* verb.

The conjugators form a small, closed, frequently-used class, while the specific verbs belong to a large, open series which is added to from time to time as the need arises.

125 The two kinds of verb forms. Although tenses are formed by the use of auxiliaries rather than inflexions, the English verb does retain certain variations in form, and the appropriate form must be used in constructing each tense. These forms fall into two main classes, and an understanding of the difference in function of these two classes is of the greatest value to the student. These two classes are known as the *finites* and the *verbals*.

Finites are the forms whose primary functions are to indicate affirmation or negation and to give the most exact indication of tense. Some of them also indicate number and person. Each tense structure contains one, and only one, finite, and when more than one verb form is used the finite is always the first of the group. It is also the form most closely linked to the subject.

Verbals are the infinitive, and the present and past participles of any verb. Though they have a subsidiary role in indicating tense they cannot form tenses by themselves.

126 Table of verb forms. In the following table the verb forms are classified according to their functions. Only the affirmative forms of the conjugating finites are shown; otherwise the list of conjugators is complete. For the specific verbs the irregular verb tə teik and the regular verb tə fil are shown as examples of all the others.

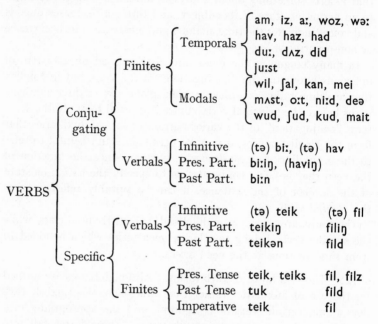

Some of these forms act in more than one capacity, thus:

Conjugating finite: hav haz had   duː dʌz did
Conjugating verbal: hav
Specific verbal: hav   had   duː
Specific finite: hav haz had   duː dʌz did

It will be seen that in the case of the specific verbs the root form does duty in three separate capacities, and that in the case of the regular verbs the past form has a dual capacity. The fact that in both these instances the same form functions either as a verbal or as a finite makes it more difficult for foreign students to grasp the English system of tense structure, but it can be mastered by studying the rules given in §153 and by remembering that in any cluster of verb forms the first is a finite and all the others are verbals, the last one being the specific verbal.

THE SPECIFIC VERBS

127 Simple and derivative verbs. It is difficult, if not impossible, to draw a rigid line of demarcation between these two kinds of specific verb. For example, verbs such as kʌm, teik, tel are obviously simple and indecomposable, while verbs such as ʌndres, blakən, riːrait, formed from existing words by means of affixes which are more or less living, are clearly derivatives. Between these two extremes, however, we find verbs such as biliːv, fəgiv, əksept, which are in practice indecomposable, while others, such as mislei, disubei, aidentifai, formed from recognizable roots (many of which are modified in form or meaning) and more or less obsolete affixes cannot be considered as simple verbs and yet do not belong to the class of derivatives that may be built up synthetically.

128 One-word verbs. The following categories, ranging almost imperceptibly from one extreme to the other, will give some idea of the various formal characteristics of verbs.

a. biː, hav, kʌm, gou, teik, put, siː, spiːk, nou, sei, tel.

b. bi'liːv, bi'grʌdʒ, bi'heiv, bi'loŋ.
     fə'giv, fə'get, fə'bid, fə'seik.
     'pʌniʃ, 'finiʃ, 'fəːniʃ, 'poliʃ, əs'toniʃ.
     ful'fil, ə'weikən, etc.

c. ək'sept, əd'vaiz, ə'tatʃ.
     kəm'peə*, kəm'pouz, kən'fəːm, kəŋ'kluːd.
     əb'dʒekt, ə'blaidʒ, əb'zəːv.
     im'pruːv, in'laːdʒ, in'list, in'tend, in'vait, iŋ'kʌridʒ, iŋ'kluːd.
     səb'skraib, sə'dʒest, sə'pouz, sə'pɔːt.
     ri'kʌvə, ri'siːv, ri'fɔːm, ri'piːt.
     di'kleə*, di'tatʃ, di'fend, di'siːv, di'skraib.
     ik'siːd, ik'spres, iks'tʃeindʒ, ig'zamin.
     'intə'rʌpt, 'intə'fiə*, 'intrə'djuːs.
     pri'siːd, pri'peə*, pri'zəːv, pri'zjuːm.
     poust'poun, trans'fɔːm, etc.

d. ˈsəːtiˌfai, ˈkwoliˌfai, aiˈdentiˌfai, ˈgloːriˌfai, ˈsatisˌfai.
ˈkʌltiˌveit, ˈheziˌteit, niˈsesiˌteit, ˈsepəˌreit.
ˈkritiˌsaiz, ˈsiviˌlaiz, məˈtiəriəˌlaiz, ˈriəˌlaiz.
ˈmisbiˈheiv, ˈmisʌndəˈstand, misˈteik, misˈlei.
ˈdisbiˈliːv, ˈdisəˈpruːv, ˈdiskənˈtinju, disˈkʌvə, disˈkʌridʒ.

e. ˈʌnˈduː, ˈʌnˈfaːsn̩, ˈʌnˈdres, ˈʌnˈluːs.[1]
ˈriːˈrait, ˈriːˈlait, ˈriːəˈreindʒ.
ˈfraitn̩, ˈwaitn̩, ˈbroːdn̩, ˈwaidn̩, ˈblakən.

Verbs used as nouns:

Certain verbs are indistinguishable in form from nouns. In some cases these appear to be words functioning usually as verbs but occasionally as nouns. Examples:

ə ˈkʌt = an incision made with a knife.
ə ˈtʃeindʒ = an alteration.
ə ˈpuʃ = an impulse made by pressing.
ə ˈdʒʌmp = a leap.
ən ˈaːnsə* = a reply.

Nouns used as verbs:

In other cases they are words functioning usually as nouns but occasionally as verbs. An almost unlimited number of common nouns may be used as verbs. Examples:

tə ˈtʃoːk = to write by means of chalk.
tə ˈpeipə* = to cover (a wall) by means of paper.
tu əˈdres = to write an address on an envelope.
tə ˈbotl̩ = to put into a bottle.
tə ˈbrʌʃ = to use a brush.

Historic compounds:

Verbs such as ˈʌndəˈstand, ˈʌndəˈteik, ˈʌndəˈgou, wiðˈdroː, wiθˈhould, ʌpˈhould, ʌpˈset, are sometimes said to be compound. This method of composition being now obsolete, all such verbs should be treated as if they were simple.

129 Group verbs. An almost unlimited number of "group-verbs" may be formed by collocations of the simpler (generally

---

[1] In this verb ʌn- is not a negative.

monosyllabic) verbs with the adverbial particles **in, aut, əwei, bak**, etc. (See Adverbial Particles, §279.)

In addition to these, it is often convenient to consider as group-verbs:

a. Combinations of **biː** and certain adjectives, in that such combinations are often semantically equivalent to simple (but often less-used) verbs:

bi ˈeib| = kan.   bi ˈglad ⎫
bi ˈsori = riˈgret   bi ˈpliːzd ⎬ = riˈdʒois.
                                    ⎭

b. Combinations of various verbs with various complements, in that such combinations are often semantically equivalent to simple (but often less-used) verbs:

ˈhav ə ˈrest   = ˈrest.   ˈmeik ˈprougres = pruˈgres.
ˈhav ˈbrekfəst. = ˈbrekfəst.   ˈmeik ˈheist   = ˈhʌri.
ˈhav ˈlʌntʃ   = ˈlʌntʃ   ˈpei əˈtenʃn̩   = əˈtend
ˈhav ə ˈdriŋk   = ˈdriŋk   ˈteik ˈkeə*   = ˈmaind.
ˈhav ə ˈgeim   = ˈplei.   ˈgou fər ə ˈwoːk = ˈwoːk

c. Combinations of verb + preposition, in that such combinations may be equivalent to simple (but often rarer or obsolete) verbs:

riˈplai tu = ˈaːnsə*   ˈluk at = riˈgaːd, kənˈsidə*
ˈweit foː = əˈweit   ˈluk foː = ˈsiːk

130 Verb inflexions. With the exception of the verb **tə biː** (dealt with in detail in §§154–5) English verbs have a maximum of five different forms, which are:

1. The root form, used in three different ways:

   a. for the Infinitive—a verbal,

   b. for all persons except the 3rd pers. sing. in the Affirmative of the Present Tense of Accomplishment—a finite,

   c. for the Affirmative of the Imperative of Accomplishment —a finite.

2. The past tense form, used for all persons in the Affirmative of the Past Tense of Accomplishment—a finite.

3. The past participle form—a verbal.

4. The s-form, used for the 3rd pers. sing. in the Affirmative of the Present Tense of Accomplishment—a finite.

5. The present participle or ing-form—a verbal.

The following table shows these five forms for some typical specific verbs. The first five are irregular verbs and the last three are regular ones.

1 Root (V or F)	2 Past Tense (Finite)	3 Past Part. (Verbal)	4 s-form (Finite)	5 ing-form (Verbal)
raiz	rouz	ˈrizn̩	ˈraiziz	ˈraiziŋ
teik	tuk	ˈteikən	teiks	ˈteikiŋ
bai	boːt	boːt	baiz	ˈbaiiŋ
kost	kost	kost	kosts	ˈkostiŋ
sel	sould	sould	selz	ˈseliŋ
kaunt	ˈkauntid	ˈkauntid	kaunts	ˈkauntiŋ
kros	krost	krost	ˈkrosiz	ˈkrosiŋ
əˈgriː	əˈgriːd	əˈgriːd	əˈgriːz	əˈgriːiŋ

131 The two regular inflexions. With the minor exceptions noted below, the ing-form and the s-form are regular in all verbs.

The ing-form.

In a few words ending in a consonant +|, the | is replaced by l in the ing-form, e.g., ˈpʌz|, ˈpʌzliŋ ; ˈkeib|, ˈkeibliŋ.

In verbs spelt with a final -r or -re, the r consonant is mute in the root form but is pronounced before the initial i of the ing-form. Such verbs as beə, ˈbeəriŋ ; hiə, ˈhiəriŋ ; ˈofə, ˈofəriŋ, may therefore be said to form this verbal by adding -riŋ to the root, while all other verbs form it regularly by adding -iŋ.

The s-form.

Apart from the verb tə biː shown in §126, only three verbs in the language show any real irregularity in forming this finite. They are: duː, hav and sei, which have the forms dʌz, haz and sez respectively. In all other verbs, whether regular or irregular in other respects, the s-form follows the rules given in §§140-5.

The above points having been placed on record, these two forms can be ignored when the irregular verbs are under consideration.

IRREGULAR VERBS

132 The two irregular inflexions. The irregular verbs constitute the most important survival from the older, inflected, stage in the development of English. Apart from the two small groups mentioned in §131, the irregularities are confined to the following two forms.

The past participle.

This verbal is formed irregularly in the case of some 150 verbs.

The past tense.

This finite is irregular in almost exactly the same number of verbs.

The phonetic irregularities occurring in these two forms can be arranged in a three-tier system. This method of classification is explained below, and lists are given of all the important verbs in each class.

133 Classification of irregularities. Irregular verbs fall into two main divisions:

I. Those whose past participle ends in a consonant other than **t** or **d**, and in most cases differs from the past tense.

II. Those whose past tense and past participle end in **t** or **d** and are always identical.

Division I

The verbs of Division I may be divided into two classes:

    A. Verbs in which the past participle is formed by adding a a nasal consonant (occasionally preceded by the vowel ə) to either the present or the past tense form or some other form, and

    B. Verbs to which no nasal consonant is added to form the past participle.

Each of these classes may be further subdivided according to the root vowel variations. The figures at the head of the following tables indicate the vowel systems and are to be interpreted as follows:

1—2—3 all three parts have different vowels.

1—2—1 the infinitive and past participle have one vowel, and the past tense another.

1—1—2 the infinitive and past tense have one vowel, and the past participle another.

1—2—2 the infinitive has one vowel, and the past tense and past participle another.

1—1—1 all three parts have the same vowel.

134 Division I, Class A. A nasal consonant is added to form the past participle.

1	2	3
duː	did ·	dʌn
gou	went	gon
flai	fluː	floun
rait	rout	ˈritn̩
raid	roud	ˈridn̩
draiv	drouv	ˈdrivn̩
raiz	rouz	ˈrizn̩

1	2	1
iːt	et *or* eit	ˈiːtn̩
fəˈbid	fəˈbad, fəˈbeid	fəˈbidn̩
giv	geiv	ˈgivn̩
fəˈgiv	fəˈgeiv	fəˈgivn̩
foːl	fel	ˈfoːlən
teik	tuk	ˈteikən
ʃeik	ʃuk	ˈʃeikən
siː	soː	siːn
droː	druː	droːn
blou	bluː	bloun
grou	gruː	groun
nou	njuː	noun
θrou	θruː	θroun

1	1	2
swel	sweld	swoulən[1]

[1] Occasionally sweld.

1	2	2
bait	bit	ˋbitn̩
haid	hid	ˋhidn̩
fəˋget	fəˋgot	fəˋgotn̩
spiːk	spouk	ˋspoukən
stiːl	stoul	ˋstoulən
wiːv	wouv	ˋwouvn̩
friːz	frouz	ˋfrouzn̩]
tʃuːz	tʃouz	ˋtʃouzn̩
weik	wouk	ˋwoukən
breik	brouk	ˋbroukən
beə*	boə*	boːn
teə*	toə*	toːn
weə*	woə*	woːn
sweə*	swoə*	swoːn
lai	lei	lein[1]

1	1	1
biːt	biːt	ˋbiːtn̩
soː	soːd	soːn
sou	soud	soun[2]
ʃou	ʃoud	ʃoun

135   Division I, Class B. No nasal consonant is added to form the past participle.

1	2	3
swim	swam	swʌm
biˋgin	biˋgan	biˋgʌn
riŋ	raŋ	rʌŋ
siŋ	saŋ	sʌŋ
spriŋ	spraŋ	sprʌŋ
siŋk	saŋk	sʌŋk
ʃriŋk	ʃraŋk	ʃrʌŋk
driŋk	draŋk	drʌŋk

[1] This word, given for the sake of reference, is rarely used in spoken English. It can usually be replaced by biːn or biːn ˋlaiiŋ.

[2] Meaning both the verb *sow* (to plant seed), and the verb spelt *sew* (to work with a needle).

1	2	1
kʌm	keim	kʌm
rʌn	ran	rʌn
biˋkʌm	biˋkeim	biˋkʌm

1	2	2
ʃain	ʃon	ʃon
haŋ	hʌŋ	hʌŋ
spin	spʌn	spʌn
win	wʌn	wʌn
stiŋ	stʌŋ	stʌŋ
swiŋ	swʌŋ	swʌŋ
dig	dʌg	dʌg
stik	stʌk	stʌk
straik	strʌk	strʌk

Division II

The verbs of Division II may be divided into three classes:

A. Verbs in which **t** or **d** is substituted for some other consonant,

B. Verbs in which **t** or **d**, already present in the root form, is retained in the past, and

C. Verbs in which **t** or **d** is added to the root to form the past.

Here also the classes are subdivided according to the root vowel variations, but since the two past forms are identical only the last two vowel systems can occur.

136   Division II, Class A.   Substitution of **t** or **d** to make the common past form.

1	2	2
katʃ	koːt	koːt
tiːtʃ	toːt	toːt
briŋ	broːt	broːt
θiŋk	θoːt	θoːt
bai	boːt	boːt
fait[1]	foːt	foːt

[1] This Class B verb is inserted here for orthographic reasons.

1	1	1
bild	bilt	bilt
bend	bent	bent
lend	lent	lent
send	sent	sent
spend	spent	spent
hav	had	had
meik	meid	meid

137   Division II, Class B.   Retention of an existing t or d in making the common past form.

1	2	2
miːt	met	met
sit	sat	sat
spit	spat	spat
get	got	got
ʃuːt	ʃot	ʃot
lait	lit	lit
fiːd	fed	fed
liːd	led	led
riːd	red	red
bliːd	bled	bled
spiːd	sped	sped
hould	held	held
slaid	slid	slid
stand	stud	stud
'ʌndəˈstand	'ʌndəˈstud	'ʌndəˈstud
baind	baund	baund
faind	faund	faund
graind	graund	graund
waind	waund	waund

1	1	1
hit	hit	hit
split	split	split
let	let	let
set	set	set
ʌpˈset	ʌpˈset	ʌpˈset
put	put	put

1	1	1
kʌt	kʌt	kʌt
ʃʌt	ʃʌt	ʃʌt
həːt	həːt	həːt
kaːst	kaːst	kaːst
kost	kost	kost
bəːst	bəːst	bəːst
rid	rid	rid
spred	spred	spred

138 Division II, Class C. Addition of **t** or **d** to make the common past form.

1	2	2
kriːp	krept	krept
kiːp	kept	kept
sliːp	slept	slept
swiːp	swept	swept
driːm	dremt	dremt (r)
liːn	lent	lent (r)
miːn	ment	ment
diːl	delt	delt
fiːl	felt	felt
niːl	nelt	nelt
liːv	left	left
luːz	lost	lost
sel	sould	sould
tel	tould	tould
hiə*	həːd	həːd
sei	sed	sed
ʃuː	ʃod	ʃod

1	1	1
spil	spilt	spilt (r)
smel	smelt	smelt (r)
spel	spelt	spelt (r)
spoil	spoilt	spoilt (r)
bəːn	bəːnt	bəːnt (r)
ləːn	ləːnt	ləːnt (r)

Verbs marked (r) may also be conjugated regularly.

REGULAR VERBS

139 Six classes. In regular verbs the past tense form (finite) and the past participle form (verbal) are identical. In the written language this common past form is made by adding -*d* or -*ed* to the root, while the s-form is made by adding -*s* or -*es*, also to the root.

In the spoken language, however, each of these terminations is pronounced in three different ways in order that it may harmonize with the final sound of the root form of each verb. This gives rise to six classes of regular verbs.

As it is obviously impossible to list and classify all the specific verbs in the English language, a representative selection has been made, based on a 2,000-word frequency list.

In the following tables about 300 of the most frequently used regular verbs are shown in their respective classes. The exact pronunciation of the two terminations is explained and examples are given at the head of each list. All the verbs in each list are inflected in exactly the same way as the specimen verbs, and all regular verbs with the same root ending take the same terminations.

140 Class Ia. Addition of -*id* to make the common past form.
      „   „ -*s* „   „   „ s-form.

In these verbs the root always ends in -t.

Example:	*Root form*	*Past form*	*S-form*	
	ək'sept	ək'septid	ək'septs	
ə'kaunt	'kaunt	'opəreit	ri'leit	səs'pekt
'akt	di'fiːt	'peint	ri'piːt	'test
əd'mit	di'rekt	'paːt	ri'poːt	'triːt
ə'dopt	'daut	pə'mit	'repri'zent	'vizit
ə'maunt	i'lekt	'point	'rest	'vout
ə'point	ig'zist	'poust	ri'zʌlt	'weit
ə'tempt	ik'spekt	pri'zent	'sepəreit	'wont
ə'trakt	'fit	pri'vent	'ʃaut	
kə'lekt	'lift	'print	'steit	
kəm'pliːt	'limit	prə'tekt	sə'dʒest	
kə'nekt	'nout	ri'flekt	sə'poːt	

141 Class 1b. Addition of -id to make the common past form.
　　　　　　　　,,　　,,　-z　,,　　,,　　,,　s-form.

In these verbs the root always ends in -d.

Example:	*Root form*	*Past form*		*S-form*
	ˈad	ˈadid		ˈadz
əˈfoːd	diˈfend	iksˈtend	prəˈvaid	səˈraund
əˈtend	diˈmaːnd	iŋˈkluːd	riˈkoːd	ˈtend
əˈvoid	diˈpend	inˈtend	riˈgaːd	ˈwuːnd
kəˈmaːnd	diˈsend	ˈland	riˈmaind	ˈjiːld
ˈkraud	diˈvaid	ˈmend	ˈsaund	
diˈsaid	ˈhand	ˈniːd	səkˈsiːd	

142 Class 2a. Addition of -t to make the common past form.
　　　　　　　　,,　　,,　-iz　,,　　,,　　,,　s-form.

In these verbs the root ends in -s or -ʃ.

Examples:	*Root form*	*Past form*		*S-form*
	əˈdres	əˈdrest		əˈdresiz
	ˈfiniʃ	ˈfiniʃt		ˈfiniʃiz
ədˈvaːns	disˈtiŋgwiʃ	ˈintrəˈdjuːs	ˈpraktis	ˈrʌʃ
əsˈtoniʃ	ˈdres	ˈmis	ˈpres	ˈstretʃ
ˈbeis	iksˈpres	ˈnoutis	prəˈdjuːs	ˈtʌtʃ
ˈbles	ˈfiks	ˈpaːs	ˈpromis	ˈwoʃ
kənˈfes	ˈfoːs	ˈpleis	ˈpuʃ	ˈwotʃ
ˈkros	ˈfəːniʃ	ˈpoliʃ	ˈriːtʃ	ˈwiʃ
disˈkʌs	iŋˈkriːs	pəˈzes	riˈdjuːs	

143 Class 2b. Addition of -t to make the common past form.
　　　　　　　　,,　　,,　-s　,,　　,,　　,,　s-form.

In these verbs the root ends in -p, -k, -f or -θ.

Examples:	*Root form*	*Past form*	*S-form*
	ˈdrop	ˈdropt	ˈdrops
	ˈaːsk	ˈaːskt	ˈaːsks
	ˈlaːf	ˈlaːft	ˈlaːfs
	ˈbaːθ	ˈbaːθt	ˈbaːθs

ˈeik ˈhelp ˈmaːk ˈslip ˈwəːk
əˈtak ˈhoup ˈpak ˈstop ˈkof
diˈveləp ˈdʒʌmp ˈpik ˈtoːk
isˈkeip ˈluk riˈmaːk ˈwoːk

144 Class 3a. Addition of -d to make the common past form.
„ „ -iz „ „ „ s-form.
In these verbs the root ends in -z or -ʒ.

Examples: Root form   Past form   S-form
          əˈkjuːz   əˈkjuːzd   əˈkjuːziz
          əˈreindʒ   əˈreindʒd   əˈreindʒiz

ˈadvəˌtaiz ˈtʃaːdʒ ˈeksəˌsaiz prəˈpouz səˈpouz
ədˈvaiz ˈsiviˌlaiz ˈdʒʌdʒ ˈreiz səˈpraiz
əˈmjuːz ˈklouz ˈmanidʒ ˈrekəgˌnaiz ˈəːdʒ
ˈkoːz kəmˈpouz əˈpouz riˈfjuːz ˈjuːz
ˈtʃeindʒ iŋˈkʌridʒ ˈpliːz ˈsiːz

145 Class 3b. Addition of -d to make the common past form.
„ „ -z „ „ „ s-form.
This is by far the largest class, containing nearly half the examples in these lists. The root ends in b, g, m, n, ŋ, l, v, ð, or any vowel.

Examples:

Root form	Past form	S-form	Root form	Past form	S-form
ˈrʌb	ˈrʌbd	ˈrʌbz	ˈberi	ˈberid	ˈberiz
ˈbeg	ˈbegd	ˈbegz	ˈaːgju	ˈaːgjud	ˈaːgjuz
ˈeim	ˈeimd	ˈeimz	ˈaːnsə*	ˈaːnsəd	ˈaːnsəz
ˈkliːn	ˈkliːnd	ˈkliːnz	ˈpei	ˈpeid	ˈpeiz
biˈloŋ	biˈloŋd	biˈloŋz	ˈflou	ˈfloud	ˈflouz
ˈboil	ˈboild	ˈboilz	əˈplai	əˈplaid	əˈplaiz
əˈpruːv	əˈpruːvd	əˈpruːvz	əˈlau	əˈlaud	əˈlauz
ˈbriːð	ˈbriːðd	ˈbriːðz	əˈnoi	əˈnoid	əˈnoiz

əˈkʌstəm	kənˈsidə*	ˈfoːm	ˈoːdə*	ˈsiːm
ədˈmaiə*	kənˈtein	ˈgein	ˈou	ˈsəːv
əˈgriː	kənˈtinju	ˈgaðə*	ˈoun	ˈsetl

111

ə'plai	kən'troul	'gʌvən	pə'fo:m	'ʃeə*
'a:m	'kʌvə*	'hand|	'plan	'sain
ə'raiv	'krai	'hapən	'plei	'smail
bi'heiv	di'kleə*	i'madʒin	'poə*	'stei
bi'li:v	di'livə*	im'pru:v	pri'fə*	'strʌg|
'bleim	dis'kraib	in'fo:m	pri'peə*	'stʌdi
'boru	di'zə:v	'dʒoin	pri'zə:v	'sʌfə*
'ko:l	dis'troi	'kil	'pru:v	sə'plai
'keə*	di'tə:min	'lei	'pul	'θretn
'kari	'dai	'lisn	ri'si:v	'tai
'tʃiə*	dis'kʌvə*	'liv	ri'fə:*	'taiə*
'kleim	'ə:n	'lʌv	ri'mein	'trein
'kliə*	im'ploi	'manju'faktʃə*	ri'membə*	'travl
'klaim	in'dʒoi	'mari	ri'plai	'trai
'klouð	'entə*	'mezə*	ri'taiə*	'tə:n
'kʌlə*	iks'plein	'mu:v	ri'tə:n	'wei
kəm'bain	'feil	'neim	'roul	'welkəm
kəm'peə*	'fiə*	əb'zə:v	'seiv	'wondə*
kəm'plein	'fil	'ofə*	'seil	'wʌndə*
kən'sə:n	'folu	'oupən	'skatə*	'wo:n

THE CONJUGATORS

146 Conjugating finites. There are 24 conjugating finites, of which 12 may be said to be tense-formers (or temporals) and 12 mood-formers (or modals). The temporals simply indicate the precise tense of the specific verb before which they are used, while the modals indicate the mood or manner of the action.

Each of the 24 conjugating finites has two forms, an affirmative one and a negative one, the latter being characterized by the termination ṇt (used when this termination is preceded by a consonant) or nt (used after vowels). The substitution of the negative form for the affirmative one is the commonest way of introducing the idea of negation into a sentence, and by their position the forms indicate interrogation—being placed before the subject in questions and after it in statements. They are thus the agents by which the four forms of the sentence are indicated: Affirmative, Negative, Interrogative and Interrogative-Negative.

The following is a table of the 24 conjugating finites, showing both affirmative and negative forms.

Temporals		Modals	
Affirmative	*Negative*	*Affirmative*	*Negative*
am	aːnt	wil	wount
iz	izn̩t	ʃal	ʃaːnt
aː*	aːnt	kan	kaːnt
woz	wozn̩t	mei	meint
wəː*	wəːnt	mʌst	mʌsn̩t
hav	havn̩t	oːt (tə)	oːtn̩t (tə)
haz	hazn̩t	niːd	niːdn̩t
had	hadn̩t	deə*	deənt
duː	dount	wud	wudn̩t
dʌz	dʌzn̩t	ʃud	ʃudn̩t
did	didn̩t	kud	kudn̩t
juːst (tə)	juːsn̩t (tə)	mait	maitn̩t

The pronunciations shown above are the strong ones, as used when the words are pronounced stressed or in isolation. In ordinary contexts most of the affirmative finites have weak forms. These are shown in detail in §16.

The infinitive that follows juːst, juːsn̩t, oːt or oːtn̩t is always preceded by tə (or tu if its first sound is a vowel). It is also usual to add tu when these finites are not followed by a specific verbal.

147 Conjugating verbals. There are four conjugating verbals that help the conjugating finites to form the more compound tenses of specific verbs. They always occupy a medial position in the verb cluster, since they follow the conjugating finite and precede the specific verbal. There is, in addition, one conjugating verbal (havin̩) that does not enter into the formation of tenses, occurring only in participial phrases.

The five conjugating verbals are:

Infinitive	*Present Participle*	*Past Participle*
(tə) biː	biːin̩	biːn
(tə) hav	(havin̩)	——

Below are shown examples of the use of the conjugating verbals in each of the tenses in which they occur. It will be seen that in some tenses two conjugating verbals are used. The numbers refer to the tense numbers given in §209.

Active Voice

	Tense No.	Example
biː	A 9	ai 'ʃaːnt bi ˯steiiŋ.
biːn	{ A 10	'havn̩t ju bin 'lisniŋ tə mi?
	A 11	ʃi d bin ˎrestiŋ bi˳foː ˏlʌntʃ.
hav	A 6	wi ʃļ əv ˎfiniʃt bai tə˳nait.
hav biːn	A 12	ai 'mʌst əv bin ˎdriːmiŋ.

Passive Voice

biː	P 3	wi 'ʃaːnt bi in·vaitid tə ðə ˯paːti.
biːiŋ	{ P 7	wi ə 'biːiŋ ˎwotʃt.
	P 8	ðə 'letə wəz biːiŋ traːnsˎleitid.
biːn	{ P 4	ðə 'ruːm ·hazn̩t bin ˎkliːnd tə˳dei.
	P 5	'hadn̩t ju bin 'woːnd əbaut it?
hav biːn	P 6	ðə 'haus ·mei əv bin ˎlet oːl˳redi.

Active Participial Phrase:

haviŋ	haviŋ 'finiʃt iz ˏwəːk, hi 'went ˎhoum.

Passive Participial Phrases:

biːiŋ	biːiŋ 'teikən bai sə˳praiz, ðei riˎtriːtid.
haviŋ biːn	haviŋ bin 'tould tə ˏweit, ai ˎweitid.

For the reasons set forth in §173 the tense classification adopted in the present work recognizes twelve tenses in the active voice and eight in the passive, or alternatively, twelve in the aspect of accomplishment and eight in the aspect of activity (see §207). The names and numbers that will be used to distinguish these tenses are given in §209. The manner in which they are constructed by varying the form and arrangement of the conjugators and the variations that are used to differentiate the affirmative, interrogative, negative and interrogative-negative forms of the sentence are tabulated in §§148–151, while the emphatic affirmative is shown in §152. For the sake of clarity the tenses are exemplified only in the 3rd person plural, but all the changes made inside each tense for the other persons are shown below each table.

148 Affirmative conjugation.

Active Voice

Accomplishment			Activity	
A		*Direct*		**A**
1	ðei ˋteik	Present	ðei ə ˋteikiŋ	7
2	ðei ˋtuk	Past	ðei wə ˋteikiŋ	8
3	ðei l ˋteik	Modal	ðei l bi ˋteikiŋ	9

A		*Perfect*		**A**
4	ðei v ˋteikən	Present	ðei v bin ˋteikiŋ	10
5	ðei d ˋteikən	Past	ðei d bin ˋteikiŋ	11
6	ðei l əv ˋteikən	Modal	ðei l əv bin ˋteikiŋ	12

Irregularities:

A 1   hiː (ʃiː, it) ˋteiks.
A 4   hiː (ʃiː) z ˋteikən; it s ˋteikən.
A 7   ai m ˋteikiŋ; hiː (ʃiː) z ˋteikiŋ; it s ˋteikiŋ.
A 8   ai (hiː ʃiː, it) wəz ˋteikiŋ.
A 10   hiː; (ʃiː) z bin ˋteikiŋ; it s bin ˋteikiŋ.

Passive Voice

Accomplishment			Activity	
P		*Direct*		**P**
1	ðei ə ˋteikən	Present	ðei ə biːiŋ ˋteikən	7
2	ðei wə ˋteikən	Past	ðei wə biːiŋ ˋteikən	8
3	ðei l bi ˋteikən	Modal	Not used	9

P		*Perfect*		**P**
4	ðei v bin ˋteikən	Present	Not used	10
5	ðei d bin ˋteikən	Past	Not used	11
6	ðei l əv bin ˋteikən	Modal	Not used	12

Irregularities:

P 1   ai m ˋteikən; hiː (ʃiː) z ˋteikən; it s ˋteikən.
P 2   ai (hiː, ʃiː, it) wəz ˋteikən.
P 4   hiː (ʃiː) z bin ˋteikən; it s bin ˋteikən.
P 7   ai m biːiŋ ˋteikən; hiː (ʃiː) z biːiŋ ˋteikən; it s biːiŋ ˋteikən.
P 8   ai (hiː, ʃiː, it) wəz biːiŋ ˋteikən.

149 Interrogative conjugation.

Active Voice

Accomplishment		Activity	
A	Direct		A
1 də ðei 'teik?	Present	ə ðei 'teikiŋ?	7
2 did ðei 'teik?	Past	wə ðei 'teikiŋ?	8
3 wil ðei 'teik?	Modal	wil ðei bi 'teikiŋ?	9

A	Perfect		A
4 həv ðei 'teikən?	Present	həv ðei bin 'teikiŋ?	10
5 həd ðei 'teikən?	Past	həd ðei bin 'teikiŋ?	11
6 wil ðei əv 'teikən?	Modal	wil ðei əv bin 'teikiŋ?	12

Irregularities:

A 1   dəz hiː (ʃiː, it) 'teik?
A 4   həz hiː (ʃiː, it) 'teikən?
A 7   əm ai 'teikiŋ?   iz hiː (ʃiː, it) 'teikiŋ?
A 8   wəz ai (hiː, ʃiː, it) 'teikiŋ?
A 10 həz hiː (ʃiː, it) bin 'teikiŋ?

Passive Voice

Accomplishment		Activity	
P	Direct		P
1 ə ðei 'teikən?	Present	ə ðei biːiŋ 'teikən?	7
2 wə ðei 'teikən?	Past	wə ðei biːiŋ 'teikən?	8
3 wil ðei bi 'teikən?	Modal	Not used	9

P	Perfect		P
4 həv ðei bin 'teikən?	Present	Not used	10
5 həd ðei bin 'teikən?	Past	Not used	11
6 wil ðei əv bin 'teikən?	Modal	Not used	12

Irregularities:

P 1   əm ai 'teikən?   iz hiː (ʃiː, it) 'teikən?
P 2   wəz ai (hiː, ʃiː, it) 'teikən?
P 4   həz hiː (ʃiː, it) bin 'teikən?
P 7   əm ai biːiŋ 'teikən?   iz hiː (ʃiː, it) biːiŋ 'teikən?
P 8   wəz ai (hiː, ʃiː, it) biːiŋ 'teikən?

150 Negative conjugation.

Active Voice

Accomplishment			Activity	
A		*Direct* ·		A
1	ðei 'dount ˇteik	Present	ðei 'aːnt ˇteikiŋ	7
2	ðei 'didn̩t ˇteik	Past	ðei 'wəːnt ˇteikiŋ	8
3	ðei 'wount ˇteik	Modal	ðei 'wount bi ˇteikiŋ	9

A		*Perfect*		A
4	ðei 'havn̩t ˇteikən	Present	ðei 'havn̩t bin ˇteikiŋ	10
5	ðei 'hadn̩t ˇteikən	Past	ðei 'hadn̩t bin ˇteikiŋ	11
6	ðei 'wount əv ˇteikən	Modal	ðei 'wount əv bin ˇteikiŋ	12

Irregularities:

A 1 hiː (ʃiː, it) 'dʌzn̩t ˇteik.
A 4 hiː (ʃiː, it) 'hazn̩t ˇteikən.
A 7 ai m 'not ˇteikiŋ; hiː (ʃiː, it) 'izn̩t ˇteikiŋ.
A 8 ai (hiː, ʃiː, it) 'wozn̩t ˇteikiŋ.
A 10 hiː (ʃiː, it) 'hazn̩t bin ˇteikiŋ.

Passive Voice

Accomplishment			Activity	
P		*Direct*		P
1	ðei 'aːnt ˇteikən	Present	ðei 'aːnt biːiŋ ˇteikən	7
2	ðei 'wəːnt ˇteikən	Past	ðei 'wəːnt biːiŋ ˇteikən	8
3	ðei 'wount bi ˇteikən	Modal	Not used	9

P		*Perfect*		P
4	ðei 'havn̩t bin ˇteikən	Present	Not used	10
5	ðei 'hadn̩t bin ˇteikən	Past	Not used	11
6	ðei 'wount əv bin ˇteikən	Modal	Not used	12

Irregularities:

P 1 ai m 'not ˇteikən; hiː (ʃiː, it) 'izn̩t ˇteikən.
P 2 ai (hiː, ʃiː, it) 'wozn̩t ˇteikən.
P 4 hiː (ʃiː, it) 'hazn̩t bin ˇteikən.
P 7 ai m 'not biːiŋ ˇteikən; hiː (ʃiː, it) 'izn̩t biːiŋ ˇteikən.
P 8 ai (hiː, ʃiː, it) 'wozn̩t biːiŋ ˇteikən.

151   Interrogative-negative conjugation.

Active Voice

	Accomplishment			Activity	
A		Direct			A
1	'dount ðei 'teik?	Present	'aːnt ðei 'teikiŋ?		7
2	'didn̩t ðei 'teik?	Past	'wəːnt ðei 'teikiŋ?		8
3	'wount ðei 'teik?	Modal	'wount ðei bi 'teikiŋ?		9

		Perfect			
A					A
4	'havn̩t ðei 'teikən?	Present	'havn̩t ðei bin 'teikiŋ?		10
5	'hadn̩t ðei 'teikən?	Past	'hadn̩t ðei bin 'teikiŋ?		11
6	'wount ðei əv 'teikən?	Modal	'wount ðei əv bin 'teikiŋ?		12

Irregularities:

A 1   'dʌzn̩t hiː (ʃiː, it) 'teik?
A 4   'hazn̩t hiː (ʃiː, it) 'teikən?
A 7   'izn̩t hiː (ʃiː, it) 'teikiŋ?
A 8   'wozn̩t ai (hiː, ʃiː, it) 'teikiŋ?
A 10   'hazn̩t hiː (ʃiː, it) bin 'teikiŋ?

Passive Voice

	Accomplishment			Activity	
P		Direct			P
1	'aːnt ðei 'teikən?	Present	'aːnt ðei biːiŋ 'teikən?		7
2	'wəːnt ðei 'teikən?	Past	'wəːnt ðei biːiŋ 'teikən?		8
3	'wount ðei bi 'teikən?	Modal	Not used		9

		Perfect			
P					P
4	'havn̩t ðei bin 'teikən?	Present	Not used		10
5	'hadn̩t ðei bin 'teikən?	Past	Not used		11
6	'wount ðei əv bin 'teikən?	Modal	Not used		12

Irregularities:

P 1   'izn̩t hiː (ʃiː, it) 'teikən?
P 2   'wozn̩t ai (hiː, ʃiː, it) 'teikən?
P 4   'hazn̩t hiː (ʃiː, it) bin 'teikən?
P 7   'izn̩t hiː (ʃiː, it) biːiŋ 'teikən?
P 8   'wozn̩t ai (hiː, ʃiː, it) biːiŋ 'teikən?

152 Emphatic affirmative conjugation.

Active Voice

Accomplishment		Direct	Activity	
A				A
1	ðei ˈduː ˌteik	Present	ðei ˈaː ˌteikiŋ	7
2	ðei ˈdid ˌteik	Past	ðei ˈwəː ˌteikiŋ	8
3	ðei ˈwil ˌteik	Modal	ðei ˈwil bi ˌteikiŋ	9

Accomplishment		Perfect	Activity	
A				A
4	ðei ˈhav ˌteikən	Present	ðei ˈhav bin ˌteikiŋ	10
5	ðei ˈhad ˌteikən	Past	ðei ˈhad bin ˌteikiŋ	11
6	ðei ˈwil əv ˌteikən	Modal	ðei ˈwil əv bin ˌteikiŋ	12

Irregularities:

A 1 hiː (ʃiː, it) ˈdʌz ˌteik.
A 4 hiː (ʃiː, it) ˈhaz ˌteikən.
A 7 ai ˈam ˌteikiŋ; hiː (ʃiː, it) ˈiz ˌteikiŋ.
A 8 ai (hiː, ʃiː, it) ˈwoz ˌteikiŋ.
A 10 hiː (ʃiː, it) ˈhaz bin ˌteikiŋ.

Passive Voice

Accomplishment		Direct	Activity	
P				P
1	ðei ˈaː ˌteikən	Present	ðei ˈaː biːiŋ ˌteikən	7
2	ðei ˈwəː ˌteikən	Past	ðei ˈwəː biːiŋ ˌteikən	8
3	ðei ˈwil bi ˌteikən	Modal	Not used	9

Accomplishment		Perfect	Activity	
P				P
4	ðei ˈhav bin ˌteikən	Present	Not used	10
5	ðei ˈhad bin ˌteikən	Past	Not used	11
6	ðei ˈwil əv bin ˌteikən	Modal	Not used	12

Irregularities:

P 1 ai ˈam ˌteikən; hiː (ʃiː, it) ˈiz ˌteikən.
P 2 ai (hiː, ʃiː, it) ˈwoz ˌteikən.
P 4 hiː (ʃiː, it) ˈhaz bin ˌteikən.
P 7 ai ˈam biːiŋ ˌteikən; hiː (ʃiː, it) ˈiz biːiŋ ˌteikən.
P 8 ai (hiː, ʃiː, it) ˈwoz biːiŋ ˌteikən.

153 Rules of tense structure. As is shown in §158, certain verb forms act sometimes as finites and sometimes as verbals. This tends to disguise the regularity of the English system of tense structure, but it is possible to draw up a guide which will facilitate identification of the various elements used in constructing tenses.

1. If a tense in a full sentence consists of only one verb form this must be a specific finite or a finite of the verb **tə biː** used as a verb of incomplete predication (§155).

2. If a tense consists of more than one verb form the first of these is always a conjugating finite. This is placed before the subject in questions and after it in statements.

3. The commonest way of adding the idea of negation to a sentence, whether question or statement, is to use the negative finite instead of the affirmative one, but if negation is added in any other way (by means of a negative subject, object or adverb) the affirmative finite must be used.   (See §§351–7.)

4. Any verb forms occupying a medial position are conjugating verbals.   There are never more than two of these.

5. The last verb form is always a specific verbal.

6. Verb forms that follow a part of the conjugating verb **tə biː** are governed by the following rules:

a. In the Active Voice the parts of the verb **tə biː** are used as conjugators only in the Aspect of Activity, and are always followed by the present participle.

b. In the Passive Voice, Aspect of Accomplishment, conjugators belonging to the verb **tə biː** are always followed by a past participle.

c. In the Passive Voice, Aspect of Activity, two conjugators belonging to the verb **tə biː** are used. The second of these is always the verbal **biːiŋ**, which is preceded by a finite of the verb **tə biː** and followed by a past participle.

7. Any verb that follows a part of the conjugating verb **tə hav** (in any voice or aspect) must be a past participle.

8. Any verb form that follows any other conjugator (that is, a part of the verb tə duː, the finite juːst, or any modal) must be an infinitive.

GRAMMAR OF THE TEMPORALS

154 Verbs that supply the temporals. The temporals are finites of the three verbs tə biː, tə hav and tə duː, to which may be added the finite juːst (tə). They indicate tenses, and most of them undergo changes of form inside the tense in order to make them agree with the number and person of the subject. These changes, which are a legacy from an earlier stage of the language, are always made by careful speakers, though they make no useful contribution to clarity of expression, as is clear from the fact that the temporals **had, did** and **juːst** and all the modals have an invariable form and function quite efficiently.

The twelve temporal finites are listed below, with the number and person with which they are used, and the tenses in which they occur.

Finite	*Person and Number*	*Tenses*
am	1st pers. sing.	A7, P1, P7
iz	3rd pers. sing.	A7, P1, P7
aː*	all persons plural	A7, P1, P7
woz	all persons singular	A8, P2, P8
wəː*	all persons plural	A8, P2, P8
hav	1st pers. sing. and all persons plural	A4, A10, P4
haz	3rd pers. sing.	A4, A10, P4
had	all persons	A5, A11, P5
duː	1st pers. sing. and all persons plural	A1
dʌz	3rd pers. sing.	A1
did	all persons	A2
juːst	all persons	Special past

This last finite is invariable for number and person. It forms a special past tense denoting habit, or permanence of a condition, often suggesting a contrast with the present.

The verbs from which the foregoing conjugating finites are taken have other, non-conjugating, functions. In order to facilitate comparison of the grammatical structures used in the two cases the non-conjugating uses of these verbs will be described in the following paragraphs.

155　Other uses of the verb tə biː.　In addition to its conjugating function, this verb is used in the following ways.

1. As a verb of incomplete predication, requiring a complement to complete the meaning of the sentence. The complement may be a noun (nominal predicate), adjective (adjectival predicate), adverb (adverbial predicate) or prepositional phrase. Examples:

ˈðat ˈman z ðə ˋprezidn̩t.	—— Noun.
joː ˈhat s ˌdəːti.	—— Adjective.
ʃi ˈwoznt ˋðeə.	—— Adverb.
wi ər in ðə ˋgaːdn̩.	—— Phrase.

2. To indicate obligation, an arrangement, an intention or some similar meaning, in which case it is followed by **tu** and an infinitive. Put into the negative this structure expresses prohibition; in this case the regular negative finites are almost always replaced by the affirmative finites followed by **not** (§159). Examples:

ˈam ai tə ˊweit fə ju?	—— Obligation.
ju ə ˈnot tə ˈgou eni ˋfəːðə.	—— Prohibition.
ˈweə z ðə ˈmiːtiŋ tə bi ˋheld?	—— Arrangement.
wi wə tu əv bin ˈmarid in ˋdʒuːn.	—— Intention.

In all these cases these finites are treated, in respect of sentence structure, word order and weakening, exactly as they are when acting as conjugators, with the single exception of the imperative. This is described in detail in §§236–8.

For the "precursory there" and "precursory it" constructions see §§231–2.

156　Other uses of the verb tə hav.　This difficult verb has developed a large variety of specific meanings, and its use is complicated by the fact that in some of these meanings it does not always follow the rules of sentence structure, though irregularities are confined to two tenses in the Aspect of Accomplishment, the Present Direct and the Past Direct, which, it should be noted, are the two tenses that have an anomalous structure in the unemphatic affirmative (see §336). The three structural patterns into which the verb tə hav enters are, then, as follows.

A. When the three finites of tə hav are used as conjugators they help to form some of the perfect tenses of other verbs and are always followed by a past participle. They are also the medium through which interrogation and negation are indicated. Examples of their use in this capacity will be found in §§165–7.

B. When tə hav is used as a specific verb with certain meanings it is conjugated like any other specific verb. That is to say, its finites (now specific finites) are used only in the unemphatic affirmative form of Tenses A1 and A2, the interrogative, negative and emphatic affirmative constructions being formed by introducing the usual conjugators: duː or dʌz for Tense A1 and did for Tense A2.

The following are the meanings in which tə hav is always conjugated regularly in this way:

To experience.

    d ju ˈhav mʌtʃ ˈdifik|ti wið ði ˈiŋgliʃ ˈvəːbz?
    ˈdʌznt i ˈhav ˈsliːplis ˈnaits?
    did ju ˈhav ə ˈgud ˈtaim on joː ˈholidiz?—ˈjes, wi ˌhad ə ˈveri
      gud ˌtaim; wi ˈdidn̩t hav ˈeni rein ət ˌoːl.

To consume.

    ai ˈdount ˈjuːʒuli hav ˌʃugər in ˌkofi.
    ˈwot ˈtaim dəz ʃi ˈhav ˌbrekfəst?
    ˈwen did ju ˈlaːst hav ə ˌmiːl?

To give birth.

    ˈhau ˈofn̩ dəz joː ˈkat hav ˈkitn̩z?

To trick or deceive.

    did mai ˈbrʌðə ˈhav ju wið ˈðat ˈould ˈtrik?

To cause something to be done.

    wi ˈdount ˈhav auə ˈnjuːspeipəz diˇlivəd.
    ˈhau ˈofn̩ dəz i ˈhav iz ˈheə ˌkʌt?
    ˈdidn̩t ju ˈhav joː ˈhaus ˈpeintid ˈlaːst ˈsʌmə?

To suffer something.

    ˈdidn̩t i ˈhav iz ˈleg ˈbroukən in ði ˈaksidn̩t?

When tə hav is followed by a noun denoting an action, thus replacing a verb of similar meaning, it is conjugated as a specific verb. Examples:

d ju 'evə hav ə ˙geim əv ˈfutbɔːl?
'wai ˙dount ˈjuː hav ə ˌgou?
did ju 'hav ə ˙luk ət ðə ˈpeipə ðis ˙mɔːniŋ?
ai 'didn̩t hav ə ˈʃeiv ðis ˌmɔːniŋ.

Also in the following idioms tə hav is conjugated as a specific verb.

'didn̩t i ˙hav it ˈaut wið iz ˙brʌðə?
d ju 'hav jɔː ˈfrendz ˙in in ði ˙iːvniŋz?
ʃi 'dʌzn̩t ˙hav 'evriθiŋ hər 'oun ˅wei.

C. When, however, tə hav has certain other specific meanings, an appreciable number of speakers use an anomalous structure in. Tenses A1 and A2. This anomaly consists in making the three finites of tə hav (which are here specific finites) do their own work of interrogation (by inverting them with their subject) and negation (by using the contracted negative forms) instead of bringing in the conjugators duː, dʌz, did and dount, dʌzn̩t, didn̩t to perform these tasks for them.

The meanings in which this structure is used are (1) a group of meanings associated with the idea of possession, i.e., to possess literally or figuratively, to be equipped with, to be in enjoyment of, to be characterized by, to exhibit, and (2) the meaning of to be obliged to and its negative, to be exempted from. The majority of native speakers of English feel instinctively that a structure that is normally associated with the conjugation of other verbs is too weak to carry the above meanings. They therefore strengthen it by adding the past participle got, thus forming the Present Perfect and Past Perfect tenses of the verb tə get, with the implication "I've obtained, therefore I have," which brings it back notionally from the perfect to the direct time reference. This structure, which conforms grammatically to Pattern A, above, is used much more consistently in the present than in the past, where Pattern B is more favoured.

For purposes of comparison examples are given below in all three patterns. It will be noticed that in Patterns B and C affirmative sentences are identical.

Possession.

A.   mai 'ʌŋk|̩ z got ən ə'tak əv ˇfluː.
B, C. mai 'ʌŋk|̩ haz ən ə'tak əv ˇfluː.
A.   ʃi z got 'bjuːtif|̩ blak ˇheə.
B, C. ʃi haz 'bjuːtif|̩ blak ˇheə.
A.   'hau meni ˇtʃildrn̩ əv ju ˌgot?
B.   'hau meni ˇtʃildrn̩ d ju ˌhav?   (Am.)
C.   'hau meni ˇtʃildrn̩ ˌhav ju?
A.   həv ju 'got ə ˊmatʃ?—ˋnou, ai m ˇsori, ai ˋhavn̩t.
B.   d ju 'hav ə ˊmatʃ?—ˋnou, ai m ˇsori, ai ˋdount. (Am.)
C.   'hav ju ə ˊmatʃ?—ˋnou, ai m ˇsori, ai ˋhavn̩t.
A.   ðei d 'got sm̩ ˇrelətivz, bət ðei 'hadn̩t got ˙meni ˇfrendz.
B.   ðei 'had sm̩ ˇrelətivz, bət ðei 'didn̩t hav ˙meni ˇfrendz.
C.   ðei 'had sm̩ ˇrelətivz, bət ðei 'hadn̩t ˙meni ˇfrendz.

Obligation.

A.   ai v 'got tə ˙weit fə ði ˇʌðəz.
B, C. ai 'hav tə ˙weit fə ði ˇʌðəz.
A.   həz i 'got tə ˙duː it wið'aut eni ˊhelp?
B.   dəz i 'hav tə ˙duː it wið'aut eni ˊhelp?
C.   'haz i tə ˙duː it wið'aut eni ˊhelp?
A.   wi 'havn̩t ˙got tə bi ˙ðeə til ˇsevn̩.
B.   wi 'dount ˙hav tə bi ˙ðeə til ˇsevn̩.
C.   wi 'havn̩t tə bi ˙ðeə til ˇsevn̩. (Provincial)
A.   'hadn̩t ju ˙got tə ˙poust ə ˊletə?
B.   'didn̩t ju ˙hav tə ˙poust ə ˊletə?
C.   'hadn̩t ju tə ˙poust ə ˊletə? (Provincial)

British speakers tend to distinguish between an obligation that is permanent or imposed repeatedly and one that is temporary or imposed only once by using Pattern B for the former and Pattern A for the latter. Examples:

A.   ai v 'got tə bi ˙ðeər ˋəːli ðis ˌmoːniŋ.
B.   ai 'hav tə bi ˙ðeər ˙əːli 'evri ˇmoːniŋ.
A.   'havn̩t ju ˙got tə ˙siː ðəm təˊdei?
B.   'dount ju ˙hav tə ˙siː ðəm 'evri ˊdei?

This distinction is not often made in American English, where most speakers may use Pattern B in all contexts.

157   Other uses of the verbs tə du: and tə juːz..   These two
verbs are used as specific verbs, but present no problems, as they
are conjugated regularly.

The verb tə duː has the meaning: to perform an action in a general
sense, as well as numerous other meanings more or less closely
connected.   Examples:

> ai 'havn̩t ˙dʌn mai ˋhoumwəːk; wil 'juː ˙help mi tə ˊduː it?
> ju məs 'duː wot ˙evribodi ˋels ˌdʌz.

The verb tə juːz has the meaning to employ something for a
purpose, and is easily distinguished from the conjugator juːst because
the latter has suffered assimilation (see §13) since it is almost always
followed by tə.   The past form of the specific verb preserves the
voiced form juːzd.   Examples:

> 'wot did ju ˙juːz tə ˋʃeiv wið?—ai 'juːzd ə ˋseifti ˌreizə.
> iz 'dʒon ˙juːziŋ mai ˊkoum?—ˋnou, hi 'oːlwiz ˙juːziz iz ˋoun.

158   Verbs that conjugate themselves.   The conjugators that
derive from specific verbs may form tenses of these same verbs,
giving rise to a combination that often puzzles students, i.e., a
repetition of the same or nearly the same verb form in a sentence.
It should be remembered that its first occurrence is as a conjugating
finite and its second as a specific verbal.   The confusion arises from
the fact that certain finites and verbals share the same form.
Examples:

> 'had i ˙had 'oːl i ˊwontid?—ˋjes, hi d 'had iˋnʌf.
> ju ʃəd 'duː it 'twais ə ˏdei.—ai ˋduː ˌduː it ˌtwais ə ˌdei.
> 'hau d ju ˏduː?   ˋduː ˌduː it əz ˌwel əz ju ˌkan.
> ai 'juːst tə ˙juːz ə ˋseifti ˌreizə, bət 'leitli ai v ˙juːzd ən iˋlektrik
> ˌreizə.

FORMS OF THE TEMPORALS

159   Weak forms.   With the exception of did and juːst all the
affirmative temporals have essential weak forms, as shown in §16.
In most cases there are several of these, and the choice between
them largely depends on the phonetic context in which the finite
occurs.

There is no weakening, properly so called, of the negative finites, but in certain phonetic contexts the final t may be elided, and in rapid speech certain assimilations may occur. These are dealt with in §172.

It should be noted that in the case of the five finites of the verb tə biː there is an alternative method of expressing negation, which consists of using the weak affirmative forms followed by a stressed 'not. This method is very seldom used in questions, where it sounds stilted. In statements it gives rather greater emphasis to the negation. The proportion in which it is used as a substitute for the regular negative construction varies from speaker to speaker, and it is used less frequently in the past tense than in the present, while in the first person singular of the present tense it is the only form used in statements (§160). Examples of the use of this alternative negative form are given in the next five sections.

A similar alternative method of expressing negation with the three finites of the verb tə hav may sometimes be heard, but this is not recommended for adoption by foreign students as it carries a dialectal flavour.

Copious examples of the use of the strong and weak forms of the temporals are given in the next twelve sections. It should be remembered that the weak forms are used far more frequently than the strong forms.

160 am — (aːnt). Used in tenses A7, P1, P7 in the 1st person singular. The negative form is used only in questions; the form used in statements is m not.

Negative form.

aːnt in all questions:
    'aːnt ai ˅dʒenərəs !   ai m ˅leit, ′aːnt ai ?
m not in all statements:
    ai m 'not ˅redi ˌjet.   ˅hiː z ˌgouiŋ, bət ˅ai m ˌnot.
    ai ˌtel ju ai m ˅not !   ai m 'not ˙teikiŋ eni ˅tʃaːnsiz.

Affirmative form in stressed positions.

am in all cases:
    'am ai tə ′weit fə ðəm ?   ai ˅am ˌglad tə ˌhiə ˌðat.
    ˅ai nou ˌweər ai ˌam.

Affirmative form in unstressed positions.

am when not followed by a complement or verbal:
   d ju 'nou huː 'ai am?   'ðei ər əz ˙taiəd əz 'ai am.

əm when preceding its subject:
   əm 'ai ðə 'fəːst?   'wot əm ai tə 'duː?
   'haːdli 'evər əm ai ˌeibļ tə ˌsiː im.

m when it follows ai:
   ai m 'weitiŋ fə ðəm.   ai 'θiŋk ai m biːiŋ 'folud.
   ai m ⌄redi.   ai m fə'bidņ tə 'muːv.

161   iz — izņt. Used in tenses A7, P1, P7 in the 3rd person singular.

Negative form.

izņt in all cases:
   ðə 'weðər ˌizņt ˌbad.   ʃi 'izņt ˙getiŋ eni ⌄betə.
   'izņt 'tiː ˙redi?—'nou, it 'izņt.

Affirmative form in stressed positions.

iz in all cases:
   it 'iz ˙ritņ ⌄badli.   it 'iz biːiŋ ə⌄tendid tu.
   it 'iz ⌄difikļt!   'iz it 'wʌn ə'klok jet?

Affirmative form in unstressed positions.

iz (1) when not followed by a complement or verbal:
   d ju 'nou wot 'ðat iz?   ai m 'mʌtʃ moː ˌtaiəd ðən ⌄hiː iz.
   'ai m biːiŋ ˌentəˌteind, bət ai 'dount θiŋk ⌄hiː iz.

iz (2) in initial positions:
   iz joːr 'ʌŋkļ kʌmiŋ?   iz 'ðat wot ju ˙miːn?

iz (3) when preceded by s, z, ʃ or ʒ:
   'ðat 'boks iz 'ful.   ðə 'vaːz iz 'broukən.
   'witʃ iz joːz?   ðə 'peidʒ iz 'toːn.

iz (4) often after a pause:
   mai 'njuː ʌm⌄brelə, witʃ 'dʒon ˌgeiv mi, iz in ðə 'hoːl.
   ðə 'wʌn 'ai ʃəd ˌlaik iz 'biːiŋ 'mendid.

s after voiceless consonants (except s and ʃ):

ˈðis kʌp s ˋdəːti.   hiz ˋhelθ s imˌpruːviŋ.
ˈwot s ˌðat?   mai ˋwaif s ˌðeə.
ðə ˋlok s ˌbroukən.   it s ˈbiːiŋ əˋtendid tu.

z in all other cases:

ðə ˈpaːsl z ˅redi.   ðə ˈsiː z ˙getiŋ ˋrʌf.
ˋðis ˌruːm z ˌwoːm.   ðə ˈdoː z biːiŋ ˌkliːnd.
ðə ˈdog z ˙tʃeind ˌʌp.   ˈweə z ˌmʌðə?—ʃi z ˋhiə.
ʃi z ˈnot ˋredi ˌjet.   ðə ˈman z ˈnot ˋlisniŋ.

162 aː* — aːnt. Used in tenses A7, P1, P7 in the 1st, 2nd and
3rd persons plural.

Negative form.

aːnt in all cases:

ˈaːnt ju ˈtaiəd?   ðei ˈaːnt ˈjuːzd ˌnauədeiz.
ˈaːnt wi biːiŋ ˈmet?—ˋnou, wi ˋaːnt.

Affirmative form in stressed positions.

aː when not followed by a vowel:

wi ˋaː biːiŋ ˌfolud.   ai ˈnou weə ju ˅aː.
ˈaː ju ˙weitiŋ fə ˈmiː?—ˋjes, wi ˋaː.

aːr when followed immediately by a vowel:

ju ˋaːr ikˌˇsaitəbl̩!   wi ˋaːr ˌaːnsəriŋ ðə ˌletə.
ˈðei ˌaːr in ə ˌhʌri!   ˈaːr ˈoːl əv ju ˙kʌmiŋ?

Affirmative form in unstressed positions.

aː when not followed by a complement or verbal:

ˈhuː d ju θiŋk ˋðei aː?   ˋai m moː ˌtaiəd ðən ˅juː aː.

ər when followed immediately by a vowel:

ər ˈoːl mai ˈfrendz ðeə?   joː ˈfrendz ər ˋaːskiŋ fə ju.

ə in all other cases:

ə ju ˈbizi?   ə ju ˈbiːiŋ lukt ˈaːftə?
wi ə ˈkwait ˅redi.   ðei ə ˈwontid iˋmiːdjətli.
ə ðei ˈkʌmiŋ təˈdei?   joː ˈfrendz ə ˋweitiŋ fə ju.
wi ə ˈnot ˋkʌmiŋ.   ðei ə ˈnot ˙gouiŋ tə ˌweit.

163   woz — wozn̩t. Used in tenses A8, P2, P8 in the 1st and 3rd persons singular. It may, however, be replaced by wəː — wəːnt in certain subordinate clauses.

Negative form.

wozn̩t in all cases:

    'wozn̩t ai 'rait?   ai 'wozn̩t ˋtould əbaut it.
    'wozn̩t ʃi ˙toːkiŋ tə 'juː?—ˋnou, ʃi ˎwozn̩t.

Affirmative form in stressed positions.

woz in all cases:

    'hiː ˎwoz ə ˌnais ˌman.   'woz it biːiŋ ˙mendid?
    'woz i ri˙fəːriŋ tə 'mi?—ˋjes, hi ˋwoz.

Affirmative form in unstressed positions.

woz when not followed by a complement or verbal:

    iz 'ðat weə ðə 'tʃəːtʃ woz?   'wiː wər əz ˙taiəd əz ˋhiː woz.

wəz in all other cases:

    ai wəz 'tould tə ˎweit.   wəz it 'biːiŋ 'mendid?
    wəz i ə'sliːp?—ˋjes, hi wəz 'teikiŋ ə ˎnap.
    hi wəz 'not ˋwoːnd.   it wəz 'not ˋwəːθ it.

164   wəː* — wəːnt. Used in tenses A8, P2, P8 in the 1st, 2nd and 3rd persons plural. In certain subordinate clauses, however, it may replace woz — wozn̩t in the singular.

Negative form.

wəːnt in all cases:

    wi 'wəːnt ˅woːnd əbaut it.   'wəːnt ju biːiŋ 'peid fə ðə ˙wəːk?
    'wəːnt ðei ˙toːkiŋ tə 'juː?—ˋnou, ðei ˎwəːnt.

Affirmative form in stressed positions.

wəːr before a vowel:

    'wəːr oːl ðə ˙buks 'sould?   wi 'nevə ˋwəːr əˌlaud tə ˎgou.

wəː in all other cases:

    'wəː ju ət ðə 'θiətə?   'ðei ˎwəː ˌpliːzd.

Affirmative form in unstressed positions.

wəː when not followed by a complement or verbal:

  d ju 'nou wot 'ðei wəː?   ˇhiː wəz əz ˌtaiəd əz ˌjuː wəː.

wər before a vowel:

  wi wər ə'loun.   ai d ˋgou if ai wər ˇaːskt.
  ðei wər ʌp'set.   wi wər ˋoːlwiz əˌlaud tə ˌgou.
  wər 'eni əv ju 'ðeə?—wi wər ˋoːl ˌðeə.

wə in all other cases:

  ðei wə biːiŋ in'spektid.   wi wə ˋnevər əˌlaud tə ˌgou.
  'wen wə ju ˙teikən ˌil?   wə 'juː ðə 'fəːst tu ə'raiv?
  wi wə 'not ˌintristid.   ju wə 'not inˌvaitid.

With singular subjects when expressing hypotheses or wishes.

  ai 'wiʃ ʃi wə ˇhiə.   ai ʃəd ˋstei if ˌai wə juː.
  hi d ˋhelp ju if i ˌwəːnt sou ˌbizi.

165 hav — havn̩t. Used in tenses A4, A10, P4 in all except the 3rd person singular.

Negative form.

havn̩t in all cases:

  'havn̩t ju bin 'rʌniŋ?—ˋnou, ai ˋhavn̩t.
  'havn̩t ðei bin ˙θroun ə'wei?—ˋnou, ai m ˋʃoː ðei ˌhavn̩t.

Affirmative form in stressed positions.

hav in all cases:

  'hav ju ˙teikən joː 'medsin?—ˋjes, ai ˌhav.
  'hav ðei bin ˙wəːkiŋ 'wel?—ˋjes, ðei ˋhav, ˋveri ˌwel.
  'hav wi bin ˙givn̩ ə 'holidi?—ˋjes, wi ˌhav.

Affirmative form in unstressed positions.

hav when not followed by a verbal

  ˇhiː ˌhazn̩t ˌsiːn it, bət ˇai hav.
  ˋʃiː z bin ˌwəːkiŋ, bət weðə ˇjuː hav iz ˋdautfl̩.
  'henri ˙hazn̩t ə'raivd, bət ði ˇʌðəz hav, 'foːtʃn̩itli.

həv in initial positions:

  həv 'eni əv ðəm ə'raivd?   həv ju bin 'weitiŋ 'loŋ?
  həv ðei bin 'noutifaid?

əv (1) after consonants:

ðə 'bɔiz əv 'gɒn tə ˅bed.   jɔː 'frendz əv bin ˋɑːskiŋ fə ju.
ðə 'rest əv bin ˙put ə˛wei.

əv (2) after interrogatives:

'huː əv ju ˛siːn?   'wai əv ai bin igˋnɔːd?
'wɒt əv ðei bin ˋduːiŋ?   'weər əv ðei bin ˋhidn̩?

əv (3) after multiple subjects:

'dʒɒn ən ˋmeəri əv ˛kʌm tə ˛siː əs.

v (1) after personal pronouns (except it):

wi v ˋdʌn ˛ðat.   ai v 'dʒʌst bin ˋriːdiŋ it.
ðei v bin ˋspoilt.   ju v 'teikən ðə ˋrɒŋ wʌn.

v (2) after huː (relative):

ə'tend tə ˙ðouz u v əˋraivd.   'eni hu v ˙siːn it kən ˛gou.

166 haz — haznt. Used in tenses A4, A10, P4 in the 3rd person singular only.

Negative form.

haznt in all cases:

'haznt ˙sʌmθiŋ bin fə'gɒtn̩? ʃi 'haznt bin ˋwəːkiŋ ˛leitli.
'haznt ðə 'milkmən ˙kʌm jet?—ˋnou, hi ˛haznt.

Affirmative from in stressed positions.

haz in all cases:

'haz i 'peid ju jet?   ˛weə 'haz i ˛put it?
it 'haz bin ˋnoun tə ˛hapən.   ai 'θiŋk ʃi ˋhaz bin ˛duːiŋ it.

Affirmative form in unstressed positions.

haz when not followed by a verbal:

ˋai ˛havn̩t ˛siːn it, bət ˅ʃiː haz.
ˋjuː v bin ˛wəːkiŋ, bət weðə ˅hiː haz iz ˋdautf|.
ˋmain ˛haznt bin ˛faund, bət ˅jɔːz haz ˙fɔːtʃn̩itli.

həz in initial positions:

həz 'enibɒdi ə'raivd?   həz i bin 'weitiŋ ˈlɒŋ?
həz i bin 'noutifaid?

əz after s, z, ʃ or ʒ:

'oːl ðə ˈkaʃ əz ˈdisəˋpiəd. mai ˈwotʃ əz bin ˋgeiniŋ.
joː ˈpleis əz bin ˋteikən. ðə ˈgaraːʒ əz bin ˌpeintid.

s after voiceless consonants (except s and ʃ):

ðə ˈkuk s ˈbəːnt ðə ˋkeik. ðə ˋruːf s bin ˌliːkiŋ.
auə ˈtrip s bin ˋkansǀd. it s bin ˋlost.

z after voiced sounds (except z and ʒ):

ðə ˋdog z ˌiːtŋ it. mai ˈbrʌðə z bin ˌtoːkiŋ tu im.
ˈðis ˈruːm z bin ˋkliːnd. joː ˋʃuː z bin ˌfaund.
ðə ˋsʌn z kʌm ˌaut. mai ˈkaː z bin ˈrʌniŋ veri ˋwel.

167 had — hadṇt. Used in tenses A5, A11, P5 in all persons.

Negative form.

hadṇt in all cases:

ai ˈhadṇt ˋhəːd əbaut it biˌfoː ˌjuː ˌtould mi.
hi ˈhadṇt bin ˋdriŋkiŋ wen i ˌhad ði ˌaksidṇt.
ju ˈgot ˈwəːs bikoz ju ˈhadṇt bin ˈkept in ˋbed.

Affirmative form in stressed positions.

had in all cases:

if ai ˋhad ˌnoun əbaut it ai ʃəd əv ˋtould ju.
ˈhad ju bin ˈθiŋkiŋ əv ˈgouiŋ əˋbroːd fə joː ˈholidiz?
ˋðei ˌhadṇt bin ˋwʌrid bai ðə ˌnoiz, bət ˅ai ˋhad.

Affirmative form in unstressed positions.

had when not followed by a verbal:

ˋwiː ˌkudṇt əv ˌdʌn it, but if ˅juː had, wi d əv ˋhelpt ju.
ˋjuː d bin ˌwəːkiŋ, bət weðə ˅hiː had iz ˋdautfǀ.
ˋðei ˌhadṇt bin ˌwʌrid bai ðə ˌnoiz, bət ˅ai had.

həd in initial positions:

həd ju ˈevə bin ˈðeə biˋfoə?
həd ˈeni əv joː ˈfrendz bin ˈtoːkiŋ əbaut it?
həd i bin ˈtould ˈwot tə ˋduː?

əd (1) after consonants:

ˋbob əd ˌteikən ði ˌʌðəz.   ðə 'tʃildrn̩ əd ˙gon tə ˌbed.
ˋtom əd bin ˌhelpiŋ əs.   ˋmain əd bin ˌeikiŋ fə ˋmʌnθs.
ˇðat əd bin ˋset|d.   ʃi 'sed it əd bin ˙teikən əˋwei.

əd (2) after interrogatives including huː used as object:

'huː əd ju ˌsiːn?   'wai əd ai bin igˋnoːd?
'wot əd ðei bin ˋduːiŋ?   'weər əd ðei bin ˋhidn̩?

əd (3) after multiple subjects:

'dʒon ən ˙meəri əd oːl'redi ˋgon.

d (1) after personal pronouns (except it):

'ai 'θoːt ju d ˋfiniʃt.   ju ˋnjuː ai d bin ˌweitiŋ fə ju.
ʃi ˋnjuː i d ˌteikən it.   wi wə 'tould ðei d bin ˋwoːnd.

d (2) after huː used as subject:

ðei 'wudn̩t ˋsei ˌhuː d ˌkʌt it. ðə 'man u d ˇdʌn it isˋkeipt.

d (3) usually after nouns ending in a vowel:

ðə ˋboi d ˌritn̩ it.   ˋhari d bin ˌpʌniʃt fər it.

168 duː — dount. Used in tense A1, in all forms of the sentence except the unemphatic affirmative (in which its place is taken by the appropriate specific finite) and in all persons except the 3rd person singular.

Negative form.

dount in all cases:

'wai dount ðei ˋaːnsə?   wi 'dount wont tə ˌgou.
'dount ju ˊlaik it?—ˋnou, ai ˌdount.

Affirmative form in stressed positions.

duː in all cases:

ai ˋduː ˌlaik ðat ˇhat!   ðei 'duː ˇwont it, ˊdount ðei?
'duː ju ˊnou ðəm?—ˋjes, wi ˌduː.

Affirmative form in unstressed positions.

duː when not followed by a specific verbal:

ˋðei dount ˌlaik it, bət ˇwiː duː.
ai 'dount ˌwont tə ˌgou, bət if ˇjuː duː ai I 'kʌm ˋwið ju.

du before vowels and w:

    du ai 'hav tə ˙gou?   du 'oːl əv ðəm bi˙loŋ tə ju?

    'weə du wi ˙put auə ˋhats?   'hau du ˋegz ˌsjuːt ju?

d before ju when unstressed:

    d ju 'laik ðəm?   'wot d ju ˙wont fə jə ˋbəːθdei?

    'hau d ju ˏduː?   d ju 'spiːk 'spaniʃ?

də in all other cases:

    də 'juː wont ˙wʌn əv ðəm?   də ði 'ʌðəz in˙tend tə ˙kʌm?

    'weə də ðei ˙wont it ˏput?   'hau də joː ˋsistəz ˌlaik it?

169 dʌz — dʌznt. Used in tense A1, in the 3rd person singular instead of duː — dount.

Negative form.

    dʌznt in all cases:

    'wai dʌznt ʃi ˋaːnsə?   ˋðat dʌznt ˏwʌri mi.

    'dʌznt i 'wont eni?—ˋnou, hi ˏdʌznt.

Affirmative form in stressed positions.

    dʌz in all cases:

    'ðat ˏdʌz luk ˌnais!   hi 'dʌz ᵛwont it, 'dʌznt i?

    'dʌz it 'matə?—ˋjes, it ˋdʌz.

Affirmative form in unstressed positions.

    dʌz when not followed by a specific verbal:

    ˋjuː ˌplei ˌbetə ðən ᵛʃiː dʌz.

    ʃi 'dʌznt ˏwont tə ˏgou, bət if ᵛhiː dʌz 'ʃiː I gou ˋwið im.

    dəz in all other cases:

    dəz 'meəri 'laik it?   'weə dəz ˋdʒon ˌwəːk?

    dəz it 'matə?   'wot ˙taim dəz ðə ˋtrein get ˌin?

170 did — didnt. Used in tense A2 in all persons and in all forms of the sentence except the unemphatic affirmative, in which its place is taken by the appropriate specific finite.

Negative form.

didṇt in all cases:

   'wai didṇt ðei ˋsei sou?   joː 'letə ˙didṇt əˋraiv in ˌtaim.
   'didṇt ʹjuː ˙breik ðis ˙kʌp?—ˋnou, ai ˋdidṇt.

Affirmative form in stressed positions.

did in all cases:

   ai ˋdid ˌlaik joː ᵥpaːti!   ju 'did ʌndəᵛstand, ˋdidṇt ju?
   'did ju ʹmiːt ðəm?—ʹjes, wi ᵥdid.

Affirmative form in unstressed positions.

did in all cases:

   did it ʹwəːk ˙propəli?   'wen did ðei ˋaːsk ju əbaut it?
   did ʹpiːtə ˙wont eni?   ʹjuː didṇt ˌsiː it, bət ᵛai did.

171   juːst — juːsṇt. Used in a special past tense which takes the place of tense A2 when it is desired to contrast past with present. It is invariable for person.

Negative form.

juːst not is often used in statements:

   ju ʹjuːst ˌnot tə ˌwʌri.   ai 'juːst not tə ˋlaik ˌswimiŋ.

juːsṇt always in questions, sometimes in statements:

   hi ʹjuːsṇt tə bi sou ˌruːd   'juːsṇt ðə tə bi ə ʹhaus hiə?
   'juːsṇt ju tə ˙plei ðə ʹpjaːnu?—ˋnou, ai ᵥjuːsṇt tu.

Affirmative form, whether stressed or unstressed.

juːst in both questions and statements:

   'juːst ju tə ˙liv ʹhiə?   ᵛwiː juːst tə ˙siː im evri ˋdei.
   'juːst ðei tu ʹwin?   ðə ᵛjuːst tə biː ə ˋtriː ðeə.
   'juːst ju tə ˙plei ðə ʹpjaːnu?—ʹjes, ai ᵥjuːst tu.

This finite can be used in the passive voice and in perfect tenses in the same way as the modals (§§176–8):

   ᵛai juːst tə bi ˋpʌniʃt fə duːiŋ ˌðat soːt əv ˙θiŋ.
   'juːsṇt ju tu əv ʹfiniʃt bai ˙ðis taim?
   wi 'juːst ˙not tə bi ˋboðəd bai ðə ˌnoiz əv ˌeəkraːft.

The same construction is used with past participles that are
functioning as adjectives:

ju ' juːst tə bi ˙pliːzd tə ˋsiː mi.
hi 'juːst ˙not tə bi sou 'wel ˋnoun.
'juːsn̩t ðə ˙siːts tə bi ri'zəːvd?

There is a popular tendency to conjugate juːst with did, thus
treating it as a specific verb. This is hard to justify logically unless
one recognizes the introduction of a new infinitive tə juːs (as opposed
to the established tə juːz = to employ). In tags, however, it may
be said that did is conjugating the specific verb that follows juːst,
as in the following examples:

ʃi 'juːst not tə ˋlaik it, 'did ʃi (like it)?—ˋnou, ʃi ˋdidn̩t (like it).
ju 'juːst tə ˙plei ðə ˋpjaːnu, 'didn̩t ju (play the piano)?—ˋjes,
    ai ˌdid (play the piano).

172 **Special elisions and assimilations.** In rapid and familiar
speech several of the temporal finites may undergo special elisions
(§12) and assimilations (§13) when they occur in certain phonetic
contexts. While foreign students of English need not adopt these
modifications (which are not often shown in phonetic transcriptions)
they should be aware of their existence. They are therefore listed
below, and examples are given of contexts in which they may be
heard.

Negative forms.

Normal	Before p, b or m	Before t, d or n	Before k or g
izn̩t	izmp, izm̩	izn̩	izŋk, izŋ̍
havn̩t	havmp, havm̩	havn̩	havŋk, havŋ̍
hazn̩t	hazmp, hazm̩	hazn̩	hazŋk, hazŋ̍
dount	doump, doum	doun	douŋk, douŋ
dʌzn̩t	dʌzmp, dʌzm̩	dʌzn̩	dʌzŋk, dʌzŋ̍

hi 'izmp ˋpleiiŋ tə͵dei.   ʃi 'hazn̩ ˋnoutist əs.
'izŋ̍ 'gladis ˙kʌmiŋ?   wi 'doun ˋnou əm.
ai 'havn̩ ˋdʌn it ͵jet.   ˋdouŋk ͵gou ə͵wei.
ðei 'havm̩ ˋmeid eni.   'dʌzm̩ ˋbob ˙wont wʌn?
ʃi 'hazŋ̍ ˋkept eni.   it 'dʌzŋ̍ ˙grou veri ˇfaːst.

Affirmative forms.

Normal	Before ʃ, ʒ or j	Before ʃ	Between t and ʃ or j
iz, z, s	iʒ, ʒ	iʃ, ʃ	ʃ
woz, wəz	woʒ, wəʒ	woʃ, wəʃ	
haz, həz, əz, z	haʒ, həʒ, əʒ, ʒ	haʃ, həʃ, əʃ, ʃ	ʃ
dʌz, dəz	dʌʒ, dəʒ	dʌʃ, dəʃ	

iʒ joː 'frend 'redi?   'witʃ əʒ jər 'aːnt ˌtʃouzn̩?
'iʃ ʃi 'weitiŋ fər əs?   'haʃ ʃi 'ritn̩ tə juː?
it ʃ 'joː ˌfoːlt.   ˋðat ʃ ˌʃokt juː!
'weə wəʒ jə ˋhat?   ˌhau 'dʌʒ jər 'aːnt ˌduː it?
wəʃ ʃi 'juːziŋ it?   'wot dəʃ ʃi ˌθiŋk əˌbaut it?

Notice also that

hav is sometimes pronounced haf before tu or tə,

əv (= have) is sometimes pronounced f between voiceless consonants,

did is sometimes pronounced dd, especially between vowels:

ai ʃl ˋhaf tə ˌgou.   'hau dd i ˙get ˌon?
ai ʃt f ˌθoːt sou.   dd i 'stei wið juː?

GRAMMAR OF THE MODALS

173 Tense nomenclature. Influenced by the grammatical structures of other languages with very different verb systems, English grammarians usually label tenses formed with wil or ʃal as "future" and "future perfect," and those formed with wud or ʃud as "conditional" and "conditional perfect," while tenses formed with the other modals are now usually left without a name.

A more accurate and comprehensive idea of the work done by the modal finites can be obtained if they are divided into three groups:

Group 1, wil, ʃal, kan, mei, which have a present or future reference;

Group 2, wud, ʃud, kud, mait, the historic past-tense forms of the above, which usually refer to a hypothetical present or future, and less frequently to a direct past;

Group 3, mʌst, oːt, niːd, deə*, which have no distinctive past tense forms and are therefore, in suitable contexts, used in either capacity.

Since it is easily demonstrable (*a*) that wil, ʃal, wud and ʃud often have just as strong modal meanings as any of the other modals, (*b*) that all the modals in Groups 1 and 3 may have the same time references and grammatical functions as wil and ʃal, while all those in Groups 2 and 3 may function like wud and ʃud, and (*c*) that even modals of Group 2 may, in suitable contexts, refer to the present or future, one is forced to the conclusion that while the modals differ fairly clearly and consistently in meaning, their references to time show a great deal of confusion and overlapping, so that any tense distinctions made between them must be largely artificial and even misleading.

There would therefore seem to be powerful reasons for effecting a very welcome simplification in the table of English tenses by postulating a single set of six "modal tenses" (three direct and three perfect) and dividing the modals themselves into the three groups shown above. One can then formulate rules to re-state the canonical "agreement of tenses," i.e., the rule which divides tenses into two sets:

a. Present, present perfect, future, future perfect,

b. Past, past perfect, conditional, conditional perfect,

and lays down that in most complex sentences tenses in different sets are mutually exclusive. The new rule would state that tenses formed with modals of Groups 1 or 3 would agree with those of set *a*, and modals of Group 2 would agree with set *b*, while modals of Group 3 would also agree with set *b* in indirect speech.

The distribution of the six modal tenses between the voices and aspects, and the names applied to them, are given in §209.

174 Grammatical functions. The time (past, present or future) to which the modals refer and their grammatical relationship to other parts of the sentence are most easily understood if the three groups mentioned in §173 are considered separately.

1. wil, ʃal, kan, mei, refer to actions taking place in either the present or the future; in many cases there is no doubt which of these is referred to, but if necessary an adverb or adverbial is used to make this clear, as may be seen in the following examples:

Present	*Future*
ai l 'siː im ət ˎwʌns.	ai l 'miːt ju ˙nekst ˎwenzdi.
hi ʃl 'hav it ˎnau.	hi ʃl 'hav it wiðin ə ˎwiːk.
wi kən 'staːt i ̍miːdjətli.	wi kən 'staːt ˙nekst ˏjiə.
ju mei 'kʌm ˋin ˏnau.	ju mei 'kʌm ˙in 'leitər ˎon.

The modal **mait** should perhaps be admitted as a part-time member of this group, as it has a present or future reference when it is used instead of the **mei** of possibility in order to suggest improbability:

Present	*Future*
it 'mei bi ˙hiər oːlˋredi.	it 'mei ə˙raiv 'nekst ˋwiːk.
it 'mait bi ˙hiər oːlˋredi.	it 'mait ə˙raiv 'nekst ˋwiːk.

2. **wud, ʃud, kud, mait**, the past-tense forms of the above, are substituted for them in indirect speech if the reporting verb is in the past tense:

Direct	*Indirect*
ai 'wount ˎweit fə ðəm.	hi 'sed i ˙wudn̩t ˎweit fə ðəm.
ai ʃl bi ˏleit.	ai ˋsed ai ʃəd bi ˏleit.
ai kən 'hiər ə ˎnoiz.	ʃi 'sed ʃi kəd ˙hiər ə ˎnoiz.
wi 'mei ˋstei hiə.	wi 'tould im wi ˙mait ˋstei ðeə.

They are also used when it is desired to give a hypothetical feeling to a sentence: such sentences are usually associated with a conditional clause, either expressed or implied.
Examples:

'wud ju ˙laik ə 'sigə′ret? (if I offered you one).
'wud ðei ˙maind ′weitiŋ? (if they were asked to).
ai ʃəd ˋlʌv tə ˏgou ðeə. (if I were invited).
'kudn̩t ju ə′foːd ə 'njuː ′kaː? (if you wanted one).
hi 'mait not ˙wont tə ˋriːd ðə ˏbuk. (if we gave it to him).

The modals **wud** and **kud**, and particularly their negatives, may be used in the direct past tense; they then have full modal meaning:

ai 'aːskt ˋevribodi, bət 'noubodi wud ˎtel mi.
hi kud ˋswim bai ðə ˏtaim i wəz ˏsiks.
ai in ̍vaitid im ˏin, bət i 'wudn̩t ˎstei.
wi 'left ðə ˙paːti bikoz wi 'kudn̩t ˙stand ðə ˙noiz eni ˎloŋgə.

3. mʌst, ɔːt, niːd, deə*, have no corresponding past-tense forms and are therefore used in both direct and indirect speech. They are not used hypothetically.

Direct	*Indirect*
ju məst ˇweit.	ai ˈtould im i məst ˌweit.
ai ˈɔːt tə ˌhelp ðəm.	ʃi ˈsed ʃi ˙ɔːt tə ˌhelp ðəm.
ju ˇniːdn̩t ˌboðə.	hi ˈtould mi ai ˈniːdn̩t ˌboðə.
ai ˈdeənt ˌdʒʌmp.	ai ˈkoːld ˙aut ðət ai ˈdeənt ˌdʒʌmp.

These four modals, like the first four, may apply equally well to the present or the future:

Present	*Future*
ðei məst ˇweit ə ˌminit.	ðei məst ˈbriŋ it ˙nekst ˌmʌnθ.
ʃi ˈɔːt tə ˙rait ət ˇwʌns.	ʃi ˈɔːt tə ˙duː it ˇsuːn.
ju ˈniːdn̩t ˙gou təˇdei.	ju ˈniːdn̩t ˙kʌm on ˇsatədi.
ai ˇdeənt ˌweit eni ˌloŋgə.	ai ˇdeənt kʌm ˌbak təˌmoru.

175 Conjugation of verbs of the five senses. When they refer to involuntary perception the verbs that specify the actions of the five senses (siː, hiə*, smel, teist and fiːl) are conjugated in the present and past tenses of the aspect of accomplishment with the help of kan and kud instead of duː (dʌz) and did. Thus:

ai kən ˈsiː ðə ˙sʌn θruː ðə ˌklaudz.
kən ju ˈhiə ðə ˇbəːdz ˙siŋiŋ?
ˈkaːnt ju smel ði ˈʌnjən in ðə ˙suːp?
ai ˈkaːnt ˙teist eni ˇʃugər in mai ˌkofi.
hi kud ˈfiːl ðət ðə ˙woːl had ə ˈrʌf ˌsəːfis.

When the senses are being used deliberately the aspect of activity is usually preferred, and luk at and lisn̩ tu are used instead of siː and hiə*. Thus:

ai m ˈlukiŋ ət ðə ˌskai, tə ˈsiː if it s ˙gouiŋ tə ˌrein.
ˈwot ə ju ˇlisniŋ tu? (Compare: ˈwot kən ju ˌhiə?)
wi ə ˈsmeliŋ ðə ˌsuːp tə ˈsiː if it ˙haz iˈnʌf ˌʌnjən.
ʃi z ˈteistiŋ ðə ˙kofi tə ˈsiː if it s ˇstroŋ inʌf.
hi wəz ˈfiːliŋ iz ˙wei əloŋ ðə ˌwoːl.

176 The six modal tenses. Regarded purely from the structural point of view the English verb possesses six modal tenses, four in the active voice and two in the passive. These tenses are formed by placing any one of the modals (which, it must be remembered, are finites) before any of the six infinitives shown in the table in §177. There are no internal complications in the tenses, as all the modals are invariable for number and person. It is worth noting that the modals cannot be used in the imperative and that the verb form immediately following them is always an infinitive.

The finites oːt and oːtn̩t are followed by the infinitive with tu. The finites niːd and deə* can be used only in sentences that contain some interrogative, negative or dubitative element, and deənt is rarely used in the passive voice.

177 Compound infinitives. The basic or lexical infinitive of any verb may be regarded as belonging to a set of six infinitives, four in the active voice and two in the passive. The other infinitives in this set are all compounds formed with the aid of conjugating verbals. The specific verb form is always a participle, the infinitive element being contributed by a conjugator. Two of the compound infinitives require two conjugating verbals; in these cases the first one is the infinitive, since the verb form immediately following a modal must always be an infinitive.

The modal tenses are formed by placing the desired modal before any of these six infinitives, and in this way all the direct and perfect modal tenses in both aspects can be composed.

The six infinitives of the verb tə teik are tabulated below.

Tense	Accomplishment	Active	Activity	Tense
A 3	(tə) teik	*Direct*	(tə) bi teikiŋ	A 9
A 6	(tu) əv teikən	*Perfect*	(tu) əv bin teikiŋ	A 12

Tense	Accomplishment	Passive	Activity	Tense
P 3	(tə) bi teikən	*Direct*	Not used	—
P 6	(tu) əv bin teikən	*Perfect*	Not used	—

Negation can be added to any of the infinitives by placing not before the tu, thus:

'not tə ˈteik   'not tu əv bin ˈteikən
'not tu əv ˈteikən   'not tə bi ˈteikiŋ
'not tə bi ˈteikən   'not tu əv bin ˈteikiŋ

178 Modal tenses with compound infinitives. The examples
below are intended to show how modal tenses are formed with these
infinitives. Tense A3, which is formed with the simple infinitive,
is included in order to make the list of modal tenses complete.
Explanations of the functions of the various tenses will be found
in §§210–24.

Active Voice

A 3 *Modal Direct of Accomplishment.*

ai ʃļ 'liːv wen˙evər ai ˎlaik.
kən ju 'kʌm ən ˙siː əs 'nekst ˊtjuːzdi?
wi ˋdeənt gou ˌin wiðaut pəˇmiʃn̩.
'wudn̩t it bi ˙betə tə 'weit til ˊfraidi?

A 6 *Modal Perfect of Accomplishment.*

ðei 'mei əv ˋleft biˌfoː wi ˌget ðeə.
'wil ju əv ˊfiniʃt bai ðə ˙taim ai get ˙bak?
hi ˋkaːnt əv ˌment tə ˌθrou it əˌwei.
'ʃudn̩t ju əv ˙tould mi əbaut it ˊjestədi?

A 9 *Modal Direct of Activity*

ai ʃļ bi ə'raiviŋ ət 'ten əˎklok.
wud ju bi 'wontiŋ ˙eniθiŋ ˊels?
wi 'ʃaːnt bi ˙gouiŋ intə ˙taun dʒʌst ˇjet.
'oːtn̩t ju tə bi ˙duiŋ joː ˊhoumwəːk?

A12 *Modal Perfect of Activity*

ðei 'mei əv bin ˙traiiŋ tə ˋfoun əs ˌoːl ðis ˌtaim.
'wil ʃi əv bin ˙wəːkiŋ in ði ˊofis tə˙dei?
hi 'oːtn̩t tu əv bin ˙laiiŋ in ðə ˋsʌn.
'kudn̩t ju əv bin ˙leiiŋ ðə ˊteibļ?

Passive Voice

P 3 *Modal Direct of Accomplishment.*

'ðis ˙medsin məs bi 'teikən wið ˙plenti əv ˎwoːtə.
kən ðə 'rest bi ˙left til tə'moru?
ju 'mʌsn̩t bi ˙teikən ˙in bai ˋðat ˌould ˌtrik.
'wount ju bi ˙peid til 'nekst ˊmʌndi?

143

P 6 *Modal Perfect of Accomplishment.*

ðei 'mait əv bin di'leid bai ðə ˅fog.
'ʃal wi əv bin ˙mist bai ði '⋀ðəz jet?
ðə 'letə 'mei not əv bin kə'rektli ə˅drest.
'ɔːtnt ʃi tu əv bin 'tould əbaut ði ˙aksidnt?

179 Modals in conditional clauses. It is often laid down that
wil, ʃal, wud and ʃud are not used in conditional clauses, that is,
in clauses introduced by if, ən'les, prə˅vaidid or some other adverb
or adverbial of condition, and rules are given for agreement of
tenses between a principal clause and a subordinate conditional
clause. A more accurate statement of the case is that modals are
used freely in conditional clauses if their modal meaning is required,
but they are not introduced merely as temporals to form a future
or conditional tense.

The following examples of modals used in conditional clauses
which are subordinate to principal clauses also containing modals
will illustrate this point, and the explanations given in brackets
(which, it will be noticed, are all in the present or past tense) will
make the function of the modal clear.

if 'ju l luk ˙aːftə ðə ˌl⋀gidʒ, 'ai l ˙get ðə ˅tikits.
        (wil = if you're willing to . . .)
if ˅hiː kən ˌduː it, 'sou kən ˅ai.
        (kan = if he's able to . . .)
if 'ai mei ˌhelp, it | ˅suːn bi ˌfiniʃt.
        (mei = if I'm allowed to . . .)
if ai ˅m⋀st ˌvout, ai ʃl 'vout ə˅geinst ju. ..
        (m⋀st = if I'm obliged to . . .)
if i ˅ɔːt tə ˌduː it, hi ˅wil.
        (ɔːt tu = if he has a moral obligation to . . .)
if ai ˅niːdnt ˌgou tə ˌwəːk, ai ˅ʃaːnt.
        (niːdnt = if I'm not obliged to . . .)
if ju 'deənt ˙spiːk ˅fraŋkli, ju l ri˅gret it ˌleitə.
        (deənt = if you're too diffident to . . .)
if ju d 'kiːp ˅stil, ai ʃəd ˅suːn ˌfiniʃ.
        (wud = if you were willing to . . .)
if i ʃəd ˅kɔːl, ai l 'giv im jɔː ˅mesidʒ.
        (ʃud = if by chance he were to . . .)

if ju kəd ˇweit ə ˌminit, ai d 'gou ˇwið ju.
   (kud = if it were possible for you to . . .)
if ai mait 'boru ə ᵛkaː, ai ʃəd ˇsuːn bi ˌbak.
   (mait = if I were allowed to . . .)

The above list includes examples of all the modals except ʃal, which is semantically unsuited for use in conditional clauses, though it is possible to imagine somewhat far-fetched cases in which it might be used.

Below are shown some of the above examples with the modal meaning removed from the subordinate clause:

if 'juː luk ˙aːftə ðə ˌlʌgidʒ, 'ai l ˙get ðə ˇtikits.
if ˇai ˌhelp, it | ˇsuːn bi ˌfiniʃt.
if ju 'dount ˙spiːk ˌfraŋkli, ju l riˇgret it ˌleitə.
if ju 'kept ˏstil, ai ʃəd ˇsuːn ˌfiniʃ.

Similarly, the modal perfect tenses are used in conditional clauses only when the modal meaning is required. The modals most used in such cases are oːt, wud, ʃud, kud and mait.

Note that in the first of the following examples d stands for wud in both clauses.

if ju d əv ˇweitid ə ˌminit, ai d əv 'gon ˇwið ju.
if ai mait əv 'borud ə ˏkaː, ai ʃəd əv bin 'bak ˇsuːnə.
if i 'oːt tu əv bin ˇwəːkiŋ təˌdei, ðei d əv ˇtould əs sou.
if ʃi kəd əv bin 'kept ˏstil, ai ʃəd əv 'finiʃt ˇsuːnə.

The following examples show these four sentences with the modal meaning removed from the subordinate clause. Since the sentences contained past tense modals the tense now used is a past perfect, and the weak form d therefore stands for had in the conditional clause.

if ju d ˇweitid ə ˌminit, ai d əv 'gon ˇwið ju.
if ai d 'borud ə ˏkaː, ai ʃəd əv bin 'bak ˇsuːnə.
if i d bin ˇwəːkiŋ təˌdei, ðei d əv ˇtould əs sou.
if ʃi d bin 'kept ˏstil, ai ʃəd əv 'finiʃt ˇsuːnə.

Except in the case of three 1—2—1 verbs (§135) and various 1—1—1 verbs (§137) there is no fear of ambiguity in the weak form d, since wud is always followed by an infinitive and had by a past participle.

MEANINGS OF THE MODALS

180 Ordinary meanings. A semantic analysis of the twelve modals is necessarily complicated, because most of them have more than one meaning and some meanings can be expressed by more than one modal. The lists below, giving the principal meanings of the modals, are followed by simple examples with paraphrases to make the meanings clear, while the variations are considered in detail in §§181–9.

Affirmative:		*Negative:*	
wil	Willingness	wount	Unwillingness
ʃal	Obligation	ʃaːnt	Prohibition
kan	Ability	kaːnt	Inability
mei	Permission	meint	Prohibition
mʌst	Obligation	mʌsn̩t	Prohibition
oːt	Advisability	oːtn̩t	Inadvisability
(niːd)		niːdn̩t	Exemption
(deə*)		deənt	Diffidence
wud	Willingness	wudn̩t	Unwillingness
ʃud	Advisability	ʃudn̩t	Inadvisability
kud	Ability	kudn̩t	Inability
mait	Permission	maitn̩t	Prohibition

Examples of the affirmative meanings, except in the cases of niːd and deə, which are shown in the negative.

hi l ˈduː it.	He's willing to do it.
hi ʃl ˈduː it.	I promise to make (*or* let) him do it.
hi kən ˈduː it.	He's able (*or* has time) to do it.
hi mei ˈduː it.	He has permission to do it.
hi məs ˈduː it.	He's obliged to do it.
hi ˌoːt tə ˈduː it.	It's advisable for him to do it.
hi ˈniːdn̩t ˌduː it.	He isn't obliged to do it.
hi ˈdeənt ˌduː it.	He's too diffident to do it.
hi d ˈduː it.	He would be willing to do it.
hi ʃəd ˈduː it.	It would be advisable for him to do it.
hi kəd ˈduː it.	He would be able to do it.
hi mait ˈduː it.	(I said) he had permission to do it.

181 **Alternative meanings.** A number of modals have these. When they are used in these meanings the affirmative forms are always stressed, and therefore have no weak pronunciation, and the contracted negatives of mei and mait are not used in statements. These devices help to show which meaning is intended in contexts where there might otherwise be ambiguity.

Affirmative:		*Negative:*	
'wil	Wilfulness	'wount	Wilfulness
'wud	Wilfulness	'wudn̩t	Wilfulness
'mei	Possibility	'mei not	Possibility
'mait	Possibility	'mait not	Possibility
'mʌst	Inference	'kaːnt	Negative Inference

Examples of the affirmative meanings, showing the stresses, and consequent strong forms of the modals.

hi 'wil ˇduː it.   He insists on doing it.
hi 'wud ˇduː it.   He insisted on doing it.
hi 'mei ˇduː it.   It's possible that he'll do it.
hi 'mait ˇduː it.   It's just possible that he'll do it.
hi 'mʌst əv ˇdʌn it.   I assume (*or* infer) that he's done it.

Negatives:

hi 'mei not ˇduː it.   It's possible that he isn't going to do it.
hi 'kaːnt əv ˇdʌn it.   I infer that he hasn't done it.

The modals ɔːt and ʃud suggest a rather less confident inference. See examples in §188.

182 **Willingness and wilfulness.** It is nearly always stated in English grammars that the meaning of wil is "wish, intention, resolution, determination or emphasis." All these renderings are misleading since affirmative conjugators are normally unstressed and the meaning of unstressed wil (with its weak forms | and l) is willingness to do something, while wount expresses unwillingness:

ai l 'send it ət ˏwʌns. = I'm willing to send it at once.
wil ju 'liːv wʌn fə ˊmiː? = Are you willing to leave one for me?
hi 'wount ˙kʌm ˏəːli. = He's unwilling to come early.

This last example might be interpreted by the more emphatic: "He's wilful, and persists in not coming early," which provides the link that probably causes the confusion of the meanings of stressed and unstressed wil, since by reversing the vocabulary we need the stressed wil:

    hi 'wil ˈkʌm ˌleit. = He's wilful, and persists in coming late.

In order to arrive at the real normal meaning of wil it is essential to envisage it, not in isolation, where there is an automatic temptation to stress it, but in context, in its normal unstressed condition.

183 Willingness and the future. While, as we have seen in §182, the usual meaning of wil—wount is willingness—unwillingness, there are contexts in which it is not logical to introduce these meanings. In such cases the modal feeling disappears and these finites express a pure future—in other words, they are reduced to the function of temporals, and are, in fact, the finites that are most frequently used to form a future tense. The question whether these finites have modal meaning or not depends in some degree upon whether the sentence is a question or a statement and upon whether the subject is in the 1st, 2nd or 3rd person. On the other hand, it is not affected by whether the subject is singular or plural, or whether the finite is affirmative or negative.

The way in which the modal and temporal functions of wil—wount are distributed in both questions and statements is tabulated below. Examples are given, with explanations of the meanings usually attached to them, and reasons are adduced for the distribution shown.

[*Meanings of* wil—wount *in Questions.*]

Modal questions	Person	Temporal questions
—	1st	—
wil juː?	2nd	wil juː?
wil ðei (hiː, ʃiː, it)?	3rd	wil ðei (hiː, ʃiː, it)?

Modal questions.

1. It is obviously absurd to ask someone else if one is willing to do something; there is therefore no modal question in the 1st person.

2. A question whether the hearer is willing to do something is very natural and common, thus:

    'wil ju 'help mi? = Are you willing to help me?

3. The hearer may be better informed than the speaker about the willingness of a third person to do something; we therefore have:

'wil ʃi 'help mi? = Is she (Will she be) willing to help me? (You know her better than I do.)

Temporal questions.

1. Again, it is absurd to ask someone what one is going to do in the future; there is therefore no temporal question in the first person except for the idioms wil ai 'duː? meaning "Am I sufficiently well dressed for the occasion?" and wil 'ai duː? meaning "Do you think I can do the job satisfactorily?"

2. Questions may be asked about what the hearer will do in the future, in contexts in which there need be no suggestion of willingness, thus:

'wil ju bi ət 'houm tə'moru 'aːftə'nuːn? = Is it part of your programme to be at home tomorrow afternoon?

When it is desired to show that no modal meaning is intended in a situation where one might be understood, the aspect of activity is often used, thus:

'wil ju 'giv ðəm ə 'miːl? = Please give them a meal.   (Modal.)
'wil ju bi 'giviŋ ðəm ə 'miːl? = A request for information without any modal meaning.

3. In 3rd person questions there are many contexts that do not admit the idea of willingness, especially if the subject is inanimate:

'wil ʃi 'laik ðə 'buk?   'wil ðei ri'membə mi?
'wil it bi 'redi in 'taim?   'wount ðei bi 'ouvə'dʌn?

[*Meanings of* wil—wount *in Statements.*]

Modal statements	Person	Temporal statements
ai (wiː) wil.	1st	—
—	2nd	juː wil.
ðei (hiː, ʃiː, it) wil	3rd	ðei (hiː, ʃiː, it) wil

Modal statements.

1. A statement that the speaker is willing to do something is very natural and common, thus:

149

ai I 'duː it ət ˏwʌns. ⎫ = ⎧ I'm willing to do these things to
ai I 'siː ju təˏmoru. ⎭   ⎩ please you or because you wish it.

2. As one cannot tell the hearer what he is willing to do there is no modal statement in the 2nd person.

3. One may know better than the hearer what a third person is willing to do, and we may therefore have:

ˏhiː I 'duː it ət ˏwʌns. ⎫ = ⎧ I've asked him, and he's expressed
ˏhiː I 'siː ju təˏmoru. ⎭   ⎩ his willingness to do these things.

Temporal statements.

1. Careful speakers do not use **wil** as a temporal in 1st person statements. The position appears to be somewhat as follows. Some speakers of English feel modal force much more strongly than others, and in particular the modal force of **wil**. They feel that a sentence like: ai I bi 'pliːzd tə ˋsiː ju means "I'm willing to be pleased to see you," which is either pontifical or nonsensical, and they would therefore say: ai ʃl bi 'pliːzd tə ˋsiː ju, which states a fact without any modal undertone. Such speakers avoid using ai wil with verbs expressing feelings or involuntary mental processes, and in other cases where it is not suitable to express willingness to perform the act. On the other hand they take care to say ai I (ai wil) and wi I (wiː wil) when the action will affect the person addressed; they feel that ʃal would be impolite, being too decided—provided, of course, that the verb is not one expressing feelings.

2. Statements without any modal implication are often made about what will happen to the hearer or about how he will react to something:

ju 'wount ˙faind im ət ˙houm ˏ/nau.   Pure information.
ju I ˋlaik ˏðat ˏnjuː ˏbuk.   An expression of opinion.

3. In the 3rd person there are many situations in which a statement is made without any modal suggestion, especially if the subject is inanimate:

hi I bi 'veri ˏaŋgri wið ju.   An expression of opinion.
it 'wount ˙laːst fər ˏ/evə.   An expression of opinion.

The modal and temporal uses of **wud** correspond closely to those of **wil**, and the former finite could be used instead of the latter in any of the examples given above. The effect would be to make the sentence sound more tentative or polite, and in some cases to suggest or introduce a condition, thus:

'wud ju 'help mi? Politely suggesting "if I asked you?"
'wud it bi 'redi in 'taim? Under certain conditions.
ai d 'duː it ət ˎwʌns. —— if I were you.
it 'wudṇt 'laːst fər ˏevə. Under certain conditions.

An affirmative idiom using unstressed **wud** gives the meaning of custom or habit in the past; this is more literary than spoken:

ðei wud 'gou fər ə ˎwoːk in ði ˏiːvniŋz. = They used to go for a walk.

There is also an idiomatic use of stressed 'wud as a direct past tense, in which case it means "to persist in":

hi 'wud ˎaːgju əbaut ˏevriθiŋ. = He persisted in arguing.

Another idiomatic use of this modal is to express a protest against another person's action and to suggest that it was typical of that person. The finite then usually takes a falling tone:

'juː ˎwud ˏduː ˏˎðat.   'ðei ˎwud ˏmis ðə ˏtrein.

184 Obligation and the future. Another finite which may form a pure future tense under certain conditions is ʃal—ʃaːnt. Though the modal meanings of these affirmative and negative forms are obligation and prohibition respectively there are contexts in which it is not logical to introduce these meanings. In such cases the modal feeling disappears and the finites express a pure future—in other words, they are reduced to the function of temporals. While the modal and temporal uses of ʃal—ʃaːnt are subject to the same factors as operate in the case of **wil**, the arrangement is different, and on the modal side there is an added complication arising from the fact that ʃal suggests that the obligation is imposed by the 2nd person in questions and by the 1st person in statements, irrespective of the person used as the subject of the verb.

The way in which the modal and temporal functions of ʃal—ʃaːnt are distributed in both questions and statements is tabulated below. Reasons are adduced for the distribution shown and examples are given, with explanations of the meanings usually attached to **them**.

[*Meanings of* ʃal—ʃaːnt *in Questions.*]

Modal questions	*Person*	*Temporal questions*
ʃal ai (wiː)?	1st	ʃal ai (wiː)?
—	2nd	—
ʃal ðei (hiː, ʃiː, it)?	3rd	—

Modal questions.

1. The modal question ʃal ai? is a most important idiom conveying an offer to do something for somebody, usually the hearer. It is used even in the United States, where other uses of ʃal have been largely abandoned.

> 'ʃal ai 'help ju? = Would you like me to help you? If so, I will.
> 'ʃal wi ˙teik ə 'taksi? = We'll take a taxi if you like.

In some cases ʃal ai? is a request for advice:

> 'witʃ wʌn ʃ| ai ˏtʃuːz?   'wot ʃ| ai ˏrait əbaut?

2. It is clearly absurd to ask someone if he will oblige himself to do something; there is therefore no modal question in the 2nd person.

3. The modal question in the 3rd person is an offer to get a third person to do something for the hearer if the latter wishes it.

> 'ʃal ðə ˙meid 'briŋ ju ə ˙kʌp əv 'kofi? = Would you like a cup of coffee? If so, I'll ask the maid to bring you one.
> 'ʃal ðə ˙matə bi 'lukt 'intu? = Do you want the matter looked into? If so, I'll have that done.

Temporal questions.

1. In certain contexts ʃal ai? loses its ordinary modal meaning and becomes a question asking for the hearer's opinion on something concerning oneself:

> 'ʃal ai bi in 'taim? Asking for information.
> 'ʃal ai 'laik ðis ˙buk? Asking for an opinion.

2. The question ʃal juː? is logically temporal and used to be employed freely, but for a good many years now it has fallen into disuse, having been replaced by 'aː ju 'gouiŋ tu?

3. There is no temporal question with ʃal in the 3rd person.

[*Meanings of* ʃal—ʃaːnt *in Statements.*]

Modal statements	Person	Temporal statements
—	1st	ai (wiː) ʃal
juː ʃal	2nd	—
ðei (hiː, ʃiː, it) ʃal	3rd	—

Modal statements.

1. One does not normally say that one is going to make oneself do something, and there is no modal statement in the 1st person.

2. In 2nd person statements ʃal—ʃaːnt are always strongly modal, conveying the idea of an undertaking given by the speaker. This may take the form of a threat of something unpleasant or a promise of something pleasant:

    ju ʃ| bi ˋpʌniʃt if ju ˌdount biˌheiv jəself.   Threat.
    ju 'ʃaːnt ˙gou tə ðə ˋpaːti if ju ə sou ˌnoːti.   Threat.
    ju ʃ| 'hav ə ˋbaisik| if ju ˌpaːs joːr igˌzam.   Promise.
    ju 'ʃaːnt ri˙gret haviŋ ˇhelpt mi.   Promise.

3. In 3rd person statements ʃal—ʃaːnt are again strongly modal in the sense that the speaker undertakes to do something that affects the subject of the verb, this again amounting to a threat or a promise, according to the nature of the action.

    hi ʃ| bi ˋpʌniʃt if i ˌdʌznt biˌheiv imself.   Threat.
    ʃi 'ʃaːnt get əˇwei wið it.   Threat.
    joː 'ʃuːz ʃ| bi ˙redi in ən ˋauə.   Promise.
    ðei 'ʃaːnt bi dis˙təːbd əˇgein.   Promise.

Temporal statements.

1. In 1st person statements careful speakers use ʃal—ʃaːnt consistently in preference to wil—wount when it is desirable to avoid any suggestion that action is being taken for the benefit of someone else or because another person (possibly the hearer) wishes it to be taken. Notice the contrasts:

    ai ʃ| 'foun ðəm ət ˌwʌns.   (On my own initiative.)
    ai l 'foun ðəm ət ˌwʌns.   (Because they want to speak to me.)
    ai ˋʃaːnt bi əˌwei ˌloŋ.   (This is for your information.)
    ai ˋwount bi əˌwei ˌloŋ.   (I know you want me back soon.)

The other case in which ʃal is to be preferred in 1st person statements (before verbs expressing feelings, etc.) has been dealt with in §183.

2, 3. The finite ʃal is always modal in 2nd and 3rd person statements.

Use of ʃal with Multiple Subjects.

If the 1st person pronoun forms part of a multiple subject ʃal is not used in statements, being replaced by wil.

'juː ənd ˙ai | bi 'hiəriŋ əbaut it ˌleitə.
'ʃiː ənd ˙ai | bi 'fiːliŋ ˋtaiəd ˌaːftə ðə ˌdʒəːni.
'dʒon, ˙meəri ənd ˙ai | 'niːd ˙moː ˋhelp.

Compare:

wi ʃl bi 'hiəriŋ əbaut it ˌleitə.
wi ʃl bi 'fiːliŋ ˋtaiəd ˌaːftə ðə ˌdʒəːni.
wi ʃl 'niːd ˙moː ˋhelp.

In questions, however, ʃal is used in most cases where it would be used with a single subject.

ʃl 'juː ənd ˙ai 'staːt ʹnau ?
ʃl 'meəri ənd ˙ai iks'pekt ju fə ʹlʌntʃ ?
ʃl 'dʒon, ˙meəri ənd ˙ai 'entə˙tein ðə ʹgests ?

The use of ʃud follows fairly closely that of ʃal, and this substitution could be made in the majority of the examples given in this section. In some cases its use would be restricted to indirect speech and in others it would suggest advisability rather than obligation. Examples:

'ʃud wi ˙teik ə ʹtaksi ? = Would it be a good idea?
'ʃud ðə ˙matə bi 'lukt ʹintu ? = Ought it to be looked into?
'ʃud ai ʹlaik ðis ˙buk ? (If I were to read it?)
hi 'sed ju ʃəd bi ˋpʌniʃt if ju ˌdidn̩t bi‚heiv jəself. (Indirect.)
ju ˋpromist ðət ðei ˌʃudn̩t bi dis‚təːbd ə‚ˏgein. (Indirect.)
ai ˋtould ju ai ˌʃudn̩t bi ə‚wei ‚loŋ. (Indirect.)

185 **Ability, opportunity, permission, possibility.** These ideas and their opposites are conveyed by the kan and mei families of modals, but there is an ever-increasing tendency for the former to encroach on the field traditionally occupied by the latter, to the extent that in the speech of some people, particularly in the United

States, the mei family is virtually disappearing and the kan family
is becoming so grossly overworked as to lead to confusion of meaning
in some cases.

There are certain limitations as to the tenses in which these
modals may be used, but the present-tense forms may always refer
to the present and the past-tense forms to the conditional, in any
of their meanings. The restrictions occur in references to the past
and the future, and examples of these tenses are given in the
following analysis, which attempts to show present-day practice
among careful speakers of English.

Ability, particularly with reference to acquired skills.

| Past | kud: | ai kəd 'woːk wen ai wəz 'tuː jiəz ˌould. |
| Fut. | None. | (Use wil (ʃal) bi eibḷ tu.) |

Inability.

| Past | kudṇt: | hi 'kudṇt ˙woːk til i wəz ˌθriː. |
| Fut. | None. | (Use wount (ʃaːnt) bi eibḷ tu.) |

Opportunity, in the sense of ability to do something because time,
one's duties or other circumstances permit it.

| Past | None. | (Use woz (wəː*) eibḷ tu.) |
| Fut. | kan: | 'kan ju ˙kʌm ənd 'siː mi ˙nekst ʹwiːk? |

Lack of opportunity.

| Past | kudṇt: | ai ᵛlukt fə him, bət ai 'kudṇt ʹfaind im. |
| Fut. | kaːnt: | ai m ᵛsori, bət ai 'kaːnt ʹsiː ju tə,moru. |

Permission. The popular use of kan in this sense is widely
accepted.

| Past | None, except in indirect speech, then mait (kud). |
| Fut. | mei (kan): ju mei (kən) 'hav wʌn tə'moru. |

Prohibition. The use of kaːnt in this sense is widely accepted.

| Past | None, except in indirect speech, then maitṇt (kudṇt). |
| Fut. | meint (kaːnt): dei 'meint (kaːnt) hav ˙eni tə˅,moru. |

Possibility. In this meaning mei and mait are always stressed,
and the latter may be used as a direct tense to suggest a more
remote possibility than mei. A falling tone on either of these
finites increases the suggestion of doubt.

Past   None, but see §§195 and 203.
Fut.   'mei: ðei 'mei bi ˙ðeə ˙nekst ˎmʌnθ.
        'mait: hi ˎmait ˏkʌm on ˎtjuːzdi.

Negative possibility. Here mait not may be used as a present
or future, to suggest a remote negative possibility.

Past   None, but see §§195 and 203.
Fut.   'mei not: ðei 'mei not bi ˋðeə ˏnekst ˏwiːk.
        'mait not: hi 'mait not ˋwont ə ˏholidi.

The substitution of kan for mei in the sense of possibility when
the subject is inanimate and cannot therefore possess any "ability"
is a comparatively modern innovation. It is admissible in the
passive voice, because it suggests that somebody has the ability
to influence the inanimate subject. Thus, ˋðat kən bi ˏdʌn means
that somebody has the ability or the opportunity to do it. On the
other hand, a sentence in the active voice, such as 'ðis sitjuˏeiʃn̩
'kan ('kud) ˙liːd tu ˎwoː suggests that the situation is endowed
with an inherent ability to lead to war if it so desires, which is
absurd. The established form used in such a case, 'ðis sitjuˏeiʃn̩
'mei ('mait) ˙liːd tu ˎwoː, merely suggests the possibility of war
developing from the situation.

186 Pleading and reproach. These two ideas are conveyed by
using a special intonation pattern with the modals mait and niːdn̩t.
The former asks for something to be done that is not being done,
and the latter asks for the cessation of something that is being
done. The special intonation pattern that gives these meanings
consists of a fall on the modal, followed by a Tune III later in
the sentence.

Pleading.

This is conveyed by using one of the three direct modal tenses,
and is a plea for something to be done—or not done—in the present
or future. It may take on the nature of a protest.

ju ˋmait ˏweit fə ˎ˯miː.   ju ˋniːdn̩t bi sou ˎ˯ruːd.
ðei ˋmait bi ˏhelpiŋ tə ˎ˯pak.   ðei ˋniːdn̩t bi ˏθroun əˎ˯wei.

Reproach.

This is conveyed by using one of the three perfect modal tenses, and is a protest against some action or lack of action in the past.

ðei ˋmait əv ˌkʌm ˎɔːliə.   ðei ˋniːdn̩t əv ˌteikən it ᵛoːl.
ju ˋmait əv bin ˎhelpiŋ mi.   hi ˋniːdn̩t əv bin ᵛtould.

For the meaning of this structure without the special tune, see §203.

187 Obligation—exemption and permission—prohibition. The relationship between these four ideas can be shown in diagrammatic form:

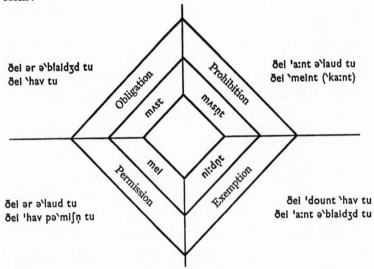

The top half of the diagram represents constraint on the subject; on the left constraint to do something (obligation) and on the right constraint not to do something (prohibition).

The bottom half of the diagram represents freedom for the subject; on the left to do what he wants to do (permission) and on the right not to do what he doesn't want to do (exemption).

The diagram also shows that though exemption is the diametrical opposite of obligation (expressed by mʌst) it is not expressed by the negative form of this modal, but by niːdn̩t, while mʌsn̩t expresses prohibition, the diametrical opposite of permission, which is expressed by mei. Stated simply:

The opposite of mʌst is niːdn̩t;
The opposite of mʌsn̩t is mei.

Other expressions that are more or less synonymous with the
four modals shown in the diagram are given in each corner. For
the affirmative modal niːd, see §198.

188 Inference. This is a secondary meaning of mʌst, oːt and
ʃud, which is differentiated from their primary meanings by their
being stressed in all cases. An example of this distinction made
by means of stress is given below. When they are used in this
sense these modals may be regarded as equivalent to the clause:
"It is logical to suppose that. . . ." They may express this meaning
before any of the six infinitives, but are probably most frequently
used before the three perfect infinitives. The modal mʌst is more
common in this sense than the other two. Examples:

it 'ʃud bi əbaut 'haːf paːst ˈnain, ˌnau, ai ˈθiŋk.
ju 'mʌs bi kənˈfjuːziŋ mi wið 'sʌmwʌn ˌels.
ðei ˈleft ət ˌveit, sou ðei ˈoːt tu əv əˌraivd bai ˌvnau.
'sʌmbədi 'mʌst əv bin ˈtoːkiŋ əbaut mi.
'ðis ˈruːm 'mʌs bi riˈzəːvd fə ˈmembəz.
ðə 'diskaunt 'mʌst əv bin ˈteikən ˈof oːlˈredi.

Notice that the fifth of the above examples means "I assume
that this room is reserved for members," whereas

'ðis ˈruːm məs bi riˈzəːvd fə ˈmembəz

means "I give orders that this room is to be reserved for members."

When making a negative inference the logic of this structure is
preserved by changing from these modals to kaːnt or kudn̩t, to
give the meaning: "It isn't possible that. . . ." Examples:

it ˈkaːnt bi əz ˌleit əz ˌvðat, ˈʃuəli!
ju ˈkaːnt bi ˌθiŋkiŋ əv ˅liːviŋ jet!
ðei 'ounli ˈleft ət ˌveit, sou ðei ˈkudn̩t əv əˌraivd ˌvjet.
ju ˈkaːnt əv bin ˌweitiŋ əz ˌloŋ əz ˅ai hav.
'ðat ˈhat ˈkaːnt bi inˌtendid tə bi ˌvwoːn!
ðə 'diskaunt ˈkaːnt əv bin ˌteikən ˌof oːlˌredi.

In American speech mʌsn̩t is in general use instead of kaːnt in
this context.

Inference of a slighter character, giving the feeling of: "It's my impression that . . .", is conveyed by an unstressed wil or wud, but care must be taken in using this structure, as in some cases it gives a dialectal flavour to the speech, especially in the direct tenses. Examples:

it | bi əbaut 'haːf paːst ˋnain, ˏnau.
'sʌmbədi | əv bin ˋtoːkiŋ əbaut mi.
ðə 'diskaunt | əv bin 'teikən ˙of oːlˋredi.
ðei 'left ət ˇeit, sou ðei d əv əˈraivd bai ˋten.

189 Contrary implication. When used before a perfect infinitive some of the modals refer to the past and carry a contrary implication, that is, the affirmative suggests that the action did not take place, while the negative supposes that it did. These modals are:

Affirmative: oːt, wud, ʃud, kud, mait.

Negative: oːtn̩t, niːdn̩t, wudn̩t, ʃudn̩t, kudn̩t, mait not.

The following are examples of sentences containing this implication:

Affirmative:

hi 'oːt tu əv bin ˋweitiŋ fər əs. (but he wasn't—or isn't)
ðə 'doktə wəd əv ˋkʌm if ju d ˏkoːld im. (but as you didn't, he didn't)
ai 'ʃud əv ˋnoun ju d bi ˏleit. (but it didn't occur to me)
wi 'kud əv bin ˋwoːkiŋ ˏhoum. (instead of waiting for a taxi)
ju 'mait əv bin 'badli ˋhəːt. (but you weren't)

Negative:

ju 'oːtn̩t tu əv ˋtould ðəm. (but you did)
ai 'niːdn̩t əv ˋwʌrid sou ˏmʌtʃ. (but I did)
it 'wudn̩t əv bin ˋbroukən if ju ˏhadn̩t ˏmuːvd it. (but you did, and it was)
ðei 'ʃudn̩t əv iksˋpektid əs. (but they did)
ju ˋkudn̩t əv bin ˏθiŋkiŋ ˯ðat! (but evidently you were)
hi 'mait not əv riˋmembəd əs. (but he did)

190 Specific verbs resembling modals. There are a few verbs that have the same form as some of the modals. They are, of course, all specific verbs, and as such have a full set of tenses and verbals, including the infinitive. They all form their past tense and past participles regularly and the 3rd person of the present tense takes the s-form. Though some of them are little used, the student should know of their existence in order that he should not be mystified when he comes across them. They are:

tə wil = to exert power over somebody or to leave property by will or testament.

tə kan = to preserve food by putting it into a sealed metal container.

tə mei = to gather hawthorn flowers in the month of May.

tə mʌst = to become musty or spoilt by damp, to moulder.

tə niːd = to want, to require.

tə deə* = to have enough courage or effrontery to do something.

The last two verbs have meanings similar to those of the corresponding modals and may be used instead of them. Unlike the modals, they can be used in affirmative sentences and are conjugated with duː, dʌz and did. They may take nouns as objects, but when they are followed by a verb in the infinitive this is preceded by tu, always after niːd and usually after deə*.

There is also a verb tə niːd (spelt knead) which means to work up a mixture of powder and liquid (e.g., flour and water) into a firm mass by pressing and moving it.

FORMS OF THE MODALS

191 Strong, weak and contracted forms. Seven of the affirmative modals have various weak forms, used in certain phonetic and grammatical contexts which are described in detail in §§192–204, examples being given of their use.

A distinction has to be made between modals whose affirmative forms are basically unstressed (i.e., unstressed unless there is a special reason for stressing them) and those that are basically stressed (i.e., always stressed, even when there is no special reason for stressing them). This distinction is important because some of the modals have more than one meaning, and the presence or

absence of stress—and consequently of weakening in some cases—
is a factor in indicating which meaning is intended.

Since the negative modals are only very occasionally unstressed
they have no weak forms properly so called, but in certain cases
they may undergo elisions or assimilations. These are described
in §204. The normal negative forms, which are otherwise invariable,
are best referred to as contracted forms, to distinguish them from
the two-word forms (consisting of the affirmative finite followed by
the adverb not) which are used in formal written English.

The twelve modals will now be considered in detail. The examples
in which the various pronunciations are given have been chosen to
present the widest possible variety of tenses, thus providing a
reasonably complete guide to the use of these important conjugators.

192 wil—wount. Weak forms |, l. When this modal is used
in the meaning of willingness—unwillingness it is basically unstressed and the weak forms are used. In the meaning of wilfulness
it is basically stressed and the weak forms are not used. In the
former meaning and as a pure future it is used freely before all
the six infinitives.

Negative form.

wount in all cases:
   ˇðei ˌwount ˌtel ju.   'wount ðei bi ˙haviŋ ˈdinə?
   'wount ʃi əv ˈweitid?   ju 'wount bi əˈlaud ˇin.

Affirmative form in stressed positions.

wil in all cases:
   'wil ju ˈweit fə mi?   'wil it əv bin disˈtroid?
   'juː ˌwil bi ˌteikiŋ ə ˌrisk!   ðei 'wil ˙peint ˙evriθiŋ ˌred.

Affirmative form in unstressed positions.

wil (1) when not followed by a specific verbal:
   ˇhiː ˌmait ˌkʌm, bət ai 'dount ˙θink ˇʃiː wil.
   ˇwiː ʃļ əv ˌfiniʃt, bət 'weðə ˇjuː wil iz ˇdautʃļ.
wil (2) in initial positions:
   wil ˈdʒon bi ˙kʌmiŋ?   wil 'juː bi ˙peid ˈtuː?
l after pronouns ending in a vowel:
   ju l 'faind it in ˌðeə.   ˇhiː l əv ˌfiniʃt ˌfəːst.
   ʃi l bi 'broːt bai ˌkaː.   'huː l bi ˙pleiiŋ ˇðis ˌpiːs?

| (or əl) in all other cases:

'witʃ | ju ˇhav?　　　　　　　　'meəri | əv bin ˋwəːkiŋ tə‚dei.
it | əv bin ˋklouzd.　　　　　　'ðis | əv 'toːt ju ə ˋlesn̩.

193 ʃal—ʃaːnt. Weak forms ʃ|, ʃl. Whether it means obligation
—prohibition or is used as a pure future this modal is basically
unstressed. It can, with certain limitations as to person, be used
before all the six infinitives.

Negative form.

ʃaːnt in all cases:

'ʃaːnt wi bi ˊleit?　　　　　　　ai 'ʃaːnt əv ˎfiniʃt.
'ʃaːnt ai bi diˊleiiŋ ju?　　　　　'ʃaːnt wi əv ˙had iˊnʌf bai ðen?

Affirmative form in stressed positions.

ʃal in all cases:

‚wot 'ʃal ai ˎduː?　　　　　　　ai 'tel ju ai ˋʃal əv ‚dʌn it!
'wiː ˎʃal bi ‚leit!　　　　　　　'ʃal ai bi ˊteliŋ im əˈbaut it?

Affirmative form in unstressed positions.

ʃal when not followed by a specific verbal:

ˋhiː ‚mei not bi ‚stʌdiiŋ, bət ˇai ʃal bi.
ˋjuː | ‚laik it, bət weðə ˇwiː ʃal iz ˋdautʃl.

ʃl sometimes before a vowel:

ʃl ˊai ˙kari it?　　　　　　　　'wot ʃl ai ˎduː?
wi ʃl əv ˋfiniʃt bai ‚ten ə‚klok.

ʃ| (or ʃəl) in all other cases:

ʃ| wi 'aːsk ðəm tə ˊtiː?　　　　　it ʃ| bi 'dʌn ət ˎwʌns.
ai ʃ| əv ˋleft bai ‚ðen.　　　　　wi ʃ| bi ˋsteiiŋ wið ðəm.
'veri ˇsuːn wi ʃ| əv bin 'weitiŋ fə ˙haːf ən ˋauə.
wi ʃ| əv bin ˋsiːn bi‚foː wi kən is‚keip.

194 kan—kaːnt. Weak form kən. Whether it means ability
—inability or opportunity—lack of opportunity, this modal is
basically unstressed. For kaːnt meaning negative inference,
see §196.

Negative form.

ka:nt in all cases:

'ka:nt ju ˙weit til tə'moru?   ʃi 'ka:nt ˙ri:d wiðaut ᵛgla:siz.
'ka:nt ju bi ˙getiŋ ˙on wið jo: 'wə:k?
ðə 'pa:s| 'ka:nt bi ˙poustid til tə`moru.

Affirmative form in stressed positions.

kan in all cases:

'kan ju ˙tʌtʃ ðə 'si:liŋ?—`jes, ai `kan.
hi ᵛkan bi ˙veri `na:sti.—'kan i?
'kan ai 'help ju?—ju 'kan if ju ᵛlaik.

Affirmative form in unstressed positions.

kan when not followed by a specific verbal:

`ðat wʌn ˌka:nt bi ˌmendid, bət ᵛðis kan bi.
`ju: ˌka:nt ˌdu: it, bət ᵛai kan.

kən in all other cases:

wi kən 'a:sk ðəm tə `ti:.   kən ʃi bi 'tould əbaut it 'nau?
ðei kən 'ounli ˙stei fər ə ᵛwi:k.
ai 'dount `θiŋk wi kən ˌdu: it, bət wi kən ᵛtrai.

195 mei—meint—mei not. No established weak forms. This modal has two regular meanings.

a. Permission—Prohibition.

When it is used in these meanings this modal is basically unstressed. It is sometimes used in the passive voice and in the aspect of activity, but never in the perfect tenses.

Negative form.

meint in all cases:

ju 'meint ˙hav eni ˌmoə.
'meint ðis ˙teib| bi 'mu:vd?—`nou, it `meint.

Affirmative form.

mei in all cases:

'mei wi 'smouk?—`jes, ju ˌmei.
`hi: ˌmʌsn̩ ˌdʒoin ˌin, bət ᵛju: mei.
mei 'ai bi 'leiiŋ ðə ˙teib| wail 'ju: ə 'kukiŋ?
mei ðə 'kla:s bi dis'mist?—it 'mei if ju ᵛlaik.

b. Possibility.

In this meaning the modal is basically stressed and the contracted negative form is not used in statements. The direct tenses refer to the present or the future, the perfect tenses to the past. All six infinitives are used.

Negative form.

meint sometimes in questions:
    'meint ʃi əv ə˙raivd wail wi wər ˈaut?
mei . . . not sometimes in questions:
    'mei ðei ˙not bi 'ðeər ɔːlˈredi?   'mei it ˙not bi 'tuː ˈleit?
mei not in all statements:
    hi 'mei not ˙wont tə ˋweit fər əs.
    'dʒon 'mei not əv əˋraivd ˌjet.
    ðei 'mei not əv bin iksˋpektiŋ əs.
    ʃi 'mei not əv bin ˙həːt veri ˌbadli.

Affirmative form.

mei in all cases:
    hi 'mei 'wont əs ðeər ˋəːli.
    ai 'mei bi 'teikiŋ ðə ˙tʃildrn əˋbrɔːd.
    ju 'mei bi ˋwontid ðis ˌaːftəˌnuːn.
    wi 'mei əv ˙mist ðə 'laːst ˌbʌs.
    ʃi 'mei əv bin ˋlukiŋ fər əs.
    it 'mei əv bin ˙sent tə ðə 'roŋ əˋdres.

196 mʌst and its opposites. Weak forms məs, məst. This modal has two regular meanings.

a. Obligation—Prohibition.

This antithesis is expressed by mʌst—mʌsn̩t, the weak forms being used, as the modal is basically unstressed. It is found frequently in the passive voice, infrequently in the aspect of activity and never in the perfect tenses.

Negative form.

mʌsn̩t in all cases:
    ju 'mʌsn̩t ˋrisk it.   ˋwai ˌmʌsn̩t ai bi ˌpleiiŋ?
    'ðis ˙buk 'mʌsn̩t bi ˙teikən əˋwei.

Affirmative form in stressed positions.

mʌst when not followed by a plosive:

ˈmʌst ju ˈmeik ˈoːl ðat ˈnoiz? ju ˈmʌst ˈstop ˈkritisaiziŋ mi.
ˈmʌst it bi ˈfiniʃt təˈdei?—ˈjes, it ˈmʌst.

mʌs before plosives:

ju ˈmʌs bi ˈmoː ˈkeəfl̩.   ˈðat s ˌsʌmθin ai ˈmʌs ˌduː.

Affirmative form in unstressed positions.

mʌst when not followed by a specific verbal:

ˈjuː ˌniːdn̩t ˌstei, bət ˈai ˈsəːtn̩li mʌst.

məst when not followed by a plosive:

wi məst ˈoːl duː auə ˈbest.   ju məst ˈweit til təˈmoru.

məs before plosives:

wi məs ˈgou ət ˌwʌns.   ai məs bi ˈgouiŋ ˌnau.
it məs bi ˈfiniʃt təˌdei.

b. Inference—Negative Inference.

These ideas are expressed by a heterogeneous collection of modals:

Affirmative:	mʌst	Negative:	kaːnt
Interrogative:	kan	Int.-Neg.:	meint

In this meaning all these modals are basically stressed and no weak forms are found. They are used freely with all the six infinitives.

Negative form in questions.

meint in all cases:

ˈwai ˌmeint ʃi əv əˌraivd?   ˈmeint it bi inˈtendid fə ˈjuː?

Negative form in statements.

kaːnt in all cases:

ju ˈkaːnt ˌmiːn ˌðat!   ðei ˈkaːnt bi ˌhoupiŋ tə ˇwin!
hi ˈkaːnt əv ˌdʌn it ˇjet.   ju ˈkaːnt əv bin ˈlisniŋ.
it ˈkaːnt bi ˌsould oːlˇredi.   ʃi ˈkaːnt əv bin ˈtould əbaut it.

Affirmative form in questions.

kan in all cases:

'kan it bi 'truː?   'kan ðei bi 'foluiŋ əs?
'kan wi əv ˈmist ðə 'təːniŋ?   'wot ˈkan ðei əv bin ˌtoːkiŋ
'kan ðei bi 'marid?   əbaut?
'kan it əv bin ˈteikən ə'wei?

Affirmative form in statements.

mʌst when not followed by a plosive:

'ðat ˈmʌst əˈnoi ðəm.   'ðat ˌmʌst əv ˌgivn̩ ðəm ə ˌʃok.
ʃi 'mʌst əv bin ˈliviŋ in ˈiŋglənd fər əbaut ə ˈjiə.

mʌs when followed by a plosive:

it 'mʌs ˈteik ə 'loŋ ˈtaim tə get ˌevriθiŋ ˌredi.
joː 'sistə ˈmʌs bi əˈtraktiŋ ə 'lot əv əˈtenʃn̩ in ˌðat ˌdres.
ju 'mʌs bi ˈtaiəd ˈaut ˌaːftə ðat ˌloŋ ˌwoːk.

197 oːt—oːtn̩t. No weak forms. This modal means, according
to context, anything from moral obligation to mere advisability.
It nearly always has some degree of stress, whatever its meaning.
It is used freely before all the six infinitives.

Negative form.

oːtn̩t in all cases:

'oːtn̩t ai tə 'foun ðəm?   ju ˈoːtn̩t tu əv ˌwʌrid əbaut ˌðat.
'oːtn̩t ju tə bi ˈgetiŋ 'redi? ʃi 'oːtn̩t tə bi əˈlaud tə ˈduː it.
'oːtn̩t ju tu əv bin ˈduːiŋ joː 'houmwəːk?
'ðis ˈsuːp 'oːtn̩t tu əv bin ˈboild sou ˌloŋ.

Affirmative form.

oːt in all cases:

'oːt ai tə 'sain ðis əˈgriːmənt?
ai 'θiŋk wi ˈoːt tə bi ˈstaːtiŋ ˌsuːn.
'oːt wi tu əv ˈkʌm sou ˈfaː wiðˈaut ˈteliŋ ði 'ʌðəz?
ai 'oːt tu əv bin ˈdigiŋ ðə ˈgaːdn̩, bət ai wəz 'tuː ˌtaiəd.
'oːt ðis ˈdiʃ tə bi ˈsəːvd 'hot oː ˌkould?
'ðis ˈwuːnd 'oːt tu əv bin əˈtendid tu ət ˈwʌns.

166

This modal is sometimes used in the affirmative instead of mʌst to suggest an inference or a probability:

ai 'θink ˙ðis ˙buk 'oːt tə bi ˙raːðər ˈintristiŋ.
ðei ˈstaːtid ˌəːli, sou ðei 'oːt tə bi ˈðeə bai ˌnau.

198 niːd—niːdn̩t. No weak forms. As shown in §187, the negative form of this modal expresses exemption from an obligation and is the opposite of mʌst. It is used before all the six infinitives, though rather less frequently with those of the aspect of activity. The affirmative form is never used unless there is an interrogative, negative, near negative or dubitative element in the sentence. This element may be in the same clause as the modal, or in a principal clause on which the modal clause depends.

Negative form.

niːdn̩t in all cases:

'niːdn̩t ai 'weit fə ðəm?—ˈnou, ju ˈniːdn̩t.
ˈwai ˌniːdn̩t ju ˌaːnsə ðə ˌletə?
'niːdn̩t 'eni əv ðə ˙men bi ˙peid?
ju ˈniːdn̩t ˌboðər əbaut ˌðat.
it 'niːdn̩t bi ˙dʌn təˇdei.

Affirmative form.

niːd in all cases:

In interrogative sentences:

'niːd ai ˙sei eni 'moə?　　　'wai niːd ju ˈboðə wið it?
'niːd ðei ˙stei eni 'loŋgə?　　'hau ˙loŋ niːd wi ˈkiːp ðəm?

With negative or near negative subject:

'noubodi niːd ˇnou əbaut it.　'ounli ˈtuː əv ju niːd ˌstei.
'niːd 'nʌn əv əs ˙weit?

With negative or near negative object:

sou ai niːd 'sei nou ˈmoə.　　ai niːd sei 'veri lit| ˇmoə.
'niːd wi ˙tʃeindʒ 'nʌθiŋ?

With negative or near negative adverb:

ju niːd 'nevə ˇwʌri əbaut it.　ai niːd 'haːdli ˙sei eni ˇmoə.
'niːd ai 'nevə ˙weit fə ðəm?　ju niːd 'skeəsli aːsk ˇwai.

After a principal clause with a negative or dubitative element:

'noubodi ˇsed ʃi niːd ˌstei.

'haːdli ˇenibodi ˌfelt wi niːd ˌaːnsə ðə ˙letə.

ðei ˌtould ˇnoubodi ðət wi niːd ˌbriŋ auə ˌtikits.

ai 'dount sə˙pouz ðei niːd 'weit eni ᵛlongə.

ai 'haːdli ˙θiŋk ju niːd 'kʌm ˙bak təᵛmoru.

ai 'daut weðə wi niːd ˇboðər əbaut it eni ˌlongə.

ai m 'not ˇʃuə weðə wʌn niːd ˇtip ðə ˌweitə.

199 deə*—deənt. No weak forms. The negative form of this
modal expresses feelings ranging from mere diffidence to outright
fear. Its use is largely confined to the present tense in the aspect
of accomplishment; it is met with occasionally in the perfect of
the same aspect, but it is very rare in the aspect of activity and
in the passive voice. The affirmative form is used only in similar
conditions to those described for niːd in §198.

Negative form.

deənt in all cases:

'deənt ju ˙tel im ðə ˈtruːθ?   ai 'deənt ˇtel ju wot ʃi ˌsed.

ˇwai ˌdeənt ju ˌtel im?   wi ˇdeənt ˌiːt eni ᵥmoə.

Affirmative form.

˙deə before consonants, deər in front of vowels.

In interrogative sentences:

d ju 'θiŋk i ˙deə ˈduː it?   'hau ˇdeə ju ˌtoːk tə mi laik ˌðat

'deər ai ˙teik ðə ˈrisk?   'deər ˈeni əv ju ˙aːnsə mi?

With negative or near negative subject:

'nouwʌn ˙deə ˇtoːk əbaut it.   'haːdli ᵛeniwʌn ˙deə ˇtrai it.

'deə ˈnʌn əv ju ˙spiːk ˙aut?

With negative or near negative object:

mai 'frendz ˙deə duː ˇnʌθiŋ.   hi 'deər ə˙tempt 'haːdli ˇeniθiŋ.

With negative or near negative adverb:

ðei 'nevə ˙deər əᵛpouz əs.   ai 'haːdli ˙deə ˇtel ju eni ˌmoə.

After a principal clause with a negative or dubitative element:

ai 'dount ˙θiŋk ʃi ˇdeə ˌgou bai əˌself.

ai 'wʌndə weðər i ˙deə ˙teik əˇnʌðə wʌn.

ai 'daut weðə ðei ˇdeər əˌkjuːz im əv disᵥonisti.

One affirmative phrase: ai ˈdeə ˌsei, survives as a common idiom meaning "I think it's possible (or likely)," and a similar idiom: ai ˈdeə ˌsweə*, is heard very occasionally.

200 wud—wudṇt. Weak forms wəd, d, ud or əd. Some speakers prefer to use ud rather than əd, especially if there is a possibility of confusion between wud and had, as is the case when a specific verb has identical forms for the infinitive and past participle, e.g., it ud kʌm (it would come) and it əd kʌm (it had come). The weak forms are not used when this modal has the meaning "insisted on." The modal is used freely before all the six infinitives.

Negative form.

wudṇt in all cases:

> ˈwudṇt it bi ˈbetə tu ꞌweit?   hi ˈwudṇt ꞌtel mi ˌwot i ˌwontid.
> ꞌjuː mait ˌlaik it, bət ꞛhiː wudṇt.

Affirmative form in stressed positions.

wud in all cases:

> ˈwud ju ꞌweit ə ˈmoumənt?   ˈðat ˌwud əv bin ə ˌgud aiˌdiə.

Affirmative form in unstressed positions.

wud when not followed by a specific verbal:

> ꞌðei wudṇt inˌdʒoi it, but ꞛjuː wud, ai θiŋk.

wəd in initial positions:

> wəd ju ˈlaik sm̩ ˈmoː ꞌtiː?   wəd ðei əv ˈlaikt ə ˈfjuː ꞌmoə?
> wəd ꞌoːl ðə ˈboiz əv bin əˈlaud ˈin?

d after vowels:

> ꞌmeəri d əv ˌlaikt ðəm.   ðei d ˈkʌm if ju ꞛaːskt ðəm.

ud (or əd) in all other cases:

> ˈwen ud ju ˈlaik tə ˌkʌm?   ˈdʒon ud bi ꞌweitiŋ fər əs.
> ꞌðat ud əv bin ˌnais.   ˈðat ud əv bin ꞛfoːsiŋ ði ˌiʃu.
> ˈwitʃ ˈgeit ud bi ˌklouzd?   ði ˈʌðəz ud əv bin ꞛteikən.

201 ʃud—ʃudṇt. Weak forms ʃəd, ʃd. This modal is basically unstressed, but must be stressed in the 1st person if it is to convey its modal meaning, since in that person the unstressed form is a normal temporal conjugator of the "conditional" tenses. In any case it is used freely before all the six infinitives.

Negative form.

ʃudn̩t in all cases:

ˈwai ˎʃudn̩t ai ˌmiːt ðəm?   ˈʃudn̩t wi bi ˙getiŋ ˊredi?
ʃi ˈʃudn̩t əv ˎweitid fə mi.   ju ˈʃudn̩t əv bin ˙draiviŋ sou ˎfaːst.
it ˈʃudn̩t bi ˙teikən əˎwei.   ˈʃudn̩t ðei əv bin ˊtould əbaut it?

Affirmative form in stressed positions.

ʃud in all cases:

ju ˈʃud əv ˎnoun ˌðat.   ˈʃud ai bi ˙putiŋ ðə ˊθiŋz əˈwei?

Affirmative form in unstressed positions.

ʃud when not followed by a specific verbal:

ˎjuː ˌwount ˌduː it əz ˌwel əz ᵛai ʃud.

ʃəd or ʃd in all other cases:

ai ʃəd ˎlaik wʌn əv ˌðouz veri ˎmʌtʃ.
wi ʃd əv ˈsiːn ᵛbetə frəm ˙ʌp ˎðeə.
wi ʃəd bi əˎraiviŋ bai ˌnau if wi d ˈstaːtid ˌəːliə.
ju ʃd əv bin ˈgetiŋ ˙redi fə ðə ˎpaːti.
ˈðat ˙medsin ʃəd bi ˙teikən in ˈplenti əv ˎwoːtə.
ai ʃd əv bin ˈdrivn̩ ˙mad bai də ˎnoiz if ai d ˌsteid.

The following two pairs of examples will show the difference between the use of the strong and weak forms in the first person:

wi ʃd əv ˎritn̩ tə ju if wi d ˌnoun joːr əˌdres.
wi ˈʃud əv ˎritn̩ tə ju, bət wi wə ˈtuː ˎbizi.
ai ʃd əv ˈteikən ˙ðat ˙medsin ˎəːliər if ju ˌhadn̩t ˌstopt mi.
ai ˈʃud əv ˙teikən ðat ˙medsin ˎəːliə, bət ai fəˎgot it.

The affirmative and negative forms of this modal can be used instead of mʌst and oːt tu to suggest an inference or a probability:

ðei ˈʃud bi ˎbak ˌsuːn.   ˎðat ˌʃud əv ˌgivn̩ ðəm ə ˌʃok.
ðei ˈʃudn̩t bi ˎloŋ, ˌnau.   ju ˎʃudn̩t ˌhav ˌmʌtʃ ˌtrʌbl̩.

202   kud—kudn̩t. Weak form kəd. This modal is basically unstressed except when it is used as a substitute for mait (but on this, see §185). It is used freely before all six infinitives.

Negative form.

kudṇt in all cases:

ai ˅lukt fər it, bət ai 'kudṇt ˎfaind it.
ʃi ˋkudṇt əv ˏdʌn it, 'iːvṇ if ʃi d ˋtraid.
'kudṇt ju bi ˙getiŋ ˙redi tə ˊstaːt?
hi 'kudṇt əv bin ˙θiŋkiŋ əv ˙wot i wəz ˋduːiŋ.
'sʌtʃ ə ˙θiŋ 'kudṇt bi ˋθoːt ov!
'kudṇt ˙ðis ˙letər əv bin 'poustid ˊjestədi?

Affirmative form in stressed positions.

kud in all cases:

'kud ju ˊhould ˙ðis fə mi? hi ˋkud əv ˏdʌn it, if i d ˅laikt.
'ðis ˙paːsl̩ ˋkud bi ˏsent bai ˋeəˏmeil.

Affirmative form in unstressed positions.

kud when not followed by a specific verbal:

ˋjuː ˏkudṇt əv ˏdʌn it, bət ˅ai kud əv.

kəd in all other cases:

'weə kəd ai ˙bai wʌn əv ˏðiːz?
ai kəd əv ˋbroːt it if ai d ˏnoun ju ˏwontid it.
wi kəd bi ˋhelpiŋ ju wail wi ə ˏweitiŋ.
ju kəd əv bin 'finiʃiŋ joː ˋwəːk inˏsted əv ˏpleiiŋ.
ðə 'miːt kəd bi ˋboild if ju priˏfəːd.
'ðis 'foutəgraf kəd əv bin inˋlaːdʒd wið ədˏvaːntidʒ.

203   mait—maitṇt—mait not. No weak forms. This modal has two regular meanings.

a. Permission—Prohibition.

When it is used in these meanings this modal is basically un-stressed, and the contracted form of the negative may be used. It occurs usually in indirect speech, replacing mei after a reporting verb in a past tense, though it also occurs in direct speech as a polite formula in making suggestions. It is very seldom found in the aspect of activity or in the perfect tenses.

Negative form.

maitṇt in most cases:

hi 'aːskt if i mait ˋteik ðəm, ənd ai 'tould im i ˋmaitṇt.

Affirmative form.

mait in all cases:

ˈai ˌtould əː ʃi mait ˌkʌm wið əs.
ai ˈaːskt ju if it mait bi ˌθroun əˌwei.
ˈmait ai səˈdʒest ə ˌkomprəmaiz?
pəˈhaps wi mait ˈliːv ðə ˈrest til təˈmoru.

b. Possibility.

In this meaning the modal is basically stressed and the contracted form of the negative is not used in statements. The modal is used indiscriminately in direct and indirect speech, and in the former it indicates more doubt than mei. It occurs freely before all the six infinitives.

Negative form.

maitn̩t in questions:

ˈmaitn̩t ðei bi ˈweitiŋ fər əs ət ðə ˈsteiʃn̩?
ˈmaitn̩t it əv bin ˈθroun əˈwei bai misˈteik?

mait not usually in statements:

ai ˈmait not ˈget tə ðə ˈsteiʃn̩ in ˈtaim tə ˈmiːt ðə ˌtrein.
ðei ˈmait not əv inˈtendid tə ˌkʌm təˌdei.
ju ˈmait not əv bin ˈtʃouzn̩ if ˌai ˌhadn̩t ˌrekəˌmendid ju.

Affirmative form.

mait in all cases:

ai ˈtould im ai ˈmait ˈluk ˈin ˈnekst ˌwiːk.
ʃi ˈmait əv ˈteikən əˈfens ət ˌwot ju ˌsed.
ðəi ˈmait bi ˈweitiŋ fər əs tə ˈfoun ðəm.
ðei ˈmait əv bin iksˈpektiŋ əs tə ˈkoːl on ðəm.
ju ˈmait bi ˈsent tu ˈafrikə ˌnekst ˌjiə.
hi ˈmait əv bin prəˈmoutid if i ˌhadn̩t riˌzaind.

204 Special elisions and assimilations. In rapid and familiar speech several of the modal finites may undergo special elisions (§12) and assimilations (§13) when they occur in certain phonetic contexts. While foreign students of English need not adopt these modifications (which are not often shown in phonetic transcriptions) they should be aware of their existence. They are therefore listed

below, and examples are given of contexts in which they may
be heard.

Negative forms.

Normal	Before p, b or m	Before t, d or n	Before k or g
wount	woump, woum	woun	wouŋk, wouŋ
ʃaːnt	ʃaːmp, ʃaːm	ʃaːn	ʃaːŋk, ʃaːŋ
kaːnt	kaːmp, kaːm	kaːn	kaːŋk, kaːŋ
mʌsṇt,	mʌsṃp, mʌsṃ	mʌsṇ	mʌsŋ̩k, mʌsŋ̩
deənt	deəmp, deəm	deən	deəŋk, deəŋ

hi ˌwoump ˌbait ju.

ju 'kaːŋk ˙get ðəm ᵛhiə.

wi 'deən ˋdriŋk it.

ai ˋʃaːmp bi ˌloŋ.

ju 'mʌsŋ̩k ˙katʃ ˌ‿kould.

ai 'ʃaːn ˙duː eni ᵛmoə.

ju ˋmʌsṃ ˌput it ˌðeə.

ðei 'wouŋ ˋgiv əs ˌeni.

wi ˋkaːn ˌteik oːl ˌðat.

ʃi ˋdeəŋ ˌgou ə‿ˌwei.

The other modal negative forms may lose their final t when they
are followed by a plosive or nasal consonant:

ju 'niːdṇ ᵛboðər əbaut it.

ai 'kudṇ ˙meik eniwʌn ˋhiə.

hi 'wudṇ ˋduː eni ˌmoə.

it 'maitṇ bi ə ˙bad aiˋdiə.

Affirmative forms.

ʃal   ʃ before wiː

'weə ʃ wi ˌgou?   'wot ʃ wi ˌduː?

ʃəd   ʃt before voiceless consonants

ai ʃt f ˌθoːt sou.   ai ʃt ˋteik it if ˌai wə ˌjuː.

mei   me or mi when used in the sense of permission

ju mi 'kʌm ˋin ˌnau.   ʃi me 'stei ˋhiər if ʃi ˌlaiks.

məs   məʃ before ʃ

ju məʃ ˋʃeər it wið im.   ju məʃ 'ʃou mi ˙wot ju ˋmiːn.

kən   kəm before p, b or m

ju kəm 'put it ˌðeə.   ai kəm 'briŋ ju wʌn 'nekst ᵛwiːk.

kən   kəŋ or kŋ̩ before k or g

ˋai kŋ̩ ˌkari it.   ju kəŋ ˋgou ˌnau.

kəd   kt before t

ai kt ˋtrai if ju ˌlaik.   wi kt 'təːn ˙raund ᵛhiə.

ANALYSIS OF THE TENSE SYSTEM

205 Kinds of specific verb. The specific verbs fall into two classes:

a. *Transitive verbs*, which take an object:

    ai 'koːld ðə ˋdoktə.   həv ju 'fild mai ʹglaːs?

    'dount 'tʌtʃ ðə ˏflauəz.   'kaːnt ju 'siː ði ʹʌðəz?

b. *Intransitive verbs*, which do not take an object:

    'sʌmbədi z ˋkoːliŋ.   'did ðei 'weik ʹʌp?

    hi 'hazn̩t əˋraivd ˏjet.   'wount ju 'kʌm təʹmoru?

The distinction between transitive and intransitive verbs is important from the structural point of view, since only transitive verbs can be used in the passive voice.

206 Voice. There are two voices:

a. *The Active Voice*, in which the grammatical subject performs the action:

    ai v 'koːld ðə ˋdoktə.   ʃl wi 'finiʃ ðə ˙haus 'nekst ʹwiːk?

    hi 'didn̩t ˋteik ðə ˏbuk.   'havn̩t ju ˙siːn ðə ʹmanidʒə?

b. *The Passive Voice*, in which the grammatical subject suffers the action:

    ðə 'buk s bin ˙teikən əˏwei.   ðə 'haus wəz ˙finiʃt 'laːst ˏwiːk.

    ðə ˋdoktə z bin ˏkoːld.   həz mai 'glaːs bin ʹfild?

Intransitive verbs cannot be used in the passive voice, as the object of the active voice sentence is needed as the subject of the passive. The subject of the active voice sentence is usually omitted, but can be expressed if necessary as an agent, preceded by the preposition "by."

        ðə 'doktə z bin ˙koːld (bai ˏmiː).

        həz mai 'glaːs bin ˙fild (bai ʹjuː)?

The chief use of the passive, however, is to make statements when it is unnecessary or undesirable to name the doer of the action. It is much used in English where an active sentence with an impersonal subject, or a reflexive sentence, might be used in other languages, as in Fr. **on dit,** Sp. **se dice,** or Ger. **man sagt** corresponding to the English passive **it is said.**

207 Aspect. Verb tenses can be classified into two aspects, whose function is to show how the speaker is looking at the action named by the verb, or in other words to indicate what his chief interest in it is. The aspects are:

a. Aspect of Accomplishment, which is used when interest is focused on the performance (or non-performance) of the action. In the active voice no part of the verb tə biː enters into the formation of any of the tenses in this aspect:

d ju 'laik 'tʃiːz?   hi 'dʌznt ˙kʌm hiər 'evri ˏdei.

'hav ðei ə'raivd jet?   wiː l 'miːt ju in ˏtaun.

b. Aspect of Activity, which is used when interest is focused on the occupation or activity (or non-activity) of the subject at the time referred to (whether explicitly or implicitly) in the sentence. Some part of the verb tə biː enters into the formation of all the tenses in this aspect, and in the active voice the tense always contains the present participle of the specific verb:

'aːnt ju 'dresiŋ jet?   ai 'havn̩t ˙bin 'lisniŋ tə ðəm.

ʃl ai bi 'siːiŋ ju ˙suːn?   wə ðei 'haviŋ 'lʌntʃ?

(Note. The tenses referred to in paragraph *b* above have been called at various times Imperfect, Continuous or Progressive Tenses. All these names are unsatisfactory, as they fail to indicate the real object of introducing the verb tə biː and the ing-form, which is to show that the speaker is interested in what the subject was, is or will be doing, and not in the accomplishment of the action.)

208 Time reference. In each Aspect there are two systems of referring to time, each with its own set of tenses. Their function is to show whether the action denoted by the verb is contemporary with, or anterior to, the time expressed or implied in the sentence. It will be convenient to refer to these tenses as:

a. The Direct (or Simple) Tenses, which refer directly to the action as being contemporary with the time in mind:

'did ju ˙si im 'jestədi?   ðei l 'gou ðeə təˏmoru.

ʃl ai 'briŋ it 'wið mi?   hi wəz 'riːdiŋ ə ˏletə.

b. The Perfect Tenses, which indicate that the action took place at a time anterior to that in mind:

həd ju ɔːl'redi 'siːn it?   ʃi 'wount əv ə'raivd ˌjet.

'havn̩t ju 'finiʃt jet?   ˋai kəd əv pə,sweidid im.

209 Tense. Strictly speaking, English has only two tenses to cover the past-present-future time continuum. In the Active Voice there are Past and Present Tenses in each Time Reference, of which there are two in each Aspect, making eight tenses in all. Apart from occasional references to the future in some subordinate clauses, the past tenses are limited to indicating past time, but the present tenses are frequently used to refer to future time, particularly in the Aspect of Activity. In these cases a future adverb is often inserted to avoid ambiguity. The modal tenses are the ones most freely used in referring to future time, either factually or hypothetically, according to the modal used.

For convenience of reference a full list of verb tenses is given below, showing the number by which each tense is being identified. Corresponding tenses in the active and passive voices are given the same numbers, the two being distinguished by prefixing the letters A and P respectively.

Active	*Name of Tense*	*Passive*
A 1	Present Direct of Accomplishment	P 1
A 2	Past Direct of Accomplishment	P 2
A 3	Modal Direct of Accomplishment	P 3
A 4	Present Perfect of Accomplishment	P 4
A 5	Past Perfect of Accomplishment	P 5
A 6	Modal Perfect of Accomplishment	P 6
A 7	Present Direct of Activity	P 7
A 8	Past Direct of Activity	P 8
A 9	Modal Direct of Activity	——
A 10	Present Perfect of Activity	——
A 11	Past Perfect of Activity	——
A 12	Modal Perfect of Activity	——

USES OF THE TENSES

210 Limitations on the aspects. There are some limitations on
the choice of one or other of the aspects.

The following are verbs which, except in the cases noted below,
are seldom, and in some cases never, used in the aspect of activity.

Mental States	*Emotional States*	*Possession, etc.*
nou	ə`doə*	hav
bi`li:v	`aidə͵laiz	pə`zes
`riə͵laiz	ri`viə*	oun
ə`pri:ʃi͵eit	`dout on	bi`loŋ
`noutis	`kʌvit	sju:t
faind	wont	ri`zembl|
`gaðə*	wiʃ	`i:kwl|
'ʌndə`stand	di`zaiə*	kən`sist ov
mi:n	lʌv	kən`tein
fi:l	praiz	di`zə:v
ri`ga:d	`valju	ri`kwaiə*
pri`zju:m	di`pend on	ni:d
sə`pouz	pri`fə:*	lak
i`madʒin	laik	
θiŋk	`fansi	*Involuntary*
fo:`si:	mis	*Perception*
iks`pekt	keə*	si:
in`tend	maind	hiə*
houp	fə`giv	smel
trʌst	'apri`hend	teist
daut	ri`zent	fi:l
dis`trʌst	dis`laik	
ri`membə*	fiə*	*Incomplete*
'rekə`lekt	di`test	*Predication*
`rekəg͵naiz	heit	bi:
ri`ko:l	louð	si:m
fə`get	`eksi͵kreit	ə`piə*
di`tə:min	ə`bomi͵neit	mi:n
`difə*	əb`ho:*	`signi͵fai
ri`fju:z		`matə*

Apart from verbs of incomplete predication, these verbs express mental or emotional states, involuntary sensory perception and possession or some other relationships.

It would appear that the reason why these verbs did not develop tenses in the aspect of activity—which is a comparatively modern phenomenon in English—is that there was no need to distinguish between a lasting and an ephemeral manifestation of the state. There is, however, a contemporary tendency, attributable to a desire to make conversation more vivid, to use the aspect of activity in a good many of the verbs that specify mental or emotional states. Further, the same aspect is used with some of the verbs when they refer to deliberate actions instead of involuntary ones.

Certain verbs that specify a state or posture of their subject are generally used to indicate the existence of the state, and not its adoption or completion. Such verbs are therefore most frequently found in the aspect of activity (which, it should be remembered, includes a state of non-activity). Verbs of this kind are:

stand	sit	lai	niːl	liːn
haŋ	skwot	krautʃ	stuːp	riˈklain

In the succeeding paragraphs the uses of each tense are listed, and, as the passive voice tenses are used in similar circumstances to those of the active voice, examples are given covering both voices. The three groups of modals referred to in a number of these paragraphs are described in §§173–4.

211 Aspect of accomplishment. In general, the tenses of this aspect are used when the speaker wishes to draw attention to the fact, either of the performance or non-performance of an action, or of the existence or non-existence of a state or condition. The emphasis is on the result of the action rather than the process, or on the existence of the state rather than on its beginning or end. In the direct present tense, however, the principal suggestion is that the action is habitual, or at least frequently repeated, and that the state is of long duration and not merely temporary.

The other direct tenses emphasize the completion of an action and not the process or activity involved in doing it. If a time is mentioned, it is for the purpose of stating that the action took place at that moment or was completed by then; if a period is named it indicates that the action lasted for that length of time.

The perfect tenses indicate the completion of an action at or before a time either mentioned or understood, or alternatively its duration for a specified period.

For the treatment of verbs expressing physical, mental or emotional states see §210.

212 Present direct of accomplishment. Tenses A1 and P1. Functions:

a. To make statements that are known to have lasting validity.

ði 'ə:θ ri`volvz on its ˙aksis in 'twenti˙fo:r ˌauəz.

'wo:tə ˙boilz ət ə 'hʌndrid di˙gri:z ˌsentigreid.

'wo:tər iz kən`və:tid intu ˌais ət 'ziərou di˙gri:z ˌsentigreid.

'peipər iz ˙meid əv ˙ragz o: ˙wud ˌpʌlp.

b. To indicate that an action is either habitual or repeated, and not merely temporary. Adverbs of frequency or repetition are therefore often associated with it.

hi 'kʌmz on ˌfraidiz.	ai 'gou ðeər ˙evri ˌdei.
d ju 'driŋk ´kofi?	dəz i 'evə ´smouk?
ʃi 'dʌznt ˌsli:p wel.	hi 'dʌznt `ofn̩ ˌlu:z ˌmʌni.
'dʌznt i ˙spi:k ´iŋgliʃ?	'dount ju ˙rait ´regjuləli?

tə'ma:tuz 'a:nt `o:lwiz ˌi:tn̩ ˌro:.

'iznt ˙ðis ˙medsin 'ju:ʒuəli ˙teikən wið ´wo:tə?

c. To refer to the future in subordinate clauses of time, duration or condition.

ai l 'si: ju wen ai 'kʌm ˙bak 'nekst ˌjiə.

ju məst 'luk fər it til ju `faind it.

'mi:t mi tə`moru ənˌles ju ˌhiə tə ðə ˌkontrəri.

it məs bi 'lukt fo: til it s ˌfaund.

ju l bi `noutifaid if ju ə ˌnot ˌni:did.

d. When it is used with the verbs listed in §210 this tense may refer to present activity or to a temporary state.

ai 'du: ˙laik jo: 'nju: ᵛhat!

dəz it 'matər if ai 'li:v ˙ðis wʌn ´aut?

'ðis ˙hat 'dʌzn̩ biˈloŋ tə ᵛmi:.

'ðount ju ´rekəgnaiz ðis ˙piktʃə?

ʃi z 'laikt fə hə ˙tʃaːmiŋ ˏmanəz.
'aːnt ðei riˈgaːdid əz ˊdeindʒərəs?

e. To refer to the future in principal clauses when one is speaking of a programme or other arrangement already decided upon.

wi 'staːt on auə ˙trip 'nekst ˏmʌndi.
də ðei əˈraiv təˈmoru oː ðə 'dei ˏaːftə?
hi 'dʌzn̩t riˈtəːn til ðə 'wiːk aːftə ˏnekst.
'dount ai ˙get eni ˊdiskaunt on ðis ˙pəːtʃis?

f. In the following cases tenses A1 and P1 are used without any implication of an habitual action. They are used in preference to A7 and P7, which would suggest that the action is going on at the moment of speaking, and are really substituted for A4 and P4, which are the tenses that would really fit the situation.

hi 'telz mi ju ə ˙teikiŋ ə ˊholidi ˏnekst ˏmʌnθ.
ai m inˈfoːmd ðət ðə ˙miːtiŋ wil bi ˙held 'nekst ˏsatədi.

213 Past direct of accomplishment. Tenses A2 and P2. Functions:

a. To indicate that an action was performed or a state existed at a time or during a period in the past which, if not already manifest or implicit, must be indicated by means of an adverbial of past time. Tenses A4 and P4 are used if no precise time or period is involved.

hi 'keim ˙in ə 'moument əˏgou.
did ju inˈvait ðəm tə ðə ˊpaːti? (When you saw them)
ai 'didn̩t ˋstei ˏmoː ðən ə ˏminit. (When I was there)
'didn̩t ʃi ˙teik hə ˊmedsin laːst ˙nait?
'ðis ˙letə wəz ˙ritn̩ 'θriː ˋdeiz əˏgou.
ðə 'kontrakt wəz ˙saind 'laːst ˏwiːk.

b. To refer to a hypothetical present or future action in the following cases:

(1) in a conditional clause dependent on a main clause containing a modal of Group 2.

ju 'mait ˙siː ðəm if ju 'went təˇmoru.
'wudn̩t ju ˊhelp mi, 'iːvn̩ if ai ˊaːskt ju?
wi 'ʃudn̩t ˙get ðeər in ˋtaim ənˏles wi ˏstaːtid ˏᵛəːliə.
'kudn̩t wi ˙staːt ət ˊsiks if wi wə ˊkoːld ˙əːli?
ʃi d 'kʌm ət ˋwʌns if ˏounli ʃi wər ˏᵛaːskt.

(2) in clauses subordinated to a present or modal main clause by the conjunctions əz if or əz dou.

hi l 'triːt mi əz ˙ðou i 'didn̩t ˋnou mi.
ai 'fiːl əz if ai ˙had ə 'bad ˎkould ˌkʌmiŋ ˌon.

(3) in clauses dependent on one of the expressions ai wiʃ, ai d raːðə*, it s taim, and the imperative of səˋpouz.

ai 'wiʃ ai had ˙taim tə 'tel ju oːl əˎˏbaut it.
ai d 'raːðə ju ˙keim ˙bak təˇmoru.
it s 'taim wi ˙went ˋhoum.
sə'pouz i ˙didn̩t ˙wont tə ˎsiː əs!

214 Modal direct of accomplishment. Tenses A3 and P3. Functions:

a. With modals of Groups 1 and 3, to indicate an action or state in the present or future, often with adverbials of present or future time respectively.

ai l 'miːt ju ət ˙wʌn əˋklok, əz ai ʃl̩ bi ˋfriː ˏðen.
'mei wi ˙kʌm ˊin, oː 'mʌst wi ˙kʌm ˙bak ðis 'aːftəˎnuːn?
ai 'niːdn̩t ˙duː it ət ˇwʌns, bət ai 'oːt tə ˙duː it təˇmoru.
'kaːnt ju ˙stei eni ˊloŋgə? ai ˋdeənt ˌstei hiər əˎˏloun.
wi 'mei bi di˙leid bai ðə ˋsnou.
'kaːnt ðə ˙ruːm bi 'kliːnd on ˊwenzdi?

b. With modals of Groups 2 and 3, to report speeches (such as those shown in examples *a* above) containing modals of Groups 1 or 3.

hi 'sed i d ˙miːt mi ət 'wʌn əˋklok.
ðei 'aːskt if ðei mait ˙kʌm ˎin.
hi ˌsed i 'niːdn̩t ˙duː it ət ˇwʌns.
ʃi 'aːskt if ai ˙kudn̩t ˎstei, əz ʃi 'deənt ˙stei ðeər əˎloun.
ai ˋtould ju wi ˌmait bi diˌleid bai ðə ˏsnou.
hi 'aːskt if ðə ˙ruːm 'kudn̩t bi ˙kliːnd on ˋwenzdi.

c. With modals of Group 2 only.

(1) to indicate a hypothetical action or state in the present or future, often with adverbials of present or future time respectively, and connected with a conditional clause in a past tense.

ai d 'gou wið ju ˋnau if ai wə ˏfriː.
kəd ju 'gou ðeə ˙nekst ˊwiːk if ðə ˙weðə wə ˙fain?

ʃi 'mait not ˇlaik it if wi ˌleft wiðaut ˌseiiŋ gud ˌbai.
'wudn̩t i ˙get ə ˙letə tə'moru if ju ˙rout it ət ˙wʌns?
ai 'ʃudn̩t bi ˙siːn ˇtoːkiŋ tu im if ˌai wə ˌjuː.
ðə 'wəːk kəd bi ˙finiʃt bai ˇfraidi if ju ˌstʌk at it.

(2) to express inclination or disinclination for a hypothetical
situation in the present or future. Often followed by an
infinitive phrase.

ai ʃəd ˇlʌv tə ˌsiː ðəm əˌgein.
joː 'brʌðə ˙mait pri˙fəːr ə 'holidi in ˇjuərəp.
ju 'kudn̩t disˇlaik ˌðis ˌbuk.
ai 'ʃudn̩t ˙keə tə ˇtrai it.
hi 'wudn̩t ˙laik tə bi in ˇjoː ˌʃuːz.
ai ʃəd ˇheit tə ˌhav tə ˌduː ðat əˌˇgein.
ai ʃəd ˇlouð ˌhaviŋ tə ˌliv əˌloun.
'wudn̩t ju bi di'laitid tə ˙siː ðəm ə˙gein?

215 Present perfect of accomplishment. Tenses A4 and P4.
Functions:

a. To indicate that an action was, or was not, performed (and,
since it is a tense of accomplishment, completed) at some unspecified
time in the past. While adverbials of duration can be used with
these tenses, adverbials of past time cannot.

ai v oːl'redi ˇritn̩ ðə ˌletə.
həv ju 'aːskt fə pə'miʃn̩ tə ˙liːv?
ðei 'havn̩t ˙spoukən tə mi fə ˇwiːks.
'hazn̩t i ˙teikən ðə 'wʌnz i ˌwontid?
ʃi z bin i'lektid ə ˙membər əv ˌpaːləmənt.
həv ðei bin in'strʌktid ˙not tə ˌkʌm ðis ˙wiːk?

b. To indicate that a state or condition that still exists began
at a certain time in the past, or has lasted for a certain period up
to the moment of speaking. This tense is used mostly with verbs
expressing a condition; with verbs expressing an activity tense A10
is usually more suitable.

wi v 'noun ˙ðat ˌfamili fə 'fiftiːn ˌjiəz.
'hau ˙loŋ əv ju ˙had ðis ˌkaː?
ju 'havn̩t bin ˙hiər əz ˙loŋ əz ˇai hav.

'haznt ʃi ˇgroun ə ˌlot ˌleitli!
ai v bin 'kept in ˇbed ˌoːl ˌðis ˌwiːk.
ðə pəˇteituz ˌhavnt bin ˌpiːld jet.

216 Past perfect of accomplishment. Tenses A5 and P5.
Functions:

a. To indicate that an action was, or was not, completed by
a moment or period denoted by an adverbial of past time.

ai d oːl'redi ˇritn ðə ˌletə wen ju ˌkeim.
həd ðei ə'raivd bai ðə ˙taim ju ˙got ðeə?
ʃi 'hadnt di˙saidid tə ˇkʌm til ai ˌspouk tə hə.
'hadnt ju ˙menʃnd it tu im bi'foə?
ðə 'faiər əd bin ˙put ˙aut bi'foː wi ˇgot ðeə.
'hadnt ðə ˙haus bin 'sould bi'foː ju ˇsoː it?

b. To suggest a hypothetical action or state in the past, in the
following cases.

(1) in a conditional clause dependent on a main clause that
contains a modal perfect tense formed with a modal of Group 2.

ju d əv 'got ðə ˙letə təˇdei if i d ˌpoustid it ˌəːliə.
'kud ju əv ˇgon if ðei d in˙vaitid ju?
ai 'ʃudnt əv ˇdʌn it if ai ˌhadnt bin ˌaŋgri.
'maitnt i əv ˇsteid if ʃi 'hadnt ə˙fendid im?
ai kəd əv ə'voidid ði ˌaksidnt if ˌounli ai d bin ˌwoːnd.
it 'wudnt əv bin ˇsould if it ˌhadnt bin ˌtestid.

(2) in clauses subordinated to a main clause by the conjunctions
əz if or əz ðou.

hi 'lukt əz if i d in˙tendid tə ˇspiːk tu əs.
it 'iznt əz ðou ju d bin ˇhaːmd in eni ˌwei.

(3) in clauses dependent on one of the expressions ai wiʃ,
ai d raːðə*, it s taim, and the imperative of sə'pouz.

ai 'wiʃ ai d ˙dʌn it bi'foː ju ˇkeim.
ai d 'raːðə ju d ˙tould mi ˇəːliə.
it s 'kwait ˙taim ðei d 'finiʃt ˙pleiiŋ ə'baut.
sə'pouz ju 'hadnt ˙faund ðəm ət ˌhoum!

217 Modal perfect of accomplishment. Tenses A6 and P6.
Functions:

a. With modals of Groups 1 and 3, to indicate that an action
or state will be complete at the moment of speaking or at some
time in the future, often denoted by adverbials of present or
future time.

ai 'mei əv ˙ritn̩ mai ˙letəz bi'fɔː ju get ˋbak.
'ʃal wi əv 'finiʃt ðə ˙geim bai ˈsʌpətaim?
ðei ˋkaːnt əv ə͵raivd ɔːlˇredi !
'wount ju əv ˙had ən 'aːnsə tə ðə ˙letə bai ˈmʌndi?
jɔː 'teligram 'mʌst əv bin diˋlivəd bai ͵nau.
'evriθiŋ | əv bin ˋiːtn̩ bai ðə ͵taim wi ͵get ðeə.

b. With modals of Groups 2 and 3, to report speeches (such as
those shown in examples *a* above) containing modals of Groups
1 or 3.

hi ͵sed i 'mait əv ˙ritn̩ ðə ˙letəz bi'fɔː wi got ˋbak.
ai 'aːskt if wi ʃəd əv 'finiʃt ðə ˙geim bai ˋsʌpətaim.
hi iks͵kleimd ðət ðei ˋkudn̩t əv ə͵raivd bai ˇðen.
wi 'aːskt if ʃi ˙wudn̩t əv ˙had ən ˙aːnsə bai ͵mʌndi.
hi 'tould mi mai ˙teligram 'mʌst əv bin diˋlivəd bai ͵ðen.
hi wəz ə'freid ˙evriθiŋ ud əv bin ˋiːtn̩ bai ðə ͵taim wi ͵got ðeə.

c. With modals of Group 2 only.

(1) to indicate a hypothetical action or state that would be
complete at some time in the past or present, often denoted by
an adverbial of past or present time or connected with a conditional clause in a past or past perfect tense.

ai kəd əv 'daːnst ˙ɔːl ͵nait wið ͵juː.
'wud ju əv ˈgest it if ai ˙hadn̩t ˙tould ju?
hi 'mait not əv ˋkʌm if i d ͵noun hau ˋfaːr it ͵woz.
'ʃudn̩t ju əv ˙got hiər ˈəːliə ðən ˙ðis?
'ðis ˙letə 'ʃud əv bin ˙sent ˙of ˋjestədi.
'kudn̩t it əv bin ˙sent bai ˈeəmeil?

(2) to express inclination or disinclination for a hypothetical
situation in the past, with the suggestion that fulfilment was
impossible, sometimes because something else was done. The
object of the verb is often an infinitive phrase or gerund.

ai ʃəd əv ˈlʌvd tə ˌsiː ðəm əˌgein.
joː ˈbrʌðə ˈmait əv priˈfəːd ə ˈholidi in ˈjuərəp.
wi ˈʃudṇt əv disˈlaikt ə ˈwiːk ət ðə ˈsiːˈsaid.
ju ˈmait not əv ˈkeəd tə ˈtrai it.
hi ˈwudṇt əv ˈlaikt tə bi in ˈjoː ˌʃuːz.
ai ʃəd əv ˈheitid tə ˌhav tə ˌduː ðat əˌgein.
ai ʃəd əv ˈlouðd ˌhaviŋ tə ˌliv əˌloun.
ˈwudṇt ju əv diˈtestid ˈhaviŋ tə ˈrʌn ə ˈhaus?

218 Aspect of activity. The tenses of this aspect are used
when the speaker wishes to concentrate his hearer's attention on
a certain actvity—or lack of activity—of the subject of the verb
rather than on the accomplishment of any particular action.

Used with an adverbial of time, they indicate that the activity
was in progress at that time, without any indication of its duration,
the only implication being that it began before, and might finish
after, the time or period mentioned.

Used with an adverbial of duration they concentrate attention
on the existence of the activity during the period mentioned, and
make no suggestion that anything was finished or accomplished.

Used without an adverbial they merely indicate the existence of
the activity, without any indication of time or duration.

The present direct of activity (tenses A7 and P7) indicates that
an activity is going on at the moment of speaking and is not
necessarily an habitual activity, or in speaking of a state, that it
is temporary and not permanent.

219 Present direct of activity. Tenses A7 and P7. Functions:

a. To indicate that the subject is—or is not—engaged in a
certain activity at the moment of speaking or during a limited
period before and after; it carries no suggestion as to when the
activity started or as to how long it will go on, but the latter point
may be conveyed by using an adverbial of present time.

ai m ˈraitiŋ ˈletəz ət ðə ˌmoumənt.
ə ju ˈweitiŋ fər ˈenibodi?
joː ˈbrʌðər ˈizṇt ˈspiːkiŋ tə mi ˌðiːz deiz.
ˈaːnt ðei ˈteikiŋ ˈiŋgliʃ lesṇz ˈðis ˈjiə?
hi z ˈbiːiŋ ˈtoːt bai ə ˈnjuː ˌmeθəd.
ˈletəz ˈaːnt biːiŋ diˈlivəd ˈregjuləli ˌnauədeiz.

b. With an adverbial of future time, to indicate that an activity will—or will not—take place at some time in the future.

wi ə 'liːviŋ fə ˋspein ˌnekst ˌmʌnθ.
iz i 'teikiŋ ðə ˙famili tə ðə ˊθiətə təˑmoru?
ʃi 'izn̩t ˋraitiŋ tə ðəm til ˌnekst ˌwiːk.
'aːnt ju ˙getiŋ ə 'njuː ˊkaː ˙suːn?
auə 'kaː z ˙biːiŋ riˋpeəd ˌnekst ˌwiːk.
ðə 'gudz ˙aːnt biːiŋ ˙sould til ˋtjuːzdi.

c. Tenses A7 and P7 of the verb tə gou, when followed by the infinitive of another verb, form a future tense which, when the subject is inanimate, makes (or asks for) a confident prediction.

it s 'gouiŋ tə ˋrein in ə ˌminit.
iz it 'gouiŋ tə bi ˊfain təˑdei?
it 'izn̩t ˙gouiŋ tə bi ˋiːzi tə ˌduː ˌðat.
'izn̩t ˙ðat ˙waiə gouiŋ tə ˊbreik ʌndə ˙ðat ˙strein?
ðə 'haus iz ˙gouiŋ tə bi ˋflʌdid if it ˌreinz mʌtʃ ˌmoə.
'ðouz ˙tuː ˙lamps 'aːnt gouiŋ tə ˙giv əs iˑnʌf ˋlait.

With animate subjects this construction expresses intention.

ai m 'gouiŋ tə ˋpʌniʃ ju if ju biˌheiv sou ˌbadli.
ə ju 'gouiŋ tə ˙stʌdi ˊiŋgliʃ ðis ˙jiə?
ðei 'aːnt ˙gouiŋ tə ˙send əs eni moː ˌmʌni.
'izn̩t ʃi ˙gouiŋ tə 'staːt ˙kliːniŋ ðə ˊhaus jet?
ju ə 'gouiŋ tə biˊ ˙givn̩ ðə 'fəːst ˌpraiz.
'aːnt ðei ˙gouiŋ tə bi əˑlaud ˊin?

In order to avoid repetition (with gou) or a clash of meaning (with kʌm) an elliptical construction, which, though formally a simple A7, is semantically still a future expressing intention, is used with these two verbs.

ai m 'gouiŋ tə ˋlʌndən ˌnekst ˌwiːk.
hi 'izn̩t ˙kʌmiŋ ˙bak til ˋwenzdi.

But the full construction may be used when it is desired to emphasize the idea of intention.

ai m ˋgouiŋ tə ˌgou tə ˌlʌndən ˌnekst ˌwiːk.
ʃi izn̩t ˋgouiŋ tə ˌkʌm ənd ˌsiː əs.

The following are some examples of contemporary speech showing how this tense is used with some of the verbs listed in §210.

hi z ri'gaːdiŋ ˙ðis əz auə 'fəːst misˌteik.

ə ju ri'membəriŋ tə ˙rait tə joː 'peərṇts ˙regjuləli?

wi ə 'wiʃiŋ wi 'hadṇt ˙teikən sou 'meni ˋrisks.

ai m fə'giviŋ ju ˇðis taim, bət ai 'ʃaːnt əˇgein.

'oːl ðə ˙famili ə ˋlʌviŋ it ˌhiər ət ðə ˌsiːˌsaid.

'ðis ˙holidi z 'sjuːtiŋ mi ˙veri ˌwel.

220 Past direct of activity. Tenses A8 and P8. Functions:

a. To indicate that the subject was—or was not—engaged in a certain activity at a moment or during a period in the past which, if not already manifest, must be implicit, or else denoted by an adverbial or clause of past time. Tense A10 is used if no precise time or period is to be understood.

hi wəz 'wotʃiŋ ˋteliˌviʒṇ ˌoːl ˌjestədi ˌiːvniŋ.

'woz it ˊreiniŋ ðis ˙moːniŋ wen ju ˙went ˙aut?

ðei 'wəːnt ˙weəriŋ ˙hats wen ˋwiː ˌsoː ðəm.

'wəːnt ju ˙steiiŋ wið ə ˊfrend əv ˙main ˙laːst ˙wiːk?

ʃi 'wozṇt biːiŋ ˙helpt wið əː ˙houmwəːk wail ˋai wəz ˌðeə.

ðei wə biːiŋ 'entəˈteind bai joː ˋmʌðər ə ˌlitḷ ˌwail əˌgou.

b. With an appropriate adverbial, to indicate that an intention, such as those shown in §219, examples *b*, was not carried out; in this case the finite often takes a stress, which may be a kinetic one.

wi wə 'liːviŋ fə ˋspein ˌnekst ˌmʌnθ. (but now we aren't)

wəz i 'teikiŋ ðə ˙famili tə ðə ˊθiətə təˈmoru?

hi 'wozṇt ˙raitiŋ tə ðəm til 'nekst ˌwiːk. (but now he will)

'wəːnt ju ˙getiŋ ə 'njuː ˊkaː ˙suːn?

hi ˋwoz biːiŋ ˌtoːt tə 'draiv ə ˋkaː. (but gave it up)

ðə 'gudz ˋwəːnt biːiŋ ˌsould til ˋtjuːzdi.

c. To refer to a hypothetical present or future activity in the following cases.

(1) in a conditional clause dependent on a main clause containing a modal of Group 2.

ju 'mait ˋhav tə ˌspiːk ˌiŋgliʃ if ju wə ˌtravliŋ əˌˋloun.

kəd ju 'juːz ˙ðat ˙wəːd if ju wə 'spiːkiŋ ˊfoːmḷ ˙iŋgliʃ?

ai 'ʃudṇt gou ˙aut if it wə ˇreiniŋ.

'wudṇt ðei bi ˙draiviŋ ˊfaːstər if ðei wə biːiŋ ˙folud?

(2) in clauses subordinated to a present or modal main clause by the conjunctions əz if or əz ðou.

it 'luks əz if ðei wə 'katʃiŋ ˅ʌp wið əs.
ai 'fiːl əz ðou ai wə ˙biːiŋ iksˋperimentid wið.

(3) in clauses dependent on a main clause containing wiʃ, wəd ˋraːðə*, it s taim, or the imperative of səˋpouz.

'dount ju ˙wiʃ ju wə 'baːskiŋ in ðə ʹsʌn ˙nau?
'wudn̩t ju ˙raːðə ðei wə 'kʌmiŋ tə'moru?
'izn̩t it ˙taim wi wə 'getiŋ ˙redi tə ʹgou?
sə'pouz ðei wə ˙briŋiŋ səm ˅vizitəz ˌwið ðəm!

Note that wəː* is used with all persons in many subordinate clauses.

221 Modal direct of activity. Tense A9. Functions:

a. With modals of Groups 1 and 3.

(1) to indicate that the subject will—or will not—be engaged in a present or future activity, a suitable adverbial being often used. When ʃal or wil are the modals used, this tense is the nearest approach to a "neutral" future, as it has the effect of stripping these finites of their modal meaning, eliminating their suggestion of willingness or obligation respectively. In concurrence with this, the finite ʃal is generally used with the first person singular and plural, even in cases where wil would be used in tense A3.

wi 'oːt tə bi ˋstaːtiŋ; ðei I bi ˋweitiŋ fər əs oːlˏredi.
kən 'juː bi ˙leiiŋ ðə ʹteibl̩; 'ai ʃl̩ bi ˙kukiŋ ðə ˅miːl.
ju 'niːdn̩t bi ˙getiŋ θiŋz ˅redi, əz ðei 'wount bi ˋkʌmiŋ.
ai 'mʌsn̩t bi ˙staːtiŋ ə˅nʌðə ˏgeim, əz wi ʃl̩ bi ˋliːviŋ ˌsuːn.

(2) to indicate that the subject will—or will not—be engaged in a certain activity at a time or during a period in the future usually indicated by an adverbial or adverbial clause.

ai ʃl̩ bi 'seiliŋ in ˋskotlənd ˌoːl ˌnekst ˌwiːk.
'hau ˙loŋ I ju bi 'steiiŋ wið joː ˋbrʌðə?
ðei 'wount bi ˙draiviŋ ðə ˙kaː wail ˙ðis ˋrein ˌlaːsts.
'oːtn̩t ju tə bi ʹwəːkiŋ ˙oːl ˙dei tə˙moru?

188

b. With modals of Groups 2 and 3, to report speeches (such as those shown in examples *a* (1) and *a* (2) above) containing modals of Groups 1 or 3.

ðei ˌsed ðei 'oːt tə bi ˏstaːtiŋ, əz ðeə 'frendz ud bi ˏweitiŋ fə ðəm.
ʃi 'aːskt if ˙ai kəd bi 'leiiŋ ðə ˏteibļ, əz 'ʃiː d bi ˙kukiŋ ðə ˏmiːl.
ai 'tould ðəm ai ʃəd bi ˙seiliŋ in ˋskotlənd ˌoːl ˌnekst ˏwiːk.
hi 'aːskt mi ˙hau ˙loŋ ai ʃəd bi 'steiiŋ wið mai ˏbrʌðə.

c. With modals of Group 2 only, to suggest a hypothetical activity in the present or future, connected with a conditional clause which is usually in one of the tenses of set *b* (§173).

wi ʃəd bi in'dʒɔiiŋ auəselvz ət ðə ˋpaːti ˏnau, if ju ˏhadņt ˏmeid
əs ˏmis ðə ˏtrein.
ju 'mait not bi ˙haviŋ sʌtʃ ən 'iːzi ˋtaim if joː 'faːðə ˙hadņt
ˋwəːkt ˏhaːd ˌoːl iz ˌlaif.
'wudņt ðei bi ˙liviŋ in ðə 'sauθ əv ˏjuərəp if ðei kəd əˈfoːd it?

222 Present perfect of activity. Tense A10. Functions:

a. With an adverbial of present time, to indicate that the subject has—or has not—been engaged in a certain activity during the elapsed portion of a period that includes the moment of speaking. Typical adverbials used in this context are **tədei, ðis moːniŋ, ðis aːftənuːn, ðis iːvniŋ.**

ʃi z bin ˋkofiŋ ə ˏlot təˏdei.
həv ju bin 'raitiŋ ˈletəz ðis ˙moːniŋ?
wi 'havņt bin ˙pleiiŋ ˋgolf ðis ˌaːftəˏnuːn.
'havņt ju bin ˙wotʃin ˈteliˈviʒņ ðis ˙iːvniŋ?

b. With the preposition (or conjunction) **sins** introducing an adverbial (or adverbial clause) of past time, to indicate that the subject has—or has not—been engaged in a certain activity in the interval between the time named and the moment of speaking. Typical adverbials used in this context are **sins ðen, sins əːli jestədi, sins laːst wiːk,** and typical clauses **sins ai soː ju laːst, sins ðei keim.**

ai v bin 'raitiŋ ˙letəz sins 'əːli ðis ˏmoːniŋ.
həv ju bin 'pleiiŋ ˙mʌtʃ ˈgolf sins ai ˙soː ju ˙laːst?
hi 'hazņt bin ˋspiːkiŋ tu əs sins wi ˏkworļd.
'hazņt ðə ˙beikə bin ˈkoːliŋ sins ˙laːst ˙wiːk?

189

c. With the preposition foː* introducing a phrase expressing duration, to indicate that the subject has—or has not—been engaged in a certain activity during a period lasting until the moment of speaking. Typical phrases are: fə ðə laːst tuː minits, fər ən auə*, fə sevr| wiːks paːst.

ai v bin 'raitiŋ ˙letəz fə 'tuː ˌauəz.
'wot əv ju bin ˎduːiŋ fə ðə ˌlaːst ˌauər oː sou?
ʃi 'haznt bin ˙teikiŋ hə ˙medsin fə 'sʌm ˎdeiz ˌnau.
'havnt ðei bin ˙liviŋ in ˙spein fə ðə 'laːst ˙tuː 'jiəz?

d. With an adverbial such as leitli, dʒʌst, sou faː, ʌp tə nau, to refer to an activity of unspecified duration lasting up to the moment of speaking.

ai v 'dʒʌst bin ˎspiːkiŋ tu im.
həv ju bin 'winiŋ ʌp tə ðə ˙preznt?
ðə 'paips 'havnt bin ˙liːkiŋ ˎsou ˌfaː.
'havnt ðei bin ˙kʌmiŋ tə ðə 'klaːs ˙riːsntli?

e. Without an adverbial, to refer to a recent activity of unspecified, but often implicit, duration.

ai v bin 'wəːkiŋ ˙veri ˎhaːd. (lately)
'wot əv ju bin ˎduːiŋ? (just now *or* since I saw you last)

223 Past perfect of activity. Tense A11. Functions:

a. To indicate that the subject had—or had not—been engaged in a certain activity at a time in the past which, if not implicit, is denoted by an adverbial of past time. There is no implication as to whether the activity ceased at the time mentioned, or whether it continued.

ai d bin 'raitiŋ ˎletəz wen ju ˌkeim.
'had ðei bin 'swimiŋ wen ju ˙met ðəm?
ai 'hadnt bin ˙fiːliŋ ˎwel bifoːr ai ˌtuk ðat ˌmedsin.
'hadnt ju bin iks˙pektiŋ ə ˙vizit frəm ðəm bi'foə?

b. To suggest a hypothetical activity in the past, in the following cases.

(1) in a conditional clause dependent on a main clause containing a modal perfect tense formed with a modal of Group 2.

ʃi d əv ˇfiniʃt bai ˌnau if ʃi d bin ˋwəːkiŋ ˌhaːdə.

ju 'mait əv ˙had ən ˋaksidn̩t if 'ai ˙hadn̩t bin ˇwotʃiŋ ju.

ju 'wudn̩t əv ˙meid sʌtʃ ə 'sili misˋteik if ju d bin ˌθiŋkiŋ əv
ˌwot ju wə ˇduːiŋ.

(2) in clauses subordinated to a main clause by the conjunctions əz if, əz ðou.

it 'izn̩t əz if i d bin 'giviŋ əs eni ˇtrʌbl̩.

hi 'luks əz ðou hi d bin ˋfaitiŋ.

(3) in clauses dependent on a main clause using wiʃ, wəd
raːðə*, or the imperative of səpouz.

ai 'wiʃ ai d bin ˇwəːkiŋ insted əv 'weistiŋ ˇtaim.

ai d 'raːðə ju d bin ˋswimiŋ ðən ˌpleiiŋ ˇfutboːl.

sə'pouz i d bin ˙traiiŋ tə ˋfoun əs ˌoːl ðis ˌtaim.

224 Modal perfect of activity. Tense A12. Functions:

a. With modals of Groups 1 and 3, to indicate that the subject
will—or will not—be engaged in an activity before the moment
of speaking or before some time in the future denoted by an
adverbial.

bai 'faiv əˈklok ʃi l əv bin 'pleiiŋ fər ən ˋauə.

'weə kən ðei əv bin ˌhaidiŋ ˌoːl ðis ˌtaim?

ju 'kaːnt əv bin prəˈnaunsiŋ ðat ˙wəːd kəˋrektli.

'oːtn̩t ju tu əv bin ˙getiŋ ˙redi fə ðə ′paːti?

b. With modals of Groups 2 and 3, to report speeches (such as
those shown in examples *a* above) containing modals of Group 1 or 3.

ai ˌsed ʃi d 'suːn əv bin ˙pleiiŋ fər ən ˌauə.

ʃi 'wʌndəd ˙weə ðei kəd əv bin ˋhaidiŋ ˌoːl ðat ˌtaim.

hi ˌsed ai 'mʌst əv bin prəˈnaunsiŋ it ˇroŋli.

ʃi 'aːskt if ai 'oːtn̩t tu əv bin ˙getiŋ ˙redi fə ðə ˇpaːti.

c. With modals of Group 2, to suggest a hypothetical activity
that would be complete at the moment of speaking or at some time
in the past denoted by an adverbial or connected with a conditional
clause in a past or past perfect tense.

ai 'mait əv bin ˙duːiŋ mai ˋhoumwəːk ˌoːl ðis ˌtaim.

'ʃud wi əv bin ə′raiviŋ ˙nau, if 'ai ˙hadn̩t ˙noun ðə ′wei?

ðei ˋkudn̩t əv bin iksˌpektiŋ əs in ˋðis ˌweðə.

'wudn̩t ′juː əv bin ˙fiːliŋ ′taiəd, if ju d 'woːkt əz ˙faːr əz ′ai hav?

TAGS

225 The conjugating finites in tags. The repetition of a specific verb that has just been used in a conversation is avoided in English by using what is often called a tag. The essential elements of a tag are a subject (usually a pronoun) and a conjugating finite, in either its affirmative or negative form, as required. The finite stands for the specific verb that has just been used, and any other essential part of the sentence, e.g., the object of a transitive verb.

Compared with the system of an invariable word or phrase used in many other languages, this system is rather more complicated for the learner, as it involves choosing the correct finite to agree with the tense and the subject, but it has the advantage of being unambiguous although the specific verb is not repeated.

Tags are used in a number of different ways, either by the speaker who used the specific verb or by another. The form of the tag varies with its meaning. Special notice should be taken of the intonation, which is important in conveying the correct meaning. All the conjugating finites are used in tags, but **juːst** is very frequently replaced by **did**.

226 Tag questions. There are five main classes of these. Examples of each class are given below.

Tag General Questions.

These are questions added to a statement by the same speaker. They are said with Tune I if the speaker is not sure of his statement, and with Tune II if he is sure of what he says. In the latter case the question is really a request for the hearer to agree with him.

ju kən 'plei ⌄krikit, ′kaːnt ju? *or* ⌄kaːnt ju?
hi z 'kʌmiŋ ⌄wið əs, ′iznt i? *or* ⌄iznt i?

Tag Questions Added to Imperatives.

With Tune I on the finite these soften the imperative. With Tune II on a finite following an imperative bearing Tune III they urge the hearer to comply with the request.

'put ðə ˙buks on ðə ˌteibl, ′wil ju?
'kʌm ⌄əːli, ⌄wount ju? 'dount bi ⌄leit, ⌄wil ju?

Tag Questions as Afterthoughts.

In these, the speaker, having made a statement, questions its validity. The finite is always affirmative, and takes a Tune II.

wi ˇʃaːnt bi ˌleit. oː ˋʃal wi?

ðei ˈjuːst tə ˙liv ˌhiə. oː ˋdid ðei?

Tag Particular Questions.

These are questions in which the second speaker asks for the identity of a subject referred to pronominally by the first speaker.

hi mei ˋgou.—ˋhuː mei? it məst bi ˋmendid.—ˋwot ˌmʌst?

Tag Questions as Comments.

Here the second speaker indicates that he has heard a statement by the first speaker, and receives it with varying degrees of interest or credulity.

ai m ˋtaiəd.—ˊaː ju? *or* ou ˋaː ju? *or* ˋou, ju ˋaːr, ˌaː ju?

ju ʃəd ˋweit.—ˊʃud wi? *or* ou, ˋʃud wi? *or* ˋou, wi ˋʃud, ˌʃud wi?

227 Tag statements.   The seven main classes of these are shown below, with examples.

Tag Answers to Questions.

These are short replies given by a speaker to either a general or a particular question.   The jes and nou always take kinetic tones.

did ju ˊriːd it?—ˋjes, ai ˋdid. *or* ˋnou, ai ˋdidn̩t.

ˈwount ðei ˊfit?—ˋjes, ðei ˋwil. *or* ˋnou, ðei ˋwount.

ˈhuː ˙wonts ˌtiː?—ˋai ˌduː. *or* ˋai ˌdount.

Tag Conditional Answers to Questions.

Here the second speaker gives a conditional affirmative reply to a question or a request by the first speaker.

ˈiz i ˙teikiŋ ðə ˊkaː?—if i ᵛmei.

ˈwil ju ˊhelp mi?—if ai ᵛkan. *or* if ai ᵛmʌst.

Tag Agreement.

Here the second speaker agrees with what the first speaker has said.

ai məst ˈliːv ˌəːli.—ˋjes, ju ˌmʌst.

ai ˈmʌsn̩t bi ˌleit.—ˋnou, ju ˋmʌsn̩t.

ʃi wəz ˋtoːkiŋ ˌtuː ˌmʌtʃ.—ˋjes, ʃi ˌwoz, ˌwozn̩t ʃi?

ʃi ˈdidn̩t ˙spiːk veri ᵛlaud.—ˋnou, ʃi ˋdidn̩t, ˋdid ʃi?

Tag Disagreement.

Here the second speaker disagrees with what the first speaker has said. Tune II is too abrupt here, and Tune III is generally used for politeness.

it s 'tuː ˋəːli tə ˏstaːt.—ˋnou, it ˏizn̩t.
wi 'niːdn̩t ᵛhʌri.—'ou, ˙jes, wi ᵛmʌst.

Tag Disagreement with an Assumption in a Question.

In these the second speaker protests that an assumption made by the first speaker is incorrect. The original question nearly always begins with wai.

'wai did ju inˋsʌlt im?—bət ai ˋdidn̩t!
'wai ˙wount ju ˋhelp ðəm?—bət ai ˋwil!

Tag Additions.

In these the second speaker adds a new subject to a verb used by the first speaker, in order to express a parallel. The addition to an affirmative statement is introduced by sou, and that to a negative statement by noː*, while there is inversion of the new subject and the finite.

ˋai l ˏhelp im.—'sou wil ˏai. *or* 'sou wil ˏdʒon.
ðei 'aːnt ˏredi.—'noːr əm ˏai. *or* 'noːr iz ˏdʒon.

Tag Contrary Additions.

In these a new subject is added to a specific verb already used, but this time to point out an antithesis. These additions, which may be made either by the original speaker or by another one, begin with bət, and there is no inversion of the new subject and the finite.

ˋhiː wəz ˏredi.—bət 'ai ˏwozn̩t. *or* bət 'juː ˏwəːnt.
'ðei ˙wəːnt ˋredi.—bət ˋwi ˏwəː. *or* bət ˋdʒon ˏwoz.

SPECIAL STRUCTURES

228 wud raːðə*. A much-used idiom expressing preference involves the use of **wud** followed by the adverb **raːðə*** and any one of the six infinitives of a specific verb. To state a preference for not doing something the affirmative finite is used before a negative infinitive. The infinitives are not preceded by **tu**.

A 3 ju d 'raːðə ˅weit, ˊwudn̩t ju?
A 3 ju d 'raːðə ˙not ˅weit, ˊwud ju?
A 6 'witʃ ud ju ˅raːðə əv ˌsiːn?
A 6 hi d 'raːðər əv ˅weitid, ˊwudn̩t i?
A 9 wi d 'raːðə bi ˙pleiiŋ ˌgolf.
A 9 'wudn̩t ðei ˙raːðə bi 'laiiŋ in ðə ˊsʌn?
A12 ai d 'raːðər əv bin ˙toːkiŋ tə ˅juː.
A12 ai d 'raːðə ˅not əv bin ˌtravliŋ in ˅ðis ˌweðə.
P 3 'wudn̩t ðei ˙raːðə bi 'teikən tə ðə ˙siːˊsaid?
P 3 ai d 'raːðə bi ˙kept in ˅ignərn̩s.
P 6 'wudn̩t ju ˙raːðər əv bin ˊtould əbaut it?
P 6 ai d 'raːðə ˙not əv bin inˌvolvd.

Negation can be incorporated in a question in two different
ways, which convey different insinuations. Notice the difference
between

wəd ju 'raːðə ˊnot ˙beið? = Would you prefer not to bathe?
'wudn̩t ju ˙raːðə ˊbeið? = You'd prefer to bathe, wouldn't you?

In a variant of this idiom the finite wud and the specific verb
have different subjects. In this case the modal, while retaining
its attributes as a conjugator (of inversion and combination with
not), acts semantically as a specific finite and is not followed by
an infinitive, while the specific verb is put into a subordinate clause
without any conjunction. Notice the tense arrangement.

If the sentence refers to present or future time the specific verb
is in the past tense:

˅fraŋkli, ai d 'raːðə ˙sʌmwʌn went ˅wið ju.
wud ju 'raːðə ði ˙ʌðəz ˙didn̩t ˅dʒoin əs?
wi d 'raːðə ju ˙sed 'nʌθiŋ əˌbaut it.
'wudn̩t ju ˙raːðər ai 'geiv ðəm əˊwei?

If the sentence refers to past time the specific verb is in the
past perfect tense:

˅fraŋkli, ai d 'raːðə ˙sʌmwʌn ˅els əd ˌgon ˌwið ju.
wud ju 'raːðər ai d 'left ði ˙ʌðəz biˊhaind?
wi d 'raːðər i ˙hadn̩t kənˊsʌltid əs in ˌðis ˌmatə.
'wudn̩t ju ˙raːðə wi d 'oːl ˙steid ət ˊhoum?

There is a variant of this idiom using the form wud suːnə*, but
most speakers seem to prefer wud raːðə*.

229 həd betə*. This well-established idiom bears a certain structural resemblance to the foregoing. It consists of **had** followed by the adverb betə*, and, like the modals, it is followed by an infinitive instead of the past participle, which is generally used after parts of the verb tə hav. It suggests that a certain course of action is (or is not) advisable, or in the best interests of the subject. To suggest the advisability of not doing something the affirmative finite is used before a negative infinitive, but the negative finite is used freely in questions. This construction occurs with all the six infinitives, though it is not very common in the perfect tenses. The infinitives are not preceded by tu.

A 3 ai d 'betə ˇtel im əbaut it, 'hadn̩t ai?
A 3 ai d 'betə ˙not ˇtel im əbaut it, 'had ai?
A 6 ju d 'betər əv ˙finiʃt bai ðə ˙taim ai get ᵛbak.
A 9 'hadn̩t wi ˙betə bi ˙getiŋ 'redi?
A 9 ðei d 'betə bi ˇstaːtiŋ ˏsuːn.
A12 ju d 'betər əv bin ˙wəːkiŋ ˇhaːd wail ai m əˏwei.
P 3 ʃi d 'betə ˙not bi 'woːnd əbaut it biᵛfoːhand.
P 3 'hadn̩t it ˙betə bi 'kukt ət 'wʌns?
P 6 ðə 'wəːk əd ˙betər əv bin in˙spektid bi'foːr ai əˇraiv.

Here again, negation can be incorporated in a question in two different ways, which convey different insinuations. Notice the difference in meaning of the two following questions:

həd ai 'betə ˙not 'gou? = Is it advisable for me not to go?
'hadn̩t ai ˙betə 'gou? = It's advisable for me to go, isn't it?

230 Causative get and hav. This structure conveys the idea that the subject of either of these verbs will (in the active) induce somebody else to do something or (in the passive) cause something to be done. In the active voice an accusative and infinitive (§234) is used, while in the passive voice a past participle is used as a predicate of result after the object. The structural patterns are:

Active	*Passive*
ai l 'get ðəm tə ˙rait ə ˏletə.	ai l 'get ə ˏletə ˏritn̩.
ai l 'hav ðəm ˙rait ə ˏletə.	ai l 'hav ə ˏletə ˏritn̩.

The passive forms are more frequently used than the active ones. Notice that in the active voice **get** takes the infinitive with **tu**, while **hav** takes the infinitive without **tu**. The use of **hav** in the active voice is more typical of American than of British English.

There is a subtle difference between the meanings of the two verbs in this context ; **get** suggests that there may be slight trouble or difficulty in arranging for the action to be performed, while **hav** treats the action as a matter of course. Examples:

Active:

hi 'gets iz ˈfaːðə tə 'help im wið iz ˈhoumwəːk.
ai v bin 'getiŋ mai ˈstjuːdn̩ts tə prəˈnauns ˌbetə.
ʃi 'mei ˈget əː ˈhʌzbənd tə 'bai ər ə ˈnjuː ˈkaː.
wi 'had ðə ˈboi ˈʃou əs ðə ˈwei tə joː ˈhaus.
ju məst 'hav ðəm ˈtiːtʃ ju 'hau tə ˈduː it.
'hav ðə ˈsekritri 'meik ə ˈkopi əv ˌðis ˌdokjumənt.

Passive:

ju 'riəli 'mʌs ˈget joː ˈheə ˌkʌt.
'kudn̩t ju ˈget ðis ˈvaːz ˈmendid?
wi ʃl̩ bi 'getiŋ ðə ˈkaː riˈpeəd təˈmoru.
ðei v bin 'haviŋ ðeə ˈhaus ˌriːˌpeintid.
'dount ˈhav eni ˈtʃeindʒiz ˌmeid til 'ai riᵛtəːn.
'ʃal ai ˈhav 'sentr| ˈhiːtiŋ inˈstoːld?

231 Precursory ðeə*. This is a device for indicating that the logical subject, which will be either a noun or a pronominal determiner, will follow the verb (nearly always the verb **tə biː** acting as a verb of incomplete predication) instead of preceding it as it normally would in statements. This is done by introducing the word **ðeə*** (almost invariably in its weak form **ðə***) in the position that would normally be occupied by the subject. When acting in this capacity it behaves as if it were a pronoun, changing places with the finite in order to form questions and taking either a singular or a plural finite according as the real subject, for which it is acting as precursor, is singular or plural.

A sentence like **ðə z ə 'buk on ðə ˈteib|** clearly meant originally **ə 'buk iz ˈðeə, on ðə ˈteib|**, the word **ðeə*** being used as an adverb of place, but in the modern use it has obviously lost all its adverbial force. For instance, in a sentence like **ðə 'kʌmz ə ˈmoumənt wen wʌn riˈbelz** it would be absurd to classify **ðeə*** as an adverb of place. Since words are now usually labelled to accord with the functions they are performing, it would seem logical, when ðeə* serves as a precursor of the real subject, to classify it as a determiner, with the label "pseudo-pronoun."

As shown in the following examples, ðeə* can be used with certain specific verbs, but is much more common with the verb tə biː. It occurs with all the conjugating finites except am and deə*.

wəz ðər ə 'buk on ðə ˙teibḷ?—ˋjes, ðə wə ˋfaiv.
'oːtṇt ðə tə bi ə'nʌðə wʌn?—ðə ᵛmait bi.
ðə 'mʌst əv bin ˙moː ðṇ ᵛðis!—ðə ˋkudṇt əv bin.
'wud ðə bi ə ˙tʃaːns əv 'siːiŋ ðəm?—ˋnou, ðə ˋwudṇt.
'haz ðə bin ən 'aksidṇt? ðə 'hadṇt bin ˋtaim fə ˌtiː.
ðə ʃḷ bi 'nou ˋaːgjuiŋ əbaut it.   ðə 'mei bi ˋtrʌbḷ.
ðə ˌsiːmz 'evri ˙riːzṇ fə səsˋpektiŋ ju.
dəz ðər ə'piə tə bi ˙eni eksplə'neiʃṇ fər it?
ðə ri,meinz 'nou ʌðə ˙koːs tə ˋteik.
ðə z 'nou ˙taim tə 'finiʃ it ᵛnau.
ðə 'wozṇt eni ˋruːm tə ˌsit ˌdaun.
'wount ðə bi ə ˙lot əv 'letəz tə bi ˙aːnsəd?
ðər ə ˋʃuə tə bi ˌlaːdʒ ᵛkraudz ðeə.
ðə z 'laikli tə bi ˋtrʌbḷ if ju ˌdount ˌstaːt ˌsuːn.
ðə kən bi 'nou ˙nouiŋ ˋhau meni misˏteiks wi ʃḷ ˌfaind.

It will be found that by replacing the verb tə biː by the appropriate tense of igzist (for states) or əkəː* (for events) any of the above examples can be rearranged in the normal order, and ðeə* can be dispensed with.

The adverbs sʌmweə*, eniweə* and nouweə* are used after precursory ðeə*, and then function as pronominal determiners, as is clear from the fact that these compounds can be replaced by the determiner-noun combination sʌm ruːm, etc., and are in fact usually replaced in American English by the combinations sʌm pleis, etc.

ðə 'mʌs bi ˋsʌmweə fər əs tə ˌsit ˌdaun.
iz ðər 'eniweə fər əs tə ˙put auə 'hats ən 'kouts?
ðə z 'nouweə fər əs tə ˋhaid frəm ðəm.

Precursory ðeə* must not be confused with such a use as 'ðeə z ə ˋbuk, 'on ðə ˋteibḷ, where ðeə* is fulfilling its normal function as an adverb of place and is therefore stressed.

232 Precursory it. This structure has a function similar to that described in §231, the difference being that while ðeə* does duty as precursor for nouns and determiners, precursory it serves in the same capacity for phrases and clauses, which, though the logical subjects of the verb, are considered grammatically as complements or adjuncts, the grammatical subject being the pronoun it. The phrases may be either infinitive or participial phrases and the clauses are noun clauses introduced either by the general conjunction ðat or by a conjunctive.

The finite used after precursory it is always singular and the verb is usually tə biː, though certain other verbs are used. Any modal except ʃal or deə* may be used in this structure. Examples:

Infinitive phrases.

    it wəz 'difik‖t tə di·said ˙wot tə ˇduː.
    it s 'iːzi tə ˇsei ‚ðat, bət 'wil ðei biˇliːv ju?
    it 'wudṇt ˙duː tə 'liːv ðə ˙doːr ʌnˇlokt.
    'didṇt it ˊəːk ju tə ˙hiə ðəm ˙toːk laik ˙ðat?

Participial phrases.

    it 'mʌs bi ˇboːriŋ ‚haviŋ tə ‚wəːk in ə ‚pleis laik ‚ðis.
    'wozṇt it diˇlaitf‖ ‚laiiŋ ‚ðeər in ðə ‚sʌn?
    it 'kudṇt əv bin ˇplezṇt ‚haviŋ tu əd‚mit ju wə ‚roŋ.
    it ˇhaz bin ə ‚pleʒə ‚toːkiŋ ‚ouvər ‚ould ‚taimz.

Clauses introduced by ðat.

    it wəz 'foːtʃṇit fər ˙ʌs ðət i 'hadṇt ˇsiːn əs.
    'izṇt it ə ˇʃeim (ðət) ju ‚didṇt ‚paːs ði ig‚zam!

Clauses introduced by conjunctives.

    it s ʌnˇsəːtṇ ˙weðə ðei ‖ bi ˙eib‖ tə ˇkʌm.
    it wəz ə 'mistəri ˙weər i ˙got iz ˇmʌni.

This structure, with it acting as a precursor to the verb's real subject, which appears later in the sentence, must not be confused with the impersonal it which is the real (and grammatical) subject of the sentence, since it refers to something, generally the weather or the time, which it is not customary to name. Examples:

    it wəz 'taim tə ‚liːv.   it 'izṇt ˙kould ˇnau.
    it s 'tuː ˇəːli tə ‚staːt.   it s ‚gouiŋ tə ˇrein.
    it ‖ 'suːn bi ˙nain ə‚klok.   ai 'θiŋk it ‖ bi ˇfain tə‚dei.

There are also, of course, the cases in which something already mentioned or identified is referred to as it, as in the following sentences.

it wəz ə 'loŋ ˙taim ə͵gou.   iᵗ s 'raːðər ə ˙loŋ ͵wei.
it 'sez ˙hiə ðət i ˈdid it.   it s ˈbaund tə sək͵siːd.

Precursory it can be identified by applying the inversion test. If the pronoun can be dispensed with by rearranging the sentence, then it is precursory. Compare the two sentences below:

a. it s ə 'gud ˙θiŋ tə ͵nou ͵ðat.   *b.* it s ə 'gud ˙θiŋ tə ͵nou.

Inversion of *a* gives: tə 'nou ͵ðat iz ə 'gud ͵θiŋ, showing that the infinitive phrase tə nou ðat is the subject of the verb. On the other hand, *b* does not make sense when inverted, showing that it is not precursory, but is the real subject, referring to something already in mind.

233 A subjunctive substitute. The finite ʃud has an important function in subordinate clauses that in many other languages would be in the subjunctive mood. When it is used in this way there is no suggestion of its modal meaning; it has a purely grammatical function as a substitute for the subjunctive, which has fallen out of use completely in spoken English with the one exception of the singular of the past tense of the verb tə biː, where woz is often replaced by wəː to indicate a hypothesis (§164).

In this structure ʃud is found in all the three persons and before all the six infinitives. By means of suitable tense adjustments it may be made to refer to the past, present or future. The clauses in which it occurs are introduced by the general conjunction ðət (expressed or understood) and are subordinated to various types of principal clause, among them:

1.   Precursory it followed by such nouns as

ə ˈwʌndə*   ə ˈpiti   ə 'gud ˈθiŋ
ə disˈgreis   ə ˈʃeim   ə 'bad ˈθiŋ

    it s ə disˈgreis ðət ʃi ʃəd əv bin in͵sʌltid laik ͵ðat.
    it s ə 'piti ðət ju ʃəd əv 'mist ˇsiːiŋ im.
    it s ə 'bad ˙θiŋ ðət ðei ʃəd bi 'pʌniʃt sou siˇviəli.

2. Precursory it followed by such adjectives as:

ˈwʌndəf| ˈrait   ˈrekəˈmendid   ˈstreindʒ   ˈʌnˈfeə*
ˈnesisri   ˈbetə*   diˈzaiərəb| səˈpraiziŋ disˈgreisf|
imˈpoːtṇt   ˈgud   ədˈvaizəb| iŋˈkredib| imˈposib|

it wəz imˈpoːtṇt ðət wi ʃəd ˈstaːt wiðaut diˌlei.

it ˈdidṇt siːm ˈrait ðət wi ʃəd bi inˌdʒoiiŋ auəselvz.

it s ədˈvaizəb| ðət ðə ˈdoː ʃəd bi ˈkept ˌlokt.

it ˈsiːmz ˈstreindʒ ðət ʃi ʃəd əv ˌsed ˌðat.

it s ˈmoust ˈʌnˈfeə ðət ˌai ʃəd əv bin iksˌkluːdid.

3. A predicate expressing feelings or attitudes:

tə bi ˈθaŋkf| tə bi səˈpraizd   tə bi ˈsori
tə bi ˈpliːzd   tə bi əsˈtoniʃt   tə bi əˈnoid
tə bi ˈglad   tə bi əˈmeizd   tə bi disˈtrest

wi ər ˈoːl ˈθaŋkf| ðət i ʃəd əv isˌkeipt wiðaut ˌindʒəriz.

ˈevriwʌn z səˌpraizd ðət ju ʃəd ˌθink ˌðat.

ai m ˈmoust əˈnoid ðət ju ˌʃudṇt əv bin iŋˌkluːdid.

4. Principal clauses containing such verbs as:

tə diˈmaːnd   tə ˈrekəˈmend   tə priˈfə*   tə ˈsiː
tu inˈsist   tə prəˈpouz   tə ˈpromis   tə riˈgret
tu ˈəːdʒ   tə səˈdʒest   tu əˈgriː   tu əbˈdʒekt

ðei ˈdidṇt inˈsist ðət ai ʃəd ˌʃeər it wið ðəm.

wi səˈdʒestid ðət ðei ʃəd ˈweit ə lit| wail.

ˈdount ju əˈgriː ðət ðə ˈpaːti ʃəd bi ˈkans|d?

ai riˈgret ðət ju ʃəd əv bin ˌfiːliŋ niˌglektid.

234 Accusative and infinitive. This is a convenient name for a collocation that foreign students should make a special point of studying and memorizing, for it does some of the work performed by the subjunctive in many other languages, and speakers of such languages often find themselves at a loss for a means of expressing their subjunctive in English. In most cases "accusative and infinitive" is the answer.

It occurs in sentences that refer to emotions or characteristics, and suggests that these will cause or enable something to be done, or (in the negative) that they will prevent its being done. Examples:

ðə ˈrivə z ˈtuː ˈwaid fər əs tə ˈswim əˌkros it.

wud ju ˈlaik mai ˈsistə tə ˈriːd tə ju?

wi ə di‵laitid fə ju tə ˌstei əˌnʌðə ˌwiːk.

'didn̩t ju ˙wont əs tə ‵weit fə ju?

‵ðis iz ˌiːzi inʌf fər ‵eniˌbodi tu ˌʌndəˌstand.

With many transitive verbs the entire accusative and infinitive phrase must be regarded as the direct object. It is obvious that in the following sentence tʃildr̩n alone is not the object of the verb.

ʃi ‵heits hə ˌtʃildr̩n tə bi ˌleit fə ˌskuːl.

The accusative and infinitive is also used in sentences having precursory subjects.

Examples with precursory ðeə*:

ðə I bi 'plenti əv ‵wəːk fə ju tə ˌduː.

'haz ðə bin i'nʌf ˙sʌn fə ðə 'fruːt tə ‵raipən?

ðə 'mei not ˙biː eni ‵buks fə ðəm tə ˌriːd.

'wozn̩t ðər ˙eniweə fə ju tə ‵sit?

ðər 'oːt tə bi i˙nʌf ˙fuːd fər ‵evriwʌn tə bi ˌsatisfaid.

Examples with precursory it:

it s ri‵dikjuləs əv ju tə riˌakt laik ˌðat.

'iz it ˙difik|t fə ðəm tə 'faind ˙taim tə ‵siː mi?

it 'wount ˙duː fə ðəm tə 'gou wiðaut ‵eksəsaiz.

'wozn̩t it ‵tʃaildiʃ əv ðəm tu ˌaːnsə laik ˌðat?

it | bi ə ‵pleʒə fər əs tu ˌentəˌtein ðəm.

THE IMPERATIVE

235 Forms of the imperative. The conjugation of the imperative is based on the infinitive, the six forms of which are set forth in the table in §177, though two of the infinitives shown there are not used in forming imperatives. The imperative has three forms:

    a. The Unemphatic Affirmative

    b. The Emphatic Affirmative

    c. The Negative.

Emphasis on the negative is increased by making changes in intonation but not in structure.

The true imperative is used only in the 2nd person, and in its basic form it is not accompanied by any pronoun, the subject **ju** being usually understood.

There is what may be called an oblique imperative for the 1st
and 3rd persons, which takes the form of the true imperative of
the verb **let**, followed by any of the object pronouns except ** juː**.
This is the English equivalent of so-called imperative forms in
other languages. Examples:

'let im ˏtrai.   'let s ˏgou.
ˌlet ə ˏweit.   'let əm ˏoːl ˌkʌm.
'let it ˏrein.   (and even: 'let mi ˏsiː).

236 The unemphatic imperative. This takes the form of the
infinitive of the specific verb without **tu**, but when it is used in this
capacity the form must be regarded as a finite. Two intonations
are common, Tune II, which is somewhat peremptory, and Tune III,
which is polite and gives the feeling of a request rather than an
order. The following structures are used.

Active Voice, Direct Imperative of Accomplishment.

'biː ˏkwaiət.   'kʌm ˏhiə.   'sit ˏdaun.
ˋbiː ˌəːli.   ˋʃʌt ðə ˌdoə.   ˋweit fə ˌmiː.

Active Voice, Perfect Imperative of Accomplishment.

'hav ˏdʌn wið ðis ˌnonsn̩s !

Active Voice, Direct Imperative of Activity.

'biː ˋweitiŋ fə mi wen ai ˌkʌm ˌbak.

Passive Voice, Direct Imperative of Accomplishment.

'biː iŋˋkʌridʒd bai joː səkˌses.

In many cases such as this the participle must be regarded as
an adjectival complement:

'biː pri·peəd fər ˋeniθiŋ.

In a familiar style of speech, which in other situations may sound
rude, the pronoun **juː** is inserted before the imperative. Probably
starting as a device for selecting from a group the person to whom
the imperative was addressed, this form is now used even when
only one person is present, to suggest a sense of urgency or emphasis.
While this structure is the same as that of a second person statement

in the present tense of accomplishment, the two meanings are distinguished because in the imperative the pronoun is always stressed, whereas in the statement it is normally unstressed.

Imperative: 'juː ˙kʌm ˌhiə.   'juː ˙sit ˌdaun.   'juː ˙weit fə ˌmiː.
Statement: ju 'kʌm ˌhiə.   ju 'sit ˌdaun.   ju 'weit fə ˌmiː.

In American English, when a speaker announces an intended course of action, the hearer often expresses approval by the formula: 'juː ˇduː ðat. The statement would be: ju ˇduː ðat.

With the verb tə biː the two structures are quite distinct:

     'juː bi ˙leiiŋ ðə ˌteibl.   ju ə 'leiiŋ ðə ˌteibl.

237 The emphatic imperative. In this case the specific verb form reverts to its infinitive status, being preceded by the finite duː. With this structure Tune II suggests impatience and Tune III pleading. The pronoun juː is not used with the emphatic imperative. The following structures are used.

Active Voice, Direct Imperative of Accomplishment.

     'duː bi ˌkwaiət.   'duː ˙kʌm ˌhiə.   'duː ˙sit ˌdaun.
     ˇduː bi ˌəːli.   ˇduː ˌʃʌt ðə ˌdoə.   ˇduː ˌweit fə ˌmiː.

Active Voice, Perfect Imperative of Accomplishment.

     'duː ˙hav ˌdʌn wið ðis ˌnonsn̩s !

Active Voice, Direct Imperative of Activity.

     ˇduː bi ˌweitiŋ fə mi wen ai ˌkʌm ˌbak.

Passive Voice, Direct Imperative of Accomplishment.

     ˇduː bi iŋˌkʌridʒd bai joː səkˌses.

238 The negative imperative. This is formed by placing **dount** before the infinitive of the specific verb. In this case Tune II is very severe and seldom used. A warning or insinuating note is given by placing an Undivided Tune III on the last stressed word of the utterance, while a pleading note is conveyed by a Divided Tune III with the fall on **dount** and the rise on the last stressed word.

Active Voice, Direct Imperative of Accomplishment.

     'dount bi ˇloŋ.   'dount ˙gou əˇwei.   'dount ˙stand ˇʌp.
     ˇdount bi ˌloŋ.   ˇdount ˌgou əˌwei.   ˇdount ˌstand ˌʌp.

'dount bi ᵛleit.   'dount ˙ʃʌt ðə ᵛdoə.   'dount ᵛweit.
ˋdount bi ˏleit.   ˋdount ˌʃʌt ðə ˏdoə.   ˋdount ˏweit.

Active Voice, Direct Imperative of Activity.

'dount bi ˙lukiŋ ˋtaiəd wen ju ˏget ðeə.
ˋdount bi ˌstaːtiŋ wið‚aut mi.

With verbs of action a common variant of this form is:

'dount ˙gou 'liːviŋ joː ˙θiŋz əᵛbaut.
ˋdount ˌgou ˏtoːkiŋ tu ˙evribodi əbaut it.

Passive Voice, Direct Imperative of Accomplishment.

'dount bi ˋnoutist if ju kən ˏhelp it.
ˋdount bi disˏkʌridʒd bai joː ˏfeiljə.

The negative imperative sometimes has the pronoun juː incorporated in familiar speech. It therefore has the same construction as the interrogative-negative, but the intonation provides a clear distinction between the two, as the imperative nearly always takes a Tune III (usually undivided), which would be extremely rare in the interrogative-negative.

'dount ˙juː 'gou əᵛwei.   'dount ˙juː 'ʃʌt ðə ᵛdoə.
'dount ˙juː ˙gou ˋtoːkiŋ tu ˏevribodi ə‚baut it.

With the verb tə biː there is again no confusion:

'dount ˙juː bi ᵛleit.   'dount ˙juː bi ˙staːtiŋ wiðᵛaut mi.
'dount ˙juː ˙biː disˋkʌridʒd bai joː ˏfeiljə.

THE SPECIFIC VERBALS

239 Forms of the verbals. The conjugating and specific verbals (§126) combine to form compound verbals, as shown below.

Infinitives. Specific verbs have six of these:

Accomplishment		Activity
	Active Infinitives	
tə teik	Direct	tə bi teikiŋ
tu əv teikən	Perfect	tu əv bin teikiŋ
	Passive Infinitives	
tə bi teikən	Direct	——
tu əv bin teikən	Perfect	——

Negative infinitives are formed by placing the negative adverb not before the tu of the infinitive ; they occur frequently in infinitive phrases, but in forming tenses negation is more usually expressed by using a negative finite. All the infinitives are used both in infinitive phrases and in the formation of tenses, but it must be remembered that intransitive verbs have no passive forms, whether infinitives or participles.

Participles. Specific verbs have seven of these:

Accomplishment		*Activity*
	Active Participles	
teikən	Direct	teikiŋ
haviŋ teikən	Perfect	haviŋ bin teikiŋ
	Passive Participles	
bin teikən	Direct	biːiŋ teikən
haviŋ bin teikən	Perfect	———

It will be noticed that the past participle is at the top of the left hand side of the table (under accomplishment) while the present participle heads the right side (under activity). It may seem strange to find these participles under these respective heads with no time distinction made between them, but since the past participle can be applied to the future (ai ʃl əv teikən) and the present participle to the past (ai wəz teikiŋ) the traditional names would seem to be unreliable guides to the functions of these verbals, which are as follows. The past participle and its compounds indicate (1) accomplishment and (2) the passive, and may refer to the past, the present or the future. The present participle and its one compound indicate activity at any time, but in the two passive tenses of activity their function is taken over by the conjugating verbal biːiŋ, since the specific verb must be in the past participle to indicate the passive.

As for the uses of the seven forms appearing in the table, we find that the four direct (i.e. non-perfect) participles all enter into the formation of tenses and, with the exception of the passive direct of accomplishment, all occur in participial phrases. On the other hand the three perfect participles (which use the conjugating verbal haviŋ as their first component) are not used in tenses but function only in participial phrases.

Negative participles, which occur chiefly in participial phrases, are formed by placing the negative adverb not before the first component of the participle.

THE INFINITIVES

240 Uses of the infinitives.   In the conjugation of specific verbs their infinitives are used in the following cases.

1. The direct infinitive of accomplishment is used in the present and past direct tenses of the aspect of accomplishment in all forms of these tenses except the unemphatic affirmative.

2. All six infinitives are used in the special past tenses formed with the finite juːst, though it should be noted that some of these tenses do not occur very frequently.

3. All six infinitives are used in forming the modal tenses.

Apart from tense formation, the infinitives are used in the following ways:

1. As subject of another verb.
2. As logical subject after precursory it or ðeə*.
3. As object or part object of another verb.
4. As complement or part complement of another verb.
5. In phrases introduced by conjunctives.
6. As adverbials of purpose.
7. In elliptical structures.

24I Infinitives as subjects of verbs.   Any of the six infinitives shown in §239 can be used in either their affirmative or their negative form as verbal nouns to form the subject of another verb, usually the verb tə biː, though many other verbs can be used in this position.   Examples:

tə 'haid ðə ˙letə wəz ðə 'wəːk əv ə ˌmoumənt.
'not tu əv inᵛvaitid ðəm wud əv əˋfendid ðəm.
tə bi 'əːniŋ ˙oːl ðat ˙mʌni 'mʌs bi ˙veri ˌgratifaiiŋ.
tu əv bin 'koːziŋ sou 'mʌtʃ ˙trʌbl̩ iz disˋgreisfl̩.
'not tə bi ˙held risᵛponsibl̩ riˈliːvd mi triˋmendəsli.
tu əv bin misˈteikən fə ᵛjuː wəz 'kwait ə ˋkomplimənt.

A sentence like the following has one infinitive as subject and another as subject complement:

tə ˈnou ˌoːl iz tə fəˈgiv ˌoːl.

This structure, which does not lend itself to the formation of questions, is more used in the written language than in the spoken, where it is almost always replaced by the precursory it structure. In the above examples the infinitive phrase is the grammatical, as well as the logical, subject of the principal verb; by moving the infinitive phrase to the end of the sentence and bringing in precursory it as the grammatical subject the sentence can be made more manageable, especially in the interrogative. The various types of this device will now be considered.

INFINITIVES AFTER PRECURSORY SUBJECTS

242 With verbs of complete predication. Certain verbs that are normally transitive are sometimes used without an object in order to give them more general application, though with some of them the indefinite pronoun wʌn is often inserted. If an infinitive phrase is the subject it is almost always displaced by precursory it. The following are among such verbs:

ˈsatisˌfai	kloi	boə*	pliːz	duː
ˈseiʃiˌeit	səˈfais	taiə*	help	pei

it səˈfaisiz tə ˈsei ðət ˈevriθiŋ z ˈgouiŋ ˌsmuːðli.
wud it ˈhelp tə ˈnou ðət joː ˈfrendz ˈsimpəθaizd?
it ud ˈnevə ˌduː tə bi ˌbiːtn̩ bai sʌtʃ ə ˌwiːk ˌtiːm.
d ju ˈθiŋk it ˈpeiz tu ˈadvəˈtaiz?

243 With transitive verbs. In this case the infinitive phrase follows the object of the verb. The following are typical of the verbs that are used in this structure.

ˈstimjuˌleit	diˈlait	taiə*	veks	inˈreidʒ
ikˈsait	ˈflatə*	ʃok	ˈsadn̩	disˈtres
əsˈtoniʃ	ˈhjuːmə*	ˈiriˌteit	griːv	ˈsikən
səˈpraiz	pliːz	ˈdisəˈpoint	boə*	disˈgʌst
əˈmjuːz	tempt	ˈwʌri	əˈnoi	ˈfraitn̩
riˈfreʃ	ˈgratiˌfai	ˈboðə*	həːt	ˈteriˌfai
ˈintrist	ˈsatisˌfai	əːk	ˈʌpˈset	ˈhoriˌfai

it ˈflatəz im tə bi ˌkoːld ˌsəː.
ˈwud it ˈintrist ju tə ˈhiə ðat ˈlektʃə?
it ˈwount ˈʃok hə tə ˌhiə ju ˌtoːk laik ˌðat.
ˈdidn̩t it əˈnoi ðəm tə bi ˈleft biˈhaind?
ˈwai dəz it inˈreidʒ ə ˈbul tə ˈsiː ə ˈred ˌrag?

There is no difficulty in putting such sentences into the passive
voice. Note that the precursory it is no longer required.

ˈwud ju bi ˈintristid tə ˈhiə ðat ˈlektʃə?
ʃi ˈwount bi ˈʃokt tə ˌhiə ju ˌtoːk laik ˌðat.

244 With adjective complements. In this case, where a verb
of incomplete predication is followed by an adjective complement
(predicative adjective) the infinitive phrase follows immediately
after the complement provided the sentence is intended to have
general or indefinite application. If, however, it is intended to
apply to a certain person or thing, a noun or determiner governed
by a preposition is inserted between the complement and the
infinitive, thus engendering one form of the accusative and infinitive
construction described in §234. The preposition used is ov if the
adjective is to apply directly to the person named, and foː* if it
is to apply to the situation. Some adjectives may apply to either,
and consequently take whichever preposition is appropriate to the
case.

The following are typical adjectives used in this construction:

With ov	*With* ov *or* foː*	*With* foː*
kaind	nais	ˈiːzi
ˈhelpfl̩	ˈriːzn̩əbl̩	ˈnoːml̩
ˈdipluˈmatik	ˈinkən̩ˈsistənt	ˈfiːzibl̩
inˈtelidʒn̩t	ˈtʃaildiʃ	ˈpraktikəbl̩
brait	ˌʌnˈriːzn̩əbl̩	ˈdifiklt̩
ˈsensibl̩	riˈdikjuləs	ˈdeindʒərəs
ˈsivl̩	əbˈsəːd	ˈjuːslis
ˈkreizi	ˈfuːliʃ	ˌabˈnoːml̩
inˈsein	ˈsenslis	imˈposibl̩
mad	ˈstjuːpid	ˈnesisri

Examples of general or indefinite application:

it wəz ˈsenslis tu əv ˌtould ðəm əbaut it.
ˈwud it əv bin ˈjuːslis tu ˈweit fə ðəm?

it 'izn̩t ˙difik|t tə bi 'teikən ᵛin bai im.
'wount it bi ˙nais tə bi 'pleiiŋ ˇgolf ə,gein!

Examples of restricted application.

it | bi ˋlʌvli fə ju tə bi ˌsteiiŋ in ðə ˌˇkʌntri.
'iz it ˙ʌn′riːzn̩əb| əv mi tə ˙wont sm̩ ˙moə?
it 'wount bi ˋfiːzib| fə ju tə ˌkʌm tə,moru.
'wozn̩t it ˋkaind əv hə tu əv in,vaitid əs!

245 With noun complements. This structure resembles the foregoing, except that the complement is a noun instead of an adjective. In the restricted version foː* is again used for the situation, but ov is replaced by on . . . paːt or on ðə paːt əv. . . . The following typical nouns used in this structure are preceded by the indefinite article.

ˋlʌkʃəri	ˋonə*	'inspi′reiʃn̩	fag	faːs
ˋblesiŋ	ˋkʌmfət	'satisˋfakʃn̩	boə*	ʃok
dʒoi	riˋliːf	'konsuˋleiʃn̩	ˋnjuːsn̩s	ˋinsʌlt
triːt	help	'afekˋteiʃn̩	əˋbjuːs	oːˋdiːl
diˋlait	ˋdjuːti	ˋplatiˌtjuːd	ˋlaib|	ʃeim
ˋpleʒə*	ˋpiti	ris'ponsiˋbiliti	ˋskand|	disˋgreis
ˋtraiʌmf	strein	'impuˋziʃn̩	əˋfens	ˋautreidʒ

Examples of general or indefinite application:

it s ə ˋʃeim ˌnot tə bi in,dʒoiiŋ ðis ˌbrait ˌsʌnʃain.
'wud it bi ə ′fag tə ˙teik ðə ˙tʃildrn̩ wið ju?
it 'wount bi ə ˋtriːt tə ˌtrav| sou ˌfaː bai ˌkoutʃ.
'wozn̩t it ə ˋpiti tu əv bin ˌbiːtn̩ bai sou ˌlit|?

Examples of restricted application:

it wəz ən ə'bjuːs on ðə ˙paːt əv ðə ˋfəːm tə dis,mis ju.
'iz it ə ′boə fə ju tə bi ˙sitiŋ ˙hiə ˙duːiŋ ˙nʌθiŋ?
it 'izn̩t ən ˙afekˋteiʃn̩ on ˌhəː paːt tə ˌsmouk.
'hazn̩t it bin ə ri′liːf fə ju tə ˙get ə˙wei fər ə bit?

The following are some nouns that are used as uncountables and are therefore not preceded by the indefinite article.

fʌn	ˋimpjudn̩s	ˋprigiʃnis	ˋfeivəritizm̩	ˋtriːzn̩
ˋraʃnis	ˋarugəns	ˋkauədis	stjuˋpiditi	ˋtoːtʃə*

Examples of general or indefinite application:

it s ˈfeivəritizm̩ tə ˌteik joː ˌsistər ən ˌnot ˌjuː.
ˈwudn̩t it bi ˈfʌn tə ˈgou əˈbroːd ðis ˌjiə?

Examples of restricted application:

it s ˈarugəns on ˌjoː paːt tə ˌtoːk laik ˌðat.
it s ˈtoːtʃə fə ˌmiː tə bi ˌweəriŋ ðiːz ˌʃuːz.

Some popular noun phrases such as the following are used in this sentence pattern:

ˈeni ˈjuːs	ˈeni ˈgud	ə ˈgud aiˈdiə	ˈlak əv ˈkonfidn̩s
ˈnou ˈjuːs	ˈnou ˈgud	ðə ˈdʌn ˈθiŋ	ˈwont əv ˈtakt
ˈfeə ˈplei	ðə ˈfaʃn̩	ˈbad ˈteist	

Examples:

it ud bi ˈnou ˈjuːs (fə ju) tə ˈkʌm ˈbak ˌleitə.
ˈiz it ˈeni ˈgud (fər əs) tə ˈtrai əˈgein?
it ˈwozn̩t ə ˈgud aiˈdiə tə ˈliːv im bai imˌself.
ˈwudn̩t it ˈʃou ˈlak əv ˈkonfidn̩s tə riˈfjuːz tə ˈgou?

246 Infinitives after precursory ðeə*. In this case the logical subject of the sentence is a noun or pronominal determiner and the infinitive functions as an attributive or predicative adjective to this. Typical nouns used in this structure are:

niːd	diˈzaiə*	prəˈpouzl̩	ˈopəˈtjuːniti	ˈriːzn̩
koːl	ˈəːdʒn̩si	riˈzolv	niˈsesiti	ˈtʃaːns
koːz	əˈtempt	inˈtenʃn̩	ˌtempˈteiʃn̩	taim
wiʃ	əˈkeiʒn̩	diˈsiʒn̩	ˈtendənsi	ˈhʌri

Examples of general or indefinite application:

ðə z ˈnou ˈkoːl tə ˈget sou ikˈsaitid əˌbaut it.
həz ðə ˈbiːn ən ˈopəˈtjuːniti tə disˈkʌs ðə ˈmatə?
ðə ˈwount bi ə ˈtʃaːns tə get ˌsəːvd.
ˈwozn̩t ðər ə diˈsiʒn̩ tu əˈboliʃ ˈðat ˈsistəm?
ðə z bin ən əˈtempt tə ˈblou ʌp ðə ˌbridʒ.

Examples of restricted application:

ðə z bin ə prəˈpouzl̩ fə ˈmiː tə ˈteik ˌouvə.
iz ðər ˈeni ˈhʌri fə ˈðis ˈwəːk tə bi ˈfiniʃt?

ðə z 'nou ni'sesiti fə ðəm tə bi in‚fo:md.

'wozn̥t ðər ə 'dʒenr| di‛zaiə fə ðə 'ski:m tə bi 'dropt?

'wil ðə bi ˙eni ˙ni:d fə mi tə 'kʌm tə'moru?

The following examples show the same structure having as its logical subject pronominal determiners instead of nouns.

General:

ðə z 'sʌmbədi tə 'si: ju.

ə ðər 'eni 'ʌðəz tə bi ˙put ə˙wei?

ðər 'izn̥t ˙mʌtʃ tə bi ˅sed fər it.

'wount ðə bi i˙nʌf tə bi 'getiŋ 'on wið?

ðər ə 'ði:z tə bi ‚finiʃt.

Restricted:

ðə I bi 'plenti fə him tə ˙du: in ðə ˅ga:dn̥.

iz ðə 'mʌtʃ 'mo: fə ðəm tə ˙teik ə˙wei?

ðə z bin 'noubədi fə mi tə 'to:k tu.

'wə:nt ðər 'eni fə ju tə ˙sta:t on?

ðə ˅mait bi 'sevr| fər əs tə ‚tʃu:z from.

INFINITIVES AFTER NORMAL SUBJECTS

247 Infinitives as objects of verbs. Infinitive phrases used after such verbs as the following may be regarded as direct objects.

'ʌndə'teik	ri'fju:z	tempt	ə'fo:d	lə:n
ri'membə*	di'ma:nd	'promis	bi'gin	tʃu:z
kən'tinju	pri'tend	fə'get	houp	

wi fə'got tə ˙mi:t ðəm ət ðə ‚steiʃn̥.

həv ðei 'promist tə ˙let əs 'boru it?

'ai ‚ka:nt ə'fo:d tə ‚smouk sou ‚mʌtʃ.

'izn̥t jo: ˙sistə 'lə:niŋ tə ˙draiv ə 'ka:?

'wil ju ri'membə tə ˙hav it ˙redi bai 'wenzdi?

Verbs such as the following also take infinitive phrases as their object:

| laik | wont | pri'fə:* | iks'pekt | heit |
| lʌv | wiʃ | di'zaiə* | in'tend | mi:n |

ai 'heit tə ‚li:v ju ‚o:l bai jo:‚self.

d ju pri'fə: 'not tu in‚vait ðəm tə ðə ‚pa:ti?

ˋai ʃudn̩t ˌlaik tə ˌbeið in sʌtʃ ˌkould ˏwoːtə.

'maitn̩t ðei bi inˑtendiŋ tə 'kʌm təˊmoru?

'wai d ju ˑwont tə 'rait ðə ˑletə joːˏself?

When restricted in application by the insertion of a noun or determiner before the infinitive, these verbs take the accusative and infinitive combination as their object.

wi ʃəd ˋlʌv ju tə ˌkʌm ən ˏstei wið əs.

ai 'dount ˑwont ju tu ʌpˇset joːself.

d ju pri'fəː ðə təˑmaːtuz tə bi 'səːvd ˊroː?

'dount ju inˑtend ðə 'njuː pəˈteituz tə bi ˊpiːld?

ai 'ment ju tə ˑkʌm ˋəːliə.

This is the structure used in the active voice form of causative get. (§230).

Another small class of verbs that may take an infinitive phrase as object includes:

riˋkwaiə*	priˋpeə*	ˋpromis	tʃuːz	aːsk
riˋkwest	diˋsaid	trʌst	niːd	beg

'ðis ˑruːm 'niːdz tə bi ˑriːˋdekəˌreitid.

did ju ri'kwest tə bi ˑtraːnsˑfəːd tə ˊlʌndən?

ai 'didn̩t ˋpromis tu əˏkʌmpəni ju.

'wudn̩t ju ˑbeg tə ˊdifər on ˑðat ˑpoint?

'wen did ju priˑpeə tə ˋteik ði igˌzamiˌneiʃn̩?

Any noun or determiner that is inserted to restrict the application of the verb becomes its object, and the infinitive then becomes a predicate of result.

ði 'aksidn̩t diˑsaidid mi tə 'giv ˑʌp ˏdraiviŋ.

də ðə 'klʌb ˑruːlz ri'kwaiə wʌn tə bi ˊsponsəd?

ai 'wudn̩t ˑtrʌst ðəm tə bi ˇpʌŋktʃuəl.

'kudn̩t ju ˑaːsk ə tə ˊweit ə ˊfjuː ˑminits?

'wai did ju ˑtʃuːz ˋmiː tə ˌhelp ju?

This is the structure used in the idiom tə ˌhav ə 'gud ˑmaind ('not) tə. . . .

The following verbs take a noun or determiner as a direct object, and this is followed by the infinitive without tu.

meik	əbˋzəːv	siː	smel	wotʃ
let	ˋnoutis	hiə*	fiːl	

ju kən 'fiːl ði ˈəːθ 'trembļ ʌndə joː ˌfiːt.

'wil ju 'meik ðə ˈtʃildrņ 'stop 'kworļiŋ?

ju 'aːnt 'wotʃiŋ mi ˌdemənstreit ˌhau tə ˌwəːk it.

'didņt ju ˈnoutis im 'heziteit in iz ˈspiːtʃ?

This is the structure used in the active voice form of causative hav (§230).

The verb help is followed by the infinitive with or without tu.

ai v bin 'helpiŋ (tə) ˈplaːnt ðeə 'rouziz.

'wil ju ˈhelp mi (tu) 'ʌnˈpak ðis 'paːsļ?

Verbs such as the following do not take the infinitive alone as their object, but require an accusative and infinitive combination in order to make sense.

'ʌndə'stand	sə'pouz	bi'liːv	teik
ək'nolidʒ	ə'sjuːm	faind	nou

ai 'ʌndəˈstand im tə bi ən 'ekspəːt in ˌðiːz ˌmatəz.

kən wi ə'sjuːm ðə ˈfigəz tə bi 'absəˈluːtli ri'laiəbļ?

ðəi 'tuk mi tə bi ə 'distənt 'relətiv əv ˌðeəz.

A passive construction is often preferred:

ʃi z bi'liːvd tu əv ˈentəd ðə ˈkʌntri i'liːgļi.

ə ðei sə'pouzd tə bi ə'raiviŋ 'əːli?

ju wə 'noun tu əv bin ˌdriŋkiŋ ˌhevili.

Another passive structure in which most of these verbs occur is precursory it heralding a subordinate clause introduced by the general conjunction ðat.

'izņt it ək'nolidʒd ðət ˈiŋgliʃ iz ˈiːzi tə ˈləːn?

it wəz 'faund ðət ðə ˈlok əd bin 'tampəd wið.

248 Infinitives as predicates. Although the following verbs are transitive they do not take the infinitive phrase as their object. They have a noun or determiner as object and the infinitive is a predicate of result.

'stimjuˌleit	in'strʌkt	ri'maind	'oːdə*	foːs
in'spaiə*	kə'maːnd	prompt	tiːtʃ	tel
iŋ'kʌridʒ	kəm'pel	əd'vaiz	tempt	bid
'priːdis'pouz	ə'blaidʒ	in'vait	kouks	pres
in'djuːs	di'rekt	im'pel	braib	get

inˈsait	prəˈvouk	inˈeibl̩	liːd	muːv
inˈtais	əˈpoint	pəˈmit	woːn	liːv
pəˈsweid	disˈpouz	əˈlau	əːdʒ	set

wi v pəˈsweidid ən ˈekspəːt tə ˈluk ˈintə ðə ˌmatə.

ˈwil ju inˈstrʌkt ðəm tə ˈkliːn ˈoːl ðə ˈwinduz?

ðei ˈdidn̩t inˈvait mi tu əˇkʌmpəni ðəm.

ˈkudn̩t ju ˈkouks ðə ˈbeibi tu ˈiːt iz ˈfuːd?

hə ˈtiːtʃə z ˈfoːsiŋ ə tə ˌduː əː ˌhoumwəːk.

Some verbs take a prepositional object before the infinitive.

wi məst ˈsend fə ðə ˈplʌmə tə ˈmend ðə ˌpaip.

ðei ˈkudn̩t priˈveil əpon mi tə ˈmeik ə ˌspiːtʃ.

ˈkaːnt ju ˈaːsk fər ə ˈkoːkskruː tu ˈoupən ðə ˈbotl̩?

Others take an adverb before the infinitive.

ʃi ˈegd im ˈon tə kriːˈeit ə disˈtəːbəns.

wiː l ˈpak it ˈʌp tə ˈsend it bai ˌpoust.

The following verbs take two objects, the first being a direct object and the second a prepositional object that combines with the infinitive to express purpose.

| giv | bai | send | teik | meik |
| lend | get | briŋ | liːv | bild |

ai v ˈmeid it fə ˈjuː tə ˌweə.

ju məs ˈbriŋ wʌn fə mi tə ˌsiː.

wil ju ˈgiv ðis ˈrekoːd ˈpleiə fər əs tə ˈrafl̩?

The indirect object may be placed first; in this case the infinitive phrase alone expresses purpose, but may also be felt to have a certain adjectival relationship towards the direct object.

wi ə ˈbaiiŋ ðə ˈgəːlz ˈnjuː ˈdresiz tə ˌweər ət ðə ˌpaːti.

ˈdidn̩t ju ˈliːv ðə ˈtʃildrn̩ eni ˈtoiz tə ˈplei wið?

ju ˈhavn̩t ˈlent mi ə ˈbuk tə ˌriːd ˌleitli.

Verbs such as the following are often followed directly by an infinitive phrase, which functions as a complement although some of the verbs are often transitive, especially those in the first two columns.

kənˈtinju	ˈtrʌbl̩	ˈheziˌteit	ˈhapən	keə*
ˈmanidʒ	ˈheisn̩	inˈdevə*	weit	deə*
əˈreindʒ	tʃaːns	əˈgriː	əˈpiə*	
riˈfjuːz	trai	kənˈsent	siːm	

ai 'tʃaːɾst te siː it in ðə ˌnjuːspeipə.
wud i 'deə tə ˙disə˙bei joːr 'oːdəz?
ju 'mʌsn̩t ə˙piə tə ˙nou 'eniθiŋ ə'baut it.
'kaːnt wi ə˙reindʒ tə 'muːv ðə ˙fəːnitʃər on 'fraidi?
'wai əv ðei ri'fjuːzd tə ˙teik əs ˌwið ðəm?

Three of the above verbs can take an accusative and infinitive
complement:

ju məst ə'reindʒ fər ˙evribodi tə bi ˌpreznt.
ʃi 'dʌznt ˙keə fər əs tə dis'kʌs ðə ˌmatə.
'didnt ðei ˙weit fə ju tə 'giv ðə 'sign|?

249 Infinitives after conjunctives. The infinitives are used after
all the conjunctives except wai and if. Examples:

ai 'kaːnt ˙θiŋk 'huː(m) tə kənˌsʌlt.
hi 'didnt ˙nou 'huːz ʌmˌbrelə tə ˌteik.
ai ˌhav 'nou ai'diə ˌwot tə ˇθiŋk əv hə.
ju məst 'aːsk ə pə˙liːsmən 'witʃ ˌbʌs tə ˌteik.
'tel mi 'weə tə ˙gou ən 'hau tə ˇget ðeə.
d ju 'nou ˙wen tə ˙riŋ ðə 'bel?
həv ju di'saidid ˙weðə tə 'gou oː ˙not?
ai 'wont tə ˙nou 'hau ˙hai tə ˇbild ðə ˌwoːl.

250 Infinitives as adverbials of purpose. Purpose is expressed
by infinitive phrases introduced by sou əz or (in oːðə) tu.

ai m 'wəːkiŋ ˇhaːd ˌnau 'sou əz tu ˙əːn ˙moː ˌmʌni.
wi 'duː ðəm ˙veri ˌkeəf|i, sou əz 'not tə ˌspoil ðəm.
in 'oːdə tə ˙get ðəm ˌtʃiːpə, hi 'boːt ðəm ˌhoulˌseil.
ri'piːt it ˙evri ˌdei, in 'oːdə ˙not tə fəˌget it.
ai v 'kʌm hiə tə ˇwəːk, ˇnot tə ˌplei.

251 Infinitives in elliptical structures. Infinitives are used in
certain constructions having no finite verb.

'wai ˌtrʌb|?   'wai not ˙teik ə ˌholidi?
tə 'tel ju ðə ˌtruːθ, ai 'dount ˇlaik im.
'oːdəz fə təˌmoru—'dʒon tə ri˙siːv ˌvizitəz, 'meəri tu ə˙tend
tə ðə 'koris'pondəns.

THE PARTICIPLES

252 Uses of the participles. In the conjugation of specific verbs, as can be seen from the tables in §§148–152, the past and present participles of these verbs are used in the following cases:

Past Participle.

> In the active voice, to form the three perfect tenses of the aspect of accomplishment.
> In the passive voice, to form all the tenses, i.e., six in the aspect of accomplishment and two in the aspect of activity.

Present Participle.

> In the active voice, to form the six tenses of the aspect of activity.

In addition to these, the following extra-temporal functions of the participles have already been discussed:

Past Participle.

> Passive participial adjectives (§§105–7).
> Predicate of result in the passive form of causative **get** and **hav** (§230).

Present Participle.

> Active participial adjectives (§§102–4).
> Nouns (§§49–50).

Other uses of the participles are:

1. In participial phrases.
2. In absolute constructions.
3. As gerund (present participles only).
4. As half-gerund (present participles only).

In considering the first two of these functions it is preferable to classify the participles by the system used in the table in §239.

253 The ing-form as a noun. When the ing-form is functioning as a noun proper, it has no verbal function. It may be used in this capacity in three ways, the first two of which present no problems.

1. *As a concrete noun.*

ðə ˈsiːliŋ	ə ˈkaːviŋ	mai ˈhandraitiŋ
ə ˈreiliŋ	ə ˈmiːtiŋ	ðə ˈrait ˈtəːniŋ
ən ˈoupniŋ	joː ˈstokiŋ	ə ˈhjuːmən ˌbiːiŋ

2. *As a verbal noun.*

ðə kəˈrektiŋ əv ðə ˌpruːfs (= the correction).
ðə ˈbildiŋ əv ðə ˌbridʒ (= the construction).
d ju ˈlaik ˈfrentʃ ˈkukiŋ? (= cookery).
ai v ˈnevə ˈsiːn sʌtʃ ˌgouiŋz ˌon. (= behaviour).

3. *As a verbal noun qualifying another noun.*

ə ˈwoːkiŋ ˌstik (a stick used when one is walking).
ə ˈweitiŋ ˌruːm (a room in which people wait).
ə ˈspiniŋ ˌwiːl (a machine for making thread).
ə ˈrokiŋ ˌtʃeə* (a chair in which one can rock oneself).
ə ˈrouiŋ ˌman (a man who often rows a boat).

These collocations must not be confused with those in which an adjectival ing-form is used to qualify a noun. Although in a few cases the same words may be used, the two collocations are distinguished by having different stress-patterns. The kinetic stress on the first component (as in the five examples given above) indicates that the thing named by the second component is intended to facilitate the action named in the first, or if a person, that he is in the habit of performing the action. If the kinetic stress is placed on the second component it indicates that the person or thing named is actually performing the action at the moment of speaking, as shown in the following examples:

ə ˈspiniŋ ˌwiːl (a wheel that is actually turning).
ə ˈrokiŋ ˌtʃeə* (a chair that is oscillating).
ə ˈrʌniŋ ˌman (a man who is running).
ə ˈweitiŋ ˌkraud (a crowd that is waiting).
ə ˈgouiŋ kənˌsəːn (an undertaking that is active).

In some cases this stress pattern does not necessarily indicate that the action is being performed at the moment, but that the person or thing named by the second component is in the habit of performing it:

ə ˈwəːkiŋ ˌmodļ (a model that will perform movements).
pəˈfoːmiŋ ˌanimļz (animals that can perform tricks).
ˈflaiiŋ ˈfiʃ (fish that can fly when pursued).
ən ˈintəˈfiəriŋ ˌbizi˛bodi (one who intrudes unnecessarily).

254 Participial phrases. Three active and three passive participles are used in participial phrases. They may be made negative by having not placed before them. Examples:

Active Voice.

Perfect participle of accomplishment (haviŋ teikən):
ˈhaviŋ ˈteikən iz ˌmedsin, hi ˈfelt ˌbetə.
ˈnot haviŋ ˈnoutist ˌenibodi, ai əˈsjuːmd ðə ˈhaus wəz ˌempti.

Direct participle of activity (teikiŋ):
ˈteikiŋ iz ˈhat ņd ʌm˛brelə, hi ˈwent ˈaut əv ðə ˌhaus.
ðə ˈmeid, ˈnot ˈwontiŋ tə ˌweik mi, ˈdidņt ˈgiv mi joː ˌnout.

Perfect participle of activity (haviŋ bin teikiŋ):
haviŋ bin ˈteikiŋ ˈmedsin fər ə ˌwiːk, ai m ˈfiːliŋ ˌbetə.
ˈnot haviŋ bin ˈpraktisiŋ iz ˌgolf, hi wəz in ˈbad ˌfoːm.

Passive Voice.

Direct participle of accomplishment (teikən):
ˈteikən bai sə˛praiz, ði ˈenəmi səˈrendəd wiðˈaut ə ˌfait.
ðə ˈhevi ˌlʌgidʒ, ˈnot ˈwontid on ðə ˌvoiidʒ, wəz ˈstoud ə˛wei.

Perfect participle of accomplishment (haviŋ bin teikən):
ˈhaviŋ bin ˈteikən ˌouvə, ðə ˈkʌmpəni wəz ˈriːˌoːgə˛naizd.
ˈnot haviŋ bin ˈwoːnd əv ðə ˌdeindʒə, wi ˈfel intə ðə ˌtrap.

Direct participle of activity (biːiŋ teikən):
biːiŋ ˈteikən ˈʌp wið iz ˌraitiŋ, hi fəˈgot iz ˌdinə.
ˈnot biːiŋ əˈlaud tə ˌsmouk, wi diˈsaidid tə ˈliːv.

When a participial phrase begins a sentence (as in the majority of the above examples) it must be followed immediately by the noun or pronominal determiner that it is intended to qualify.

255 Participles in absolute constructions. This structure is more typical of the written language. It resembles the participial phrase, but begins with a noun (or sometimes with a pronominal determiner), and the participle applies to this and not to the subject of the main clause. The absolute construction may either precede or follow the main clause.

219

Active Voice.

Perfect participle of accomplishment (haviŋ teikən):
ðə 'men haviŋ di'saidid tə ˌstraik, ðə 'faktri wəz ˌklouzd.

Direct participle of activity (teikiŋ):
ai 'rapt maiself ˙ʌp ˌwoːmli, ðə 'nait biːiŋ ˙veri ˌkould.

Perfect participle of activity (haviŋ bin teikiŋ):
ði 'ʌðəz haviŋ bin ˙digiŋ ˙oːl ˌdei, 'wiː ˙tuk ˌouvə.

Passive Voice.

Direct participle of accomplishment (teikən):
hiz 'wəːk ˙finiʃt fə ðə ˌdei, ðə 'leibərə ˙went ˌhoum.

Perfect participle of accomplishment (haviŋ bin teikən):
ðə 'piːsiz ˙not haviŋ bin ˌkept, wi 'kudn̩t ri'peə ðə ˌvaːz.

Direct participle of activity (biːiŋ teikən):
ðə 'klaːs wəz ˌkans|d, 'moust əv əs biːiŋ ˙niːdid elsˌweə.

256 Gerunds. This name is applied to the participles of verbs when they are used as nouns while still retaining some of their verbal function. Being nouns, gerunds may act in a sentence as the grammatical subject, logical subject after precursory it or ðeə*, direct object or prepositional object. When their meaning is to be restricted to a person or thing other than the subject of the sentence they are preceded by a possessive determiner or by a noun in the genitive, though this last is rarely used in the spoken language. In their verbal capacity gerunds may take an object and be modified by adverbials.

Four of the participial compounds tabulated in §239 may function as gerunds, and negative gerunds may be formed by prefixing **not**.

The following are the four participial compounds used as gerunds:

Active Voice.

Perfect gerund of accomplishment (haviŋ teikən):
ai ri'membə haviŋ ˋteikən ðis ˌfoutəgraf (the fact that I took it).

Direct gerund of activity (teikiŋ):
ai ri'membə ˋteikiŋ ðis ˌfoutəgraf (the occasion).

Passive Voice.

Perfect gerund of accomplishment (haviŋ bin teikən):
ai ri'membə haviŋ bin ˙teikən ˈil ˌlaːst ˌnait. (the fact).

Direct gerund of activity (biːiŋ teikən):
ai ri'membə biːiŋ teikən ˈil ˌlaːst ˌnait. (the occasion).

The following further examples of gerunds are classified by function. In the first set the gerund has a general application.

As subject:

ˌhaviŋ kəm'pleind ˌwount ˌduː ju eni ˌgud.
'getiŋ ˈrid əv it ud bi ðə ˈbest ˌθiŋ.

After precursory **it**:

it ud bi 'wəːθ ˙wail 'traiiŋ tə ˈsiː im.
it s ˈwʌriiŋ biːiŋ ˌrʌŋ ˌʌp sou ˌleit ət ˌnait.

After precursory ðeə*:

ðə z 'nou ˙getiŋ ˈrid əv im.
ðə z 'tuː ˙mʌtʃ ˈtoːkiŋ in ðə ˌklaːs.

As direct object:

ai ri'gret ˙not haviŋ bin ˈfoutəgraft wið im.
'wai did ju ˙sʌdn̩li ˙stop ˈraitiŋ tə mi?

As prepositional object:

ju ʃəd bi'gin bai ˙riːdiŋ ən ˙eliˈmentri ˌbuk.
did ju 'teik ˙ðat ˙buk wið'aut ˙aːskiŋ pə'miʃn̩?

In the second set of examples the application of the gerund is restricted by the insertion of a possessive determiner or a noun in the genitive before it.

As subject:

ðə 'manz ˙konstənt ˈgrʌmbliŋ ət ˌθiŋz ə'noiz mi.
joː 'haviŋ ˙got ˈrid əv it ˌwount ˌhelp.

After precursory **it**:

it | bi 'nou ˙gud joː ˙haviŋ kəmˇpleind əbaut it.
'izn̩t it ə ˈʃeim joː ˌfaːðəz riˌfjuːziŋ tə ˌkʌm!

As direct object:

ˋai ˌdount ˌmaind iz ˌhaviŋ bin ˌfoutəgraft wið mi.
iksˋkjuːz mai ˌnot haviŋ ˌgot ˌredi ˯əːliə.

As prepositional object:

'wəːnt ju əʹnoid ət hiz ˙not biːiŋ inˑvaitid tə ðə ˈwediŋ?
dəz 'enibodi əbˈdʒekt tu 'auə ˈpaːtiz ˈdʒoiniŋ ʹjoːz?

257 Half-gerunds. This term was suggested by Sweet to distinguish the popular use in speech of a direct object instead of a possessive before the gerund to restrict its application to a person other than the subject of the main clause. Fowler used the term Fused Participle for this structure. The difference between the gerund and the half-gerund will be clear from the following examples:

Gerund: ai ri'membə ðeə ˯duːiŋ it.   'fansi joː ˯miːtiŋ əs !
Half-gerund: ai ri'membə ðəm ˯duːiŋ it.   'fansi juː ˯miːtiŋ əs !

The half-gerund is frowned upon by most grammarians, but it is so widely used that its existence has to be recognized. While it sounds absurd in some contexts it is more inoffensive in others, and perhaps the best advice that can be given is to avoid it when it would be the grammatical or logical subject of the sentence and also when it is the object of a verb expressing emotions. The following series of examples gives a range of possible uses of the half-gerund.

Undesirable.

'juː ˈhaviŋ got ˋrid əv it ˌwount ˌhelp.
it s ˋimpjudn̩s, ˌðem ˌtoːkiŋ tu əs laik ˌðat
ai ˋheit ju ˌhaviŋ ˌhad tə ˌweit sou ˈloŋ.

Doubtful.

'wəːnt ju əˌnoid ət 'him ˈnot biːiŋ inˑvaitid tə ðə ʹwediŋ?
ˋai ˌdount ˌmaind ˌhim haviŋ bin ˌfoutəgraft wið mi.
it s 'nou ˈjuːs 'juː ˈkariiŋ ˈon laik ᵛðat.

Less objectionable.

ai ri'membə ju ˈklaimiŋ ðat ˋtriː ˌlaːst ˌjiə.
ai kən 'ʌndəˋstand ju ˌhaviŋ bin ˯angri wið im.
iksˋkjuːz mi ˌmeikiŋ ju ˌweit.
'wot d ju ˈθiŋk əbaut 'him ˋdʒoiniŋ əs?
ai kən 'dʒʌst iˋmadʒin ðəm ˌtraiiŋ tə ˌduː it.

E. Adverbs

FORMAL CLASSIFICATION

258 Varieties of adverbs. Formally, adverbs may be classified
as simple, derivative, compound and group-adverbs. It is difficult,
if not impossible, to draw a rigid line of demarcation between these
classes. Adverbs such as tuː, kwait, jet are obviously simple and
undecomposable, while adverbs such as ˋnaisli, ˋhapili, ˋdeili are
clearly formed from existing words by means of the living affix -li.
But between these two extremes we find adverbs such as biˋlou,
əˋloŋ, which are for all practical purposes undecomposable, while
others, such as ˋprezn̩tli, diˋrektli, ˋhaːdli, are formed from recognizable roots, but so differ in meaning from the words from which
they are derived that they cannot be said to be built up synthetically.

The compound and group-adverbs also show various degrees of
transition between undecomposable words such as ˌhauˋevə* and
compounds such as ˋsʌmˌtaimz. Moreover, the distinction between
derivative and compound adverbs is by no means obvious.

The following categories, ranging almost imperceptibly from one
extreme to the other, will give some idea of the various formal
characteristics of adverbs:

a. not, in, aut, bai, bak, daun, faː*, of, on, θruː, ʌp, mʌtʃ, kwait,
sou, az, stil, jet, hiə*, ðeə*, ðen, nau, suːn, faːst, wel.
əˋbʌv, ˋouvə*, ˋʌndə*, ˋəːli, ˋaːftə*, ˋveri, ˋlitl̩, ˋpriti, iˋnʌf,
ˋraːðə*, ˋofn̩, ˋseldəm, pəˋhaps (*or* praps).

b. wʌns, ˋounli, ˋoːlwiz, ˋoːlmoust, ˌoːlˋredi, ˌhauˋevə*, twais,
ˋjestədi, təˋmoru, biˋlou, təˋgeðə*, əˋkros, əˋloŋ.

c. ˋhaːdli, ˋskeəsli, ˋniəli, ˋdiːpli, ˋfuli, ˋʃuəli, ˋleitli, ˋriːsn̩tli,
iˋmiːdjətli, diˋrektli, ˋprezn̩tli, ˋʃoːtli, ˋaːftəwədz, paːst,
ˈoːltəˋgeðə*, təˋdei.

d. ˋsʌmˌweə*, ˋeniˌweə*, ˋnouˌweə*, ˋevriˌweə*, ˋsʌmˌtaimz.

e. ˋmoustli, ˋdeili, ˋwiːkli, ˋmʌnθli, ˋjiəli, ˋsəːtn̩li, ˋsimpli, ˋiːzili,
ˋsoftli, ˋkwaiətli, ˋnaisli, ˋkwikli, ˋslouli.

The only distinction between certain compound adverbs and
certain group-adverbs is that the former are written as one word

and the latter as two or more words—a mere orthographic distinction which has no linguistic importance.

Some group-adverbs are practically indistinguishable from adverbial phrases, and these again are not always easily distinguishable from adverbial clauses. All these may conveniently be termed *Adverbials*.

259 Comparison of adverbs. A large number of adverbs, notably adverbs of manner, possess degrees of comparison similar to those used with adjectives.

The comparative of superiority is formed by placing moə* before and ðən after the adverb:

'hi: ˙wə:ks mo: ˋregjuləli ðən ᵛju: du:.

The comparative of equality is formed by placing the adverb əz before and the conjunction əz after the adverb:

ˋai kən ˌdu: it əz ˌi:zili əz ᵛju: kan.

The comparative of inferiority is formed by placing les before and ðən after the adverb:

'ai ˙si: im 'les ˋfri:kw̥ntli ðən ᵛju: du:.

The superlative of superiority is formed by placing moust before the adverb:

ˋhi: z ðə ˌwʌn u ˌraits ðə ˌmoust kəˌrektli.

The superlative of inferiority is formed by placing li:st before the adverb:

ˋʃi: z ðə ˌwʌn ai ˌsi: ˋli:st ˌofŋ.

The following adverbs, however, form their comparative and superlative degrees inflexionally:

Positive	*Comparative*	*Superlative*
wel	ˋbetə*	best
ˋbadli	wə:s	wə:st
ˋə:li	ˋə:liə*	ˋə:liist
leit	ˋleitə*	ˋleitist
niə*	ˋniərə*	ˋniərist
fa:*	ˋfa:ðə*, ˋfə:ðə*	ˋfa:ðist, ˋfə:ðist
mʌtʃ	moə*	moust
ˋlitļ	les	li:st
su:n	ˋsu:nə*	ˋsu:nist
fa:st	ˋfa:stə*	ˋfa:stist

Many speakers use the inflexional comparison for certain other adverbs, notably:

ˋslouli	ˋslouə*	ˋslouist
ˋkwikli	ˋkwikə*	ˋkwikist
ˋoᶠn̩	ˋofn̩ə*	ˋofn̩ist

FUNCTIONAL CLASSIFICATION

260 Functions of adverbs. The only general statement that can be made concerning the functions of adverbs is that they serve to modify. To describe what or how they modify is more difficult. In some cases they modify individual words such as other adverbs, verbs, adjectives and nouns. In other cases they modify the sentence as a whole, or are sentences in themselves. Some adverbs are so intimately associated with verbs that the combinations thus formed may be considered as group-verbs, while many others (notably those of place) are adverb complements, analogous to other complements.

It is useful to classify adverbs in four different respects, these being according to:

A. *Meaning* (manner, time, degree, etc.).

B. *Grammatical function* (what parts of speech they modify).

C. *Position* in the sentence.

D. *Footing* in the sentence—whether they are incidental components (epithets) or essential components (complements).

261 Catalogue of adverbs. In many respects any functional classification of units of so heterogeneous a character must be defective. However, the information given in §§262–3 should prove of practical utility to the student, if only in providing lists of some of the most important categories of adverbs.

Adverbs that function as connectives (whether conjunctives, relatives or interrogatives) will not be found in the lists; they are fully dealt with in §§316, 320 and 328.

The table below forms a key to the lists; the numbers in the four lettered sections of the table correspond to those used in the four columns of the two lists and in §§264–288 in which the various classes of adverbs are described.

A Meaning	1 2 3 4 5 6 7	Manner Place, Direction, Distance Time, Duration Frequency, Repetition Degree, Quantity, Precision Affirmation, Probability, Negation Miscellaneous
B Grammatical Functions	1 2 3 4 5 6 7	Modifying Verbs Modifying Adjectives and Adverbs Modifying Nouns and Determiners Modifying Sentences Adverbs which may be Sentences Adverbs used as Complements Adverbial Particles
C Position	1 2 3 4 5	Before the Subject Between Finite and Verbal After the Object Before an Adjective Miscellaneous
D Use or Footing	1 2	As Incidental Components As Essential Components

262 Adverbs. The following list contains only adverbs proper (i.e. one-word adverbs). It is based on a 2,000-word frequency list and contains 267 adverbs.

	A Meaning (1 2 3 4 5 6 7)	B Function (1 2 3 4 5 6 7)	C Position (1 2 3 4 5)	D Use (1 2)
ˈabsəˌluːtli	5 6	2 3 4 5	2 4	1
ˈaksiˈdentli	1	1 4	2 3 4	1 2
ˈaktivli	1	1	2 3 4	1 2
ˈaktʃuəli	6	1 2 3 4	2 4 5	1
ˈaz (əz)	5 7	2	4 5	2
ˈaiðə* ... (ɔː*)	7	1 2 3 4	1 2 4 5	1
ˈaut	2 5	1 3 6 7	3	2
ˈautˈsaid	2	1 3 6	3	2
ˈaːftə*	3	1 4	3	2
ˈaːftəwədz	3	1 4	1 3	1 2
ˈbadli	1 5	1	3	2
ˈbai	2 3	1 6 7	1 3	2
ˈbak	2 3	1 6 7	1 3	2
biˈfoə*	3	4	3	2
biˈlou	2	1 3 6	3	2
ˈbouldli	1	1	2 3	1 2
ˈbouθ ... (ənd)	7	1 2 3	2 3 4 5	1
ˈbraitli	1	1	2 3	1 2
ˈbreivli	1	1	2 3	1 2
ˈdaun	2	1 3 6 7	1 3	2
ˈdaunˈsteəz	2	1 6	3	2
ˈdeili	4	4	3	2
ˈdifrṇtli	1	1	3	2
diˈrektli	1 3	1 4	3	2
diˈsaididli	5 6	2 4 5	4	1 2
ˈdiːpli	1 5	1 2	2 3 4	1 2
ˈdʌbli	5	2	4	2
ˈdʒenrəli	4	4	2 3 4	1 2
ˈdʒentli	1	1	2 3	1 2
ˈdʒʌst	3 5	1 2 3	2 4 5	1
ˈðeə*	2	1 3 5 6	1 3	2

	A Meaning							B Function							C Position					D Use	
	1	2	3	4	5	6	7	1	2	3	4	5	6	7	1	2	3	4	5	1	2
ˋðeəfɔ:*							7				4				1	2		4	5	1	
ˋðen			3				7			3	4				1	2	3				
ˋels					5		7	1		3	4				1		3		5		2
ˋenihau	1						7	1			4				1		3		5		2
ˋeniweə*		2						1	2						1		3	4			2
ˋeniwei	1							1			4				1		3		5		2
ˋevə*		2	3	4							4					2				1	
ˋevriweə*		2						1				5	6				3		5		2
əˋbaut (əproksimitli)					5		7		2	3								4	5	1	
əˋbaut (hiər ən ðeə)		2						1						7			3				2
əˋbi:djəntli	1							1				5					3			1	2
əˋbrɔ:d		2						1		3		5	6				3				2
əˋbʌv		2						1		3			6				3				2
əˋkeiʒn̩li				4							4	5			1	2	3	4		1	2
əˋkɔ:diŋli							7				4				1	2	3			1	
əˋkros		2						1					6	7			3				2
əˋlaik	1									3			6				3				2
əˋloŋ		2								3				7			3				2
əˋloun	1							1		3			6				3		5		2
əˋpa:t	1	2								3			6				3				2
əˋraund		2						1		3				7					5		2
əˋridʒin̩li	1										4				1	2				1	
əˋsli:p	1									3			6				3				2
əˋwei		2						1		3			6	7	1		3				2
ˋə:dʒn̩tli	1							1				5					3			1	2
ˋə:li			3					1				5					3				2
ˋfa:*		2			5		7	1		3							3				2
ˋfa:st	1							1									3				2
ˋfeəli (dʒʌstli)	1							1									3				2
ˋfeəli (modəritli)					5				2			5				2		4		1	
ˋfə:st		2	3					1				5	6		1	2	3				2
ˋfə:stli							7				4				1					1	
ˋfo:tʃn̩itli	1										4	5			1	2		4		1	
ˋfraitf̩li	1				5				2									4			2
ˋfri:kwn̩tli				4							4	5				2				1	2

	A Meaning							B Function							C Position					D Use	
	1	2	3	4	5	6	7	1	2	3	4	5	6	7	1	2	3	4	5	1	2
ˈfuli	1				5			1								2	3	4		1	
ˈfuːliʃli	1							1	2			5				2	3			1	2
ˈfʌnili	1							1									3				2
ˈgladli	1							1				5				2	3			1	2
ˈgreitʃli	1							1								2	3			1	2
ˈgreitli					5			1								2	3			1	
ˈhapili	1							1			4	5			1	2	3			1	2
ˈhaːdli					5			1	2	3		5				2		4		1	
ˈhaːf					5			1	2	3						2		4	5	1	
hauˈevə*	1				5			1	2		4				1			4		1	
ˈhiə*		2						1				5	6		1	2	3			1	2
ˈhoulli					5			1	2							2		4	5	1	
igˈzaktli					5	6			2	3		5				2	3	4	5	1	2
ikˈstriːmli					5				2			5						4			2
ikˈstroːdn̩rili					5				2									4			2
iˈmiːdjətli			3								4	5				2	3			1	2
ˈin		2						1		3			6	7	1		3				2
ˈindiˈpendəntli	1							1									3				2
ˈindiˈrektli	1							1			4	5				2	3			1	2
inˈdiːd						6	7		2	3	4	5			1	2		4	5	1	
ˈinˈsaid		2						1		3		5	6		1		3				2
inˈtaiəli					5	6		1	2							2		4		1	
inˈtenʃn̩li	1							1								2	3	4			2
iˈnʌf					5			1	2			5	6				3		5		2
iˈsenʃli					5	6			2	3								4		1	2
isˈpeʃli					5	6				3	4					2		4	5	1	2
ˈiːkwəli	1				5			1	2							2	3	4		1	
ˈiːvn̩					5	6		1	2	3	4					2	3	4		1	
ˈiːzili	1				5			1	2			5				2	3				2
ˈjes						6						5							5		2
ˈjestədi			3								4	5			1		3				2
ˈjet			3					1			4					2	3				2
ˈjiəli				4							4	5					3				2
ˈjuːʒuəli				4							4	5			1	2		4		1	
ˈkaːmli	1							1				5				2	3			1	2

	A Meaning							B Function							C Position					D Use	
	1	2	3	4	5	6	7	1	2	3	4	5	6	7	1	2	3	4	5	1	2
ˈkeəʃli	1							1				5				2	3			1	2
ˈkeəlisli	1							1				5				2	3			1	2
kəmˈpliːtli	1				5			1	2			5				2		4		1	2
kənˈsidərəbli					5				2									4		1	
kənˈtinjuəli	1			4				1	2			5				2	3	4		1	2
kənˈviːnjəntli	1				5				2									4		1	2
kəˈrektli	1							1				5				2	3			1	2
ˈkjuəriəsli	1				5			1	2		4						3	4		1	
ˈklevəli	1							1			4	5			1	2	3			1	
ˈkliəli	1							1			4	5			1	2	3			1	2
ˈkoːʃəsli	1							1								2	3			1	2
ˈkruəlli	1							1								2	3			1	2
ˈkuːlli	1							1								2	3			1	2
ˈkʌmfətəbli	1				5			1	2			5				2	3				2
ˈkwaiətli	1							1	2			5				2	3			1	2
ˈkwait					5			1	2	3		5						4	5	1	
ˈkwikli	1							1				5				2	3			1	2
ˈlaitli	1							1				5				2	3			1	2
ˈlaːdʒli					5				2	3		5				2		4		1	
ˈlaːst							7				4	5	6			2	3			1	2
ˈleit	1		3					1			4	5	6				3				2
ˈleitli			3								4	5					3			1	2
ˈles					5			1	2	3		5					3	4			2
ˈliːst					5			1	2								3	4			2
ˈloŋ			3						2	3	4						3	4			2
ˈlʌkili	1										4	5			1		3			1	
ˈmiəli					5			1	2	3	4					2	3	4	5	1	
ˈmoə*					5			1	2	3							3	4			2
ˈmoust					5			1	2							2	3	4			2
ˈmoustli					5					3	4	5				2	3	4	5	1	
ˈmʌnθli				4							4	5					3				2
ˈmʌtʃ					5			1	2							2	3	4		1	
ˈnatʃrəli	1					6		1			4	5			1	2	3	4		1	2
ˈnaiðə* ... (ˈnoː*)						6		1	2	3	4				1	2		4	5		2
ˈnaisli	1							1				5					3				2

230

	A Meaning							B Function							C Position					D Use	
	1	2	3	4	5	6	7	1	2	3	4	5	6	7	1	2	3	4	5	1	2
ˈnaitli				4							4	5					3				2
ˈnau			3				7				4	5			1	2	3			1	2
ˈnekst							7	1			4	5	6		1	2	3			1	2
ˈnesisrili						6					4	5				2		4		1	
ˈnevə*				4		6					4	5				2		4		1	2
ˈniə*		2						1		3			6	7			3	4			2
ˈniəli					5			1	2	3		5				2		4		1	
ˈniːdlisli	1							1	2			5					3	4		1	2
ˈnot						6		1	2	3	4				1	2		4	5	1	
ˈnou						6			2		4	5			1			4	5	1	2
ˈnoubli	1							1				5				2	3			1	2
ˈnouweə*		2				6		1				5	6				3				2
ˈof		2						1		3			6	7	1		3				2
ˈofn̩				4					2		4	5			1	2	3			1	2
ˈon		2						1		3			6	7	1						2
ˈonərəbli	1							1				5				2	3			1	2
ˈonistli	1							1				5				2	3			1	2
ˈounli					5			1	2	3	4				1	2		4	5	1	
ˈouvə*		2	3		5			1		3			6	7	1		3				2
ˈoːfli					5				2			5						4			2
ˈoːkwədli	1							1				5					3			1	2
ˈoːlmoust					5			1	2	3		5				2		4		1	2
ˌoːlˈredi			3								4	5				2	3	4		1	2
ˈoːltəˈgeðə*	1				5		7	1	2	3	4				1		3	4	5	1	2
ˈoːlwiz				4					2		4	5				2		4		1	2
ˈpaːst		2						1		3			6	7			3				2
ˈpaːtli					5			1	2	3	4	5				2		4		1	2
ˈpeinfli	1				5			1	2			5					3	4		1	2
ˈpeiʃn̩tli	1							1				5				2	3			1	2
pəˈhaps (or ˈpraps)						6					4	5			1	2			5	1	
pəˈlaitli	1							1				5				2	3			1	2
pəˈtikjuləli					5			1	2		4					2	3	4		1	
ˈpəːfiktli	1				5			1	2			5					3	4			2
ˈpəːpəsli	1							1								2	3			1	2
ˈpəːsn̩li	1							1			4				1		3			1	2

	A Meaning 1 2 3 4 5 6 7	B Function 1 2 3 4 5 6 7	C Position 1 2 3 4 5	D Use 1 2
ˈpjuəli	5	2 3	3 4	1 2
ˈpleinli	1	1 4 5	1 2 3	1 2
ˈposibli	6	4 5	1 2 4 5	1
ˈpraktikli	1 5	1 2 3 4 5	2 4	1
ˈpraudli	1	1	2 3	1 2
ˈprezn̩tli	3	4 5	3	1 2
ˈpriti	5	2	4	1 2
ˈprobəbli	6	4 5	1 2 4 5	1
ˈpromptli	1	1	2 3	1 2
ˈpropəli	1 5	1 4	2 3	1 2
ˈrapidli	1	1	2 3	1 2
ˈrait (direktli)	2 5	2	3	2
ˈrait (kərektli)	1 6	1 6	3	2
ˈrait (hand said)	2	1 3	3	2
ˈraund	2	1 3 6 7	1 3	2
ˈrɑːðə*	5	1 2 5	2 4	1
ˈregjuləli	1 4	1 4 5	2 3	1 2
ˈreəli	4	1 5	2 3	1 2
ˈriəli	6	1 2 3 4 5	1 2 4 5	1
ˈriːsn̩tli	3	4 5 6	2 3	1 2
ˈroŋli	1	1 5	3	1 2
ˈruːdli	1	1 5	2 3	1 2
'satisˈfaktərili	1	1 5	3	2
ˈsaundli	1	1 5	2 3	1 2
ˈsekəndli	7	4	1	1
ˈseldəm	4	4 5	2 4	1 2
ˈselfiʃli	1	1 5	2 3	1 2
ˈsensibli	1	1 5	2 3	1 2
ˈsepəritli	1	1 5	3	2
ˈseifli	1	1 5	3	1
səˈfiʃn̩tli	5	1 2 5	3 4	2
səkˈsesfl̩i	1	1 5	3	1 2
ˈsəːtn̩li	6	4 5	1 2 4 5	1
ˈsimpli	1 6	1 2 3 4	2 3 4 5	1 2
sinˈsiəli	1 6	1 2 4 5	2 3 4 5	1 2

	A Meaning							B Function							C Position					D Use	
	1	2	3	4	5	6	7	1	2	3	4	5	6	7	1	2	3	4	5	1	2
si'viəli	1				5			1	2								2	3			1	2
'siəriəsli	1							1			4	5					2	3			1	2
'skeəsli					5			1	2			5					2		4		1	
'slaitli	1				5			1	2			5						3	4		1	2
'slouli	1							1				5					2	3			1	2
'smu:ðli	1							1				5					2	3				2
'softli	1							1				5					2	3			1	2
'sou (manner)	1					6	7	1	2			5	6		1			3	4	5	1	2
'sou (degree)					5				2										4			2
'speʃli	1							1	2								2	3	4		1	2
'stedili	1							1				5					2	3			1	2
'stifli	1							1				5					2	3				2
'stil (mouʃn̩lis)	1							1		3			6					3				2
'stil (i:vn̩ 'nau)			3								4				1	2	3	4			1	2
'stju:pidli	1							1									2	3			1	2
'streindʒli	1				5			1	2									3	4			2
'stroŋli	1				5			1				5					2	3			1	
'su:n			3								4	5	6		1	2	3				1	2
'sʌdn̩li	1							1			4	5			1	2	3	4			1	2
'sʌmtaimz				4							4	5			1	2	3	4			1	2
'sʌmweə*		2						1		3		5	6				3					2
'swiftli	1							1				5					3					2
'ʃa:pli	1							1				5					2	3			1	2
'ʃo:t	1							1										3				2
'ʃo:tli			3					1				5						3				2
'ʃuəli						6					4	5			1	2					1	
'taidili	1							1				5						3				2
'taitli	1							1				5						3				2
'tendəli	1							1				5						3				2
'teribli					5				2			5						3	4		1	2
'teistfʃli	1							1				5						3			1	2
tə'dei			3								4	5			1		3					2
tə'geðə*	1	2	3					1		3	4	5	6		1		3					2
tə'moru			3								4	5			1		3					2
tə'nait			3								4	5			1		3					2

	A Meaning							B Function							C Position					D Use	
	1	2	3	4	5	6	7	1	2	3	4	5	6	7	1	2	3	4	5	1	2
ˈtruːli	1					6		1	2		4	5			1	2		4		1	2
ˈtʃiəf‍li	1							1								2	3			1	2
ˈtʃiːf‍li					5	6		1			4					2	3	4		1	2
ˈtʃiːpli	1							1								2	3			1	2
ˈtuː (oːlsou)						6			2	3	4		6	7			3				2
ˈtuː (iksesivli)					5				2	3								4			2
ˈtwais				4							4	5			1	2	3			1	2
ˈθəːdli							7				4				1						1
ˈθoːtf‍li	1							1								2	3			1	2
ˈθruː		2						1		3			6	7			3				2
ˈθʌrəli	1				5			1	2			5				2	3	4		1	2
ˈʌndə(ˈniːθ)		2						1		3			6	7			3				2
ˌʌnˈkomənli					5				2									4			2
ˈʌp		2					7	1		3			6	7	1		3				2
ˈʌpˈsteəz		2						1		3		5	6				3				2
ˈʌtəli					5				2			5						4			2
ˈveri					5				2			5						4			2
ˈwaizli	1							1								2	3			1	2
ˈwel	1				5			1				5				2	3				2
ˈwilf‍li	1							1				5				2	3			1	2
ˈwiliŋli	1					6		1			4	5				2	3			1	2
ˈwiːkli (weakly)	1							1									3			1	2
ˈwiːkli (weekly)				4							4	5					3				2
ˈwoːmli	1							1				5				2	3			1	2
ˈwʌndəfli	1				5			1	2			5					3	4			2
ˈwʌns				4							4	5			1	2	3			1	2

263 Adverbials. The following is a selection of adverb phrases consisting of two or more words, tabulated in the same way as the adverbs.

	A Meaning							A Function							C Position					D Use	
	1	2	3	4	5	6	7	1	2	3	4	5	6	7	1	2	3	4	5	1	2
'bai ən 'bai			3								4	5			1		3				2
bai 'nau			3								4				1		3				2
'dʒʌst 'ðen			3								4				1		3				2
'dʒʌst 'nau			3								4	5			1		3				2
'dʒʌst 'sou	1						7					5	6				3				2
'evri 'dei				4							4	5					3				2
'evri ʌðə 'dei				4							4	5			1		3				2
ə 'lit|					5			1	2			5					3	4			2
ə 'lit| 'tuː					5				2									4			2
ə 'loŋ 'wei		2					7	1					6				3				2
ən'til 'ðen			3								4				1		3				2
ə 'ʃoːt 'wei		2						1					6				3				2
ət 'ðat 'taim			3								4				1		3				2
ət 'fəːst			3								4				1		3			1	2
ət 'laːst			3								4	5			1	2	3			1	2
ət 'liːst					5		7			3	4				1	2	3	4	5	1	
ət 'oːl				4	5	6			2	3	4						3	4		1	2
ət 'preznt			3								4				1		3				2
ət 'wʌns			3								4					2	3		5	1	2
əv 'koːs						6					4	5			1				5	1	
əz 'wel							7				4						3				2
'faː 'tuː					5				2	3								4			
'faː 'moː*					5			1	2	3							3	4			2
'feəli 'wel	1							1				5				2	3				2
'haːdli 'evə*				4				1			4	5				2				1	
in 'fjuːtʃə*			3								4				1		3				2
'insaid 'aut		2						1		3	4		6				3				2
'leitər 'on			3								4	5			1		3				2
'niəli 'oːlwiz				4							4	5				2		4		1	2
'nou 'daut						6					4	5			1	2			5	1	
'oːl ət 'wʌns	1							1			4				1		3				2

235

	A Meaning							B Function							C Position					D Use	
	1	2	3	4	5	6	7	1	2	3	4	5	6	7	1	2	3	4	5	1	2
ˋsʌm ˌdei			3								4	5			1		3				2
ˈskeəsli ˋevə*				4							4	5				2		4		1	2
ˈslaitli ˈtuː					5				2									4			2
ˋsou ˌfaː*		2	3				7	1			4	5		7	1	2	3				2
sou ˋmʌtʃ					5			1								2	3				2
sou ˋveri					5				2									4			2
ˈsuːn ˋaːftə*			3								4	5					3				2
ˈsuːnər oː ˋleitə*			3								4	5			1		3				2
ˈtuː ˋfaː*		2			5		7			3	4		6				3				2
ˈtuː ˋmʌtʃ					5					3			6				3		5		2
ˈtuː ˋofn̩				4							4						3				2
ˈtwais ə ˋdei (etc.)				4							4	5			1		3				2
ˈθriː ˋtaimz				4							4	5					3				2
ˈθriː ˈtaimz ə ˋdei				4							4	5			1		3				2
ˈʌpsaid ˋdaun		2						1		3		5	6				3				2
ˈʌp tə ˋnau			3								4	5			1		3				2
ˋveri ˌwel						6						5							5		2
ˈveri ˋwel	1				5			1				5	6				3				2
ˈwʌn ˋdei			3								4	5					3	4			2
ˈwʌns ə ˋdei (etc.)				4							4	5			1		3				2

MEANING

264 Grouping by meaning. From the point of view of their meaning, adverbs may be roughly grouped into classes according as they may constitute answers to various questions such as those shown in the respective sections below. It must, however, be realized that any such classification must be arbitrary, for the classes shade into one another, and a very large number of adverbs may be used with two or more meanings, according to context and word order.

A convenient scheme of classification is to divide adverbs into seven groups according to their intrinsic meanings:

A1 Adverbs of *Manner* (123).
A2 Adverbs of *Place, Direction* and *Distance* (39).
A3 Adverbs of *Time* and *Duration* (29).
A4 Adverbs of *Frequency* and *Repetition* (20).
A5 Adverbs of *Degree, Quantity* and *Precision* (75).
A6 Adverbs of *Affirmation, Probability* and *Negation* (31).
A7 *Miscellaneous* Adverbs (20).

The figures in brackets after each class show the total number of one-word adverbs listed in §262 as funcioning in that capacity.

265 Adverbs of manner (AI). Adverbs belonging to this, the largest group in the list, may serve as answers to questions beginning with hau, e.g., 'hau did ju ˅duː it? 'hau ə ðei ˋtriːtiŋ ju? They usually modify either verbs or sentences, and the position they occupy varies from C1 (before the subject) to C2 (between the finite and the verbal) or C3 (after the object). Some of them are restricted to one of these positions but many may be found in more than one. Examples:

'sʌdn̩li it əd ˙disə˅piəd   'onistli ai 'dount ˅nou.
it əd 'sʌdn̩li ˙disə˅piəd.   hi 'spouk ðə ˙wəːdz ˌkwaiətli.
it əd 'disə˙piəd ˌsʌdn̩li.   'aːnt ðei di'livəd ˊkwikli?
'hau dəz i ˌwəːk?—hi 'wəːks ˅slouli bət ˋstedili.

266 Adverbs of place, direction and distance (A2). Adverbs of place may serve as answers to such questions as ˅weə?, 'weərə-ˋbauts? The simple adverbs of place merge almost imperceptibly into phrases and clauses. Adverbs of direction, which answer such questions as 'witʃ ˅wei?, are usually adverbial phrases and clauses, and so are adverbs of distance, except for the adverb faː* (which is replaced in affirmative sentences by ə 'loŋ ˅wei). These answer such questions as 'hau ˅faː? The adverbials and adverbs in this class, which may modify a whole sentence or any part of it, usually occupy position C3 (after the object). Examples:

'weərə˙bauts wil ju ˌbiː?—ai ʃl bi 'ouvə ˋðeə.
'witʃ ˙wei iz ʃi ˋgouiŋ?—ʃi z 'gouiŋ ˋðat ˌwei.
'hau ˙faː did ju ˅wəːk?—wi 'didn̩t ˙wəːk veri ˅faː.
wen ju 'briŋ mai ʌm˙brelə ˌbak 'put it autˌsaid, in ðə ˌhoːl.

267 Adverbs of time and duration (A3). Adverbs of time and duration should not be confused with adverbs of frequency (§268), as the two classes occupy different positions in the sentence.

Adverbs of time, which may serve as answers to such questions as ˈwen ?, merge imperceptibly into adverbial phrases and clauses. Adverbs of duration, which may serve as answers to such questions as ˈhau ˈlɔŋ ?, are usually adverbial phrases or clauses, except for the adverb lɔŋ (which is replaced in affirmative sentences by ə ˈlɔŋ ˈtaim).

The adverbs and adverbials in this class, which may modify a whole sentence or any part of it, usually occupy position C3 (after the object), but are frequently placed in position C1 (before the subject) either for emphasis or in order to avoid an awkward construction when the object is a long one. Examples:

ˈwen | ju bi ˈliːviŋ ?—wi ʃ| bi ˈliːviŋ ˈlʌndən təˈmoru.

ai ˈsiː wot ju ˈmiːn, ˌnau.   ˈnau ai ˌsiː wot ju ˈmiːn.

ˈhau ˈlɔŋ did ðə ˈfilm ˌlaːst ?—it ˌlaːstid ˈtuː ˌauəz.

268 Adverbs of frequency and repetition (A4). These may serve as answers to the questions ˈhau ˈofṇ and ˈhau meni ˈtaimz ? respectively. They usually modify the whole sentence and occupy position C2 (between finite and verbal). They are generally used as incidental rather than essential components of the sentence and are frequently modified themselves by adverbs of degree, etc. Examples:

ˈhau ˈofṇ əz ʃi ˈaːskt ju tə ˌtiː ?—ʃi z ˈnevər ˌaːskt mi.

ˈhau meni ˈtaimz əv ju ˈsiːn im ?—ai v ˈsiːn im ˈmeni ˌtaimz.

ai v ˈhaːdli ˈevə ˈspoukən tu im.—ˇai ˈnevə ˌhav.

Adverbial phrases and clauses expressing frequency or repetition usually occupy position C3 (after the object). For details of word order in position C2 see §282.

269 Adverbs of degree, quantity and precision (A5). These may serve as answers to such questions as ˈhau ˈlaːdʒ iz it ?, dəz i ˌwəːk ˈtuː ˌmʌtʃ, oː ˈnot iˌnʌf ? or ˈhau ˌfluəntli dəz i ˌspiːk ? Examples:

ˈhau ˌlaːdʒ iz it ?—it s ˈveri ˌlaːdʒ.

hi ˈwəːks tuː ˌmʌtʃ.   hi ˈdʌzṇt ˈwəːk iˈnʌf.

ðei ə ˌraːðə ˋgud.   it ˈizn̩t ˋwait iˌnʌf.

it s ˋounli ə ˌboi.   ai pəˇtikjuləli ˙wontid tə ˋsiː ju.

270 Adverbs of affirmation, probability and negation (A6).
This class includes all adverbs equivalent to jes, pəhaps and nou.
They are frequently used as sentences in themselves, but when
they are used in contexts their grammatical functions and position
are very varied. Certain adverbs marking prominence may conveniently be included in this class, typical ones being tʃiːfli, ispeʃli
and noutəbli. Examples:

ˈpraps ju | ˋsiː im.   ai ˋsəːtn̩li ˌdidn̩t ˌteik it ˌðen.

it s ˇobviəsli imˋposibl̩.   ai ˈnevə sed ˈeniθiŋ əv ðə ˌkaind !

əv ˋkoːs ai ˌtould im sou.   ˋjes, it wəz in ˋparis, ˋnot in ˌlʌndən.

271 Miscellaneous adverbs (A7). It is possible to define and
classify other and minor categories of adverbs, such as *ordinals*
(sekəndli), adverbs of *concession* (stil), of *consequence* (sou), etc.,
but it will probably be more convenient to gather them together
under the above heading. Examples:

ˈfəːstli wi ˙hav tə kənˈsidə ði iksˌpens ; ˈsekəndli wi məs ˈteik
intu əˈkaunt ðə ˌdifikl̩tiz . . . *etc.*

ju ˋmei bi ˌrait, ˋstil, ai ˈwudn̩t ˇkaunt on it.

ai ˈsoː i wəz ˋbizi, sou ai ˈkeim əˋwei.

GRAMMATICAL FUNCTION

272 Functional limitations. Under the heading of grammatical
function consideration is given to the way in which adverbs modify
various classes of words (parts of speech, etc.). It is necessary,
for instance, for the foreign student to know that veri may modify
an adjective, but not a verb ; that deili may modify a verb, but
not an adjective ; that pəːfiktli may modify either verbs or adjectives,
etc. It is also well for him to know which adverbs may be used
by themselves as sentences. The group of adverbs used predicatively
(i.e. as complements) and the group of adverbial particles are also
included in this section.

On this basis, we may distinguish the following seven functions,
which, of course, are not mutually exclusive:

B1   Adverbs modifying *verbs* (185).
B2   Adverbs modifying *adjectives* and *adverbs* (84).
B3   Adverbs modifying *nouns* and *determiners* (64).
B4   Adverbs modifying *sentences* (98).
B5   Adverbs that may be *sentences in themselves* (143).
B6   Adverbs *used as complements* (43).
B7   *Adverbial particles* (20).

The figures in brackets after each functional class show the total number of one-word adverbs listed in §262 as performing that function.

273 Adverbs modifying verbs (B1). This is the most usual function of adverbs. Examples:

ðei v 'dʒʌst əˌraivd.   əm ai 'spiːkiŋ ˈtuː 'kwikli?
ʃi wəz 'woːkiŋ ˋslouli.   joː 'sistə ˋraits ˌwel.
həv ju 'evə ˈsiːn im ˊakt?   ˋai ʃəd ˌduː it ˋdifrṇtli.

274 Adverbs modifying adjectives and adverbs (B2). The adverbs that modify adjectives or other adverbs are nearly always those of Degree, Affirmation or Manner. Examples:

Modifying adjectives	*Modifying adverbs*
ðat s 'veri ˌgud.	ðei 'spiːk 'kwait ˋdifrṇtli.
ʃi z 'aktʃuəli ˋredi!	hi ˌdid it 'riəli ˌwel.
˅ðiːz ə ˊfraitfḷi ˌbad.	wi 'keim 'speʃḷi ˌəːli.
ðei ə 'pəːfiktli ˌlʌvli!	ðei ə'raivd ˈdʒʌst ˌenihau.
ʃi z ə˅keiʒṇḷi fəˋgetfḷ.	it s ik'siːdiŋli ˈwel ˌdʌn.
ai wəz inˈtenʃṇḷi ˌkəːt.	wi ˅faund it 'feəli ˋiːzili.

For adverbs requiring a special word order when modifying adjectives or adverbs see §284.

275 Adverbs modifying nouns and determiners (B3). In most cases when an adverb modifies a noun, an article (usually the indefinite one) is inserted between the two. Examples:

hi z 'kwait ə ˋman, ˌnau.   it ˋsiːmz tə bi ˌkwait ə ˋbaːgin.
ʃi z 'miəli ə biˋginə.   it s 'iːvṇ ðə ˋbest ˌwei tə ˌduː it.
it wəz ˋounli ə ˅piktʃə.   it wəz ˋounli ðə ˌmilkmən.

When the word modified is a determiner the article is generally
not used:

iz it 'riəli 'main? ðər ə 'beəli ə ˌdʌzn̩.
it s ˇounli ˌmiː. ðə z 'iːvn̩ ˇplenti.

Other examples of adverbs modifying nouns and determiners will
be found in §59f and §67.

276 Adverbs modifying sentences (B4). When it modifies a
complete sentence the adverb is usually placed at the beginning.
Examples:

ˇʃuəli hi ˌiznt ᵛil! 'aiðə ju ˇduː ˌlaik it, oː ju ˇdount.
pəˇhaps ju ə ˌrait. ᵛposibli i ˙haznt riˇsiːvd ðəm.
ˇstil, ju ˇmait ˌᵥtrai! inˇdiːd, ai ˙didn̩t ˇnou i wəz ˌðeə.

Many would classify these as conjunctions.

277 Adverbs that may be sentences themselves (B5). These
adverbs fall into two classes:

a. Those that are frequently used in conversation as reactions
to or comments upon a situation or a remark, or as imperatives
or exclamations. Examples:

'autˇsaid! ˇbak! ˇdaun! diˇsaididli. ᵛfaːstə!
igˇzaktli. ˇhiə! ᵛlʌkili. ˌnekst. ˇriəli!

b. Those used as a self-contained answer to a question. Most
of the adverbs of manner are among these, e.g., 'hau did i biˌheiv?
—pəᵛlaitli. Examples of other possible answers to questions:

ˇgladli. ᵛhaːdli. ˇjes. kəmˇpliːtli. ᵛmoustli.
ˇnau. ˇnevə! ˌnou. ᵛoːlmoust. ˇsəːtn̩li!

Another view held regarding these adverbs is that they are
modifying words in alogistic (or unexpressed) sentences that can
be supplied only from the context, since, if they were sentences
in themselves, they would contain a completed thought apart from
any context.

278 Adverbs used as complements (B6). A certain number of
adverbs may be used as subject complements, i.e., as complements
to the verb tə biː and other verbs of incomplete predication. Some
of these are almost adjectival in their nature (e.g., əˇfreid, əˇlaiv,

əˈsliːp, əˈweik, əˈweə*). Others are the adverbs of place and the
adverbial particles. Examples:

hi z əˈbrɔːd.   ˈðiːz ˈtuː ˈθiŋz ər əˈlaik.
it s ˈhiə.   hi ˈmʌst bi ˈaut.

Most of these may be used also as object complements. Examples:

ˈput on jɔː ˌhat.   *or*   ˈput jɔː ˌhat on.
hi ˈtuk ər əˈbrɔːd.   ˈpul ðə ˌkɔːk aut.

279 Adverbial particles (B7). These correspond to the "separ-
able particles" of other Germanic languages. The most used
ones are:

aut	daun	əloŋ	in	ouvə*	θruː
bak	əbaut	əraund	of	paːst	ʌnðə*
bai	əkros	əwei	on	raund	ʌp

There is considerable similarity in form and meaning between
these adverbs and certain simple and compound prepositions of
place:

hi ˈkeim ˌaut.   hi ˈkeim ˈaut əv ðə ˌhaus.
hi ˈkeim ˌbak.   hi ˈkeim ˈbak tə ˌlʌndən.
hi wəz ˈwɔːkiŋ əˌloŋ.   hi wəz ˈwɔːkiŋ əˈloŋ ðə ˌroud.
hi ˈwent əˌwei.   hi ˈwent əˈwei frəm ˌlʌndən.
hi ˈwɔːkt ˌin.   hi ˈwɔːkt intə ðə ˌhaus.
it ˈfel ˌof.   it ˈfel ˈof ðə ˌteibl̩.

In addition to one or more fairly stable and specific meanings,
many of these adverbs (notably aut, daun, əwei, of, on, ʌp) express
ideas that are difficult to define.

In some cases they reinforce the idea expressed by the verb:

ˈstand ˈʌp   ˈlai ˈdaun   ˈtəːn ˈraund   ˈskriːm ˈaut

In other cases while they express a distinct and independent idea
the meaning of the compound is perfectly clear to anyone who
understands the general meaning of the individual words:

ˈkʌm ˈaut   ˈbriŋ ˈbak   ˈteik əˈwei   ˈgou ˈin

In many other cases they combine with a verb to form a compound
with a purely arbitrary meaning that cannot easily be deduced from
that of the individual words. These combinations may be regarded

242

as compound verbs, which the student would do well to learn as integral wholes, as he does such compounds as fəget, ouvəteik, ʌndəstand, ʌndəteik, ʌpset and wiðdrɔː.

While the meanings of such compounds are to be looked for in the dictionary rather than the grammar, a few representative samples are explained below.

'fɔːl ˋaut (= kworl)	'blou ˋʌp (= disˈtroi bai iksˋplouʒŋ)
'pik ˋaut (= tʃuːz)	'botl ˋʌp (= iŋˈklouz az in ə ˋbotl)
'giv ˋin (= jiːld)	'brik ˋʌp (= ˈʃʌt in wið briks)
'liːv ˋof (= stop)	'giv ˋʌp (= əˈbandən əˋtempts)

The position in the sentence of the adverbial particle varies with the structure of the sentence.

When the sentence contains no direct object the particle is placed immediately after the verb:

ju kən ˋɔːlwiz ˌkʌm ˏbak.   ðei 'tould mi tə ˙gou əˏwei.
hi 'went ˙in ət ˏwʌns.   did ju 'siː ðəm ˙raid ˊpaːst?

When the sentence contains a direct object in the form of a personal pronoun (or most of the other types of determiners) the particle is placed immediately after the pronoun or determiner:

'put it ˏaut.   ai ʃl 'aːsk im ˏin.
'teik ˙ðat ˏof.   ju məst 'send ˙ðiːz ˏbak.

When the sentence contains a direct object other than those in the above classes the particle may be placed immediately after the verb:

'teik ˙of jɔː ˏhat.   ju v 'put ˙on jɔː 'best ˏʃuːz.
'put əˈwei ˙ðouz ˏbuks.   ai l 'briŋ ˙daun ə 'fjuː ˏtʃeəz.

Alternatively, and especially in natural and familiar speech, the particle may be placed after the object:

'teik jɔː ˏhat ˌof.   ju v 'put jɔː ˙best ˏʃuːz ˌon.
'put ði ˏʌðə wʌn ˌθruː.   ai ʃl 'aːsk mai ˏfrend ˌouvə.

In exclamatory statements (as used in lively narrative) and in exclamatory imperatives (usually of a slightly jocular or familiar nature) the particle is placed at the beginning of the sentence and is pronounced with a high level or falling tone. If the subject is a personal pronoun it follows the particle and precedes the verb, which takes a low rising tone. If the subject is not a pronoun it follows the verb and takes a low rising tone. Examples:

Adverb + Subject + Verb	Adverb + Verb + Subject
ˋin ðei ˎwent !	'in ˙went ði ˌʌðəz !
ˋof it ˎkeim !	'of ˙keim ðə ˎwiːl !
ə'wei hi ˎfluː !	ə'wei ˙fluː ðə ˎboi !
'daun ju ˎgou !	'daun ˙fel ðə ˎbot∣ !
'aut ju ˎkʌm !	'aut ˙went ðə ˎlait !

Note in this connection such elliptical expressions as:

　　ˋof wið iz ˎhed !　　　　　　　ˋdaun wið it !

In some cases the adverbial particles may be compounded with hiə* or ðeə*.

'in ˋhiə*	'in ˋðeə*	ə'loŋ ˋhiə*	ə'loŋ ˋðeə*
'aut ˋhiə*	'aut ˋðeə*	ə'kros ˋhiə*	ə'kros ˋðeə*
'bak ˋhiə*	'bak ˋðeə*	'θruː ˋhiə*	'θruː ˋðeə*
'daun ˋhiə*	'daun ˋðeə*	'ouvə ˋhiə*	'ouvə ˋðeə*
'ʌp ˋhiə*	'ʌp ˋðeə*	'raund ˋhiə*	'raund ˋðeə*

All the adverbial particles except əbaut and əraund may be modified by rait (which acts as an intensifier suggesting the idea of "extremity") and by dʒʌst or ounli dʒʌst (meaning "so far and not more"):

　　it s 'rait ˎin (əz 'faːr əz it ∣ ˎgou).
　　ai ˌpuʃt it 'rait ˎdaun (tə ðə 'louist ˎpoint).
　　it s 'rait ouvə ˎðeə (əz 'faːr əz ju kən ˎsiː).
　　it s 'ounli ˙dʒʌst ˎin (it ˋmait ˎgou 'stil ˋfaːðə).
　　ju l ˌsiː it 'dʒʌst ʌp ˎðeə (ˋnot veri ˎfaːr ʌp).
　　hi ˌlivz 'dʒʌst raund ˎhiə ('kwait ˎklous).

POSITION

280 Analysis of adverb positions. The positions occupied in the sentence by adverbs may be roughly divided into the following five classes:

C1　*Before the subject* (91).
C2　*Between finite and verbal* (141).
C3　*After the object* (202).
C4　*Before an adjective* (99).
C5　*Miscellaneous* (36).

The figures in brackets after each class show the total number of one-word adverbs listed in §262 as occupying that position.

Some of the terms employed above to identify the five positions are generalizations and cover certain variations which, though minor in position, are important in syntax. These variations are described below.

281 Before the subject (C1). Two possible orders are included under this heading. In the first one the adverb begins a normal sentence:

ᵛridʒin|i ai in'tendid tə ˙gou əˋbroːd ðis ˏsʌmə.
ᵛjestədi wi ˙went tə ðə 'siːˋsaid.

In the second case, which occurs chiefly with adverbs having a negative or near negative connotation, the adverb begins the sentence and is followed by an inverted finite and subject. In tenses A1 and A2 the conjugating finite duː, dʌz or did is introduced in affirmative statements. (See also §357.)

'nouweə kən ju ˙faind 'betə ˙kukiŋ ðən in ˋfraːns.
'haːdli ˋevə həv ai ˏsiːn sʌtʃ ə'poːliŋ ˏweist.
'wel du ai ri˙membə ˋmiːtiŋ him.

282 Between finite and verbal (C2). This heading covers several variants in word order, which depend upon the structural composition of the tense and the incidence of the stress, as shown below.

a. If the tense consists of a specific finite only (i.e., tenses A1 and A2 in their affirmative form only) the adverb is placed between the subject and the specific finite:

hi 'oːlwiz ə˙raivz ˏleit.   ai 'fuːliʃli ˙weitid 'tuː ˏloŋ.

b. If the tense consists of a conjugating finite followed by a specific verbal, the adverb is placed between the finite and the verbal, though **probəbli** and **səːtnli** precede negative finites:

dəz i 'evər ə˙raiv ˊleit?   ai ʃl 'nevə fə˙get ᵛðat.
wi wə 'juːʒuəli ə˙laud ˋmoə.   ʃi z ˋoːlwiz ˏteliŋ ˏlaiz.
ju v 'probəbli ˋsiːn it.   ju 'probəbli 'havn̩t ˏsiːn it.
ai ʃl ˋsəːtn̩li ˏweit.   ai ˋsəːtn̩li ˏʃaːnt ˏweit.

   c. If the tense consists of a conjugating finite, one or two conjugating verbals and a specific verbal, the adverb is placed between the finite and the first verbal if it is modifying the whole sentence:

it s ˋofn̦ bin sə‚plaid ˋfriː.   ai ʃl ˋoːlwiz bi ‚θiŋkiŋ əv ˬjuː.
it kəd ˋnevər əv bin ˬmendid. ʃi z 'nevə bin ˙lukiŋ sou ˬwel.

   d. If the conjugating finite used in structure *c* above is stressed, or if it stands by itself as representing a specific verb or a complement (as in some tags), the adverb is placed before the finite:

ai 'nevə ˋkud ʌndə‚stand joːr ‚atitjuːd.
'onisti z ðə ˙best ⌄polisi.—it 'oːlwiz ˋwoz. (it ˋoːlwiz iz).

   e. When the adverb in these multi-verbal tenses modifies the specific verb rather than the whole sentence, which occurs most frequently in the passive voice and with adverbs of manner, it is usually placed immediately before the specific verbal:

hi l bi 'dʒʌst ə'raiviŋ ‚nau.   ai wəz biːiŋ 'slouli ˌsʌfəkeitid.
ðei d əv bin 'waizli ˬjuːzd.   it | əv bin 'speʃli ˬmeid fə ju.

These changes in adverb position, sometimes aided by a change in the intonation, may modify the meaning of the sentence. Notice the difference between:

it ʃəd ⌄riəli əv bin ˋkukt; *and* it ʃəd əv bin 'riəli ˬkukt.

It is worth noting that the determiners bouθ and oːl, when used in the collocations shown in the first column of the list given in §96, follow the same rule of position as the adverbs of frequency, thus:

  a. wi 'bouθ ə˙raivd ˬleit.   *c.* ju v ˋoːl bin ‚givn̦ wʌn.
  b. ðei wər 'oːl ə˙laud ˬmoə.   *d.* 'hau meni əv ju ˬsoː mi?—
                             wi ˋoːl did.

283 After the object (C3). If the verb is an intransitive one there is of course no object and the adverb is placed immediately after the specific verb:

  hi z 'gon ə'broːd.   ʃi 'smaild ˬhapili.

If the verb is followed by a prepositional object the position of the adverb usually depends on the logic of the case:

hi z 'gon ə'broːd wið ðəm.   ai l 'plei wið ˋjuː ‚nekst.
ʃi 'smaild ət im ˬhapili.   *or* ʃi 'smaild ˋhapili ‚at im.
wi v 'lukt fər it ˋevriweə.   *or* wi v 'lukt ˋevriweə ‚foːr it.

If the verb is a transitive one the adverb is placed after, and *not* before the object:

hi 'spiːks ˙ingliʃ ˌwel.   ʃi 'pʌniʃt ðə ˙tʃaild siˇviəli.

hi 'dʌz iz ˙wəːk ˋkeəfˌli.   ju v 'ritη ðis ˙letə 'veri ˌwel.

There are cases in which an adverb may separate a verb from its object, but they are not common in spoken English and should be resorted to only by students who understand the reason for this departure from the usual practice, as the insertion of adverbs between a verb and its object is one of the most characteristic mistakes made by foreigners in English. (See also §372.)

a. The adverbs or adverbials that normally occupy this position are those of Manner, Place and Time, and if more than one of these classes is present in the same sentence they are usually placed in the above order:

hi 'spouk ˋbriljəntli ət ðə ˌmiːtiη ˙laːst ˙nait.

wi 'wʌn ˋiːzili in ðə ˌbout reis on ˙satədi.

b. If more than one adverb of either Place or Time is used, the more particular precedes the more general:

ai m 'liːviη ˙əːli təˌmoru.   hi z in ðə 'litl̩ ˙ruːm ʌpˌsteəz.

c. When used with specific verbs expressing movement, adverbs and adverbials of place take precedence over adverbs of manner:

ju l 'get ðeər ˙iːziər ən ˇkwikə bai ˋtrein.

ðei l ə'raiv hiər ˋeniwei in ˌtaim fə ˇlʌntʃ.

d. In the passive tenses, adverbs of manner nearly always precede the specific verbal; especially if this has a partly adjectival function.

ðə 'buks əv bin kən'viːnjəntli ə˙reindʒd bai ˋsʌbdʒikts.

'ðiːz ˙toiz 'mʌst əv bin 'veri ˙tʃiːpli prəˇdjuːst.

e. If an adverb and an adverbial of manner occur in the same sentence the former precedes the latter, and they are generally connected by a co-ordinating conjunction.

ai ʃl̩ 'spiːk tə ðəm ˇkliəli ənd in 'nou ʌn˙səːtn̩ ˌtəːmz.

hi 'dʌz iz 'wəːk ˇkwikli bət wið 'greit ˌkeə.

284 Before an adjective (C4). This position is occupied by adverbs modifying the adjective, and those modifying another adverb also precede the word modified. Examples:

> hi wəz 'kwait sə`praizd.   ju ə 'wɔːkiŋ 'tuː ˅faːst fə ˌmiː.
>
> ju ər 'absəluːtli ˌrait.   ʃi 'tuk it ˅feəli ˌkaːmli.

Important exceptions to the above rule are the adverbs els, indiːd and inʌf, which nearly always follow the word they qualify.

els forms adverbial collocations with the adverbs sʌmweə*, eniweə*, nouweə*, evriweə*, and less frequently with sʌmhau and enihau.

> it 'izn̩t ˅hiə, it 'mʌst bi ˙sʌmweər ˅els.
>
> ðə z 'nouweər ˙els ðət wi kən ˅gou.
>
> wi ʃl 'hav tə ˙sit ˅hiə, 'evriweər ˙els is ˅ful.

indiːd is generally used to reinforce the adverb of degree veri when it is modifying another adverb or an adjective. In this case the word being modified is preceded by veri and followed by indiːd.

> it s 'veri ˙nais inˏdiːd.   hi ˏspouk 'veri ˙wel inˏdiːd.

inʌf is often associated with kwait, niəli, or a negative adverb or finite.

> ˅ðis iz ˏgud inʌf fə ˌmiː.   ʃi z ˅kwait ˏwel inʌf tə ˌgou.
>
> 'ðat s not ˅niəli ˏgud inʌf.   ðei 'aːnt ˙wəːkiŋ ˅faːst inʌf.

285 Miscellaneous positions (C5). As will be seen from the list in §262, quite a number of adverbs may occupy various positions in the sentence. In some cases the choice of position depends on the meaning in which the adverb is being used or on the part of speech which it is modifying. The following examples illustrate this point:

> ˅natʃrəli ai ˏwont tə ˏspiːk.   ˅stil, ju 'mait əv ˅weitid.
>
> ai ˅natʃrəli ˏwont tə ˏspiːk.   ju 'stil mait əv ˅weitid.
>
> ai ˅wont tə ˏspiːk, ˅natʃrəli.   ju mait 'stil əv ˅weitid.
>
> ai 'wont tə ˙spiːk ˏnatʃrəli.   ju ˅mait əv ˏweitid 'stil ˅loŋgə.

The tendency in modern spoken English is to prefer position C2 (between finite and verbal) for adverbs which may occupy various positions, the typical case being that of ounli. If it modifies the subject this adverb takes position C1 (before the subject), but in other cases it most frequently takes position C2, the word it modifies being identified by placing the nuclear tone upon it (§40). Examples:

'ounli ðə ˋmen əv bin ˌaːskt tə ˌsain ðə piˌtiʃn̩. (not ðə ˅wimin).
ðə 'men əv ˙ounli bin ˋaːskt tə ˌsain ðə piˌtiʃn̩. (not ˅oːdəd).
ðə 'men əv 'ounli bin ˙aːskt tə ˋsain ðə piˌtiʃn̩. (not ˅rait it).
ðə 'men əv 'ounli bin ˙aːskt tə 'sain ðə pi˅tiʃn̩. (not ðə di˅maːnd).
həz 'ounli ˊjoː ˙waif ˙siːn ðə ˙plei? (not joː ˊbrʌðəz ˙waif?).
həz 'ounli joː ˊwaif ˙siːn ðə ˙plei? (not joː ˊdoːtə?).
həz joː 'waif ˙ounli ˊsiːn ðə ˙plei? (not ˊred it?).
həz joː 'waif 'ounli ˙siːn ðə ˊplei? (not ðə ˊfilm?).

In the written language it is preferable, and more usual, to place **ounli** immediately before the word it modifies, since in writing there is normally no indication of where the nuclear tone is intended to fall.

USE

286 Classification by function. Under this heading adverbs may be divided into two groups according to their footing in the sentence and the two ways in which they perform their modifying function. These are:

D1 Epithets, or *incidental components* of sentences (161).

D2 Complements, or *essential components* of sentences (214).

The figures in brackets after each class show the total number of one-word adverbs listed in §262 as having that footing.

The following examples will help to show the difference between these two uses of adverbs.

Incidental components	*Essential components*
wi wə 'kwaiətli ˙gouiŋ əˌwei.	wi wə 'gouiŋ ə˙wei ˌkwaiətli.
ai i'miːdjətli kəˌrektid it.	ai kə'rektid it iˌmiːdjətli.
hi l 'simpli ˙rait ðə ˌletə.	hi l 'rait ðə ˙letə ˌsimpli.
ðei 'onistli ˙wont tə ˌwəːk.	ðei 'wont tə ˙wəːk ˌonistli.
ʃi ˋnatʃrəli ˌred ðə ˌletə.	ʃi 'red ðə ˙letə ˌnatʃrəli.
ʃi 'regjuləli inˌdʒoid əself.	ʃi in'dʒoid əself ˌregjuləli.

The distinction between these two classes is a most useful one, and should be thoroughly grasped by the foreign student, if only to help him in determining the position of adverbs in the sentence.

Many adverbs can be used only as incidental components, others can be used only as essential components, and others again may be used in both manners, though they generally vary considerably in meaning according as they are used in one way or the other.

287 Incidental components. When they are used as incidental components adverbs have a casual, almost parenthetical, footing in the sentence. In most cases they may be added or omitted without changing the meaning of the modified word or sentence in any appreciable degree, but they usually add intensity to the sentence, and for this reason are sometimes felt to suggest dramatic or emotional speech. When they function in this way they are rarely of sufficient semantic prominence to require a nuclear tone, though in cases of special emphasis they may do so. They occupy positions C1 or C2, the latter being the more frequent. Examples:

C1 *Before the subject*	C2 *Between finite and verbal*
ˋsəːtn̩li hi l ˌkʌm.	hi l ˋsəːtn̩li ˌkʌm.
'dʒʌst ˙weit til ai ˋkatʃ ju !	wi 'miəli ˙wont tə ˋnou.
ˇaktʃuəli, ðei 'left ˋjestədi.	ai 'kwikli ˙lokt ðə ˌdoə.
diˋsaididli ju məs ˌkʌm əˌgein.	ðei wə 'kliəli ˙ment fə ˋmiː.
'hapili wi v 'nevə ˙feild ˇjet.	ai ə'koːdiŋli ˙keim tə ˋsiː ju.

288 Essential components. When adverbs have a footing as essential components of the sentence they state explicitly and prominently in what manner or degree the action is performed. They are often adverbial complements and differ little from prepositional phrases used as adverbs. They are felt to be an integral part of the sentence, and are usually of sufficient importance to take the nuclear tone. Sentences change appreciably in meaning according as such adverbs are included or omitted. These adverbs generally occupy position C3. Examples:

hi wəz 'wəːkiŋ ˙veri ˌpeiʃn̩tli.   ʃi ri'fəːd tə ju ˙indiˇrektli.

ʃi 'kʌmz tə ˙siː mi ˇsʌmtaimz.   hi ˌdid it 'slouli ən ˌkeəfli.

ðə 'wil wəz ˙wəːdid iks'triːmli ˙kliəli ən priˌsaisli.

hi 'spiːks ˙iŋgliʃ ˌwel, ən prə'naunsiz ˙veri kəˌrektli.

ˋsʌm piːp| ˌduː ðəm ˋiːzili ; ˇʌðəz ˌduː ðəm wið ˋdifik|ti.

Note that the opposite of the adverb iːzili is the prepositional phrase wið difik|ti, as shown in the last example above.

F. Prepositions

289 Form and meaning. Formally, prepositions may be

Simple prepositions, consisting of a single word, or
Group prepositions, consisting of more than one word.

Semantically, both simple and group prepositions fall into various classes, as shown in the following lists, in which those marked † may take the end-position in the circumstances described in §294.

In these lists simple prepositions are given their strong forms, with their weak forms in parentheses, while group prepositions are shown with the stresses and weak forms that would characterize them in normal use.

Place, movement and direction.

†at (ət)	†biˈtwiːn	†from (frəm)	†raund
ˈautˈsaid	†daun	†in	†təˈwoːdz
†bai	†əˈbaut	ˈinˈsaid	†tuː (tu, tə)
biˈfoə*	†əˈbʌv	†ˈintu (intə)	†θruː
†biˈhaind	†əˈkros	†niə*	θruˈaut
biˈjond	†əˈgeinst	†of	†ˈʌndə*
biˈlou	†əˈloŋ	†on	ˈʌndəˈniːθ
biˈniːθ	†əˈmʌŋ	†ˈouvə*	†ʌp
†ˈaut əv	†ət ðə ˈkoːnər əv	†ˈklous tə	
ˈautˈsaid əv	†ət ðə ˈsaid əv	†ˈʌp tə	
†bai ðə ˈsaid əv	†in ˈfrʌnt əv	†əˈwei frəm	
†ət ðə ˈbak əv	†in ðə ˈmidl əv	tə ˈloŋ ˈwei frəm	
†ət ðə biˈginiŋ əv	†on ˈtop əv	†faː frəm	
†ət ðə ˈbotəm əv	†ˈbak tə	†ˈfaːr əˈwei frəm	
†ət ði ˈend əv	†ˈdaun tə	əz ˈfaːr əz	

Time and duration.

†at (ət)	ˈdjuəriŋ	†in	θruː
†ˈaːftə*	əˈbaut	†on	θruˈaut
†bai	ənˈtil	sins	
biˈfoə*	†foː* (fə*)	til	
biˈtwiːn	†from (frəm)	tuː (tu, tə)	
†ət ðə biˈginiŋ əv	ət ðə ˈtaim əv	ˈdaun tə	
†ət ði ˈend əv	†in ðə ˈmidl əv	ˈʌp tə	

Relationship.

`az fə*	ə`kɔːdiŋ tə	†wið `refrŋs tə
`az tə	kən`səːniŋ	wið ri`gaːd tə
†ə`baut	ri`gaːdiŋ	wið ris`pekt tə

Motive, cause and agency.

| on ə`kaunt əv    | bi`koz əv | bai `miːnz əv |
| fə ðə `seik əv   | `ouiŋ tə | in `spait əv |

Addition.

| bi`saidz | †in ə`diʃŋ tə | tə`geðə wið |

Reservation.

| bʌt (bət) | `bʌt fə* | ik`sept | ik`septiŋ |

Miscellaneous.

| †fɔː* (fə*) | †laik | †ov (əv) | †wið | †wið`aut |

290 Function. Both simple and group prepositions are followed by a noun or determiner, which it is their function to relate to some other word or to the rest of the sentence. This noun or determiner that follows the preposition is said to be its "object," and when this object is one of the five personal pronouns that have a special form for the oblique case (§68), this form is used. The preposition and its object constitute a "prepositional phrase," and this may be used either adjectivally, to qualify nouns or determiners, or adverbially, to modify verbs or sentences.

These two uses of prepositional phrases are exemplified in the next two sections. It should be understood that the vertical lines inserted in the examples have no other function than to indicate where the prepositional phrase begins or ends.

291 Adverbial phrases. In modifying verbs or sentences these phrases have the various semantic functions shown in §289, and examples of each are given below. Adverbial phrases may be placed at either the beginning or the end of the sentence, though the latter is far more frequent, and essential in many cases.

Place, movement and direction.

ʃi 'livz | bai ðə ˏrivə.   hi 'woːkt | əˑkros ðə ˏruːm.
'put it | on ðə ˏteibḷ.   ai m 'gouiŋ | tə ðə ˏsteiʃṇ.
ðei 'liv | ət ðə ˑbotəm əv ðə ˏhil.
ðər ə səm ˋtriːz | in ˏfrʌnt əv ðə ˏhaus.
'put ˑðis ˑbuk | on 'top əv ði ˏʌðəz.
ai m əˈfreid wi ə ˑstil | ə 'loŋ ˑwei frəm ˇhoum.

Time and duration.

'kʌm | ət 'haːf paːst ˏtuː.   ai l 'siː ju | ˑaːftə ˏskuːl.
wi ʃḷ bi 'bak | in səp ˏtembə.   ai 'soː im | djuəriŋ ðə ˏholidiz.
hi wəz 'hiə | fər ən ˋauə.   ju v bin 'aidḷ | θruˑaut ðə ˏdei
'ʌp tə ðə ˑprezṇt | ðei v dʌn ˋnʌθiŋ abaut it.
wi ʃḷ 'miːt əˑgein | ət ði 'end əv ðə ˏjiə.
ai m 'staːtiŋ mai ˑholidiz | in ðə 'midḷ əv ˏoːgəst.

Relationship.

iŋ'kwaiər | ˑaz tu iz 'kwolifiˋkeiʃṇz fə ðə ˏdʒob.
'witʃ ˑaksidṇt | ə ju ˋtoːkiŋ | əbaut?
əˈkoːdiŋ tə ðə ˇtaimteibḷ | wi 'oːt tə bi əˋraiviŋ ˏsuːn.
ai v ˋritṇ tə ðəm | wið ˏrefrṇs tə ðə ˏkontrakt.

Motive, cause and agency.

'wai dount ju ˑduː it | fə ðə 'seik əv ði ˏʌðəz?
'ouiŋ tə ðə ˑbad ˏweðə | ðə 'gaːdṇ ˑpaːti wəz ˏkansḷd.
in ˋspait əv ˏwot ai ˏsed | hi kən'tinjud tə ˏwʌri mi.

Addition.

ðə wə 'θriː ˋʌðə piːpḷ ˏðeə | bi ˏsaidz mai ˏself.
'ðiːz ˇteligramz | təˈgeðə wið ðə 'priːviəs ˏletəz | ˋsetḷ ðə ˏmatə.

Reservation.

'bʌt fə 'joː mis ˏteik | wi ʃəd əv bin ˋðeə bai ˏnau.
ˋevribodi ˏsoː it | ik ˏsept ˏmiː.

Miscellaneous.

ə 'pen z ˑjuːzd | fə ˏraitiŋ.   'wai dount ju ˑspiːk | fə jəˋself?
'wot ʃl ai ˋduː | wið it?   hi 'wəːks | laik ə ˋtroudʒṇ.
wi ʃḷ 'gou | wiðˇaut ju.   həv ju 'got ˑrid | əv joː 'kould?

292 **Adjectival phrases.** In qualifying nouns or determiners these phrases are frequently used for the purpose of identifying a person or thing when no suitable adjective is available. They are shorter than the relative clauses that might perform the same function, and more elegant than *ad hoc* adjectives that might be formed to replace them, thus:

Adjective: ðə 'griːn-dʒʌmpə-klad ˌwumən.
Adjectival Phrase: ðə 'wumən wið ðə ˈgriːn ˌdʒʌmpə.
Adjectival Clause: ðə 'wumən hu z ˈweəriŋ ðə 'griːn ˌdʒʌmpə.

Examples of adjectival phrases:

Qualifying determiners	*Qualifying nouns*
'nʌθiŋ | ˈaut əv ði ˅oːdn̩ri.	ðə 'man | biˈhaind ðə ˌkauntə.
'ðouz | ʌndəˈniːθ ðə ˌpiktʃə.	ðə 'buk | on ðə ˌteibl̩.
ðə 'nekst | bət ˌwʌn.	ðə 'bridʒ | ouvə ðə ˌrivə.
səm 'moə | laik ði ˌʌðəz.	ðə 'noiz | ˈklous tə ðə məʃiːnz.
'sʌmbədi | wið ə ˌpaip.	ðə 'kʌlər | əv ðə ˌɡraːs.
ðə 'wʌn | wiðˈaut ə ˌpatən.	ðə 'kʌp | wiðˈaut ə ˌhandl̩.

It will be noticed that adjectival phrases follow the noun or determiner that they qualify. Further examples will be found in §60*d*.

293 **Verbal nouns after prepositions.** The verbal noun that is used after prepositions is the gerund. Examples:

ðei ə 'not əˈbʌv 'teikiŋ ˈʌnfeər ədˈvaːntidʒ əv ju.
'kaːnt ju ˈstop im frəm 'meikiŋ ˈoːl ðat ˈnoiz?
ai 'koːt ðis ˈkould θruː 'gouiŋ ˈaut wiðˈaut ə ˈkout.
wi ər in ðə 'midl̩ əv ˈtʃeindʒiŋ ˅hauziz.
˅weit ə ˌwail biˌfoː ˌteikiŋ eni ˌakʃn̩.
'az fər əˈ˅polədʒaiziŋ, ai 'ʃudn̩t ˈdriːm əv it.
˅dount ˌdʒʌst ˌtoːk fə ðə ˌseik əv ˈseiiŋ ˌsʌmθiŋ.
biˈsaidz ˅raitiŋ, wi 'sent ə ˈteligram.

The infinitive particle.

The word **tu** which usually precedes the infinitives of verbs does not perform the functions of a preposition. Its chief use is to point out that the verb form following it is an infinitive and not a finite, and it is therefore best referred to as the Infinitive Particle. It occurs either alone or in the collocations sou əz tu and in ɔːdə tu, which are always followed by an infinitive. Examples:

ai 'ʌndə'stand ðət ʃi 'gouz ðeə tə 'ləːn ˌiŋgliʃ.
wi 'duː it ᵛðis wei sou əz tə 'seiv 'taim.
ðei 'staːtid ˌəːli in 'ɔːdə tə 'get ðeər ˌəːli.

The gerund after tu.

The preposition tu does not usually take a gerund as its object, but a few special cases occur when tu is the final element in expressions such as:

tə 'teik ə 'laikiŋ tə	tə bi ə'kʌstəmd tə	tə bi 'juːst tə
tə 'hav 'nou əb'dʒekʃn̩ tə	tə bi 'ʌnə'kʌstəmd tə	tə bi 'givn̩ tə
tə 'teik ə dis'laik tə	tə bi 'prefrəbl̩ tə	tə bi ə'vəːs tə
tu əb'dʒekt tə	tə bi sju'piəriə tə	

həv ju 'eni əb·dʒekʃn̩ tə mai 'boruiŋ 'ðis 'buk?
ai 'wont 'sʌmwʌn hu z ə'kʌstəmd tə 'weitiŋ ət ˌteibl̩.
'travliŋ bai 'trein z 'prefrəbl̩ tə 'travliŋ bai ᵛbʌs.
ai m 'not ə·vəːs tə 'getiŋ ʌp 'əːli prə'vaidid it 'izn̩t ᵛdaːk.

294 Position. The general rule for any preposition is that it is placed before its object:

wil ju bi 'ðeə bai 'eit?	hi 'livz ə'kros ðə ˌrivə.
ðei 'kʌt it wið ə 'naif.	ai m 'not 'tɔːkiŋ əbaut ˌdʒon.

In certain circumstances, however, the prepositions marked † in the lists in §289 do not follow this rule. Nearly always in speech and very often in writing they are separated from their object if this is a conjunctive, relative or interrogative word. These three classes of connectives (§295) occupy the initial position in their clauses, but the preposition governing them remains in its normal late position, which, in the absence of a following object, now becomes final in the sentence or clause.

The following examples of this word order show that the relatives (except wot) may be omitted and that the preposition, though usually unstressed, has no weak form when it is in the final position.

Prepositions governing interrogatives (§§313–7).

> 'huː(m) did ju ˅giv it tu?
> 'wot əv ju bin ˌlukiŋ at?
> 'hau ˙mʌtʃ wil ðei ˌsel it foː?
> 'witʃ ˅ʃop did ju ˌget ðə ˌkeik from?

Prepositions governing conjunctives (§§318–20).

> ai 'dount ˙nou 'witʃ ˙aksidṇt ju ə ˌtoːkiŋ əbaut.
> hi 'wudṇt ˙tel mi 'weər it əd ˌkʌm from.
> ai d bin ˅wʌndəriŋ ˌwot ju wə ˌlukiŋ at.
> wi l 'trai tə ˙faind ˙aut 'hau ˙mʌtʃ ðei l ˅sel it foː.

Prepositions governing relatives (§§321–8).

> ˅ðat ˌizṇt wot wi ˌwontid tə ˌtoːk əbaut.
> 'izṇt ˊðat ðə ˙wʌn (ðət) ju wə ˙lukiŋ at?
> 'wil ju ˙intrə˙djuːs mi tə ðə 'gəːl (ðət) ju wə ˙haviŋ ˊtiː wið?
> ðei 'mei əv ˙left it ʌndə ðə 'triː (ðət) ðei wə ˅haidiŋ bihaind.

The alternative construction for three of the above examples is shown below. It will be seen that this follows the general rule for the placing of prepositions, but students are advised to be chary of using it, as it sounds unnatural, stilted, and in some cases even clumsy.

> frəm 'witʃ ˅ʃop did ju ˌget ðə ˌkeik?
> ai 'dount ˙nou əbaut 'witʃ ˙aksidṇt ju ə ˅toːkiŋ.
> ˅ðat ˌizṇt ˌðat əbaut witʃ wi ˌwontid tə ˌtoːk.

When such sentences are put into the passive, the preposition almost invariably occupies the end position.

> 'witʃ ˅ʃop wəz ðə ˌkeik ˌgot from?
> wi l 'trai tə ˙faind ˙aut 'hau ˙mʌtʃ it | bi ˅sould foː.
> 'izṇt ˊðat ðə ˙wʌn ðət wəz biːiŋ ˙lukt at?

When verbs taking a prepositional object are used in the passive, the preposition takes the end position, even in principal clauses.

> ðə 'miːl z oːl'redi bin ˅peid foː.
> kən joː 'brʌðə bi ri'laid on?
> 'nou di˙siʒṇ wəz ə˅raivd at.
> 'havṇt ðei bin ˊritṇ tu?

G. Connectives

295 Classification. These are words that connect clauses, phrases, and sometimes individual words.[1] They fall into five main classes, each of which has sub-divisions. These classes are:

1. Co-ordinating conjunctions
2. Subordinating conjunctions
3. Interrogatives
4. Conjunctives
5. Relatives.

The difference between the first two classes is that co-ordinating conjunctions join clauses that are independent of one another while subordinating conjunctions join a dependent clause to a principal clause. Another difference is that if two co-ordinate clauses have the same subject it is seldom necessary to repeat it in the second clause, whereas subordinate clauses must always have their subject expressed. Compare:

Co-ordinate: ai l ˈsiː im ən ˈtel im ˈwot tə ˈduː.

Subordinate: ˈwen ai ˌsiː im ai l ˈtel im ˈwot tə ˈduː.

The Interrogatives, Conjunctives and Relatives form three closely parallel series.[2] This, and the further fact that while, strictly speaking, the Interrogatives do not join clauses of the same sentence, they do introduce Special Questions (§41) and form the link between these and the sentence that answers them, may justify their inclusion here. There are pronominal, adjectival and adverbial words in all three sets of connectives, as may be seen from the following table, which is intended as a guide to the sections (§§313–328) in which the functions of these words are described.

[1] "The term Connective is used to comprise all words, whether Pronouns, Adjectives, Adverbs or Conjunctives, which serve to connect clauses or sentences." *Recommendation XXXI of the Committee on Grammatical Terminology.*

[2] "The interrogative pronouns are also used as conjunctive pronouns in English." "All the interrogative adverbs are used relatively and conjunctively as well." Sweet's *New English Grammar.*

Function	Interroga-tives	Conjunc-tives	Rela-tives	Reference
Pronominal	ˈhuː	ˈhuː	huː	Persons
	(ˈhuːm)	(ˈhuːm)	(huːm)	Persons
	ˈhuːz	ˈhuːz	——	Possessive
	ˈwot	ˈwot	wot	Things
	ˈwitʃ	ˈwitʃ	witʃ	Selective
Adjectival	ˈhuːz	ˈhuːz	huːz	Possessive
	ˈwot	ˈwot	wot	Things
	ˈwitʃ	ˈwitʃ	——	Selective
Adverbial	ˈhau	ˈhau	——	Manner
	ˈweə*	ˈweə*	weə*	Place
	ˈwen	ˈwen	wen	Time
	ˈwai	ˈwai	wai	Cause
	'hauˈ...	'hauˈ...	——	Degree

In addition to the above there are three connectives that have only one position in the above table:

if   which is a conjunctive (and a subordinating conjunction —§302),

weðə*   which is a conjunctive only,

ðət   which is a relative referring to persons or things (and a general conjunction—§311).

CO-ORDINATING CONJUNCTIONS

296 Forms and functions. The comparatively few co-ordinating conjunctions join clauses or words of equal status in the sentence. They express various relationships between the elements that they join.

Addition: and (ənd, ən, n̩d, n̩)

> 'woːk ˈslouli ən ˌkeəfl̩i.   'blak ən ˈwait ˌfoutəgrafs | ˌduː.
> ai ˌwont 'ðis ˈand ði ˌʌðə.   'wount ju ˈhav sm̩ 'bred n̩ 'bʌtə?
> ai v ˈritn̩ ðə ˌletə tə joːr ˌʌŋkl̩ ən 'teikən it tə ðə ˌpoust.

Alternatives: oː* (ə*)

> wəz it ˈwel oː ˈbadli ˌdʌn?   wəz ðə ˌlait ˈred, oː ˌgriːn?
> ʃl̩ wi ˌteik ˈdis oː ˌðat?   ai ˌsoː 'wʌn ə ˈtuː ˌswoluz.
> d ju ˌwont tə 'stei ˈin ðis ˈiːvniŋ, oː 'gou ˌaut?

Note that questions containing the conjunction ɔː* have a special intonation: a rising tone before the ɔː*, and a falling tone after it. They are often known as Alternative Questions.

Addition to a negative: nɔː* (with inversion in the second clause)

ˎai m ˌnot ˌil, 'nɔː z ˎhiː.   ˎjuː ˌwount ˌlaik it, 'nɔː ʃl ˎai.

Opposition: bʌt (bət); jet

ˎjuː ˌkaːnt ˌriːd ˌfrentʃ, bət ˎai ˌkan.
ʃi 'keim tə ˇsiː əs, bət 'didn̩t ˎstei ˌloŋ.
hi had ə ˇstrikt, bət 'welˇmiːniŋ, ˎfaːðə.
ai 'spouk ˇslouli, jet 'kudn̩t ˙meik im ˙ʌndəˎstand.
ʃi z riˇzəːvd, jet ˎpopjulə.

Motive: fɔː* (fə*)

ai 'ʃaːnt ˇbai it, fər ai 'kaːnt əˎfoːd it.

Correlative conjunctions.

These are pairs of co-ordinating conjunctions used in each of two clauses in the same sentence. It is important to preserve "parallelism" with them, i.e., to see that each conjunction of the pair is followed by the same part of speech. They belong to the first two of the above classes.

Addition: bouθ . . . ənd; not ounli . . . bət ɔːlsou

hi 'spiːks bouθ 'frentʃ ənd ˌingliʃ.
hi bouθ 'weid ðə ˌrisks ən 'feist ðə ˌkonsikwn̩siz.
ðei ˌwəːk bouθ mi'tikjuləsli ənd ˎakjuritli.
jɔː 'brʌðə z ˙bouθ ə 'helpfl̩ ˌneibər n̩d ə kən'dʒiːnjl̩ kəmˌpanjən.
ai 'not ounli disˇlaik im, bət 'ɔːlsou əˎvoid im wen ai ˌkan.
hi z 'not ounli ˇtriki, bət 'ɔːlsou disˎonist.
ai m ˌtoːkiŋ 'not ˙ounli tə ˇjuː, bət 'ɔːlsou tə ði ˎʌðəz.

Alternatives: aiðə* . . . ɔː*; naiðə* . . . nɔː*

ju məs ˌduː it aiðə ˌpropəli ɔː 'not ət ˎɔːl.
ʃi z ˌaiðər 'il ɔː ˎleizi.
ju məs ˌbai aiðər 'ɔːl əv ðəm, ɔː 'nʌn ət ˌɔːl.
ðei ə ˌkʌmiŋ 'naiðə bai ˌtrein 'nɔː bai ˌbʌs.
hi z ˌaiðə 'mist ðə ˌtrein, ɔː di'saidid ˙not tə ˎkʌm.
'aiðə ju məs ˙gou ət ˌwʌns, 'ɔː ju l ˙hav tə 'stei ðə ˎnait.

The last two of the above examples show clearly how parallelism works with the correlative conjunctions. With all the other co-ordinating conjunctions except **foː***, if the same subject applies to both clauses it need not be repeated in the second clause. The same usually applies to any conjugators that may be common to both clauses; this excludes, of course, cases in which there is a change of tense or from affirmative to negative. In the following examples the words in parentheses are better omitted; it will be seen that in the third and fourth sentences only the subject can be dispensed with.

ai ʃĺ əv 'finiʃt mai ˙letər ənd (ai ʃĺ əv) ˋpoustid it bai ˌsiks.

ʃĺ 'mʌst əv bin ˙weitiŋ ən (ʃi ˙mʌst əv bin) 'wʌndəriŋ ˙weə wi ˋwəː.

ai v bin pri'peəriŋ fə ðə ˌtrip, ənd (ai) ʃĺ bi 'staːtiŋ təˋmoru.

ðei v 'dʌn ðə riˇpeəz, bət (ðei) 'havn̩t ˙finiʃt ðə ˋpeintiŋ jet.

SUBORDINATING CONJUNCTIONS

297 Classification. There are considerable numbers of conjunctions that join subordinate clauses to principal ones, but they can be conveniently classified according to the type of clause that they introduce and the type of question that the clause answers. On this basis we have subordinating conjunctions introducing adverbial clauses of:

1. Manner	4. Condition	7. Reservation	10. Degree
2. Place	5. Motive	8. Concession	11. Comparison
3. Time	6. Effect	9. Proportion	12. General

Subordinating conjunctions are considered in detail in §§299–312.

298 Tenses in subordinate clauses. In clauses introduced by some of the subordinating conjunctions, more particularly those of Time, Condition, Proportion, Duration and Frequency, the modal finites are not used as temporals to form future or conditional tenses, but are introduced only if their modal meaning is required. Examples illustrating this point in respect of the conjunction **if** will be found in §179. The conjunctions that are subject to this rule are marked † in the sections that follow.

299 Adverbial clauses of manner. These answer the question
ˇhau. The preposition laik must not be used as a substitute for az.
əz if
  it 'luks əz if it | ˇrein.   hi 'aktid əz if i wər əˇfreid.
əz ðou
  hi 'did it əz ˙ðou i ˇlaikt it.   it 'luks əz ˙ðou i l 'kʌm təˇmoru.
az (əz)
  hi 'did it əz ˇai did.   'nekst ˙jiə, hi l 'duː əz i ˌlaiks.

300 Adverbial clauses of place. These answer the question
ˇweə*? When the verb is one expressing movement the idea of
direction is added to that of place.
weə*
  'juː ˙stei weə ju ˌlaik.   ju kən 'stei weə ju ˇlaik.
  ju ʃl 'gou weə ju ˌlaik.   wi 'gou weə wi ə ˙best ˌsəːvd.

301 Adverbial clauses of time. These answer the question
ˇwen? They may precede the principal clause instead of following
it, in which case the conjunction is usually stressed and the strong
form of az is used.
† wen
  ai 'did ˙ðat wen ai əˇraivd.   ai l 'duː it wen ai ˙hav ˌtaim.
† wenˇevə*
  wen'evər ai ˇsiː im ai ˌsei ˌðat.
  ai l 'lisn̩ tu it wen'evər ai get ə ˌtʃaːns.
† wail
  ai l 'duː it wail ai m ˇhiə.   ju məst 'rait it wail ju ə ˇhiə.
† biˇfoə*
  'duː it bi˙foː ju ˌgou.   ai ˇoːlwiz ˌduː it biˌfoːr ai ˌgou.
† ˇaːftə*
  'aːftə ju v ˌritn̩ it 'let mi ˇsiː it.
  ai ˇoːlwiz ˌlet ju ˌsiː ðəm ˌaːftər ai v ˌritn̩ ðəm.
† diˇrektli
  diˈrektli ai ˇsoː it ai ᵛrekəgnaizd it.
  ai ʃl 'rekəgnaiz it di˙rektli ai ᵛsiː it.
† az (əz)
  ai riˈmembəd it əz ai wəz ˙kʌmiŋ ˌbak.
  'az wi ˙gou əˌloŋ ai l iksˇplein it tə ju.

† sins

   'sins ai ˈkeim ˌbak ai v ˈritn̩ 'θriː ˌletəz.

   'sins ai ˈkeim ˌbak ai v bin 'raitiŋ ˌletəz.

302 Adverbial clauses of condition. These answer the questions in 'wot ˈkeis? or on 'wot kənˈdiʃn̩z?

In clauses introduced by some of these conjunctions ʃud is used (in all persons) to suggest doubt that the condition will be fulfilled. Similarly wəː tu is used (also in all persons) to emphasize the sense of condition. As shown in brackets below, the conjugation if may be replaced by inversion of wəː, had or ʃud with the subject.

† if

   ai I 'duː it təˈmoru if ai ˌhav ˌtaim.

   ai d 'duː it təˈmoru if ai ˌhad ˌtaim. (ˌhad ai ˌtaim.)

   ai d əv 'dʌn it ˈjestədi if ai d ˌhad ˌtaim. (ˌhad ai had ˌtaim.)

   if ju 'siː ˌdʒon 'tel im ai ˌwont im.

   if ju ʃəd 'siː ˌdʒon 'tel im ai ˌwont im. ('ʃud ju ˈsiː . . .)

   if ju wə tə 'gou ˌnau, ju d ˈsiː im. ('wəː ju tə 'gou . . .)

† if ˈounli or if . . . ˈounli

   if 'ounli ju d ˈtould mi ˌðat, ai 'ʃudn̩t əv ˈritn̩.

   if ju d 'ounli ˈkiːp ˅kwaiət, ai ʃəd 'finiʃ in ˈnou ˌtaim.

   if ju d 'ounli ˈkept ˅kwaiət, ai ʃəd əv ˈfiniʃt bai ˌnau.

† prəˈvaidiŋ or prəˈvaidid (ðət)

   ai I 'kʌm prəˈvaidiŋ ju 'let mi ˈnou in gud ˌtaim.

   prəˈvaidid ju ˈdraiv ˅keəfli, ai I 'let ˈjuː ˌteik ˌouvə.

† səˈpouz or səˈpouziŋ (ðət), usually in front position and followed by a question in the main clause. In all these cases ʃəd may replace ʃl.

   səˈpouz ai ˌsiː im, 'wot ʃl ai ˌtel im?

   səˈpouziŋ i ˈisn̩t ˈin, ʃl ai 'liːv ə ′nout?

   səˈpouziŋ i ʃəd bi ˌaut, ʃl ai 'liːv ə ′nout?

   'wot ʃl ai ˌtel im, səˌpouziŋ ai wə tə ˌsiː im?

† on kənˈdiʃn (ðət)

   ju kən 'teik it ˈnau on kənˌdiʃn̩ (ðət) ju riˌtəːn it təˌmoru.

   on kənˈdiʃn̩ ju bi˅heiv jəself ai I 'let ju ˈgou əˈloun.

† əz ˈloŋ əz (the use of this conjunction in adverbial clauses of cause—§303a—is an Americanism).

   ai 'dount ˈmaind ˈhau ju ˌduː it əz ˌloŋ əz ju ˌduː it ˅kwikli.

   əz 'loŋ əz ju ˈduː it ˅kwikli it 'dʌzn̩ ˈmatə ˈhau ju ˌduː it.

† ən'les (compare these with the if clauses and notice the insertion
of the negation, and the change of intonation).

ai 'ʃaːnt ˙duː it təˈmoru ənˈles ai ˙hav ᵛtaim.

ai 'ʃudṇt ˙duː it təˈmoru ənˈles ai ˙had ᵛtaim.

ənˈles ju ˙gou ᵛnau, ju 'wount ˋsiː ðəm.

ənˈles ju ˙went ᵛnau, ju 'wudṇt ˋsiː ðəm.

303 Adverbial clauses of motive. The clauses that explain
the motive for a certain course of action fall into three sub-divisions.

a. Clauses of cause, answering the question ᵛwai?

biˋkoz

biˈkoz ʃi ᵛwontid it ʃi ˋtuk it.

ai ʃ| ᵛteik it bikoz ai ˋwont it (*or* ʃ| ˋwont it).

sins

wi 'mei əz wel ˋliːv, sins ðə z 'nou ˙point in ᵛsteiiŋ.

ˌsins ju 'kaːnt ˋfiniʃ it in ˌtaim, 'wai not ˙giv ˋʌp?

əz (az)

ai 'ʃaːnt ˋgou ˌnau, əz it s 'tuː ˙leit tə 'duː eni ˋgud.

əz wi 'havṇt ᵛhəːd frəm ðəm ai səˈpouz ðei l bi ˋkʌmiŋ.

'nau (ðət)

'wot d ju ˋθiŋk əv im, 'nau (ðət) ju v ˋsiːn im?

'nau (ðət) ai m ᵛhiər ai d 'betə ˋstei.

'siːiŋ (ðət)

'wot ə ju ˙gouiŋ tə ˋduː, ˌsiːiŋ (ðət) ðei 'wount əˋgriː?

'siːiŋ ðət ai m ˙kʌmiŋ təᵛmoru, ai 'θiŋk ai l ˋgou ˌnau.

in 'vjuː əv ðə ˙fakt ðət

ai l ˋwaiə ðəm, in ˌvjuː əv ðə ˌfakt ðət ai ˌmist ðə ˌpoust.

in 'vjuː əv ðə ˙fakt ðət ˋʃiː z ˌhiə, wi priˈfəː tə ˌliːv.

b. Clauses of contingency, also answering the question ᵛwai?

in ˋkeis

ai l 'teik mai ʌmˋbrelə, in 'keis it ˋreinz.

in 'keis it ʃəd ˌrein, ai l 'teik mai ʌmˋbrelə.

it 'mei ˋrein; ai l 'teik mai ʌmˋbrelə in ˋkeis.

c. Clauses of purpose, answering the question 'wot ˋfoː?

ˌsou ðət

ai v 'put it ˋhiə, ˌsou ðət i kən 'siː it wen i ˌkʌmz.

ai l 'put it ˋhiə, ˌsou ðət i l 'siː it wen i ˌkʌmz.

in 'ɔːdə ðət

ai l ˌhav 'evriθiŋ ˌredi, in 'ɔːdə ðət ðə ʃl bi 'nou diˌlei.
'wil ju 'aːsk im tə ˌsiː mi, in 'ɔːdə ðət wi mei 'setl ðə matə?

304 Adverbial clauses of effect. These do not answer any specific question.

'sou . . . (ðət)

ai wəz 'sou ˙taiəd (ðət) ai 'went tə ˙bed ət ˌwʌns.
ju l bi 'sou ˙taiəd (ðət) ju l 'hav tə ˙gou tə ˙bed ət ˌwʌns.

'sʌtʃ . . . ðət

hi 'kept mi ˙weitiŋ 'sʌtʃ ə ˙loŋ ˌtaim ðət ai 'went ə'wei.
it wəz 'sʌtʃ ə ˌhevi wʌn ðət ai 'kudn̩t ˌkari it bai maiˌself.

305 Adverbial clauses of reservation. These do not answer any specific question.

ik'sept ðət

ai d 'gou ðeə 'nau ikˌsept ðət ai m ˌtuː ˌtaiəd.
ai d əv 'gon ðeə 'jestədi ikˌsept ðət ai wəz 'tuː ˌbizi.

ik'septiŋ ðət

ai d 'gou ðeə tə'moru ikˌseptiŋ ðət ai ˌʃaːnt ˌhav ˌtaim.

306 Adverbial clauses of concession. These do not answer any specific question.

ðou

ðou i 'dʌzn̩t ᵛlaik mi hi 'puts ˋʌp wið mi.
ai l ˋtrai tə ˌduː it, ðou ai 'havn̩t ˙mʌtʃ ˙houp əv səkˋsiːdiŋ.

ɔːlˈðou

hi z 'veri ᵛklevər ɔːlðou i 'dʌzn̩t ˌluk it.
ai l 'rait tu im tə'nait, ɔːlðou ai ʃl ˋsiː im tə,moru.
ɔːlˈðou ai ˙had ə 'bad ˌnait, ai 'got ʌp ˋəːli ðis ˌmɔːniŋ.

† 'iːvn̩ if

ai 'ʃaːnt hav ˙taim tə ᵛsiː im ˙iːvn̩ if i ˋkʌmz.
'iːvn̩ if i ˋkeim ai ˌʃudn̩t hav ˌtaim tə ˌsiː im.
ˋðat ˌwount ˌmeik eni ˌdifrn̩s, 'iːvn̩ if it s ˋtruː.
'iːvn̩ if 'ðat wə ˋtruː, it 'wudn̩t 'meik eni ˌdifrn̩s.

weərˋaz

ᵛðis wʌn z 'njuː, weərˌaz ði ᵛʌðə wʌn z ˙kwait ˋould.
weərˌaz 'ai wəz ˙tould tə ᵛstop, 'juː wə ˌtould tə ˙gou ˋon.

264

hauˋevə* (followed by a determiner, adjective or adverb).
   hi l ˋnevə ˌləːn it ˌpropəli hauˋevə ˌmʌtʃ i ˌstʌdiz.
   hauˈevə ˋgud i ˌiz hi ˈnevə gets ˙eni iŋ˅kʌridʒmənt.
   hi ˈnevə kəm˙pleinz əv ðə ˅fuːd, hauˋevə ˌbadli it s ˌkukt.
in ˋspait əv ðə ˌfakt ðət
   hi ˈwent ˌaut in ˈspait əv ðə ˙fakt ðət i ˈwozn̩t ˏwel.
   in ˈspait əv ðə ˙fakt ðət ʃi ˅laiks ju, ʃi əˋvoidz ju.

307 Adverbial clauses of proportion. These do not answer any
specific question. Of the two clauses, the first is the subordinate
and the second the principal. Many combinations of comparative
determiners, adjectives and adverbs are used; only a few examples
are given here.
   † ðə ˈmoə* . . . ðə ˋmoə*; ðə ˈmoə* . . . ðə ˋles
   † ðə ˈles . . . ðə ˋmoə*; ðə ˈles . . .ðə ˋles.
   † ðə ˈloŋgə* . . . ðə ˋbetə*; ðə ˈmoː ˙keəfʃi . . . ðə ˈles ˋsatisfaid.
   ðə ˈmoər ai ˌgiv ju, ðə ˈmoə ju ˋwont.
   ðə ˈles ju ˌteik, ðə ˈmoə ju l ˙hav ˋleft.
   ðə ˈloŋgər ai ˌstei, ðə ˈbetər ai ˋlaik it.
   ðə ˈloŋgə ju ˌstei, ðə ˈbetə ju l ˋlaik it.
   ðə ˈmoː ˙keəfʃi ʃi ˌwəːks, ðə ˈles ˋsatisfaid ðei aː.

308 Adverbial clauses of degree. These clauses, all of which
can answer questions beginning with **hau** followed by an adjective
or an adverb, cover a very wide range of subjects. In many cases
questions of this kind prompt a comparison; the clauses are then
introduced by one of the conjunctions listed in §309. These clauses
of degree fall into various sub-divisions, of which the following
may be distinguished:

a. Clauses of distance, answering the question ˈhau ˋfaː ?

ˈʌp tə ˋweə*
   ðə θəˈmomitə z gon ˙ʌp tə ˈweər it ˙woz ˋjestədi.
ˈdaun tə ˋweə*
   ˈriːd ˙daun tə ˈweə wi ˙stopt ˋlaːst ˌtaim.

b. Clauses of duration, answering the question ˈhau ˋloŋ ?

   † til *or* ənˋtil
   hi ˈjuːst tə ˙weit ˙hiər əntil ai ˈkeim ˋbak.
   hi ˋoːlwiz ˌweits ˌhiər əntil ai ˌkʌm ˌbak.

'tel im tə ˙weit ˙hiə til ju ˈkʌm ˌbak.

ai ʃ| bi ˈwəːkiŋ ˙hiə til ju ˌkoːl fə mi.

† sins

ai v ˈritn̩ ə ˇlot əv ˌletəz ˌsins ai got ˌbak.

ˈsins ai ˙got ˌbak ai v ˙dʌn ˈnʌθiŋ bət ˙rait ˌletəz.

† ˈevə sins

ai v bin ˈraitiŋ ˇletəz ˌevə sins ai ˌgot ˌbak.

ˈevə sins ai ˙got ˌbak ai v bin ˈraitiŋ ˇletəz.

† ˈoːl ðə ˇtaim (ðət)

ˈoːl ðə ˙taim (ðət) i wəz ˌhiə hi did ˈnʌθiŋ bət ˌgrʌmb|.

hi ˈgrʌmb|z ˈoːl ðə ˙taim i z ˇhiə.

ai ʃ| bi ˈraitiŋ ˇletəz ˌoːl ðə ˌtaim ðət ai m ə̩ˌwei.

c. *Clauses of frequency*, answering the question ˈhau ˇofn̩ ?

† wen

ai ˈteik ə ˙rest wen ai ˇkan.

ˈwen ai ˙hav ˌtaim ai l ˇrait tə ju.

† wenˇevə*

ˌðat s wot ˇai ˌsei wen˙evər ai ˇsiː im.

wenˈevə wi ˌkud, wi ˙juːst tə ˇvizit ðəm.

wi l ˈgou ən ˌsiː ðəm wenˈevə wi ˙hav ˌtaim.

† əz ˇofn̩ əz

ai ˈrout tə ju əz ˙ofn̩ əz ai ˇkud.

ˈkʌm ən ˙siː mi əz ˈofn̩ əz ju ˌlaik.

wil ju ˈrait tu əs əz ˙ofn̩ əz ju ˇkan?

309 Adverbial clauses of comparison. These may answer questions beginning with ˈhau followed by a determiner, an adjective or an adverb. The three forms that comparisons may take are explained in §§108–110, and the following examples show some of the qualities, etc., that may be compared.

Comparisons using determiners

Quantity

ˇmoː ðən	ˈdount ˙trai tə duː ˈmoː ðən ju ˇkan.
əz ˇmʌtʃ əz	ˈteik əz ˙mʌtʃ əz ju ˌwont.
ˇles ðən	ˌai v got ˈles ˙miːt ðən ˇjuː hav.

Number

ˈmoː ðən	ˌðiːz ə ˈmoː ðən wi kən ˌmanidʒ.
əz ˈmeni əz	ðə ˈwəːnt əz *(or* sou) ˙meni əz ai ˈθoːt.
ˈfjuːə ðən	ai ˌgot ˈfjuːə ðən ai ˌdid ˈlaːst ˌtaim.

Comparisons using adjectives

Dimensions

ˈlaːdʒə ðən	it s ˈlaːdʒə ðən ai ˈθoːt it woz.
ˈloŋgə ðən	it s ˈraːðə ˙loŋgə ðən i ˈsed it woz.
əz ˈlaːdʒ əz	it ˈiznt əz ˙laːdʒ əz ai ˈθoːt it woz.

Qualities of all kinds

ˈbetə ðən	it s ˈmʌtʃ ˌbetə ðən ai ˈθoːt it ˌwoz.
ˈheviə ðən	it s ˈheviə ðən ai iksˈpektid it tə ˌbiː.
ˈmoː ˈfit ðən	hi ˌluks ˈmoː ˙fit ðən ai v ˈevə ˈsiːn im.
əz ˈgud əz	it s ˈkwait əz ˌgud əz ai ᵛθoːt.
əz ˈhevi əz	ˌmain z əz ˌhevi əz ˌjoːz iz.
əz ˈfit əz	ʃi ˌluks əz ˈfit əz ai v ˙evə ˈsiːn əː.

Comparisons using adverbs

Manner

ˈbetə ðən	ˈhiː kən ˌduː it ˌbetə ðən ˌjuː kan.
əz ˈwel əz	hi ˈdid it əz ˙wel əz i ᵛkud.

Distance

† ˈfəːðə ðən	hi went ˈmʌtʃ ˌfəːðə ðən ai ᵛaːskt im tu.
† əz ˈfaːr əz	ai ʃl ˌgou əz ˈfaːr əz ai ˙fiːl iŋˈklaind tu.

Time

ʲ ˈsuːnə ðən	ai ʃl bi ˈðeə ˙suːnə ðən ju ˈθiŋk.
† əz ˈsuːn əz	ai l ˈduː it əz ˙suːn əz ai ᵥkan.

Duration

† ˈloŋgə ðən	it ˌtuk ˈloŋgə ðən ai ˈθoːt it ˌwud.
† əz ˈloŋ əz	ju ʃl ˈstei ˙hiər əz ˈloŋ əz ju ˌlaik.

310 Case after əz and ðən. In many instances the clauses introduced by these two conjunctions of the comparative may be reduced to phrases or even single words, the finite that they might contain being omitted as understood. Thus, in sentences like the following the words shown in brackets are usually left out.

'ai v dʌn ˈmoː ðən ˏjuː (hav).

ˈai v dʌn əz ˏmʌtʃ əz ˏjuː (hav).

ˏai v dʌn ˈles ðən ᵛjuː (hav).

ˏðis wʌn z ˈlaːdʒə ðən ˏðat (wʌn iz).

ai ˈlaik ᵛðis wʌn əz ˈwel əz (ai laik) ˈeni əv ðəm.

ˈðis wʌn ˈizn̩t əz (or sou) ˈlaːdʒ əz ᵛðat (wʌn iz).

This raises the question as to whether in such cases ðən and əz are functioning as prepositions rather than subordinating conjunctions. Sweet, in his *New English Grammar*, §380, stated the case for this point of view, which, if accepted, means that when one of the five pronouns having special forms for the oblique case is needed in this position, that special form will be used, thus:

hi z ˈtoːlə ðən ˏmiː.   ˈwiː v ˏgon əz ˏfaːr əz ˏðem.

While many grammarians adhere to the view that this practice is ungrammatical, it has to be recognized that it is extremely widely used. Some speakers, in order to avoid involvement in the controversy, prefer to retain the finites, thus justifying the use of the nominative form of the pronoun:

hi z ˈtoːlə ðən ˈai ˏam.   ˈwiː v ˏgon əz ˏfaːr əz ˏðei hav.

311 The general conjunction. In addition to its use in combination with other words to introduce adverbial clauses (§§302–6 and 308), the word ðət is used as a general conjunction to introduce noun clauses. These may be either the subject or the object of the verb in the principal clause. Many of these clauses resemble, and may replace, some of the infinitive phrases described in §§241–250. The following are some examples.

a. As subject of a verb

ðət ju ʃəd ˈəːn ˈoːl ˈðat ˏmʌni ˈmʌs bi ˈveri ˏgratifaiiŋ.

ðət ai wəz ˈnot ˈheld risᵛponsibl̩ riˈliːvd mi triˈmendəsli.

b. With precursory ðeə*

ðə z ˈnou diˈmaːnd ðət ju ʃəd riˈzain frəm joː ˏpoust.

ðə z bin ˈnou prəˈpousl̩ ðət ði əˈgriːmənt ʃəd bi ᵛkansl̩d.

c. With precursory it and adjective complement

it s ˈʌndiˈnaiəbl̩ ðət joː ˏfaːðə z ˏdʒenərəs.

it wəz ˈfoːtʃn̩it ðət ai wəz ˏnot ˏheld ris ˏponsibl̩.

d. With precursory it *and noun complement*

    it s ə ˈʃeim ðət wi ˌkaːnt bi inˌdʒoiiŋ ðis ˌbrait ˌsʌnʃain.
    it s ə ˈnjuːsn̩s ðət ai ˌkaːnt ˌstaːt til ˌnekst ˌwiːk.

e. As object of a verb

    ˈpliːz riˈmembə ðət ju məst ˈhav it ˈredi bai ˈwenzdi.
    ai ˈdidn̩t ˈpromis ðət ai d əˌkʌmpəni ju.

f. As predicate

    ˈwil ju ˈtel ðəm ðət ˈoːl ðə ˈwinduz məs bi ˈkliːnd?
    ai riˈmaindid əː ðət ʃi ˈhad tə ˈget ˈʌp ˈəːli.

In clauses of types *d, e* and *f* the general conjunction is frequently
omitted, giving rise to what is called a Contact Clause, thus:

    d. it s ə ˈnjuːsn̩s ai ˌkaːnt ˌstaːt til ˌnekst ˌwiːk.
    e. ˈpliːz riˈmembə ju məst ˈhav it ˈredi bai ˈwenzdi.
    f. ˈwil ju ˈtel ðəm ˈoːl ðə ˈwinduz məs bi ˈkliːnd?

In American English the conjunction is often omitted in clauses
of types *b* and *c*, as well as in those mentioned above.

In sentences such as the following the general conjunction is
never expressed:

    ai ˈwiʃ i d ˇweit!   ai ˈhoup it ˈdʌzn̩t ˈrein təˌmoru.
    ai ˈwiʃ i d ˇweitid!   ai ˈtrʌst i ˈhazn̩t fəˇgotn̩ it.
    it s ˈtaim wi wə ˌgouiŋ.   ai d ˈraːðə ju ˈstaːtid təˇmoru.

Notice that in the two examples on the last line past tenses are
used with a future or present reference. They are acting as substitutes for a subjunctive expressing a hypothesis.

312 The ing-form after conjunctions. In §§256 and 293 examples were given of gerunds as prepositional objects. In some cases
the ing-form follows words which may be either prepositions or
conjunctions, and it is sometimes a moot point whether in these
cases it is a gerund or not. Examples:

bifoə* ju d ˈbetə ˈfiniʃ ˈðis ˌwəːk biˌfoː ˌstaːtiŋ eniθiŋ ˌels.
əntil   əntil ˈtiːtʃiŋ ˌiŋgliʃ ai ˈnevə ˈriəlaizd its ˌdifikˌtiz.
aːftə* aːftə ˈhiəriŋ ði ˈʌðə ˌsaid ai ˈgeiv ˈmai əˌpinjən.
sins   ai v ˈtʃeindʒd mai ˈmaind sins ˌriːdiŋ ˌðat ˌbuk.

When the connective cannot in any circumstances be regarded as a preposition, it is clear that the ing-form is not a gerund, but is forming part of an adverbial phrase:

wen	wen 'spiːkiŋ ˌiŋgliʃ, hi 'ofn̩ ˙meiks misˋteiks.
wail	ai 'vizitid ðə ˙britiʃ mjuˋziəm wail ˌsteiiŋ in ˌlʌndən.
ðou	ðou ə'griːiŋ wið ðə ᵛfigəz, ai 'kaːnt əkˊsept ðə kəŋˋkluːʒn̩z.

In either case this is a somewhat formal construction, not much used in spoken English, where it is usually replaced by adverbial clauses as shown below.

. . . biˌfoə ju ˌstaːt eniθiŋ ˌels.	'wen i ˙spiːks ˌiŋgliʃ . . .
əntil ai ˋtoːt ˌiŋgliʃ . . .	. . . wail ai wəz ˌsteiiŋ in
'aːftər ai dˊhəːd ði 'ʌðə ˌsaid . . .	ˌlʌndən.
. . . sins ai ˌred ˌðat ˌbuk.	ðou ai ə'griː wið ðə ᵛfigəz . .

INTERROGATIVES

313 Characteristics. The interrogatives, which may be pronominal, adjectival or adverbial in nature, introduce the sentences known as Particular (or Special) Questions. As was explained in §43, such questions normally take a Tune II. The nuclear tone is usually placed on the last stressed word of the sentence, but may fall on the interrogative word if there is no later word that can accommodate it. As the interrogatives are nearly always stressed they have no weak forms. A classified list is given in §295.

A very important structural point to note is that when an interrogative is the subject of the verb an affirmative construction must be used:

'huː ˙got hiə ˌfəːst?	'witʃ 'buk ə'piːlz tə ju ˌmoust?
'wot ˙meid ˙ðat ˌnoiz?	'hau ˙meni əv ju │ ˌgiv mi wʌn?

Compare these sentences with the following in which the interrogative is the object of the verb, and an interrogative construction is used:

'huː(m) did ju ˌsiː ðeə?	'witʃ ˙buk d ju ˙laik ˌbest?
'wot wə ju ˌmeikiŋ?	'hau ˙meni əv ðəm wil ju ˌgiv mi?

As explained in §294, certain prepositions take the end position when their object is an interrogative word.　Here are further examples:

　　'huː(m) did ju ˌspiːk tu?　　'witʃ ˙buk iz i ˌtoːkiŋ əbaut?
　　'wot did ju duː ˋðat wið?　　'hau meni ˙piːpl ə ju ˌkeitəriŋ foː?

The prepositions that take this end position are marked † in the lists given in §289.

314 Pronominal interrogatives: huː (huːm), huːz, wot, witʃ. With the exception of huːm these may function as subject, subject-complement, direct object or prepositional object.　They are used as follows:

huː

This refers to persons only, and may be singular or plural.　While it was originally used only as a subject or subject-complement, it has for very many years replaced huːm as an object, especially in natural conversation.

　　'huː ˙tould ju ˌðat?　　'huː z ðə ˙tʃeəmən əv ðə ˌmiːtiŋ?
　　'huː əv ju ˌritn̩ tu?　　'huː did ju ˙siː ət ðə ˌpaːti?

It is used to ask about a person's identity:

　　'huː ˌiz i?—hi z mistə ˋsmiθ.　　hi z ðə ˋprezidn̩t.

huːm

This refers to persons only, and may be singular or plural. Though nominally the correct form for the direct and prepositional objects, it is avoided by the great majority of speakers, who prefer to use huː in all cases.　It is, however, to be met with in written English and in a ceremonial style of speech.　When it is used, any preposition that governs it is usually placed before it instead of in the end position.

　　'huːm əv ju ˌsiːn?　　'huːm did ðei ˙hould ˌprizn̩ə?
　　fə 'huːm wə ju ˌpliːdiŋ? *or* 'huːm wə ju ˌpliːdiŋ foː?

huːz

This refers to possession by persons and, though usually adjectival, may be used pronominally.

　　'huːz iz ðat ˌbuk?　　'huːz did ju ˌboru?

wot

This refers to things, and may be either singular or plural. It
is invariable for case.

    ˈwot ˈmeid ˈðat ˌnoiz?   ˈwot s ðə ˌtaim?
    ˈwot did ju ˌsei tə ðəm?   ˈwot did juː ˈduː ˋðat foː?
    ˈwot ə ˋðouz θiŋz?   ˈwot ə ðə ˌvizitiŋ auəz?

It is used to ask about a person's nationality, social standing
or profession.

    ˈwot ˋiz i?—hi z ə ˋspanjəd.   hi z ə ˋtiːtʃə.

witʃ

This is selective, asking for one or more members of a class to
be picked out from the rest. It may refer to either persons or things,
and may be either singular or plural. It is invariable for case,
and is more frequently adjectival than pronominal. When used
as a pronoun it is frequently followed by a participial phrase indicating the class from which the choice is to be made.

    ˈwitʃ əv ˈðouz ˈmen iz joː ˌbrʌðə? *or* ˈwitʃ iz joː ˌbrʌðə?
    ˈwitʃ əv ˈðiːz ˈpiktʃəz ˈgeiv ju ðə ˈmoust ˌpleʒə?
    ˈwitʃ əv ˈðouz ˈtuː ˈbuks did ju ˈfaind ˈmoust ˌintristiŋ?
    ˈwitʃ əv ðə ˈboiz əv ju ˌspoukən tu?

hau mʌtʃ, hau meni, hau litl, hau fjuː

Though generally adjectival, these collocations may be used
pronominally.

    ˈhau ˈmʌtʃ d ju ˌwont?   ˈhau ˈmeni did ju ˌsiː?
    ˈhau ˈlitl ˌwoz ðə?   ˈhau ˈfjuː kən ju ˌduː wið?

315 Adjectival interrogatives: huːz, wot, witʃ. These have
the same references as when they are pronominal.

huːz

This refers to possession (of persons or things) by persons.

    ˈhuːz ˈdoktər əˌtendid ju? ˈhuːz ˈtʃildrn̩ wə ju ˌpleiiŋ wið?
    ˈhuːz ˈhoːs iz ˌðat?   ˈhuːz ʌmˋbrelə həv ju ˌteikən?

wot

This usually refers to things, but is occasionally used for persons.
It is used in asking for selection when the choice is felt to be
unlimited.

'wot 'idiət 'tould ju ˯ðat?   'wot ˯aːnsə did ju ˌgiv ðəm?
'wot ˵medsin ə ju ˌteikiŋ?   'wot kən'seʃŋz əv ju ˵aːskt foː?

witʃ

This refers to persons or things, and is used in asking for selection
when the choice is from a limited class.

'witʃ 'boi 'wʌn ðə ˯praiz?   'witʃ 'ruːmz əv ðei ˯kliːnd?
'witʃ 'wei iz ðə ˯ʃoːtist?   'witʃ 'trein ə ðei ˯kʌmiŋ bai?

hau mʌtʃ, hau meni, hau litļ, hau fjuː

The following are examples of these collocations used adjectivally.

'hau mʌtʃ ˯tiː əv ju ˌgot?   'hau meni 'piːpļ ə ˯kʌmiŋ?
'hau litļ ˯milk iz ðə?   'hau fjuː mis˯teiks did ju ˌmeik?

The interrogative hau is also collocated with adjectives.

'hau 'laːdʒ iz joː ˯gaːdņ?   'hau 'gud wəz ðat ˯film ju ˌsoː?

316   Adverbial interrogatives: hau, weə*, wen, wai. These have
their usual meanings.

hau

Adverb of manner, also used in inquiring after someone's health.

'hau d ju 'laik joː ˯tiː?   'hau dəz i 'get 'θruː sou 'mʌtʃ ˯wəːk?
'hau d ju ˯duː?   'hau z joː ˯brʌðə?
'hau ˵aː ju?   'hau ər 'oːl ðə ˯famili?

weə*

Adverb of place and direction.

'weər ˯iz it?   'weə did ju 'put mai ˯buk?
'weər ˵aː ðei?   'weər ə ju 'gouiŋ fə jə ˯holidiz?

wen

Adverb of time.

'wen did ju ˯miːt ðəm?   'wen | ði '˵ʌðəz bi ˌredi?

wai

Adverb of motive or cause.

'wai 'kaːnt ju ˯weit fə mi?   'wai dəz it ˯rein sou ˌmʌtʃ ˌhiə?

The interrogative hau is often collocated with adverbs of various
kinds.

Manner	'hau 'fluːəntli dəz ʃi 'spiːk ˯iŋgliʃ?
Distance	'hau 'faːr iz ˯lʌndən frəm ˌhiə?
Time	'hau 'suːn kən ju 'let mi ˯hav it?

Duration   ˈhau ˈloŋ did it ˌteik?
Frequency   ˈhau ˈofn̩ dəz i ˈkʌm tə ˌsiː ju?

317   Interrogatives with evə* and els. Most of the interrogatives
may be intensified by combining them with **evə***, while alternatives
are expressed by adding **els**. Both these elements take a stress,
and **els** usually takes the nuclear tone, which, since the question
begins with an interrogative word, will normally be a Tone II.

evə*	els
Pronominal	
huː ˈevə z ˌðat?	ˈhuː ˌels ˌwonts wʌn?
——	ˈhuː(m) ˌels əv ju ˌsiːn?
——	ˈhuːz ˌels əv ju ˌteikən?
wot ˈevə ˈmeid ju ˌduː it?	ˈwot ˌels iz ˌniːdid?
witʃ ˈevə did ju ˌteik?	ˈwitʃ ˌels d ju ˌwont?
Adjectival	
wot ˈevə ˈjuːs wəz ˋðat?	ˈwot pleis ˌels kəd it ˌbiː?
witʃ ˈevə ˈbuk s ˌðat?	ˈwitʃ buk ˌels d ju ˌwont?
Adverbial	
hau ˈevə d ju ˋduː it?	ˈhau ˋels kən ai ˌduː it?
weər ˈevər ə ju ˌgouiŋ?	ˈweər ˋels kəd it ˌbiː?
wen ˈevə did ju ˌsiː im?	ˈwen ˌels kəd ju ˌmiːt mi?
wai ˈevə did ju ˋduː it?	ˈwai ˌels ʃəd ai ˌwont wʌn?

Though the collocations **huːm ˈevə*** and **huːz ˈevə*** exist, they
are very seldom used. In place of the former, many speakers
would use the subject form, thus:

huː ˈevə did ju ˋtel əbaut it?

For the possessive form a paraphrase would be used, e.g.,

huː ˈevə dəz ˋðis biˌloŋ tu?

In popular speech the possessive **ˈhuːz ˌels** is usually replaced
by **ˈhuː ˌelsiz**, so that the example on the third line of the above
table would become:

ˈhuː ˌelsiz əv ju ˌteikən?

This practice arises from the feeling that **huː els** is a unit of the
type referred to in §57.

CONJUNCTIVES

318 The particular conjunctives. This term is a convenient
one to designate a class of words which are closely parallel to the
interrogatives in form but which are used to introduce subordinate
noun clauses when the principal clause conveys such mental states
as interrogation, wonderment, ignorance, uncertainty or reticence.
The principal clause may be a statement, an imperative or a
question, and, like the interrogatives, the conjunctives may have
a pronominal, an adjectival or an adverbial nature.

In most cases the subordinate noun clause represents a particular
(or special) question that has been converted into an indirect
question ; the introductory interrogative word of the direct question
changes its role to become the conjunctive introducing the subordinate clause, thus :

'huː ˌiz it?	>	ai 'dount ˙nou 'huː it ˌiz.
'weə z i ˌgouiŋ?	>	ai 'wʌndə ˙weər i z ˌgouiŋ.
'hau did ʃi ˈduː it?	>	'tel mi ˙hau ʃi ˌdid it.

It is important to notice that the interrogative construction of
the direct question is converted into a statement construction in
the indirect question. A common mistake of foreign students of
English is to retain the interrogative construction in the indirect
question.

Unlike the interrogatives, conjunctives cannot be intensified by
evə*, and, unlike the relatives, they usually bear some degree of
sentence stress, and they have no antecedent.

319 The general conjunctives. This term may be applied to
the two conjunctives **if** and **weðə***, which do not correspond to
any interrogative word, but serve to introduce subordinate noun
clauses representing general questions (§41) that have been converted into indirect questions, thus :

ə ju ə'weər əv ˙ðat?	>	ai 'wʌndə ˙weðə ju ər əˌweər əv ˌðat.
həz i 'siːn ðəm?	>	'let mi ˙nou if i z ˅siːn ðəm.
kən ðei 'weit?	>	'wil ju ˙tel mi if ðei kən 'weit?

As will be seen from the above examples, the principal clause
may be a statement, an imperative or a question.

A certain difference in meaning between **if** and **weðə*** should be noticed. While **if** means "in the case that", **weðə***, with its suggestion of duality or alternation (compare **aiðə***, **naiðə***, **ʌðə***), means "in this case or the other". In certain contexts, therefore, **if** may be ambiguous, and **weðə*** is to be preferred. Example:

ˈwaiər if ai m tə ˌkʌm. = If I'm to come, send me a telegram.

ˈwaiə ˈweðər ai m tə ˌkʌm. = In any case send me a telegram saying whether I'm to come or not.

The difference in intonation suggests that the if-clause is felt to be adverbial, while the whether-clause is felt to be a noun clause.

320 Substitution tables. The tables given below show how and in what contexts the conjunctives work.

With reference to the intonation marking, it should be noted that, while the nucleus (§37) falls in the subordinate clause, the tone it takes is governed by the nature of the principal clause. If this is a statement or an imperative the nucleus may be Tone II (as shown) or sometimes Tone III, while questions usually take Tone I High (§31). To facilitate the making of the necessary changes, imperatives are marked (!), questions (?), and statements are left unmarked.

The general conjunctives.

This table gives fifty examples of the use of the two general conjunctives.

Principal Clause		Conjunctive	Subordinate Clause
ðə z ˈnou ˈnouiŋ		if	ai m tə ˈgou təˌdei
ðei ˈwount ˈtel mi		ˈweðə*	it s ˌredi
it s ˈhaːd tə ˈsei			ʃi ˈwonts eni ˌmoə
ˈtrai tə riˈmembə*	(!)		ðei v ˌteikən it
ˈwount ðei ˈtel ju	(?)		hi z əˌraivd

The particular conjunctives.

This table gives more than a thousand examples of the use of the particular conjunctives. The elements in the second and third columns are divided into five sections and are interchangeable only inside these sections, but the elements in the first column may be used with any of those in the other columns.

Principal Clause		*Conjunctive*	*Subordinate Clause*
ai ˈdount ˈnou		ˈhuː	it ˌiz
ai ˈkwait fəˈget		ˈwitʃ	ˋðis iz
ai ˈwʌndə		ˈwot	ˋðat iz
ai ˈwont tə ˈnou		ˈhuːz	ðei ˌaː
it əd bi ˈnais tə ˈnou		ˈhuː(m)	ju ˌsoː
ai l ˈtrai tə ˈfaind ˈaut		ˈwitʃ	ðei ˌwont
ai m ˈnot ˈsəːtn̩		ˈwot	ʃi ˌdid it wið
ai hav ˈnou aiˈdiə			i ˌrout it foː
ai ˈkaːnt ʌndəˈstand		ˈhuːz	ˋhat ðis ˌiz
it s ə ˈmistəri tə ˈmiː		ˈwitʃ	ˈdei əv ðə ˌwiːk it ˌiz
ai m əˈfreid tə ˈsei		ˈwot	ˌbuk ðei v ˌteikən
wi ˈtould ˈnoubodi		ˈhau	ju ə ˌgouiŋ
ˈaːsk im	(!)	ˈweə	ʃi ˌsoː it
ˈtel mi	(!)	ˈwen	ðei ˌdid it
ˈdount ˈtel ˈenibodi	(!)	ˈwai	wi ˌgeiv it tə ðəm
ˈrait n̩ ˈlet mi ˈnou	(!)	ˈhau	ˈmʌtʃ wəz ˌsent
ˈdeənt ðei ˈsei	(?)		ˈmeni ðei ˌtuk
ˈwount ʃi iksˈplein	(?)		ˈfaː wi ˌwoːkt
həz ˈevriwʌn bin ˈtould	(?)		ˈloŋ wi ˌsteid
ˈdount ju ˈnou	(?)		ˌhai it ˌwent

In contexts like those shown below the connectives follow principal clauses that neither contain words that might act as antecedents nor suggest uncertainty. In such cases the connective nearly always bears some stress, and it is therefore preferable to regard it as a conjunctive rather than a relative, which would be unstressed.

ˋðat s ˌhuː ʃi ˌiz.

ˏðat s ˙wot ai ˋtould ju.

ai ˋgeiv ðəm ˌwot ai ˌkud.

ˋðis iz ˌhau it wəz ˌdʌn.

ˋðat s ˌweər ai ˌfaund it.

ˋðat wəz ˏwen it ˋhapənd.

'ðat s ˙wai ai ˋtuk it.

ju 'nou ˙hau ˏruːd ʃi ˌiz.

ai 'nou ˙huː ˋels wonts wʌn.

ju 'nou ˙witʃ wʌn ˋai ˌtuk.

ðə z 'nou ˙daut 'huːz it ˇiz.

ai l 'tel ju ˙hau ai ˋhəːd əv it.

ðei ˋtould ju ˌweər it ˌwoz.

ju ˋnjuː ˌwen ðei wə ˌkʌmiŋ.

ˋai ˌnou ˌwai ðei ə ˏleit.

ˋðat ˌʃouz ˙hau ˋraip ðei ˌaː.

RELATIVES

321 Function. Comparison of the lists of conjunctives and relatives given in §295 will show that the relatives do not include the forms if and **weðə***, but do include **ðət**, which is identical in pronunciation and spelling with the general conjunction (§311).

Though they introduce subordinate clauses, the relatives have a different function from that of the subordinating conjunctions in that they link their clauses with a specific antecedent in the principal clause. This antecedent is usually the noun or pronominal determiner immediately preceding the relative.

The relatives do not take sentence stress.

322 Defining and non-defining clauses. The clauses introduced by the relatives fall into two classes, known as defining (or restrictive) clauses and non-defining (or parenthetical) clauses. It is important to distinguish between these two classes, as they differ in function, in tonetic treatment, and usually in structure.

Defining clauses play an essential part in the sentence of which they form part, since they provide information whereby their antecedent may be picked out from among a class ; in fact they function as a kind of determiner and might more consistently be called Determining Clauses. Tonetically they are fully incorporated into the sentence ; they form part of the main tune of the sentence and there are no pauses before or after them.

Non-defining clauses are not essential to the meaning of the sentence, since their antecedent is always of such a nature as to identify or determine the person or thing referred to; they are used to convey an additional piece of information about their antecedent. They are tonetically independent of the principal clause, being marked off from it by pauses before and after them and by having their own tune. This parenthetical insertion causes the tune of the principal clause to be broken into two parts, so that the part preceding the non-defining clause normally ends in a tone that finishes with a low rise (Tones IL, III or V). This tonetic independence is indicated in the written language by commas placed before and after the clause; these commas are not present in the case of the defining clause.

It is possible to find instances in which the two kinds of clause have identical wording; the following example will show how intonation (in speech) and punctuation (in writing) help in differentiating them.

Defining Clause.

ðə ˈfaɪə wɪtʃ ˈstaːtɪd ˈhɪə dɪsˈtrɔɪd ˈsɪks ˌhauzɪz.

In this case there was more than one fire, and the one referred to is identified by stating where it started. The relative clause contains information that is essential to the proper understanding of the sentence.

Non-defining Clause.

ðə ˇfaɪə, wɪtʃ ˈstaːtɪd ˇhɪə, dɪsˈtrɔɪd ˈsɪks ˌhauzɪz.

In this case there was only one fire, and the parenthetical relative clause gives additional—but inessential—information as to where it started.

323 The independent relative. The relative **wot** has been called the independent relative as it is used without an antecedent; in fact it is felt to contain its own antecedent and to be roughly synonymous in the singular with the combination ðat wɪtʃ and in the plural with the phrase ðə θɪŋz wɪtʃ. It may be the subject, direct object or prepositional object of its clause. It is generally pronominal, but is sometimes used adjectivally, especially in a more formal style. Normally it refers to things in the singular, but it may, especially when adjectival, have a plural reference, and also be applied to persons.

Pronominal use.

ˈlaitniŋ z wot ˌskeəz ˌmiː.   ðei l ˈduː wot ðei ˈkan ˌfoː ju.

ˈðat s wot ˌgivz ju ˌhikʌps.   ˈluk wot ju v ˈdʌn tə mai ˌbuk!

ˈlaitniŋ z wot ˈai diˌtest.   ˈlaitniŋ z wot ˈai m əˌfreid ov.

hi ˈtould mi wot i ˌwoz.   ˈai ˌdount ˌnou wot ju ˌmiːn.

ˈhaiə ˈweidʒiz ə wot ðei ə ˌstraikiŋ ˈfoː.

Adjectival use.

ˈðis iz wot ˌwəːk wi v ˌdʌn.   ˈðiːz ə wot ˌfakts əv ˌkʌm tə ˌlait.

hi ˈwoːnd wot ˌpiːp‖ i ˌkud.   ai v ˈrʌŋ ʌp wot ˌfrendz ai ˌhav.

Subject clauses may begin with wot.

wot ˈai ˌsei ˈdʌzn̩t ˈmatə.   wot ˅pʌz‖z mi iz ðə ˈvəːdikt.

wot ju ˌniːd iz ˈmoː ˈhelp.   wot ai ˅wont iz tə bi ˈdʌn wið it.

wot ðei ˅θiŋk ˈdʌzn̩ ˈkaunt; it s wot ðei ˈduː ðət ˌmatəz.

Students must resist the temptation to use wot after oːl. The normal relative after oːl is ðət for persons or things, though huː is sometimes used for persons. When the relative is objective it is often omitted.

ˈðis iz ˈoːl ðət wəz ˌleft.   ai v ˈgivn̩ ju ˌoːl (ðət) ai ˌhad.

ˈoːl ðət (*or* hu) ˈwont tə ˌgou məs bi ˈredi bai ˈnain əˌklok.

The normally pronominal relatives huː and huːm are occasionally used as independent relatives when certain well-known literary quotations are used in conversation. In such cases they are assumed to contain their own antecedent; thus in the examples below huː = hiː huː and huːm = ðouz huːm.

huː ˈstiːlz mai ˈpəːs ˈstiːlz ˈtraʃ.

huːm ðə ˈgodz ˌlʌv, ˈdai ˈjʌŋ.

324 Pronominal relatives. The antecedents of these may be singular or plural nouns or determiners. While the relatives themselves are invariable for number, they are assumed to be singular or plural to agree with their antecedent and must be followed by the appropriate form of any finite that has different forms in singular and plural.

ˈðis iz ðə ˌman u ˌwonts tə ˌsiː ju.

ˈðiːz ə ðə ˌmen u ˌwont tə ˌsiː ju.

The various pronominal relatives are described below.

huː (weak forms uː, hu, u) refers to persons or to personified animals or things. It is used only as the subject of its verb and occurs in both defining and non-defining clauses.

ˋðat s ðə ˌgəːl u ˌdid it !   iz ˈðat ðə ˙man u ˈkoːld ˈjestədi?
mai ˇfaːðə, hu z ˈniəli ˇeiti, ˈlivz in ˌlʌndən.

huːm (occasional weak forms hum, um) is the oblique form of huː, and is used as a direct or prepositional object. It is found only in literary English or in ceremonious speech.

ˋðat s ðə ˌman hum ai ˌsoː.   iz ˈðat ðə ˙man tə ˙huːm ju ˈspouk?
mai ˇfaðə, huːm ju l ˈmiːt təˌmoru, ˈlivz in ˌlʌndən.

witʃ (no weak form) refers to animals and things. It serves as either subject or object. While ðət is usually preferred in defining clauses, witʃ is always used in non-defining ones.

iz ˈðat ðə wʌn witʃ ˈbrouk?   ˋðat s ðə ˌbuk witʃ ai v ˋred.
mai ˇkaː, witʃ ˈjuːʒuəli ˙rʌnz veri ˌwel, iz ˈgiviŋ ˋtrʌbl ˌnau.
ˈðis ˌbuk, witʃ ai ˈboːt fər ə ˌpaund, iz ˌwəːθ ˋtuː paundz ˌnau.

The antecedent of witʃ may be a whole clause instead of a noun or determiner; in that case it functions more like a conjunction.

ai ˈsed ˌnʌθiŋ, witʃ ˈmeid im ˙stil ˌmoːr ˌaŋgri.
hi ˈsed it wəz ˋreiniŋ, witʃ ai ˈdidnt biˌliːv.

ðat (weak form ðət, which is the only pronunciation used in connected speech) may refer to either persons or things. It is used only in defining clauses, where it is usually preferred to witʃ, but not to huː, except in the contexts described below. It is usually omitted when it is the object of its clause. Examples:

iz ˈðis ðə ˙paːs| ðət əˈraivd ðis ˈmoːniŋ?
ˈʃou mi ðə ˙boi ðət ˈwʌn ðə ˈfəːst ˌpraiz.
iz ˈðis ðə ˙paːs| (ðət) ai ˈsoː on ðə ˈteibl ðis ˙moːniŋ?
ai ˈwont tə ˈtoːk tə ðə ˈboi (ðət) ju ˌpʌniʃt ˌjestədi.
iz ˈðis ðə ˙buk (ðət) ju wə riˈfəːriŋ tu?
ˈintrəˈdjuːs mi tə ðə ˈman (ðət) ju ˙had ˋdinə wið ˌlaːst ˌnait.

When the antecedent is a person and the relative is the subject of its clause, many speakers prefer to use ðət rather than huː in the following contexts:

a. After precursory it (§232).

it wəz iz ˈwaif ðət ˌkept im ˌgouiŋ.

it s ðə ˈraudi ˌpiːpl ðət ˌkoːz oːl ðə ˌtrʌbl.

b. After a superlative.

hi z ðə ˈbest ˈfutboːlə ðət s ˈevə ˈpleid fər əs.

c. After determiners expressing uniqueness or totality.

ju ə ði ˈounli ˈpəːsn̩ ðət ˈwount əˌgriː tu it.

ə ˈðiːz ˈoːl ðə ˈboiz ðət əv ˈtəːnd ˈʌp təˈdei?

325 Choice of pronominal relative. In order to show clearly the different ways in which pronominal relatives and their substitutes are used, the following classified sets of simple sentences are given for comparison.

Defining Clauses.

Except in the first pair of examples below, most speakers prefer the second of each pair, and usually omit the word ðət in those cases where it is shown in brackets.

1. When the antecedent is a person.

Subject: ˈðis iz ðə ˌman u ˌsoː ju.
              ˈðis iz ðə ˌman ðət ˌsoː ju.

Object: ˈðis iz ðə ˌman hum ju ˌsoː.
              ˈðis iz ðə ˌman (ðət) ju ˌsoː.

Prep. Obj.: ˈðis iz ðə ˌman tə huːm ai ˌgeiv it.
              ˈðis iz ðə ˌman (ðət) ai ˌgeiv it tu.

2. When the antecedent is a thing.

Subject: ˈðis iz ðə ˌkaː witʃ ˌbrouk ˌdaun.
              ˈðis iz ðə ˌkaː ðət ˌbrouk ˌdaun.

Object: ˈðis iz ðə ˌkaː witʃ wi ˌboːt.
              ˈðis iz ðə ˌkaː (ðət) wi ˌboːt.

Prep. Obj.: ˈðis iz ðə ˌkaːr in witʃ wi ˌkeim.
              ˈðis iz ðə ˌkaː (ðət) wi ˌkeim in.

Non-defining Clauses.

These are usually avoided in spoken English, being replaced by other constructions such as those shown as the second example of each of the following pairs.

1. When the antecedent is a person.

Subject:

mai ˅niːs, hu 'met ju ˌjestədi, 'livz in ˌlʌndən.

ju ri'membə mai ˙niːs ˙met ju ˊjestədi? ʃi 'livz in ˌlʌndən.

Object:

mai ˅niːs, hum ju 'met ˌjestədi, 'livz in ˌlʌndən.

ju ri'membə ˙miːtiŋ mai 'niːs ˊjestədi? ʃi 'livz in ˌlʌndən.

Prepositional Object:

mai ˅niːs, tə huːm ju wə ˋspiːkiŋ dʒʌst ˌnau, 'livz in ˌlʌndən.

ai 'soː ju ˙spiːkiŋ tə mai ˋniːs dʒʌst ˌnau. ʃi 'livz in ˌlʌndən.

2. When the antecedent is a thing.

Subject:

mai ˅haus, witʃ əz 'dʒʌst bin ˌdekəreitid, ˌluks 'veri ˌnais.

mai ˌhaus əz 'dʒʌst bin ˌdekəreitid ənd ˌluks 'veri ˌnais.

Object:

mai ˅haus, witʃ ai v 'dʒʌst ˌmodərnaizd, iz 'veri ˌkʌmfətəbl̩.

ai v 'dʒʌst ˋmodənaizd mai ˌhaus, ənd it s 'veri ˌkʌmfətəbl̩.

Prepositional Object:

mai 'njuː ˌhaus, witʃ ai v 'dʒʌst ˅muːvd intu, iz 'tuː ˌsmoːl.

ai v 'dʒʌst ˙muːvd intə mai 'njuː ˌhaus, ənd 'faind it ˙tuː ˌsmoːl.

3. When the antecedent is a clause.

ai v ˋbroukən it, witʃ iz ə ˋnjuːsn̩s.

'wot ə ˌnjuːsn̩s! ai v ˋbroukən it!

326 The comparative relative. In cases where the idea of comparison or similarity is introduced into the main clause by the use of either of the determiners ðə seim or sʌtʃ, the relatives huː, huːm (referring to persons) or ðət (referring to persons or things) are replaced by az (weak form əz). This rule applies irrespective of whether the determiner is functioning pronominally or adjectivally. Unlike the true pronominal relatives, əz is never omitted when it is the object of its clause. The following pairs of examples show the substitution of əz for other relatives.

Pronominal Determiner.

ðə 'membəz hu ˏvoutid ə 'ðouz u əˋgriː wið əs.
ðə 'membəz hu ˏvoutid ə 'sʌtʃ əz əˋgriː wið əs.
ðə 'piːpl̩ hu v ˏkʌm ə ðə 'wʌnz (hum) ju ˙soː ˋjestədi.
ðə 'piːpl̩ hu v ˏkʌm ə ðə 'seim əz ju ˙soː ˋjestədi.
ðə 'buks ai ˙wont ə 'ðouz (ðət) ju kən ˏspeə.
ðə 'buks ai ˙wont ə 'sʌtʃ əz ju kən ˏspeə.

Adjectival Determiner.

'oːl ðə ˙vizitəz u d 'steid ˙on wə 'hʌd|d ˙raund ðə ˏfaiə.
'sʌtʃ ˙vizitəz əz əd 'steid ˙on wə 'hʌd|d ˙raund ðə ˏfaiə.
ˋðis ˏizn̩t ðə ˏbʌs (ðət) wi ˏtuk ˏjestədi.
ˋðis ˏizn̩t ðə ˏseim ˏbʌs əz wi ˏtuk ˏjestədi.
'let mi ˙hav 'eni ˙buks (ðət) ju kən ˏspeə.
'let mi ˙hav sʌtʃ ˙buks əz ju kən ˏspeə.

Notice also such constructions as (*or* constructions such as) the following:

ˋteik it, ˏsʌtʃ əz it ˏiz.   wi 'pikt ˋʌp ˏsʌtʃ əz ðə ˏwəː.

327 Adjectival relatives. The relatives wot, witʃ and huːz may be used adjectivally. The first of these was dealt with in §323, and as witʃ is used adjectivally only in a very formal style it need not be considered here.

huːz (weak forms uːz, huz, uz) normally refers to possession by persons. It is used in both defining and non-defining clauses.

ˋðat s ðə ˏman uːz ˏhaus wi wə ˏlukiŋ at dʒʌs ˙nau.
iz ðər 'enibodi ˙hiə huz 'neim ˙hazn̩ bin ˋkoːld?
hi z ˋoːlwiz ˏkwor|iŋ wið ˏpiːpl̩ uz ai,diəz ˏdifə frəm iz ˏoun.
mai ˇfaːðə, huz 'houm iz in ˏlʌndən, iz 'spendiŋ ə ˙wiːk ˏhiə.
mai ˇsistə, huz 'dog ju ˙soː ˏjestədi, iz ˋfond əv ˏanim|z.

Sometimes, when it is desired to avoid a clumsy construction, huːz is used for possession by things.

ai 'laik tə ˙riːd ˙buks uz 'oːθəz ˙nou ðeə ˋsʌbdʒikt.

This avoids the awkward:

ai 'laik tə ˙riːd ˙buks ði 'oːθəz əv witʃ 'nou ðeə ˋsʌbdʒikt.

It is often preferable, however, to use a prepositional phrase instead of a relative clause, as shown in the following pairs of examples:

ðə 'dog uz ˋleg z ˌbroukən iz ˋfoluiŋ əs.
ðə 'dog wið ðə ˙broukən ˌleg z ˋfoluiŋ əs.
ai 'sliːp in ə ˙ruːm uz 'winduz ˙luk ˙on tə ðə ˋstriːt.
ai 'sliːp in ə ˙ruːm wið 'winduz ˙lukiŋ ˙on tə ðə ˋstriːt.

328 Adverbial relatives. The relatives weə*, wen and wai have an adverbial function. Their antecedents are nouns indicating place, time or cause, respectively.

weə*, referring to place, used in both defining and non-defining clauses.

'ðis iz ðə ˙haus weər ai wəz ˌboːn.
ðə ˋsekəndri ˌskuːl, weər ai 'juːst tə ˌtiːtʃ, iz 'ouvə ˌðeə.

wen, referring to time, used in both defining and non-defining clauses.

'ðat wəz ðə ˙jiə wen ai 'went tu əˋmerikə.
wi I dis'kʌs it in ði ˋintəv|, wen ðə I bi 'les ˋnoiz.

wai, referring to cause, used only in defining clauses.

ˋðat s ðə ˌriːzn̩ wai ʃi ri'fjuːzd tə ˋkʌm.

The above three connectives and hau are also used in a similar structure, in which the antecedent is omitted.

ˋðis iz ˙weər ai wəz ˌboːn.
ˋðat wəz ˙wen ai ˋwent tu əˋmerika.
ˋðat s ˌwai ʃi ri'fjuːzd tə ˋkʌm.
ˋðis iz ˌhau it ˌʃud bi ˌdʌn.

In such cases the connective takes a partial stress, and might be better classed as a conjunctive (§318) than as a relative.

H. Interjections and Exclamations

329 Interjections. These are words, having no syntactical relation to the sentence, used to express emotion. Some of the commonest are shown below and, as they naturally depend greatly on intonation for their meaning, they are classified by tunes (§§37–9). The feelings suggested by the various tunes are roughly as follows:

I   Suprise, or a query.
II   A reaction that is definitely approving or disapproving, according to the word used.
III   A hesitant or apologetic reaction.
IV   A more colourful reaction, which may be either arch or enthusiastic, according to the situation.

I	′wel !	′wot !	in′diːd !	‾hʌ‿lou !
II	‵ou !	hu‵rei !	‵nonsn̩s !	'ou ‿nonsn̩s !
	‵aː !	in‵diːd!	‵fansi !	'wot ə ‿piti !
	‵wel !	'wel ‿wel !		'wel wel ‿wel !
III	ˇaː !	ˇou !	ˇwel !	
IV	˄ou !	˄fansi !	in˄diːd !	‿wot ə ˄piti !
	˄aː !	‾ai ˄sei !		

The following are used more particularly by women.

II	‵gudnis !	‾ou ‿diə !	‾diə ‿miː !	'wel ai ‿nevə !
	‵greiʃəs !	‾ou ‿mai !		
IV	‾ou ˄diə !	'ou ˄mai !	′diə ˄miː !	‾ou ˄boðə !

The following are used more particularly by men.

II	'dʒoli ‿gud !	'bles mai ‿soul !
III	‾nou ‿fiə !	
IV	′ou ˄loːd !	′gud ˄loːd !

In addition to the above an indefinite number of exclamations, both facetious and violent, are to be heard in the speech of educated persons.

330 Exclamatory sentences. These fall into two main types, which are distinguished by their structural differences.

Type 1.

These begin with an exclamatory **hau** or **wot**, and use a Tune II or IV. Preference is shown for Tune II in exclamations expressing regret or disgust and for Tune IV in exclamations of pleasure; both kinds usually have either a high prehead (§34) or a rising head (§46).

hau is used before adjectives not qualifying a noun, and before adverbs:

II   ⁻hau ʌnˏplezn̩t !   ′hau ˏbadli ʃi ˏspiːks !
       ′hau disˏgʌstiŋ !   ⁻hau ˏoːkwəd ju ˏaː !

IV   ⁻hau ^nais !   ′hau ^gud əv ju !
       ′hau ik^saitiŋ !   ⁻hau ^kwikli ju ˏwəːk !

wot is used before nouns that are uncountables, and before countables in the plural. **wot ə** is used before countables in the singular. In all cases the noun may be qualified by a preceding adjective:

II   ⁻wot ə ˏnjuːsn̩s !   ⁻wot ′naːsti ˏweðə !
       ⁻wot ə ˌʃeim !   ′wot ə ˌʃeim !

IV   ⁻wot ′lʌvli ˏˏflauəz ðouz ˏaː !
       ′wot ə ′nais ^gaːdn̩ ju v ˏgot !

Type 2.

These begin with a front-shifted adverbial. This is usually an adverbial particle, but it is often supplemented by an adverbial phrase of place or direction. These sentences may take the form of either statements or imperatives. In the latter case they generally express either good-humoured abruptness or mock severity. The nuclear tone is usually a lowered Tone I, and this is preceded by a rising tone on any preceding words that require sentence stress.

The following structural variations should be noticed.

If the subject is a personal pronoun, it is placed before the verb:

       ′hiə ʃi ˏkʌmz !   ′of ju ˏgou !
       ′ðeə ðei ˏgou !   ′in ju ˏdʒʌmp !

If the subject is not a personal pronoun, it is placed after the verb:

ʹhiə kʌmz ðə ˌman !   əʹwei went ðə ʹhoul ˌkraud !
ʹbak keim ði ˌʌðəz !   ʹof gouz ðə ˌplein !

If the adverbial particle is accompanied by a further adverbial element, the former is placed at the beginning of the sentence while the latter generally occupies its usual position at the end:

ʹof ðei ʹran tə ˌskuːl !   əʹwei ðei ʹwent tə ðə ˌsteiʃn̩ !

But in a more literary construction the whole of the adverbial may take the front-shifted position:

ʹof tə ʹskuːl ðei ˌran !   əʹwei tə ðə ʹsteiʃn̩ ðei ˌwent !

A substitute imperative is sometimes formed using the preposition wið after an adverbial particle:

əʹwei wið ju !   ʹaut ˌwið it !   ʹof wið iz ˌʃəːt !

PART III

Sentence Structure

TENSE TABLES

331 Sentence pattern formula. The established formula for showing basic word order in the sentence is S — V — O (Subject —Verb—Object). This is often amplified to S — v — V — O (Subject—auxiliary verb—Principal Verb—Object), with the use when necessary of C (Complement) and A (Adverbial). Adhering to the same principle this system can easily be adapted to show details of tense structure by using symbols having the following meanings:

$$S = \text{Subject}$$
$$f = \text{Conjugating finite}$$
$$v = \text{Conjugating verbal}$$
$$V = \text{Specific verbal}$$
$$F = \text{Specific finite}$$
$$O = \text{Object}$$

The relative positions of the symbols for subject and conjugating finite will indicate whether the sentence is a statement or a question, but it is also desirable to indicate the presence or absence of negation. This can be done by means of the following amplifications of the symbol for the conjugating finite:

$$af = \text{Affirmative conjugating finite}$$
$$nf = \text{Negative conjugating finite}$$

Using these symbols the following arrangements will represent the various forms of the sentence.

Affirmative	S — af — (v) — V — (O, C, A)
Interrogative	af — S — (v) — V — (O, C, A)
Negative	S — nf — (v) — V — (O, C, A)
Interrogative-negative	nf — S — (v) — V — (O, C, A)
Anomalous affirmative	S — F — (O, C, A)

The tables in the next four sections give examples of the basic affirmative, interrogative, negative and interrogative-negative structures of each of the twelve active and eight passive tenses of the verb, while §§336-7 show the anomalous conjugation. The numbering of the tenses corresponds to that given in §209. The letter A prefixed to a tense number means that the tense is in the active voice, while the letter P indicates that it is in the passive. For practical reasons all parts of the sentence that follow the specific verbal are lumped together under the head O, C, A.

332 The affirmative. This is widely regarded as the basic sentence structure, though it might be difficult to find a logical reason for this, as a statement is frequently a reply to a question, and questions are usually followed by a statement containing the information asked for. In affirmative statements the subject precedes all verbal forms and (except in Tenses A1 and A2) is followed immediately by an affirmative conjugating finite.

Tense No.	S	af	v	V	O, C, A
A 1	(See §336)				
A 2	(See §336)				
A 3	ʃi	məs		'teik	ˋðiːz.
A 4	ju	v		ˋfiniʃt	ðə ˌbuk.
A 5	ʃi	d		ˋmendid	it.
A 6	it	'mait	əv	biˋloŋd	tə ˋdʒon.
A 7	hi	z		ˋlisniŋ	tə mi.
A 8	'ðat	wəz		ˋhəːtiŋ	ju.
A 9	ðei	'ʃud	bi	ˋraitiŋ	ˌnau.
A10	ai	v	bin	ˋθiŋkiŋ	əbaut it.
A11	'dʒon	əd	bin	ˋtoːkiŋ	tə ðəm.
A12	ðei	l	əv bin	'əːniŋ	ˌsʌmθiŋ.
P 1	'ðat	s		˙riəlaizd	bai ˋevriwʌn.
P 2	ðei	wər		'oːdəd	tə ˌliːv
P 3	it	kən	bi	'pakt	in ˌhiə.
P 4	ju	v	bin	ˋrobd.	
P 5	'ðouz	əd	bin	fəˋgotn̩.	
P 6	ʃi	d	əv bin	ˋmist.	
P 7	hi	z	biːiŋ	ˋkwestʃn̩d	əbaut it.
P 8	ʃi	wəz	biːiŋ	'toːt	tə ˌswim.

Intonation and Stressing.

It will be noticed that the nuclear tone is either Tone II, Tone III or Tone IIID, and that it falls either on the specific verbal or on the object or adverbial.   The affirmative finites are unstressed except in two instances where stress is needed for semantic reasons.

333 The interrogative. This is formed by placing an affirmative conjugating finite before the subject instead of after it, as in affirmative statements.   In the case of Tenses A1 and A2 the specific finite used in the affirmative (see §336) is replaced by the infinitive of the same verb, and one of the affirmative conjugating finites **duː, dʌz,** or **did** is placed before the subject.

Tense No.	af	S	v	V	O, C, A
A 1	dəz	'dʒon		˙drɪŋk	ˊkofi ?
A 2	did	ðei		ˊsiː	əs ?
A 3	məst	ʃi		'teik	ˊðiːz ?
A 4	həv	ju		ˊfiniʃt	ðə ˙buk ?
A 5	həd	ʃi		ˊmendid	it ?
A 6	'mait	it	əv	biˈloŋd	tə ˊdʒon ?
A 7	iz	i		ˊlisnɪŋ	tə mi ?
A 8	wəz	'ðat		ˊhəːtɪŋ	ju ?
A 9	'ʃud	ðei	bi	ˊraitɪŋ	˙nau ?
A10	həv	ju	bin	ˊθɪŋkɪŋ	əbaut it ?
A11	həd	'dʒon	bin	ˊtoːkɪŋ	tə ðəm ?
A12	wil	ðei	əv bin	ˊəːnɪŋ	˙eniθɪŋ ?
P 1	iz	'ðat		˙riəlaizd	bai ˊevriwʌn ?
P 2	wə	ðei		'oːdəd	tə ˊliːv ?
P 3	kən	it	bi	'pakt	in ˊhiə ?
P 4	həv	ju	bin	ˊrobd ?	
P 5	həd	'ðouz	bin	fəˊgotn̩ ?	
P 6	wəd	ʃi	əv bin	ˊmist ?	
P 7	iz	i	biːɪŋ	ˊkwestʃn̩d	əbaut it ?
P 8	wəz	ʃi	biːɪŋ	'toːt	tə ˊswim ?

Intonation and Stressing.

The nuclear tone is now IH. Except for the two that are stressed for semantic reasons, the finites are shown unstressed. They would be given high level stress if it were desired to infuse a feeling of greater interest into the questions. (See §343.)

334 The negative. This has the same structure as the affirmative, the only change being the substitution of the negative finite for the affirmative one, except in Tenses A1 and A2, where the specific finite that is used in the affirmative (see §336) is replaced by the infinitive of the same verb, while one of the negative conjugating finites **dount, dʌznt** or **didnt** is placed immediately after the subject. Other exceptions to this rule will be found in §§155, 160 (tə biː), 171 (juːst tə), 195*b* (mei) and 203*b* (mait).

Tense No.	S	nf	v	V	O, C, A
A 1	'dʒon	˙dʌznt		ˋdriŋk	ˌkofi.
A 2	ðei	'didnt		ˋsiː	əs.
A 3	ʃi	'mʌsnt		˙teik	˅ðiːz.
A 4	ju	'havnt		ˋfiniʃt	ðə ˌbuk.
A 5	ʃi	'hadnt		ˋmendid	it.
A 6	it	'mait not əv		biˋloŋd	tə ˌdʒon.
A 7	hi	'isnt		ˋlisniŋ	tə mi.
A 8	ˋðat	ˌwoznt		ˌhəːtiŋ	ju.
A 9	ðei	'ʃudnt	bi	˙raitiŋ	˅nau.
A10	ai	'havnt	bin	ˋθiŋkiŋ	əbaut it.
A11	'dʒon	˙hadnt	bin	ˋtoːkiŋ	tə ðəm.
A12	ðei	'wount	əv bin	˅əːniŋ	˙eniθiŋ.
P 1	ðat	'iznt		˙riəlaizd	bai ˅evriwʌn.
P 2	ðei	'wəːnt		˙oːdəd	tə ˅liːv.
P 3	it	'kaːnt	bi	˙pakt	in ˅hiə.
P 4	ju	ˌhavnt	bin	ˌrobd.	
P 5	ˋdouz	ˌhadnt	bin	fəˌgotn.	
P 6	ʃi	'wudnt	əv bin	˅mist.	
P 7	hi	'iznt	biːiŋ	˅kwestʃnd əbaut it.	
P 8	ʃi	'woznt	biːiŋ	˙toːt	tə ˅swim.

In a formal written style and in very formal or emphatic speech the negative finite may be split into its component parts, i.e., affirmative finite + **not**, the latter word taking the stress (less consistently in British than in American English, where this formal structure is more favoured than it is in Britain).

Intonation and Stressing.

Tune III occurs more frequently than it did in the affirmative. All the negative finites are stressed.

Other methods of introducing negation into statements will be found in §§351–7.

335 The interrogative-negative. This has the same form as the interrogative, the only change being the substitution of the negative finite for the affirmative one.

While this form of the sentence is rare in the written style, it is much more common in speech than is generally realized. Its neglect in most text-books is unjustified, for in lively conversation as many as a third of the general questions may contain a negative finite. It is widely used for making questions rhetorical, protesting or merely indicative of the speaker's attitude, and it is therefore recommended to the student's attention.

Tense No.	nf	S	v	V	O, C, A
A 1	'dʌznt	˙dʒon		'driŋk	ˈkofi?
A 2	'didn̩t	ðei		ˈsiː	əs?
A 3	'mʌsn̩t	ʃi		˙teik	ˈðiːz?
A 4	'havn̩t	ju		ˈfiniʃt	ðə ˙buk?
A 5	'hadn̩t	ʃi		ˈmendid	it?
A 6	'maitn̩t	it	əv	biˈloŋd	tə ˈdʒon?
A 7	'izn̩t	i		ˈlisniŋ	tə mi?
A 8	'wozn̩t	˙ðat		ˈhəːtiŋ	ju?
A 9	'ʃudn̩t	ðei	bi	ˈraitiŋ	˙nau?
A10	'havn̩t	ju	bin	ˈθiŋkiŋ	əbaut it?
A11	'hadn̩t	'dʒon	bin	ˈtoːkiŋ	tə ðəm?
A12	'wount	ðei	əv bin	ˈəːniŋ	˙eniθiŋ?
P 1	'izn̩t	˙ðat		'riəlaizd	bai ˈevriwʌn?
P 2	'wəːnt	ðei		˙oːdəd	tə ˈliːv?
P 3	'kaːnt	it	bi	˙pakt	in ˈhiə?
P 4	'havn̩t	ju	bin	ˈrobd?	
P 5	'hadn̩t	˙ðouz	bin	fəˈgotn̩?	
P 6	'wudn̩t	ʃi	əv bin	ˈmist?	
P 7	'izn̩t	i	biːiŋ	ˈkwestʃn̩d	əbaut it?
P 8	'wozn̩t	ʃi	biːiŋ	˙toːt	tə ˈswim?

In very formal speech the subject is occasionally preceded by an affirmative finite and followed by not (e.g., dəz 'dʒon ˙not ˙drink ˈkofi?), but most good speakers feel that this style is stilted and unnatural.

Intonation and Stressing.

The intonation is the same as for the interrogative, but all the finites are stressed.

Other methods of introducing negation into questions will be found in §§358–63.

336 The anomalous conjugation. In this structure the tense is indicated by a finite of the specific verb instead of by the usual conjugating finite. Though it is used only in the imperative and in Tenses A1 and A2, all these are of such frequent occurrence that the structure is still important.

Formerly in general use in all four forms of the sentence in these two tenses and in the negative imperative as well as the affirmative, it is now restricted to the unemphatic imperative and the unemphatic affirmative form of Tenses A1 and A2 and to certain special sentence arrangements that are described in §§349, 356 and 363. Its most common uses are in the imperative, described in §236, and in the Present and Past Tenses of the Aspect of Accomplishment (Tenses A1 and A2), set forth below.

337 Anomalous affirmative. This occurs only in the unemphatic affirmative form of Tenses A1 and A2.

Tense No.	S	F	O	A
A 1	'dʒon	˙driŋks	ˋkofi	ət ˏnait.
A 1	hi	'laiks	ˋoːl əv ðəm	ˏnau.
A 1	ðei	'grou	ˋflauəz	in ðə ˏgaːdn̩.
A 1	wi ˋoːl	ˏnou	ði ˏaːnsə	tə ˏðat.
A 2	ðə 'gəːlz	˙soː	ˋmeəri	in ˏtaun.
A 2	it	'meid	˙sens	tə ˅miː.

ANALYSIS OF STRUCTURES

338 Variant sentence patterns. The form of the sentence, whether in affirmative, interrogative, negative or interrogative-negative, does not always follow the normal pattern shown in §§332–5. For instance, Tenses A1 and A2 have the exceptional structure shown in the previous section, questions do not always have an interrogative structure, and negation can be expressed without using a negative finite. Differences in meaning may also be expressed by changes of stress and intonation.

These variations in the sentence pattern will be examined in the following sections, each form of the sentence being taken in turn.

AFFIRMATION

339 Variations in the affirmative. It has been shown in §332 that ordinary affirmation is expressed in all tenses except A1 and A2 by placing an affirmative finite after the subject, the finite being nearly always unstressed.

Affirmative statements may, however, be treated in other ways, involving changes in the stress and intonation patterns, and in particular in the form of some of the conjugators, while in Tenses A1 and A2 a normal structure is sometimes employed instead of the anomalous one described in §§336–7.

The most usual change in the stress and intonation pattern involves using the strong form of the conjugating finite and giving it a strong stress. This may take either of two forms, one of which merely makes the statement emphatic while the other gives it a sense of contradiction.

340 Emphasis. When it is desired to emphasize the general truth of an affirmative statement, perhaps also emphasizing some particular idea that it contains, a high level stress is placed on the conjugating finite. In Tenses A1 and A2 the specific finite used in the unemphatic affirmative (§337) is replaced by the infinitive of the specific verb while the approprate conjugating finite in its stressed form is inserted between the subject and the infinitive. The nuclear tone, which falls later than the finite, may be a Tone II, III or IIID.

Tense No.	S	af	v	V	O, C, A
A 1	ˌdʒon	ˈdʌz		˙driŋk	ˬkofi.
A 3	ʃi	ˈmʌs		˙teik	ˇðiːz
A 5	ʃi	ˈhad		ˇmendid	it.
A 7	hi	ˈiz		ˇlisniŋ	tə mi.
A 9	ðei	ˈʃud	bi	ˎraitiŋ	ˌnau.
A11	ˌdʒon	ˈhad	bin	ˇtoːkiŋ	tə ðəm.
P 1	ðat	ˈiz		˙riəlaizd	bai ˎevriwʌn.
P 3	it	ˈkan	bi	˙pakt	in ˎhiə.
P 5	ˌðouz	ˈhad	bin	fəˎgotn̩.	
P 7	hi	ˈiz	biːiŋ	ˇkwestʃn̩d	əbaut it.

341 Contradiction. If the emphatic affirmative is intended as a contradiction of a previous statement or the reversal of a previous negative attitude, a Tone II is used on the conjugating finite, its prominence being enhanced by the weakening or lowering in pitch of all the other stresses. If it is desired to give the impression of complete certainty, all the succeeding stresses are low level ones, which makes the Tone II on the finite the nuclear tone of the sentence. In cases of less certainty, or to soften the statement for politeness' sake, one of the succeeding stresses may take a low rising tone, thus converting the nucleus into a Tone IIID.

Tense No.	S	af	v	V	O, C, A
A 2	ðei	ˋdid		ˌdriŋk	ˌkofi.
A 4	ju	ˋhav		ˌfiniʃt	ðə ˌbuk.
A 6	it	ˋmait	əv	biˌloŋd	tə ˌdʒon.
A 8	ˌðat	ˋwoz		ˌhəːtiŋ	ju.
A10	ai	ˋhav	bin	ˌθiŋkiŋ	əbaut it.
A12	ðei	ˋwil	əv bin	ˌəːniŋ	sʌmθiŋ.
P 2	ðei	ˋwəːr		ˌoːdəd	tə ˌliːv.
P 4	ju	ˋhav	bin	ˌrobd.	
P 6	ʃi	ˋwud	əv bin	ˌmist.	
P 8	ʃi	ˋwoz	biːiŋ	ˌtoːt	tə ˌswim.

INTERROGATION

342 Kinds of question. Questions fall into two main classes, which differ in both structure and intonation. They are:

1. *General Questions*, which begin with a conjugating finite and usually take Tone I as their nucleus. They are the ordinary interrogative forms of the sentence, and can be answered by **jes** or **nou**. They are dealt with in §§333 and 335.

2. *Special Questions*, which begin with an interrogative word and usually take Tone II as their nucleus. They need a specific answer and cannot be answered by **jes** or **nou**. They are dealt with in §§345–9.

Alternative Questions, which contain one of the two conjunctions **oː*** or **noː*** and present two or more alternatives from which the hearer is asked to make a selection or an identification, form a subsidiary class. They may be formed from either General or Special Questions. (See §350.)

343 Emphatic general questions. In the examples of the interrogative given in §333 the large majority of the conjugating finites are shown unstressed and in their weak forms. In some situations this pattern may suggest a certain perfunctoriness or lack of interest on the part of the speaker. This can be eliminated by using the strong forms of the finites and giving them a full high level stress while leaving the rest of the sentence more or less unmodified except for certain stress adjustments.

Tense No.	af	S	v	V	O, C, A
A 2	ˈdid	ðei		ˈsiː	əs?
A 4	ˈhav	ju		ˈfiniʃt	ðə ˈbuk?
A 6	ˈmait	it	əv	biˈloŋd	tə ˈdʒon?
A 8	ˈwoz	ˈðat		ˈhəːtiŋ	ju?
A10	ˈhav	ju	bin	ˈθiŋkiŋ	əbaut it?
A12	ˈwil	ðei	əv bin	ˈəːniŋ	ˈeniθiŋ?
P 2	ˈwəː	ðei		ˈoːdəd	tə ˈliːv?
P 4	ˈhav	ju	bin	ˈrobd?	
P 6	ˈwud	ʃi	əv bin	ˈmist?	
P 8	ˈwoz	ʃi	biːiŋ	ˈtoːt	tə ˈswim?

344 Rhetorical general questions. These have something of the nature of the contradictions mentioned in §341. They are used to express surprise or incredulity in the face of some affirmative statement that has been made. They differ from emphatic general questions in that the nuclear Tone I is placed on the finite at the beginning of the sentence while the rest of the question forms the rising tail.

Tense No.	af	S	v	V	O, C, A
A 1	ˈdʌz	ˈdʒon		ˈdriŋk	ˈkofi?
A 3	ˈmʌst	ʃi		ˈteik	ˈðiːz?
A 5	ˈhad	ʃi		ˈmendid	it?
A 7	ˈiz	i		ˈlisniŋ	tə mi?
A 9	ˈʃud	ðei	bi	ˈraitiŋ	ˈnau?
A11	ˈhad	ˈdʒon	bin	ˈtoːkiŋ	tə ðəm?

297

Tense No.	af	S	v	V	O, C, A
P 1	ˈiz	˙ðat		˙riəlaizd	bai ˙evriwʌn ?
P 3	ˈkan	it	bi	˙pakt	in ˙hiə ?
P 5	ˈhad	˙ðouz	bin	fəˈgotn̩ ?	
P 7	ˈiz	i	biːiŋ	˙kwestʃn̩d əbaut it ?	

345 Special questions. An interrogative structure is used provided the interrogative word is not the subject of the sentence, which means in effect that it may be an adverb or, in the active voice only, the object of the verb. Examples:

Interrogative word as object or part thereof.

Tense No.	O	af	S	v	V
A 1	ˈwot	dəz	ˋdʒon		ˌdriŋk ?
A 2	ˈwitʃ	did	ˋmeəri		ˌwont ?
A 3	ˈhau meni	mei	ai		ˏteik ?
A 4	ˈwitʃ əv ðəm	əv	ju		ˏfiniʃt ?
A 5	ˈhuː(m)	əd	ʃi		ˏsiːn ?
A 6	ˈwot ˏels	kən	ðei	əv	iˌmadʒind ?
A 7	ˈwot	s	i		ˋduːiŋ ?
A 8	ˈhuː(m) ˏels	wə	ju		iksˌpektiŋ ?
A 9	ˈhau mʌtʃ	ʃəd	wi	bi	ˏjuːziŋ ?
A10	ˈwot	əv	ju	bin	ˋduːiŋ ?
A11	ˈwitʃ ˙buks	əd	ðei	bin	ˏriːdiŋ ?
A12	ˈwot		ʃi	əv bin	ˋθiŋkiŋ ?

Interrogative word as adverb.

Tense No.	A	af	S	v	V
A 2	ˈhau ˙ofn̩	did	ʃi		ˏrait ?
A 4	ˈhau ˙faːr	əv	wi		ˏwoːkt ?
A 6	ˈwen	kəd	ai	əv	ˏkʌm ?
A 8	ˈweə	wə	ðei		ˏsteiiŋ ?
A10	ˈhau ˙wel	əz	i	bin	ˏwəːkiŋ ?
A12	ˈwai	ʃəd	ju	əv bin	ˋrʌniŋ ?
P 1	ˈwen	ə	ju		iksˏpektid ?
P 3	ˈweə	kəd	it	bi	ˋhidn̩ ?
P 5	ˈhau	əd	ðei	bin	ˏkukt ?
P 7	ˈwai	z	ʃi	biːiŋ	ˏskouldid ?

346 Special questions with statement structure. When the interrogative word that introduces Special Questions is (or is associated with) the subject of the sentence, a statement structure is used. Examples:

Tense No.	S	af	v	V	O, C, A
A 1	(See §349)				
A 2	· (See §349)				
A 3	'huː ˏels	məst		ˌliːv	ˌəːli?
A 4	'witʃ əv ju	əv		ˋfiniʃt	ðə ˌbuk?
A 5	'huː	d		ˏmendid	it?
A 6	'hau ˙meni	‖	əv	ə'raivd	oːlˏredi?
A 7	'witʃ əv ju	ə		˙juːziŋ	ˋpens|z?
A 8	'wot	wəz		ˏhəːtiŋ	ju?
A 9	'witʃ ˙gəːl	ʃəd	bi	'gouiŋ	ˏnau?
A10	'huː	z	bin	ˏtoːkiŋ	əbaut it?
A11	'witʃ ˙boi	əd	bin	ˏhelpiŋ	ju?
A12	'huː	kən	əv bin	˙iːtiŋ	ðə ˏkeik?
P 1	'wot ˏels	iz		ˌnoun	əbaut it?
P 2	'witʃ wʌn	wəz		ˏstoulņ?	
P 3	'hau ˙mʌtʃ	‖	bi	'pakt	in ˋhiə?
P 4	'huː	z	bin	˙oːdəd	tə ˌliːv?
P 5	'huː ˏels	əd	bin	fəˌgotņ?	
P 6	'hau ˙meni	‖	əv bin	˙sent	bai ˏnau?
P 7	'huː	z	biːiŋ	˙aːskt	tə ˏhelp?
P 8	'wot	wəz	biːiŋ	ˋsed	əbaut it?

347 Emphatic special questions. Emphasis is often added to Special Questions by placing the nuclear Tone II on the finite instead of on one of the more meaningful words (usually either the subject or the specific verbal) that come later in the sentence. This conveys the speaker's feeling that an unnecessary mystery is being made of the facts; alternatively, it may suggest impatience at being given irrelevant facts, e.g., ai 'nou ˙wot ˋwozn̩t ˌdʌn, 'tel mi ˙wot ˋwoz ˌdʌn. In some cases, also, it may convey a contrast of tenses or of modals, e.g., ai 'nou ˙wot ˋʃud əv bin ˌdʌn, 'tel mi ˙wot ˋhaz bin ˌdʌn. The falling nuclear tone on the finite may be either high or low. When the interrogative word is (or forms part of) the subject there is no inversion of subject and finite.

The sentences below are modifications of some of the examples given in §§345-6.

Interrogative word as object or part thereof.

Tense No.	O	af	S	v	V
A 1	'wot	ˌdʌz	ˌdʒon		ˌdriŋk?
A 2	'witʃ	ˌdid	ˌmeəri		ˌwont?
A 4	'witʃ əv ðəm	ˈhav	ju		ˌfiniʃt?
A 6	'wot ˈels	ˈkan	ðei	əv	iˌmadʒind?
A 7	ˌwot	ˈiz	i		ˌduːiŋ?
A 9	'hau ˈmʌtʃ	ˌʃud	wi	bi	ˌjuːziŋ?

Interrogative word as adverb.

Tense No.	A	af	S	v	V
A 2	ˌhau ˌofņ	ˈdid	ʃi		ˌrait?
A 6	ˌwen	ˈkud	ai	əv	ˌkʌm?
A10	'hau ˈwel	ˌhaz	i	bin	ˌwəːkiŋ?
P 3	'weə	ˌkud	it	bi	ˌhidņ?
P 5	'hau	ˌhad	ðei	bin	ˌkukt?

Interrogative word as subject.

Tense No.	S	af	v	V	O, C, A
A 4	'witʃ əv ju	ˌhav		ˌfiniʃt	ðə ˌbuk?
A 5	ˌhuː	ˈhad		ˌmendid	it?
A 8	ˌwot	ˈwoz		ˌhəːtiŋ	ju?
A10	ˌhuː	ˈhaz	bin	ˌtoːkiŋ	əbaut it?
P 4	ˌhuː	ˈhaz	bin	ˌoːdəd	tə ˌliːv?
P 7	'huː	ˌiz	biːiŋ	ˌaːskt	tə ˌkʌm?

348 Rhetorical special questions. When Special Questions are asked rhetorically in order to suggest surprise or dismay at something that has been said, the nuclear tone is changed to a Tone I and placed on the interrogative word, while the rest of the question becomes the rising tail of the tune. Again there is no inversion of subject and finite if the interrogative word is (or forms part of) the subject.

Interrogative word as object.

Tense No.	O	af	S	v	V
A 1	′wot	dəz	ˈdʒon		ˈdriŋk?
A 4	′witʃ əv ðəm	əv	ju		ˈfiniʃt?
A 5	′huː(m)	əd	ʃi		ˈsiːn?
A 7	′wot	s	i		ˈduːiŋ?
A 9	′hau ˈmʌtʃ	ʃəd	wi	bi	ˈjuːziŋ?
A11	′witʃ ˈbuks	əd	ðei	bin	ˈriːdiŋ?

Interrogative word as adverb.

Tense No.	A	af	S	v	V
A 2	′wen	did	i		əˈraiv?
A 4	′hau ˈfaːr	əv	wi		ˈwoːkt?
A12	′weə	ʃəd	ai	əv bin	ˈsitiŋ?
P 1	′hau ˈsuːn	ə	ju		iksˈpektid?
P 7	′wai	z	i	biːiŋ	ˈskouldid?

Interrogative word as subject.

Tense No.	S	af	v	V	O, C, A
A 4	′hau ˈmeni	əv		ˈfiniʃt	ðə ˈbuk?
A 5	′huː	d		ˈmendid	it?
A11	′witʃ ˈboi	əd	bin	ˈhelpiŋ	ju?
P 2	′huː	wəz		ˈoːdəd	tə ˈliːv?
P 4	′wot	s	bin	ˈstouln?	
P 7	′huː	z	biːiŋ	ˈaːkst	tə ˈkʌm?

349 Anomalous interrogative. This occurs in Tenses A1 and A2 in a similar case to that explained in §346, i.e., when the interrogative word is (or forms part of) the subject of the sentence, and provided no negative finite is required. Examples:

Tense No.	S	F	O	A
A 1	′huː	ˈdriŋks	ˈkofi	ət ˌnait?
A 1	′wot	ˈkoːziz	ðə ˌtaidz?	
A 1	′hau ˈmeni əv ju	ˈgrou	ˈflauəz	in ðə ˌgaːdn?
A 1	′witʃ əv ju	ˈnou	ði ˌaːnsə?	
A 2	′witʃ ˈgəːlz	ˈsoː	ˈmeəri	in ˌtaun?
A 2	′hau meni	ˈkeim		tə ðə ˌpaːti?

Emphatic Special Questions.

The type of emphasis referred to in §347 causes the above tenses to adopt the normal structure, since the conjugating finite is brought in to take the nuclear tone:

Tense No.	S	af	V	O	A
A 1	'wot	ˋdʌz	ˌkoːz	ðə ˌtaidz?	
A 1	'witʃ əv ju	ˋduː	ˌnou	ði ˌaːnsə?	
A 2	'witʃ ˙gəːlz	ˋdid	ˌsiː	ˌmeəri	in ˌtaun?

Rhetorical Special Questions.

On the other hand, in the rhetorical questions described in §348 the conjugating finite is not required, and the anomalous structure is retained in these two tenses:

Tense No.	S	F	O	A
A 1	ˊhuː	˙driŋks	˙kofi	ət ˙nait?
A 1	ˊhau ˙meni əv ju	˙grou	˙flauəz	in ðə ˙gaːdn̩?
A 2	ˊhau meni	˙keim		tə ðə ˙paːti?

350 Alternative questions. These questions, which are defined in §342, present no structural complications, but do require special tonetic treatment. They usually carry a rising tone on all the alternatives except the last, which takes a falling tone to indicate that it is the last alternative offered for consideration. Examples:

> iz i ət ˊhoum, oːr ət ði ˌofis?
> wil ju ˌhav ˊhʌni, oː ˈdʒam, oː ˋmaːməˌleid?
> d ju priˌfəː ˌtravliŋ bai ˊroud, ˊreil, ˊsiː oːr ˌeə?

If, however, it is desired to indicate that the alternatives mentioned do not necessarily constitute a complete series, but are open to additions, the last one mentioned, as well as the others, will have a rising tone:

> iz i ət ˊhoum, oːr ət ði ˊofis ...?
> wil ju ˌhav ˊhʌni, oː ˈdʒam, oː ˊmaːmə˙leid ...?

Alternative Special Questions.

Most of the Special Questions may have a list of alternatives added to them to indicate the field from which the speaker expects the answer to come. Examples:

'witʃ iz ðə ˌbetə, 'ðis oː 'ðat?
'wen ə ðei iks'pektiŋ ju, tə'dei oː təˌmoru?
'witʃ wʌn wəz ˌstoulṇ, ðə 'big wʌn oː ðə ˌlit| wʌn?
'huː ˙got ðeə ˌfəːst, 'dʒon oː ˌmeəri?
'weər | i ˌbiː, ət 'houm, oːr ət ði ˌofis?

NEGATION

351 Vehicles of negation. The introduction of negation into
a sentence by means of a negative conjugating finite was discussed
and exemplified in §§334–5. There are, however, four other ways
in which negation may be added to a sentence. They and their
symbols are:

nS = Negative Subject	nC = Negative Complement
nO = Negative Object	nA = Negative Adverbial

The expression of negation by any of the above vehicles instead
of by a negative finite has the effect of emphasizing the negative
idea, and it will be noticed in the examples given in the following
sections that they frequently take the nuclear tone of the sentence.

In each of these classes there are a few near-negative elements
which are subject to the same rules as the fully negative elements.

It is most important to realize that negation is not cumulative
in English, as it is in many other languages. In other words, two
negative elements in the same clause do not reinforce the idea of
negation; on the contrary, they cancel each other out and produce
a sort of affirmative. One may therefore lay down the principle
that negative and near-negative elements in the sentence are nearly
always mutually exclusive.

This provides many pitfalls for students who are in the habit of
using cumulative negation in their own languages; they need to
take great care not to use more than one type of negation or near-
negation in English to convey a negative or near-negative idea.
They must also avoid the temptation to think that the indefinite
partitive **eni** and its compounds contain in themselves a negative
element. When asked questions like **'hau meni 'buks aː ðər on
ðə ˌteib|?** they are inclined to give a negative answer the form
'eni, instead of 'nʌn.

352 Negative subjects. The words used as negative subjects are the pronominal determiners naiðə*, nʌn, noubodi, nouwʌn, nʌθiŋ, and the adjectival determiners naiðə*, nou, not ə, not ən followed by a noun or by certain other determiners.

Words used as near-negative subjects are the pronominal determiners eni, enibodi, eniwʌn, eniθiŋ preceded by haːdli or skeəsli, and expressions like not oːl, not evri, not evribodi, not evriwʌn, not evriθiŋ, not mʌtʃ, not meni, not ə litļ, not ə fjuː. Examples:

Tense No.	nS	af	v	V	O, C, A
A 1	(See §356)				
A 2	(See §356)				
A 3	'not ˋevribodi	kən		ˌiːt	ˌfiʃ.
A 4	ˋnʌn əv ju	əv		ˌʌndəˌstud	ðə ˌlesn̩.
A 5	'nouwʌn	əd		ˋmendid	it.
A 6	'not ˋoːl əv it	kəd	əv	biˌloŋd	tə ˌdʒon.
A 7	'not ˋwʌn əv ju	z		ˌlisniŋ	tə mi.
A 8	ˋnoubədi	wəz		ˌhəːtiŋ	ju.
A 9	ˋnou ˌkandidits	ʃəd	bi	ˌraitiŋ	ˌnau.
A10	'nouwʌn	z	bin	ˋθiŋkiŋ	əbaut it.
A11	'nʌn əv ˋʌs	əd	bin	ˌθretniŋ	ðəm.
A12	'noubodi	ļ	əv bin	inˋdʒoiiŋ	ðə ˌplei.
P 1	'not ˋmeni	ər		iksˌpektid	tə ˌdʒoin.
P 2	'nʌθiŋ	wəz		ˈheld	ˌbak.
P 3	'nou ˈmoː	kən	bi	'pakt	in ˌhiə.
P 4	'not ˋmʌtʃ	əz	bin	ˌstoulṇ.	
P 5	'noubodi	d	bin	fəˇgotṇ.	
P 6	'not ˇevriwʌn	kəd	əv bin	diˋpendid	əˌpon.
P 7	'nou ˈpriznəz	ə		biːiŋ	riˌliːst.	
P 8	'nʌn əv əs	wə		biːiŋ	ˋfoːst	tə ˌwəːk.

353 Negative objects. Most of the words used as negative and near-negative subjects are also used as objects in the tenses of the active voice:

Tense No.	S	af	v	V	nO
A 1	(See §356)				
A 2	(See §356)				
A 3	ʃi	niːd		'briŋ	'nʌθiŋ ˇels.
A 4	ju	v		'finiʃt	'skeəsli ˋeni.
A 5	ʃi	d		'mendid	'nʌθiŋ ət ˋoːl.
A 6	it	kəd	əv	'satisfaid	ˋnoubodi.
A 7	hi	z		'riːˉraitiŋ	ˋnʌn əv it.
A 8	'ðat	wəz		ˉhəːtiŋ	'haːdli ˋeniwʌn.
A 9	ju	ʃəd	bi	'raitiŋ	ˋnʌθiŋ.
A10	ðei	v	bin	'giviŋ	'nou ˇtrʌbḷ.
A11	'dʒon	əd	bin	ˉdriŋkiŋ	'haːdli ˏeniθiŋ.
A12	ðei	l	əv bin	'əːniŋ	ˋnʌθiŋ.

In the passive tenses the same words may be used as agents to indicate who performed the action.

Tense No.	S	af	v	V	n Agent
P 1	ju	ə		'θretṇd	bai ˏnouwʌn.
P 2	hi	wəz		bi'liːvd	bai 'haːdli ˋenibodi.
P 3	ðei	l	bi	'wontid	bai ˏnʌn əv əs.
P 4	it	s	bin	'stʌdid	bai 'nouwʌn ˇels.
P 5	ai	d	bin	fə'gotṇ	bai ˋnoubodi.
P 6	wi	'mei	əv bin	ˉfraitṇd	bai ˋnʌθiŋ.
P 7	ðei	ə	biːiŋ	'helpt	bai ˏnʌn əv əs.
P 8	ðə 'bel	wəz	biːiŋ	ˉrʌŋ	bai ˋnoubodi.

For the treatment in the passive of verbs taking two objects, see §§378–81.

354 Negative complements. These occur after verbs of incomplete predication, and particularly after the verb tə biː. They
are frequently to be found in the precursory ðeə* structure.
Examples:

Tense No.	S	af	v	nC
A 1	(See §356)			
A 2	(See §356)			
A 3	ðə	l	bi	'nouwʌn ˘els.
A 4	ðə	z	bin	'nʌθiŋ ˘njuː.
A 5	ðə	d	bin	'nou ˘rein.
A 6	ˋðat	ud	əv bin	ˌnou ˌnov|ti.

355 Negative adverbials. Such words as not, nevə*, not ət oːl,
nouweə* are classed as negative adverbials, while seldəm, reəli,
skeəsli, beəli, skeəsli evə*, haːdli, haːdli evə* are near-negative
adverbials. The adverb not is usually confined to tenses in which
finites of the verb tə biː are used and to the special cases mentioned
in §§171, 195 and 203.

In the following examples notice the position of the negative
adverbs, after the finite and before any verbals.

Tense No.	S	af	nA	v	V	O, C, A
A 1	(See §356)					
A 2	(See §356)					
A 3	ju	l	'beəli		˙katʃ	ðə ˎbʌs.
A 4	ðei	v	'nevə		ˋsiːn	ˌsnou.
A 5	wi	d	'haːdli evə		ˋmet	ðəm.
A 6	ai	ʃəd	'nevər	əv	ˋnoun	əbaut it.
A 7	hi	z	'not		ˋlisniŋ	tə ju.
A 8	ʃi	wəz	'skeəsli		˙iːtiŋ	ˋeniθiŋ.
A 9	ðei	d	'haːdli	bi	˙steiiŋ	ˌhiə.
P 1	ˌðat	s	'not		˙set|d	ət ˋoːl
P 2	wi	wə	'reəli		˙aːskt	tə ˇstei.
P 3	it	kən	'haːdli	bi	˙pakt	in ˌhiə.
P 4	hi	z	'seldəm	bin	˙meid	tə ˌweit.
P 5	ai	d	'nevə	bin	˙robd	biˇfoə.
P 6	ʃi	d	'skeəsli	əv bin	ˇmist.	

The negative adverb **nouweə***, being an adverb of place, follows
the specific verbal, or the object if there is one:

Tense No.	S	af	V	O	nA
A 3	ai	kən	'faind	im	ˋnouweə.
A 7	wi	ə	'gouiŋ		ˋnouweər in pə‚tikjulə.

356 Anomalous negative. This occurs in Tenses A1 and A2 in
statements in which the negation is expressed in some other way
than by a negative finite, i.e., by a negative subject, object,
complement or adverbial. Examples:

Negative Subject.

Tense No.	nS	F	O	A
A 1	'haːdli ˋenibodi	‚drinks	‚kofi	ət ‚nait.
A 1	ˋnʌθiŋ	sək‚siːdz		laik sək ˇses.
A 1	ˋnʌn əv ðəm	‚grou	‚flauəz	in ðə ‚gaːdn̩.
A 1	ˋnʌn əv ju	‚nou	ðə ‚lesn̩	‚propəli.
A 2	ˋnoubodi	‚soː	‚meəri	in ‚taun.
A ˙2	'haːdli ˋeniθiŋ	‚meid	‚sens	tə ‚miː.

Negative Object.

Tense No.	S	F	nO	A
A 1	'dʒon	˙driŋks	'haːdli ˋeniθiŋ	ət ‚nait.
A 1	hi	'laiks	ˋnʌn əv ðəm.	
A 1	ðei	'grou	ˋnou ‚flauəz	in ðə ‚gaːdn̩.
A 1	wi	'nou	ˋnoubodi	in ‚ðis ˙taun.
A 2	ðə 'gəːlz	˙soː	'haːdli ˋenibodi	in ‚taun.
A 2	it	‚meid	'nou ˙sens	tə ˇmiː.

Negative Complement.

Tense No.	S	F	nC
A 1	'dʒon	˙siːmz	'not tə bi ‚redi.
A 1	ðə 'gəːlz	˙saund	'not veri in˙θjuːziˋastik.
A 2	ðei	'lukt	'nou ˙betə ðən ði ˋʌðəz.

Negative Adverbial.

Tense No.	S	nA	F	O	A
A 1	ˈdʒon	ˈhaːdli ˋevə	ˌdriŋks	ˌkofi	ət ˏnait.
A 1	hi	ˋnevə	ˌkʌmz		tə ˬlʌndən.
A 1	ðei	ˋseldəm	ˌgrou	ˌflauəz	in ðə ˬgaːdn̩.
A 1	ju	ˋnevə	ˌstei		wið ˏʌs.
A 2	wi	ˋseldəm	ˌsoː	ˌmeəri	in ˬtaun.
A 2	ʃi	ˈhaːdli ˋevə	ˌgeiv	ˌeniθiŋ	əˌwei.

See, however, §357 for circumstances under which the anomalous structure is not used in Tenses A1 and A2 with a negative adverbial.

357 Inversion after initial adverbs. The placing of adverbs at the beginning of a sentence in order to emphasize them or to create a more graphic effect is a traditional device in English, though in modern conversation the number and type of adjectives so displaced are fewer than they used to be. In the written language it is still possible to place many of the adverbials given in the list in §§262–3 at the beginning of the sentence.

When some of these adverbials are placed in the initial position no other change is made in the sentence, but with others the subject and finite are nearly always inverted, while in Tenses A1 and A2 the appropriate conjugating finite is resorted to, since inversion with specific finites is not accepted in modern English.

The adverbials that induce inversion are the negative and near-negative adverbials listed in §355, some adverbs of manner, and adverbs of frequency such as ofn̩, friːkwəntli, sʌmtaimz, oːlwiz, twais, θriː taimz, meni taimz, tuː ofn̩. There is no inversion when adverbs of time or place take the initial position.

When this structure is used the adverbial generally takes the nuclear tone, unless this is needed on the specific verbal. Examples:

Tense No.	A	af	S	v	V	O, C, A
A 1	ˈhaːdli ˙evə	du	ai		ˋtravl̩	bai ˌbʌs.
A 2	ˋseldəm	did	ðei		ˌaːsk	fə ˬhelp.
A 3	ˋnevə	ʃl̩	ai		fəˌget	joː ˏkaindnis.
A 4	ˈtuː ˋofn̩	əv	wi		ˌtould	ju əbaut it.
A 5	ˋnouweər	əd	i		ˌsiːn	sʌtʃ ə ˌθiŋ
A 6	ˈθriː ˋtaimz	kəd	ʃi	əv	ˌgot	əˌwei.

Tense No.	A	af	S	v	V	O, C, A
P 1	ˋseldəm	iz	i		əˌlaud	tə ˌgou ˌaut.
P 2	ˋmeni ˌtaimz	wə	ju		ˌwoːnd	tə bi ˌkeəfļ.
P 3	ˋofņ	kəd	ʃi	bi	ˌhəːd	ˌsiŋiŋ.
P 4	ˈnouweərˋelsəv		ðei	bin	ˌhauzd	souˌwel.
P 5	ˈnevə biˋfoːr	əd	ai	bin	ˌrobd.	
P 6	ˈskeəsli ˋevə	wud	ʃi	əv bin	ˇmist.	

NEGATIVE INTERROGATION

358 Negation in general questions. It was explained in §335 that the interrogative-negative form of the sentence is normally formed with the help of a negative conjugating finite ; this is sometimes replaced by the other vehicles of negation listed in §351. These often take the nuclear tone of the question, as they are used to focus attention on the negation of the idea that they convey. As is the case in statements, these negative and near-negative elements are mutually exclusive in questions.

Examples of General Questions containing these elements of negation are given below.

Negative Subjects.

Tense No.	af	nS	V	O
A 1	dəz	ˊnoubodi	˙wont	it ?
A 2	did	ˈhaːdli ˊenibodi	əkˈsept	ðəm ?
A 4	həz	ˊnaiðər əv ðəm	˙siːn	mi ?
A 8	wəz	ˈskeəsli ˊeniθiŋ	˙muːviŋ ?	
P 2	wəz	ˈnʌθiŋ ˊmoː	˙dʌn ?	

Negative Objects.

Tense No.	af	S	v	V	nO
A 1	d	ju		ˈlaik	ˊnʌn əv ðəm ?
A 2	did	ʃi		ˈgriːt	˙haːdli ˊenibodi ?
A 3	ʃəd	wi		iksˈpekt	ˊnaiðər əv ðəm ?
A 6	wil	ðei	əv	ˈteikən	˙nʌn ət ˊoːl ?
A10	həz	i	bin	ˈgiviŋ	ju ˊnʌθiŋ ?

Negative Agent in the Passive.

Tense No.	af	S	v	V	n Agent
P 1	iz	i		'wontid	bai 'noubodi?
P 3	wil	it	bi	ə'fektid	bai 'nʌθiŋ?
P 5	həd	ʃi	bin	'woːnd	bai 'nʌn əv ju?
P 7	ə	ðei	biːiŋ	'met	bai 'nouwʌn?

Negative Complements.

Tense No.	af	S	v	V	nC
A 1	də	ðei		'siːm	'not tə 'maind?
A 2	did	ʃi		ə'piə	˙not ˙tuː 'pliːzd?
A10	həz	i	bin	'lukiŋ	˙nou 'betə?

Negative Adverbials.

Tense No.	af	S	nA	V	O, C, A
A 1	də	ðei	'nevə	˙spiːk	'iŋgliʃ?
A 2	did	ju	'reəli	˙win	ə 'praiz?
A 3	məst	wi	'haːdli ˙evə	˙hav	ə 'holidi?
A 5	həd	ʃi	'seldəm	˙noutist	ju bi'foə?
A 8	wəz	i	'beəli	bi'giniŋ	tə ˙wəːk?
P 1	əm	ai	'not	ə˙laud	in'said?
P 2	wə	ðei	'not ət ˙oːl	'teikən	ə'bak?

359 Negation in special questions. Negation may be inserted in Special Questions by using a negative conjugating finite or any of the other vehicles of negation listed in §351. When the latter are used the nuclear tone usually falls either on them or on the. interrogative word.

As the interaction of the interrogative and negative elements in these questions is somewhat complicated it may be as well to tabulate the possible combinations.

	Negative Subject	*Negative Object*
Int. Subj.	——	'huː ˙soː ˎnʌθiŋ?
Int. Obj.	'wot did ˎnoubodi ˌsiː?	——
Int. Adv.	ˎwai did ˌnoubodi ˌsiː it?	ˎwai did ju ˌsiː ˌnʌθiŋ?

	Negative Adverb	*Negative Finite*
Int. Subj.	'huː ˎnevə ˌsoː it?	'huː ˎkaːnt ˌsiː it?
Int. Obj.	'wot did i ˎnevə ˌsiː?	'wot ˎkaːnt ju ˌsiː?
Int. Adv.	——	ˎwai ˌkaːnt ju ˌsiː it?

360 Interrogative word as subject. Special Questions containing a negative element follow the rule given in §346 regarding the use of a statement structure when the interrogative word is the subject (or part of the subject) of the sentence. In such questions the negation may be introduced through the finite, the object or the adverbial, and in the passive voice the vehicle may be a negative agent.

When a negative conjugating finite is used, Tenses A1 and A2 use the same sentence pattern as the other tenses, but they retain the anomalous structure when any of the other vehicles are used.

Negation in the Agent.

Tense No.	S	af	v	V	n Agent
P 1	ˋwot	s		ˌθretn̩d	bai ˌnouwʌn ?
P 2	ˋhuː	wəz		biˌliːvd	bai ˌhaːdli ˌenibodi ?
P 3	'witʃ	ǀ	bi	˙wontid	bai ˋnʌn əv əs ?
P 4	'witʃ	əz	bin	˙juːzd	bai ˋnʌn əv ju ?
P 5	'wot	əd	bin	fəˈgotn̩	bai ˋnoubodi ?
P 6	'huː	d	əv bin	˙fraitn̩d	bai ˏnʌθiŋ ?
P 7	'wot	s	biːiŋ	˙stʌdid	bai 'nouwʌn ˏels ?
P 8	'huː	wəz	biːiŋ	˙helpt	bai ˏnʌn əv ðəm ?

Negation in the Adverbial.

Tense No.	S	af	nA	v	V	O, C, A
A 1	(See §363)					
A 2	(See §363)					
A 3	ˋhuː	ǀ	ˌbeəli		ˌkatʃ	ðə ˌbʌs ?
A 4	'huː	z	ˋnevə		ˌsiːn	ˌsnou ?
A 5	'witʃ əv ju əd		˙nevə		ˏmet	ðəm ?
A 6	ˋhuː	wud	ˌseldəm əv		ˌtoːkt	əbaut it ?
A 7	'huː	z	˙not		ˋlisniŋ	tə mi ?
A 8	'witʃ ˈgəːl	wəz	'skeəsli		˙iːtiŋ	ˏeniθiŋ ?
A 9	'huː	ǀ	˙reəli	bi	˙puliŋ	iz ˏweit ?
P 1	'witʃ əv ju ə		ˋnot		ˌsetˌld	jet ?
P 2	ˋhuː	wəz	ˌreəli		ˌaːskt	tə ˌstei ?
P 3	ˋwot	kən	ˌskeəsli	bi	ˌpakt	in ˌhiə ?
P 4	ˋhuː	z	ˌseldəm bin		ˌmeid	tə ˌweit ?
P 5	'wot	əd	ˋnevə	bin	ˌstouln̩	biˌfoə ?
P 6	ˋhuː	wud	ˌhaːdli	əv bin	ˌmist ?	

Negation in the Finite.

Tense No.	S	nf	v	V	O, C, A
A 1	'huː	ˋdʌznt		ˌdriŋk	ˌkofi?
A 2	'witʃ əv ju	ˋdidn̩t		ˌsiː	ˌmeəri?
A 3	'hau meni	ˋniːdn̩t		ˌliːv	ˌəːli?
A 4	'witʃ əv ju	ˋhavn̩t		ˌfiniʃt	ðə ˌbuk?
A 5	'huː	ˋhadn̩t		riˌsiːvd	ə ˌpraiz?
A 6	'hau meni	ˋwount	əv	ˌfiniʃt	in ˌtaim?
A 7	'witʃ ˈboiz	ˋaːnt		ˌjuːziŋ	ˌpenz?
A 8	'wot	ˋwozn̩t		ˌfitiŋ	ˌwel?
A 9	'huː	ˋwudn̩t	bi	ˌhoupiŋ	tə ˌwin?
A10	'huː	ˋhazn̩t	bin	ˌtoːkiŋ	əbaut it?
A11	'huː ˋels	ˌhadn̩t	bin	ˌhelpiŋ	ju?
A12	'huː	ˋwount	əv bin	ˌdroːiŋ	kəŋˌkluːʒn̩z?
P 1	'wot ˋels	ˌisn̩t		əˌlaud?	
P 2	'witʃ wʌn	ˌwozn̩t		ˌdamidʒd?	
P 3	'hau mʌtʃ	ˌkudn̩t	bi	ˌfitid	ˌin?
P 4	'witʃ əv ju	ˌhavn̩t	bin	ˌoːdəd	tə ˌliːv?
P 5	'witʃ əv ðəm	ˈhadn̩t	bin	ˈtraid	biˌfoə?
P 6	'wot	ˋwount	əv bin	ˌteikən	əˌwei?
P 7	'huː	ˌizn̩t	biːiŋ	ˌaːskt	tə ˌhelp?
P 8	'wot	ˋwozn̩t	biːiŋ	ˌsed	əbaut əs?

Negation in the Object.

Tense No.	S	af	v	V	nO
A 1	(See §363)				
A 2	(See §363)				
A 3	'huː	məst		ˈiːt	ˌnʌθiŋ?
A 4	'witʃ əv ju	əv		ˈfiniʃt	'skeəsli ˌeni?
A 5	'huː	d		ˈmendid	ˌnʌθiŋ?
A 6	'hau ˈmeni	l	əv	ˈsiːn	'nʌθiŋ ət ˌoːl?
A 7	'witʃ əv ju	ə		ˈduːiŋ	ˌnʌn əv it?
A 8	'huː	wəz		ˈjuːziŋ	'haːdli ˌeniθiŋ?
A 9	'witʃ ˈboiz	ʃəd	bi	'raitiŋ	ˌnʌθiŋ?
A10	'huː	z	bin	ˈduːiŋ	'nʌθiŋ ˌels?
A11	'witʃ əv ju	əd	bin	ˈdriŋkiŋ	ˌnʌθiŋ?
A12	'huː	l	əv bin	ˈhelpiŋ	ˌnoubodi?

361 Interrogative word as object. When the interrogative word introducing a Special Question is the object of the sentence a question structure is used and Tenses A1 and A2 do not take the anomalous structure.
Negation may be introduced through the finite, the subject or the adverbial.

Negation in the Finite.

Tense No.	O	nf	S	v	V
A 1	ˈwot	ˋdʌzn̩t	ˌdʒɔn		ˌdriŋk?
A 2	ˈwitʃ wʌn	ˋdidn̩t	ˌmeəri		ˌsiː?
A 3	ˈhuː(m)	ˋmʌsn̩t	wi		inˌvait?
A 4	ˈhau meni	ˌhavn̩t	ju		ˌmaːkt?
A 5	ˈwitʃ əv ðəm	ˋhadn̩t	ðə ˌboiz		ˌfiniʃt?
A 6	ˈhuː(m)	ˋwudn̩t	ðei	əv	əkˌseptid?
A 7	ˈwot	ˋizn̩t	i		ˌduːiŋ?
A 8	ˈwitʃ əv əs	ˋwəːnt	ju		iksˌpektiŋ?
A 9	ˈwitʃ wʌn	˙wount	ju	bi	ˌjuːziŋ?
A10	ˈwot	ˋhavn̩t	ai	bin	ˌduːiŋ?
A11	ˈwitʃ ˙buks	ˈhadn̩t	ʃi	bin	ˌriːdiŋ?
A12	ˈwot	ˋwount	ðei	əv bin	ˌθiŋkiŋ?

Negation in the Subject.

Tense No.	O	af	nS	v	V
A 1	ˈwot	dəz	ˋnouwʌn		ˌdriŋk?
A 2	ˈwit əv ðəm	did	ˋnʌn əv ju		ˌsiː?
A 3	ˈhuː(m)	kən	ˋnoubodi		ˌstand?
A 4	ˈwot	əv	˙nʌn əv ju		ˈʌndəˌstud?
A 5	ˋwitʃ ˌplei	əd	ˌhaːdli ˌenibodi		inˌdʒoid?
A 6	ˈwitʃ əv ju	wil	ˋnouwʌn	əv	inˌvaitid?
A 7	ˈwot	ə	ˋnʌn əv ðəm		ˌiːtiŋ?
A 8	ˈwot ˙geim	wəz	ˈskeəsli ˋeniwʌn		ˌpleiiŋ?
A 9	ˋwitʃ wʌn	ʃəd	ˌnoubodi	bi	ˌjuːziŋ?
A10	ˈwot	əv	ˋnʌn əv əs	bin	ˌθiŋkiŋ?
A11	ˈwitʃ ˙buk	əd	ˋnoubodi	bin	ˌriːdiŋ?
A12	ˈwot	ǀ	ˋnʌn əv ðəm	əv bin	iksˌpektiŋ?

Negation in the Adverbial.

Tense No.	O	af	S	nA	v	V
A 1	'wot	dəz	˙dʒon	ˋnevə		ˌdriŋk?
A 2	'huː(m)	did	˙meəri	ˌseldəm		ˌsiː?
A 3	'witʃ	ʃl	wi	˙haːdli ˌevə		ˌniːd?
A 4	'wot	əv	ðei	˙skeəsli		ˎtraid?
A 5	'witʃ əv ðəm əd	ju		ˋnot		ˌmet?
A 6	'huːz ˙neim	wud	ju	'nevər	əv	ˎgest?
A 7	ˋwot	ə	ðei	ˌbeəli		ˌtraiiŋ?
A 8	ˋwot	wəz	ʃi	ˌhaːdli		ˌtəːniŋ?
A 9	'witʃ		ju	˙nevə	bi	ˌjuːziŋ?
A10	'huː(m)	əv	ðei	˙haːdli	bin	ˌsiːiŋ?
A11	'witʃ 'buk	əd	i	ˋnot	bin	ˌriːdiŋ?
A12	'wot	˙mei	ʃi	ˋnot	əv bin	ˌseiiŋ?

362 Interrogative word as adverb. When the interrogative word introducing a Special Question is an adverb a question structure is used and Tenses A1 and A2 do not take the anomalous structure.

Negation may be introduced through the finite, the subject, the object or, in the passive voice, through the agent.

Negation in the Finite.

Tense No.	A	nf	S	v	V	O, C, A
A 1	'wai	˙dʌznt	'dʒon		˙driŋk	ˋkofi?
A 2	ˋwai	ˌdidnt	ˌmeəri		ˌsiː	ðə ˌgəːlz?
A 3	'weə	ˋwount	ju		ˌfaind	wʌn?
A 4	'weə	ˋhaznt	ʃi		ˌlukt	fər it?
A 5	'wai	˙hadnt	ðei		ˎweitid	fə mi?
A 6	'wai	˙kudnt	ˋai	əv	ˌhad	wʌn?
A 7	'wen	ˋiznt	it		ˌreiniŋ	ˌhiə?
A 8	'weə	ˋwoznt	it		ˌreiniŋ?	
A 9	'wen	˙wount	ðei	bi	ˌniːdiŋ	ju?
A10	'wai	˙havnt	ðei	bin	ˋweitiŋ	fər əs?
A11	'wen	ˋhadnt	i	bin	ˌwəːkiŋ?	
A12	'wai	˙kudnt	ʃi	əv bin	'duːiŋ	hə ˋwəːk?

Negation in the Subject.

Tense No.	A	af	nS	v	V	O, C, A
A 1	'wai	dəz	˙noubodi		'driŋk	ˌkofi?
A 2	'wai	did	˙nʌn əv ju		'siː	ˌmeəri?
A 3	'weə	wud	˙noubodi		ˋfaind	it?
A 4	'weər	əv	˙nʌn əv əs		ˋlukt	fər it?
A 5	'wai	əd	˙noubodi		ˌkoːld	fə mi?
A 6	'wai	ʃəd	ˋnʌn əv əs	əv	ˌhad	wʌn?
A 7	'wen	iz	ˋnʌθiŋ		ˌhapniŋ	ˌhiə?
A 8	ˋweə	wəz	ˌnʌθiŋ		ˌhapniŋ?	
A 9	'hau ˙suːn |		ˋnouwʌn	bi	ˌniːdiŋ	it?
A10	'wai	əv	˙nʌn əv ju	bin	ˋwəːkiŋ?	
A11	'wai	əd	˙nʌn əv ðəm bin		ˋweitiŋ	fər əs?
A12	'wai	ʃəd	˙noubodi	əv bin	ˋlisniŋ	tə mi?
P 1	'weər	iz	'nou ˙moː		ˌniːdid?	
P 2	'wen	wəz	'nʌθiŋ ˙els		ˌleft?	
P 3	'wai	kən	˙nʌθiŋ ˋmoː	bi	ˌdʌn	fə him?
P 4	sins 'wen	əz	ˋnouwʌn	bin	ˌsiːn	ˌðeə?
P 5	'wai	əd	˙nʌθiŋ	bin	ˌdʌn	fə ðəm?
P 6	'wai	kəd	˙nou ˋmoːr	əv bin	ˌfaund?	
P 7	'wai	iz	˙nʌθiŋ	biːiŋ	ˌsed	əbaut it?
P 8	'wai	wəz	˙noubodi	biːiŋ	ˋbleimd	fər it?

Negation in the Object.

Tense No.	A	af	S	v	V	nO
A 1	'wai	dəz	˙dʒon		'driŋk	ˌnʌθiŋ?
A 2	'wai	did	˙meəri		'siː	ˋnʌn əv ju?
A 3	'wen	|	ju		˙ou	ˌnʌθiŋ?
A 4	sins ˋwen	əv	ju		ˌfaund	ˌnou ˌruːm?
A 5	'wai	əd	ʃi		˙aːskt	ˌnoubodi?
A 6	'wai	ʃəd	wi	əv	˙noutist	ˌnouwʌn?
A 7	'wai	z	ʃi		˙juːziŋ	'nou ˋsoːlt?
A 8	ˋwen	wəz	i		ˌdriŋkiŋ	ˌnʌθiŋ?
A 9	'hau ˙suːn |		ðei	bi	'peiiŋ	ˋnoubodi?
A10	sins ˋwen	əz	i	bin	ˌouiŋ	ˌnʌθiŋ?
A11	'wai	əd	ðei	bin	˙seiiŋ	ˋnʌθiŋ?
A12	ˋwai	ʃəd	wi	əv bin	ˌiːtiŋ	ˌnou ˌbred?

315   M

Negation in the Agent.

Tense No.	A	af	S	v	V	n Agent
P 1	'wai	iz	it		'juːzd	bai 'nouwʌn ˏels?
P 2	ˋwen	wə	ju		əˏmjuːzd	bai ˏnʌθiŋ?
P 3	'wen ǀ		it	bi	'wontid	bai ˋnoubodi?
P 4	'wai	əz	ʃi	bin	əˋkjuːzd	bai ˋnʌn əv ju?
P 5	'wai	əd	it	bin	riˋmembəd	bai ˋnoubodi?
P 6	'wen	ud	ʃi	əv bin	'fraitn̩d	bai ˏnʌθiŋ?
P 7	'wai	iz	it	biːiŋ	'stʌdid	bai 'nouwʌn ˏels?
P 8	'wai	wə	wi	biːiŋ	'helpt	bai ˏnʌn əv ju?

363 Anomalous interrogative-negative. This occurs in Tenses A1 and A2 when the interrogative word is (or forms part of) the subject of the Special Question, provided the negation is not expressed by a negative finite. Since interrogative words do not contain a negative element, the negation can in effect be introduced only by an object, an adverbial or a complement.

Negation in the Object.

Tense No.	S	F	nO	A
A 1	'hau 'meni əv ju	'driŋk	ˋnʌθiŋ	ət ˏnait?
A 1	'huː	'grouz	ˋnou ˏflauəz	in ðə ˏgaːdn̩?
A 2	'witʃ 'gəːlz	'soː	ˋnoubodi	in ˏtaun?

Negation in the Adverbial.

Tense No.	S	nA	F	O
A 1	'hau 'meni əv ju	ˋseldəm	ˏdriŋk	ˏkofi?
A 1	'huː	'haːdli ˋevə	ˏgrouz	ˏflauəz?
A 2	'witʃ 'gəːlz	ˋnevə	ˏsoː	ˏmeəri?

Negation in the Complement.

Tense No.	S	F	nC
A 1	ˋhuː	ˏsiːmz	ˏnou ˏbetə?
A 1	'witʃ 'gəːlz	'luk	'not ˋikwǀ tu it?
A 2	'hau 'meni əv ðəm	əˋpiəd	'not tə ˏmaind?

BYWAYS OF NEGATION

364 Degrees of negation. A scale of five different degrees ranging from a full affirmative to a full negative is provided by certain compound determiners and by compounds of the adverb weə*. Many of these are formed with the aid of the partitives (§§75–8). The following table shows the five degrees.

Full Aff.	Partial Aff.	Indefinite	Partial Neg.	Full Neg.
oːl	sʌm	eni	not oːl	nou, nʌn
evribodi	sʌmbodi	enibodi	not evribodi	noubodi
evriwʌn	sʌmwʌn	eniwʌn	not evriwʌn	nouwʌn
evriθiŋ	sʌmθiŋ	eniθiŋ	not evriθiŋ	nʌθiŋ
evriweə*	sʌmweə*	eniweə*	not evriweə*	nouweə*
bouθ		aiðə*		naiðə*

The word nou is adjectival, while nʌn is pronominal; all the other words on the first and last lines of the table may be used in either capacity. All compounds of -bodi, -wʌn and -θiŋ are pronominal, while compounds of weə* are normally adverbial but can be used as pronouns (§231). With the determiners expressing duality only one intermediate degree is possible.

365 Uses of the degrees of negation. The behaviour of the various forms shown in the table in §364 will now be described.

The fully affirmative forms.

These are used freely, with one exception, as subjects or objects, in questions or statements, and with affirmative or negative finites.

'kan 'evribodi ˈjuːz ðəm?	ˋevribodi məs ˌteik wʌn.
'mʌst wi inˈvait 'evriwʌn?	ju məst iŋˈkluːd ˌevriwʌn.
'dʌznt 'evribodi ˈlaik ˈkofi?	————
'havṇt ju ˈsiːn 'evriθiŋ?	ju 'havṇt ˈsiːn ˇevriθiŋ.

The exception referred to above is the use of these forms as subjects of a negative finite. Though this structure may often be heard in familiar speech, careful speakers avoid it on account of its ambiguity. Thus sentences such as

ˋoːl ˌizṇt ˌgould ðət ˌglitəz. *or* ˋevribodi ˌwount ˌdriŋk ˌðat.

are usually intended to mean

'not ˋoːl ðət ˌglitəz iz ˌgould. *and* 'not ˋevribodi | ˌdriŋk ˌðat.

whereas their logical meanings are

ˋnʌθiŋ ðət ˌglitəz iz ˌgould. *and* ˋnoubodi | ˌdriŋk ˌðat.

Though the use of a suitable intonation (as shown above) may go a little way towards determining the meaning, it is obviously better to use the unambiguous structure that has the partially negative determiner as subject of an affirmative finite.

The partially affirmative forms.

The most frequent use of these is in statements containing affirmative finites.

ˈsʌmwʌn z ˈweitiŋ tə ˈsiː ju.   ai ʃəd ˈlaik ˈsʌmθiŋ ˌdifrn̩t.

They are used as subjects of negative finites in such statements as the following.

ˈsʌmwʌn ˈdʌzn̩t ˈlaik ju.   ˈsʌm əv ðəm ˈdidn̩t get ˈkukt.

They are also used in questions that are intended to suggest, invite or press for an affirmative answer, and particularly with a negative finite.   In extending invitations they are used for politeness in preference to the indefinite forms.

ˈhazn̩t ˈsʌmwʌn ˈmeid ə misˈteik? wud ju ˈlaik sm̩ ˈkofi?
wil ju ˈgiv mi sm̩ ˈmoː ˈtiː?   ˈwudn̩t ju ˈlaik ˈsʌmθiŋ ˈels?

The indefinite forms.

These are not normally used as subjects in statements.   In other capacities they are used in the following cases.

In most questions except those using the partially affirmative forms described above:

həv ju ˈfiniʃt ˈeni əv ðəm?   ˈwount ˈenibodi ˈhelp ju?

In dubitative statements:

ai ˈwʌndər if ˈenibodi z ˌðeə. ai ˈdount ˈnou if ðər ˈaːr ˌeni.

In statements containing a negative finite or other negative element:

wi ˈhavn̩t ˈgot ˌeniθiŋ ˌmoə. hi ˈdʌzn̩t ˈlaik ˈaiðər əv ðəm.
ˈnoubodi ˌwonts eni ˌtʃiːz.   ˈnouweə wə ðər ˌeni tə bi ˌsiːn.

But when they are used in definite statements with an affirmative finite they have the special meaning of "no matter who (what, which, where)".   They can then be used as subjects.

ˈenibodi kən ˌduː ˌðat.   hi I ˌgiv ðəm ˈeniθiŋ ðei ˌwont.
ˈteik ə ˈsiːt ˈeniweə.   ju kən ˈhav ˈaiðər əv ðəm.

The partially negative forms.
These are used almost exclusively as subjects of statements using an affirmative finite. In questions and as objects they are nearly always replaced by a fully affirmative form with a negative finite, as shown above in the paragraph dealing with the fully affirmative forms.

ˈnot ˋoːl ðei ˌsei iz ˌtruː.   ˈnot ˋevriwʌn kən ˌswim ˌwel.

The fully negative forms.
These are used in both questions and statements, but only with affirmative finites. They may serve as subjects or objects.

wil ˈnouwʌn ˙hav eni ˊmoə?   ˋnoubodi ˌlaiks ˌðat.
did ju ˈsiː ˙nʌθiŋ ət ˊoːl?   wi v ˈteikən ˋnaiðər əv ðəm.

366 Choice of negation. It has been seen (§351) that negation can be expressed in various ways other than by a negative finite, and that the other vehicles of negation, most of which are determiners compounded with partitives, are more emphatic than the negative finites.

It may be useful to give some indication of the factors that influence a speaker's choice between the following structures:

 a. An indefinite determiner with a negative finite.
 b. A negative determiner with an affirmative finite.
 c. Precursory ðeə* before a negative finite.
 d. Precursory ðeə* before a negative determiner.

If the determiner is the subject of the sentence, structure *b* is the one most favoured, but if this is felt to be too emphatic structure *c* may be substituted for it in order to soften the statement.

b	*c*
ˋnouwʌn ˌkoːld ˌjestədi.	ðə ˈwozn̩t ˋeniwʌn u ˌkoːld ˌjestədi.
ˈnʌθiŋ ˙els ˋmatəz.	ðər ˈizn̩t ˙eniθiŋ ˙els ðət ˋmatəz.
ˈnʌn əv ðəm ˋwont it.	ðər ˈaːnt ˙eni əv ðəm ðət ˋwont it.
ˋnou ˌʃops ər ˌoupən ˌnau.	ðər ˋaːnt eni ˌʃops ˌoupən ˌnau.

When sentences of this type are turned into questions structure *a* is generally preferred, though some speakers favour structure *b*.

                              a   b
'didn̩t 'eniwʌn 'koːl 'jestədi?   did 'nouwʌn 'koːl 'jestədi?
'dʌznt 'eniθiŋ 'els 'matə?   dəz 'nʌθiŋ 'els 'matə?
'dount 'eni əv ðəm 'wont it?   ðə 'nʌn əv ðəm 'wont it?
'aːnt 'eni 'ʃops 'oupən 'nau?   ə 'nou 'ʃops 'oupən 'nau?

If the determiner is not the subject of the sentence, structure *a* is the one normally used in statements, but a speaker wishing to be emphatic will use structure *b*.

                     a   b
wi 'havn̩t 'siːn 'enibodi.   wi v ˌsiːn 'noubodi.
ai 'kaːnt 'faind 'eniθiŋ.   ai kən ˌfaind 'nʌθiŋ.
hi 'didn̩t 'sei 'eniθiŋ.   hi ˌsed 'nʌθiŋ.
ʃi 'dʌznt 'laik 'aiðər əv ðəm.   ʃi 'laiks 'naiðər əv ðəm.

Structure *a* is also usually preferred in questions in this case, as structure *b* tends to sound stilted.

                     a   b
'havn̩t ju 'siːn 'enibodi?   həv ju 'siːn 'noubodi?
'kaːnt ju 'faind 'eniθiŋ?   kən ju 'faind 'nʌθiŋ?
'didn̩t i 'sei 'eniθiŋ?   did i ˌsei 'nʌθiŋ?
'dʌznt ʃi 'laik 'aiðər əv ðəm?   dəz ʃi ˌlaik 'naiðər əv ðəm?

When precursory ðeə* is used in statements the impersonal nature of the sentence makes it improbable that an emphatic construction will be impolite and structure *d* is therefore generally favoured. Furthermore, the negative determiners provide a more definite subject than do the indefinite ones, and they are therefore more suited to the precursory ðeə* structure.

ðə z 'nʌθiŋ tə bi 'dʌn əbaut it.   ðə l bi 'nouwʌn 'ðeə ˌjet.
ðə wəz 'nou 'moː ˌbred ˌleft.   ðə v bin 'nou ᵛaksidn̩ts.

When precursory ðeə* is used in questions structure *c* is generally preferred, as structure *d* sounds rather stilted.

                     c   d
'izn̩t ðər 'eniθiŋ tə bi 'dʌn?   iz ðə 'nʌθiŋ tə bi 'dʌn?
'wozn̩t ðər 'eni moː 'bred left?   wəz ðə 'nou moː 'bred left?
'wount ðə bi 'eniwʌn 'ðeə jet?   wil ðə bi 'nouwʌn 'ðeə 'jet?
'havn̩t ðə bin eni 'aksidn̩ts?   həv ðə bin 'nou 'aksidn̩ts?

367 Negative infinitives. Most of the infinitive phrases described in §§241–50 can be used in their negative forms, and in many cases they give a more definite meaning than does a negative finite. Compare, on the one hand

ʃi l iks'pekt ju tə ˎgou.   ʃi 'wount iks·pekt ju ˋnot tə ˌgou.

and on the other hand

ʃi l iks'pekt ju 'not tə ˎgou.   ʃi 'wount iksˋpektˉju tə ˌgou.

It is clear that the first of each pair, which contains the affirmative finite, is more decided in feeling than the second, containing a negative finite.

The following are more examples of negative infinitive phrases incorporated in sentences.

ju məst 'wəːk ˎhaːd, sou əz 'not tə ·feil in ði igˎzam.
wi pə'sweidid ðəm ·not tə ·weit eni ˎloŋgə.
'wudn̩t it əv bin ə 'piti ·not tu əv ·gon?
ju wə ˋstjuːpid ˌnot tu əv ˌweitid fə ˌmiː.
it ud ˇpei ju 'not tə bi ·faund 'weistiŋ ˋtaim.
ai ˌhav 'nou aiˋdiə ˌhau ˌnot tə bi ˌdroːn ˌintu it.
'didn̩t it ə'noi ðəm ·not tu əv bin in·vaitid?
ðə wəz ə 'dʒenr| di·zaiə 'not tə bi ə·traktiŋ əˋtenʃn̩.
in 'oːdə ·not tu inˌtruːd, ai 'kept in ðə ˎbakgraund.
hi pri'tendid ·not tu əv bin ˋlisniŋ tu əs.

368 Negative participles. Many of the participial adjectives described in §§101–7 may have **not** prefixed to them in order to reverse their meaning. In particular, those already having the prefix ʌn- and suggesting a quality are frequently used with a prefixed **not** in order to convey a qualified affirmative opinion. Examples of these are given in the third column below.

'not kənˋvinsiŋ	'not iniksˋpiəriənst	'not ʌnˋsatisfaiiŋ
'not səˋpraiziŋ	'not ·self-diˋdʒestiŋ	'not ʌniksˋpektid
'not ·ʌndəˋdʌn	'not ·badli ˋbilt	'not ʌnˋintristiŋ
'not ·faːˋsiːiŋ	'not iŋˋkʌridʒiŋ	'not ʌnˋkoːldˌfoː
'not ˋhʌrid	'not ·wel ˋfitiŋ	'not ʌnˋnoun
'not ˋkraudid	'not ·wel-inˋfoːmd	'not ʌndiˋzəːviŋ

Examples of the use of **not** to make participles negative when they are used in participal phrases, in absolute constructions or as gerunds or half-gerunds are given in §§254–7.

When participles are used as specific verbals to form tenses in the Aspect of Activity (i.e., Tenses A7 to A12 and P7 and P8), any negation that is required is added in the ways described in §§351–5, and these usually exclude the use of negative participles.

369 Double negatives. The presence of two negatives in a clause gives an affirmative meaning. Any of the vehicles of negation mentioned in §351 may be combined with any other, though the most frequent combinations are probably a negative finite combined with one of the other vehicles.

Although double negatives used cumulatively (i.e., intended to bear a negative meaning) may be heard from some native English speakers, foreign students are warned that this is regarded as a feature of sub-standard speech in all English-speaking countries.

When two negatives are correctly used antithetically a special intonation (Tune III) is generally used on the sentence; this helps to indicate that the two negatives are meant to cancel each other out. If a negative adverb begins the sentence the subject and finite are inverted, as explained in §357.

The following examples show some of the ways in which double negatives are correctly used.

ju ˋkaːnt əv ˌsiːn ˏnoubodi ˌoːl ðə ˌmoːniŋ	(nf |nO)
ðə z 'haːdli ˋenibodi hu ˏdʌzn̩t dis ˌlaik im.	(nS | nf)
ai 'havn̩ ˙teikən 'oːl ðat ˙trʌbl̩ fə ˏnʌθiŋ.	(nf |nA)
'not fə ˋnʌθiŋ həv ai ˌteikən ˌoːl ðat ˌtrʌbl̩.	(nA|nA)
ai 'ʃudn̩t ˙laik tə ˙liːv ˋnʌθiŋ fə ˌjuː.	(nf |nO)

ACTIVE AND PASSIVE

370 Use of the passive. The passive voice is used when the doer of an action is (1) obvious, (2) unknown or imprecise, or (3) being deliberately kept anonymous for some reason or other. Examples:

1. ðə pə'liːs əv əˋrestid im.   hi z bin əˋrestid.
2. 'sʌmwʌn məst ˋmend ˌðis.   'ðis məs bi ˋmendid.
3. ai 'mʌst əv ˙meid ə misˋteik.   ə misˋteik ˌmʌst əv bin ˌmeid.

The doer of the action is occasionally named when the passive is used. This may be done in order to change the focus of interest of the sentence, or to give it a neater structure or smoother intonation.

> *Active:*   'dʒonz ˋsistə ˌtoːt im tə ˌswim.
> *Passive:*   'dʒon wəz ˙toːt tə ˙swim bai iz ˋsistə.

In this case the passive allows a more rhythmical distribution of the stresses and enables the nuclear tone on sistə to occupy its normal place at the end of the sentence.

It must also be remembered that, for the reasons mentioned in §206, the passive is used more frequently in English than in many other languages.

The essential element in forming the passive voice tenses is some part of the verb tə biː followed by the past participle of the specific verb. There are, however, cases in which the past participle, instead of forming part of a passive tense, functions as an adjectival complement to the verb tə biː acting as a verb of incomplete predication. In some borderline cases it is difficult to decide which of the two functions it is fulfilling.

The classification of sentences as between these two structures may depend on the tense that is being used; after the present and past tenses of the verb tə biː the participle tends to have an adjectival function rather than the verbal one it would have in the same semantic context but in other tenses. Compare:

ʃi l əv bin 'disə`pointid.    ʃi z 'disə`pointid.
ðə 'kʌp əd bin `broukən.    ðə 'kʌp wəz `broukən.

A past participle that might otherwise be considered as adjectival must be regarded as a verbal forming a passive tense when it is followed by certain adverbial phrases, particularly those naming the agent. Compare:

ai wəz sə`praizd.   wi wə sə'praizd bai ði ˌenəmi.
'ðis ˈsiːt s ri`zəːvd.          'ðis ˈsiːt s ri'zəːvd fə `juː.

While many of the passive participials listed in §105 are frequently used as verbals in passive voice tenses, the compound passive participials of §107 act much more rarely in that capacity.

371 Conversion from active to passive. When active voice sentences are converted to the passive certain changes, in addition to the details of tense structure, become necessary. The form of the finite may have to be adjusted for person or number, and if the modals ʃal or wil are involved in statements, there will probably have to be an interchange if one of the subjects is in the first person. If an adverb of manner is used its position will be after the object in the active but before the specific verbal in the passive, as shown in some of the following examples below.

Affirmative.

A > P

ðei 'koːld on im tə ˌspiːk.	2	hi wəz 'koːld on tə ˌspiːk.
wi I ə˟tend tu it.	3	it ʃl bi ə˟tendid tu.
ju v 'ritn̩ it ˟badli.	4	it s bin 'badli ˌritn̩.

Interrogative.

A > P

d ju 'ʌndə'stand ˙ðat?	1	iz 'ðat ˙ʌndə'stud?
'ʃud wi ig'noːr im?	3	'ʃud i bi ig'noːd?
həv ðei 'finiʃt ðə ˙wəːk?	4	həz ðə 'wəːk bin 'finiʃt?
'oːt wi tu əv 'tould im?	6	'oːt i tu əv bin 'tould?
iz i 'weiiŋ ðəm 'keəf‖i?	7	ə ðei biːiŋ 'keəf‖i 'weid?

Negative.

When the active sentence contains a negative or near-negative subject this is of course lost in the passive, and the negation must be introduced in some other way. This is usually effected by using a negative finite or a negative or near-negative adverb.

If the active sentence has a negative object this automatically becomes the negative subject of the passive and no further change is necessary, but when partitives or semi-pronouns compounded with them are used adjustments may have to be made, as in the first example below.

If the active sentence contains a negative or near-negative adverb no adjustment is necessary.

Negative Finite > Negative Subject, or No Change.

A > P

wi 'havn̩t ˙teikən ˟eni.	4	˟nʌn əv bin ˌteikən.
ðei 'wəːnt ˌhelpiŋ im.	8	hi 'wozn̩t biːiŋ ˌhelpt.

Negative Subject > Negative Adverb or New Negative Subject.

A > P

'nʌθiŋ ˟fraitn̩d im.	2	hi wəz 'nevə ˟fraitn̩d.
'haːdli ˙eniwʌn kən ˟muːv it.	3	it kən 'haːdli bi ˟muːvd.
'nouwʌn z ˙wʌn eni ˌpraiziz.	4	'nou ˟praiziz əv bin ˌwʌn.

Negative Object > Negative Subject.

A > P

ðei ˌsed 'haːdli ˌeniθiŋ.	2	'haːdli ˌeniθiŋ wəz ˌsed.
wi ə 'teliŋ ˟noubodi.	7	˟noubodi z ˌbiːiŋ ˌtould.

Negative Adverb—No Change in Vechicle of Negation.

A > P

wʌn 'haːdli ˙evə ˋsiːz im.   1   hi z 'haːdli ˙evə ˋsiːn.

wi v 'nevə ˋhəːd əv it.   4   it s 'nevə bin ˋhəːd ov.

Interrogative Negative.

The changes in vehicles of negation shown above are also to be found in the interrogative-negative, as can be seen from some of the following unclassified examples.

A > P

dəz 'nʌθiŋ sə˙praiz ju?   1   ə ju 'nevə sə˙praizd?

'didn̩t ðei 'niːd it?   2   'wozn̩t it 'niːdid?

məst wi 'tel 'noubodi?   3   məst 'noubodi bi ˙tould?

'havn̩t ðei 'siːn əs?   4   'havn̩t wi bin 'siːn?

'hadn̩t ʃi 'saind it?   5   'hadn̩t it bin 'saind?

'ʃudn̩t wi əv 'poustid it?   6   'ʃudn̩t it əv bin 'poustid?

iz 'noubodi 'wotʃiŋ əː?   7   'izn̩t ʃi ˙biːiŋ 'wotʃt?

wə ðei 'duːiŋ ˙nou 'wəːk?   8   wəz 'nou ˋwəːk ˙biːiŋ ˙dʌn?

WORD ORDER IN PREDICATES

372 Objects and adverbials. It is a general rule of English syntax that if a verb is followed by an object and an adverbial, the former must precede the latter except in a few cases where there are special reasons for reversing the order. This is a rule that gives a great deal of trouble to foreign students of English, because in a number of languages the practice is the exact opposite. The following are typical of incorrect constructions often used by such students:

d ju 'laik ˙betə ði 'ʌðə wʌn?   wi 'krost ˙tuː ˙suːn ðə ˎrivə.

'stʌdi ˋkeəfʃi ðis ˌlesn̩.   hi 'spiːks ˙fluəntli ˌfrentʃ.

ðei 'spred θru˙aut ðə ˙kʌntri ðeə 'laŋgwidʒ ənd ˌkʌstəmz.

The accepted word order in these cases is:

d ju 'laik ði 'ʌðə wʌn ˙betə?   wi 'krost ðə ˙rivə 'tuː ˋsuːn.

'stʌdi ðis ˙lesn̩ ˌkeəfʃi.   hi 'spiːks ˙frentʃ ˌfluəntli.

ðei 'spred ðeə ˙laŋgwidʒ ənd ˙kʌstəmz θru'aut ðə ˎkʌntri.

373 Indirect objects and prepositional objects. When an adverbial phrase introduced by tu or foː* follows a direct object in order to indicate the person or thing for whose sake the action is performed, this adverbial phrase is often referred to as a "prepositional object". Examples:

ai l 'bai ə ˈbuk fə ðə ˌboi.   wi 'sent sm̩ ˈflauəz tə joː ˌmʌðə.

This "prepositional object" may be placed between the specific verbal and its direct object, provided the preposition is omitted. It is then known as an indirect object, and the structure has the form: Subject + verb + indirect object + direct object. Examples:

ai l 'bai ðə ˙boi ə ˈbuk.   wi 'sent joː ˙mʌðə sm̩ ˈflauəz.

It might be less confusing, while retaining the term "indirect object", to refrain from using the expression "prepositional object" and to refer to this feature as an adverbial of movement, direction, motive, cause, or whatever other semantic function it may perform for the verb with which it happens to be used. This would serve to maintain a clearer distinction between the two structures, which are often confused by foreign students. This step would seem to be justified by the fact that the adverbial may be placed for emphasis (or for contrast with some other recipient) before the subject, a position that is admissible for adverbials but distinctly unusual for objects. Examples:

fə ðə ˅boi ai l 'bai ə ˈbuk.   tə joː ˅mʌdə wi 'sent sm̩ ˈflauəz.

374 Choice of structures. The verbs involved in these structures indicating that an action is performed for the sake of some person or thing fall into three classes:

    a. Verbs requiring the indirect object.
    b. Verbs admitting either structure.
    c. Verbs rejecting the indirect object.

The largest of these classes is Class *b*, where the speaker is given an option between the two structures. With these verbs it is usual to give the first position to whichever object is shorter or weaker, thus:

Indirect Object: *Adverbial Phrase:*

ai 'geiv im ðə ˌbuk.   ai 'geiv it tə ˌdʒon.

ai 'geiv ˙dʒon ðə ˌbuk.   *or*   ai 'geiv ðə ˙buk tə ˌdʒon.

ai 'geiv ˙dʒon ðə 'red ˌbuk.   ai 'geiv ðə ˙buk tə mai ˌfaːðə.

These three classes of verbs will now be considered in detail.

375 Verbs requiring the indirect object. The following are the most important of the few verbs with which the indirect object must be used:

tel	**aːsk**	**əlau**	**tʃaːdʒ**	**envi**

Examples:

'tel mi ðə ˎtruːθ.	**ðei l 'tʃaːdʒ əs ə ˬpaund.**
wi v ə'laud im ˎθriː.	**ai 'aːskt ju ə ˎkwestʃn̩.**
hi 'enviz ju joː 'lʌvli ˎgaːdn̩.	

376 Verbs admitting either structure. While the rule given in §374 regarding the choice between the two structures is of general application, exceptions are made, very often for the purpose of emphasizing either the person or the thing involved. The examples in this paragraph will therefore be given in both structures.

These verbs may be divided into three classes: those after which the adverbial phrase is introduced by **tu**, those after which **foː*** is used, and those after which either can be used—usually with a slightly different meaning.

Since verbs may be followed by all sorts of adverbial phrases, some of which will obviously be introduced by one of the two prepositions under discussion here, it is clearly necessary to apply a test before admitting verbs to these classes. The test here applied is whether the adverbial phrase is convertible into an indirect object.

Adverbial introduced by **tu**

ou	**pei**	**θrou**	**hand**	**tiːtʃ**
ʃou	**giv**	**diːl**	**send**	**poust**
sel	**paːs**	**ofə***	**lend**	**rekəmend**

Indirect + Direct Objects:	*Direct Object + Adverbial:*
ʃi 'ouz ˋevriwʌn ˌmʌni.	**ʃi 'ouz ˙mʌni tu ˋevriwʌn.**
ʃl̩ ai 'giv ˊðem ˙sʌm?	**ʃl̩ ai 'giv ˙sʌm tə ˊðəm?**
hi 'sould mi iz ˎhaus.	**hi 'sould iz ˙haus tə ˋmiː.**
ju məst ˋofər im ˌwʌn.	**ju məst 'ofə ˙wʌn tə ˋhim.**
ai l ˋlend ju ðə ˌbuk.	**ai l 'lend ðə ˙buk tə ˇjuː.**
wi l 'tiːtʃ ði ˋʌðəz ˏðat.	**wi l 'tiːtʃ ˙ðat tə ði ˋʌðəz.**

Adverbial introduced by either **tu** *or* **foː***

riːd   rait   liːv   siŋ   briŋ   teik

Indirect + Direct Objects:	*Direct Object + Adverbial:*
'riːd mi ði ˌaːnsə.	'riːd ði ˌaːnsə fə (tə) mi.
ai v 'ritn̩ ðəm ə ˌletə.	ai v 'ritn̩ ə ˌletə tə (fə) ðəm.
hi 'left mi iz ˌhaus.	hi 'left iz ˙haus tə ˋmiː.
hi 'left mi ə ˌnout.	hi 'left ə ˌnout ˌfoː mi.
'siŋ ðm̩ ə ˌsoŋ.	'siŋ ə ˌsoŋ ˌfoː (tə) ðm̩.
ai v 'broːt ju ə ˌpreznt.	ai v 'broːt ə ˌpreznt ˌfoː ju.
ˋbriŋ mi it.	'briŋ it tə ˋmiː.
wi l 'teik ðm̩ sm̩ ˌtoiz.	wi l 'teik sm̩ ˌtoiz tə (fə) ðm̩.

Adverbial introduced by **foː**

bai   get   seiv   meik   grou   faind

duː   wei   spel   bild   gaðə*   pripeə*

The indirect object structure is probably more common with the verbs on the first line than with those on the second, though there is the very common expression ˋduː mi ə ˌfeivə.

Indirect + Direct Objects:	*Direct Object + Adverbial:*
'didn̩t ju ˙bai ´miː eni?	'didn̩t ju ˙bai eni fə ´miː?
ʃi məs 'gaðə ˋðem ˌsʌm.	ʃi məs 'gaðə ˙sʌm fə ˇðem.
ai m 'meikiŋ ju sm̩ ˋtiː.	ai m 'meikiŋ sm̩ ˌtiː ˌfoː ju.
ðei v 'faund ju əˋnʌðə.	ðei v 'faund əˋnʌðə ˌfoː ju.
ai l 'get ju wot ai ˇkan.	ai l 'get wot ai ˋkan ˌfoː ju.
'dount ˙wei mi eni ˇtiː.	'dount ˙wei eni 'tiː fə ˇmiː.
wil ju ´spel mi ˙ðat ˙wəːd?	wil ju ´spel ˙ðat ˙wəːd fə mi?
pri'peə ðəm ə ˙gud ˌmiːl.	pri'peər ə ˙gud ˌmiːl fə ðəm.

377 Verbs rejecting indirect objects. There are, of course, large numbers of transitive verbs which may be modified by adverbial phrases introduced by **tu** or **foː*** but which do not admit the conversion of the adverbial into an indirect object. As the equivalents in some languages of certain of these verbs do take indirect objects, students are prone to use inadmissible structures in English, and should take particular note of the following:

sei   spiːk   sədʒest   oupən   diskraib   iksplein

Correct usage with these verbs is:

ˋdount ˏsei ˏðat tu im ə˪gein.
'wai ˙dount ju 'spiːk ˋiŋgliʃ tə mi?
ai I sə'dʒest ən iksˏtʃeindʒ tə ðəm.
ʃI ai 'oupən ðis ˈletə fə ju?
ai 'kudn̩t disˋkraib ðə ˅siːn tə ju.
kən ju iks'plein ðə ˙miːniŋ əv ðis ˈsentəns tə mi?

In the case of the verb tu intrədjuːs, referring to two persons, while either may be the direct object, neither may be made an indirect object, and the person not named as the direct object must be brought in by means of an adverbial phrase:

'intrə˙djuːs joː ˏfrend tə mi. *or*
'intrə˙djuːs mi tə joː ˏfrend.

WORD ORDER IN THE PASSIVE

378 Choice of two structures. When verbs such as those considered in §§373–7 are used in the passive they again fall into three classes:

a. The indirect object must be used as the subject of the passive.
b. Either object may be used as the subject of the passive.
c. The direct object must be used as the subject of the passive.

In Classes *a* and *c* there are a few verbs that do not always follow the rule, but these exceptions are not important. In Class *b* the indirect object of the active voice is usually preferred as the subject of the passive, since it gives a smoother structure. This sentence pattern is a source of some trouble to certain foreign students of English.

379 Indirect object must become the subject. The most important verbs belonging to this class are:

tel   aːsk   əlau   tʃaːdʒ   envi

Examples:

ai məs bi 'tould ðə ˋtruːθ.   wi ʃI bi 'tʃaːdʒd ə ˅paund.
ju wər 'aːskt ə ˋkwestʃn̩.   ju ər 'envid joː ˙gud ˋteist.
hi z bin əˋlaud ˏθriː əv ðəm.

329

380 Either object may become the subject. In the case of verbs that admit either object of the active voice as subject of the passive certain preferences are observable. At times the choice is determined by semantic factors.

With the following verbs the indirect object is often preferred:

ʃou	pei	diːl	hand	tiːtʃ
sel	giv	liːv	lend	ofə*

Indirect Object as Subject:

hi wəz ˋpeid iˏnʌf.
ju ʃ| bi ˈgivn̩ ˏmoə.
ʃi z bin ˈhandid əː ˏtikit.
ai ˋmei bi ˏleft ə ˋfoːtʃn̩.
ðei ə biːiŋ ˋofəd ˏhelp.

Direct Object as Subject:

iˈnʌf wəz ˇpeid tu im.
ˋmoː ʃ| bi ˏgivn̩ tə ju.
hə ˈtikit s bin ˇhandid tu ə.
ə ˋfoːtʃn̩ ˏmei bi ˏleft tə mi.
ˈhelp s biːiŋ ˇofəd tə ðəm.

With the following verbs the direct object is often preferred:

ou	get	riːd	send	faind
duː	bai	seiv	briŋ	rekəmend

Direct Object as Subject:

ə ˋlot iz ˏoud tə ðəm.
ˈwʌn z biːiŋ ˋboːt fər əs.
sm̩ ˋsʌpə z bin ˏseivd fə ju.
ə ˈnout ʃ| bi ˏsent tə hə.
ə ˈdʒob z bin ˏfaund fər im.

Indirect Object as Subject:

ðei ər ˈoud ə ˋlot.
wi ə biːiŋ ˋboːt wʌn.
ju v bin ˈseivd səm ˇtrʌb|.
ʃi ʃ| bi ˈsent ə ˏnout.
hi z bin ˈfaund ə ˏdʒob.

381 Direct object becomes the subject. When the direct object of the active voice is used as the subject in the passive the other person or thing involved must be introduced in an adverbial phrase beginning with either **tu** or **foː***. The following are typical verbs with which this structure is used:

sei	paːs	spiːk	poust	sədʒest
wei	meik	teik	oupən	diskraib
siŋ	spel	rait	gaðə*	iksplein
bild	θrou	grou	pripeə*	intrədjuːs

Examples:

P1 joː 'letə z ˈpaːst tu 'ʌs fər ˎakʃn̩.
P1 ði 'apl̩z ə ˈweid fə ju in ˎsaks.
P2 'ðis ˈhaus wəz 'bilt ˋspeʃl̩i foːr əs.
P2 ðə 'doː wəz ˈoupənd fə ðəm bai ə ˎsəːvn̩t.
P3 ðə 'letər | bi ˈritn̩ tə ˋmiː.
P3 'nʌθiŋ məs bi ˇsed tə ðəm.
P4 ə 'paund əv təˈmaːtuz əz bin ˋweid fə ju.
P4 'ðat ˈwəːd z bin 'spelt fə ju oːlˋredi.
P5 joː 'plan əd bin səˈdʒestid tə ðə ˋmanidʒə.
P5 ðə 'man əd oːl'redi bin disˋkraibd tə mi.
P6 ðə 'peipəz | əv bin ˋpoustid tə ju bai ˏnau.
P6 ðə 'paːsl̩ ˈmʌst əv bin ˈteikən tə joːr ˋaːnt.
P7 ðə 'difikl̩tiz ə biːiŋ iksˈpleind tə joː ˋsistə.
P7 sm̩ ˋgreips ə biːiŋ ˌgaðəd foː ju.
P8 wəz ðə 'suːp biːiŋ ˈmeid fə joː ˊmʌðə?

The treatment of the verb tu intrədjuːs when referring to two persons is similar to that described for the active voice in §377.

joː 'kʌzn̩ ʃəd əv bin ˈintrəˈdjuːst tə di ˋʌðəz.
ði 'ʌðəz ʃəd əv bin ˈintrəˈdjuːst tə joː ˋkʌzn̩.

ST. JOSEPH'S COLLEGE OF EDUCATION
TRENCH HOUSE
BELFAST 11

Index

References are to paragraphs

occupying miscellaneous positions, 285; of affirmation, probability and negation, 270; of degree, quantity and precision, 269; of frequency, 268; of manner, 265; of place, direction and distance, 266; of time and duration, 267; placed after the object, 283; placed before an adjective, 284; placed before the subject, 280; placed between finite and verbal, 282; that may be sentences, 277; used as complements, 278; varieties of, 258

Advisability (həd betə), 229; (oːt tu), 197

Affirmation, etc., 339–341

Affirmative, anomalous, 337; conjugation, 148, 332; contradiction in the, 341; partitive, the, 75; variations in the, 339

Affricates, 3

Alternative questions, 342, 350

Analysis of structures, 338–363; of the tense system, 205–209

Anomalous affirmative, 337; conjugation, the, 336; interrogative, 349; interrogative-negative, 363; negative, 356

Apologies, intonation of, 41, 44

Article, the absolute, 74; the definite, 73, 74; the indefinite, 73, 74

Article-analogues, 79–82; definition of, 79; denoting duality, 80; denoting selection, 82; denoting totality, 81

Articles, forms of the, 73; table of the, 78; use of the, 74

Aspect, definition of, 207; of accomplishment, 211; of activity, 218

Aspects, limitations on the, 210

Assimilation, 13

Body, 33, 36

Case after əz and ðən, 310; of pronouns, 69; the genitive, 52, 55–57

Catalogue of adverbs, 261–263

Causative get and hav, 230

Choice of structures with two objects, 374

Classification of adverbs, 260–264

Clauses, defining and non-defining, 322; introduced by ðət, 232; introduced by conjunctives, 232

Clear and dark l, 7

Collectives, 90

Collocations of bouθ, 96; of els, 67; of evri, 97; of oːl, 96; of sʌtʃ, 98; of ʌðə, 95, 97; of nouns, 50

Comparison of adjectives, 108–115; of adverbs, 259

Compound infinitives, 177, 239; nouns, 50; participles, 239; tunes, 46

Conditional clauses, modals in, 179; perfect tenses, 173; tenses, 173

Conjugating finites, 146; verbals, use of the, 147; verbs, 124, 146–147; verbs, formal classification of, 146–147

Conjugation, affirmative, 148, 332; emphatic affirmative, 152; interrogative, 149, 333; interrogative-negative, 151, 335; negative, 150, 334

Conjugators, the, 124, 126, 146–204; table of the, 146; see also finites and verbals

Conjunction, the general (ðət), 311

Conjunctions, co-ordinating, 296; correlative, 296; subordinating, 297–310; subordinating, classification of, 297

Index

Index

Index

Relative, the comparative (əz), 326; the independent (wot), 323

Relatives, adjectival, 327; adverbial, 328; choice of pronominal, 325; function of, 321; pronominal, 324

Restricted use of mʌtʃ and meni, 92

Rhetorical general questions, 344; special questions, 348

Rhythm, 26

Salutations, intonation of, 41, 43, 45

Semi-pronouns, 65–66; compound, 67

Semi-vocalic r, 8

Semi-vowels, the, 3

Sentence-pattern formula, 331

Sentence-patterns, variant, 338

Sentence stress, 27

Simple tenses, 208

Sounds, consonant, 3; vowel, 4

Special questions, 342, 345–349; alternative, 350; emphatic, 347, 349; negation in, 359–363; rhetorical, 348–349; with statements structure, 346

Special structures, 228–234; accusative and infinitive, 234; causative get and hav, 230; həd betə, 229; precursory ðeə, 231; precursory it, 232; subjunctive substitute (ʃud), 233; wud raːðə, 228

Special weak forms of modals, 204; of temporals, 172

Specific finites, 126

Specific verbals, 239–257; forms of the, 239

Specific verbs, 124, 127–145; classification of irregularities, 133; expressing postures, 210; expressing mental states, 210;

formal classification of, 127–145; inflexions of, 130; intransitive, 205; past participle of, 132; past tense of, 132; regular and irregular forms of, 132; resembling modals 190; simple and derivative, 127; the ing-form of, 131; the s-form of, 132; transitive, 205

Statements, intonation of, 41, 43–44, 46

Static tones, 29

Stress, 21; kinetic, 22–25; level, 22; marks, tonetic, 31; moving, 22; multiple word, 25–26; sentence, 27; static, 22–23, 25; word, 24

Structures, analysis of, 338–363; choice of, 374; special, 228–234

Subjunctive substitute (ʃud), 233

Subordinate clauses, tenses in, 298

Subordinating conjunctions, 297–312

Substitution tables, 320

Syllabic consonants, 6

Symbols, miscellaneous, 6; phonetic, 2–6; tonetic, 31

Tables: articles, 78; connectives, 295; demonstratives, 78; infinitives, 177; noun categories, 61; partitives, 78; possessives, 71; pronouns, 68; specific verbals, 130; substitution, 320; tense structures, affirmative, 332; tense structures, anomalous affirmative, 337; tense structures, interrogative, 333; tense structures, interrogative-negative, 335; tense structures, negative, 334; verb forms, 126, 131; weak forms, 15–19

Tag questions, 226; statements, 227

Tags, nature of, 225

Index